Heritage Values in Site Management

Four Case Studies

Marta de la Torre

Margaret G. H. MacLean

Randall Mason

David Myers

Edited by Marta de la Torre

The Getty Conservation Institute, Los Angeles

The Getty Conservation Institute

Timothy P. Whalen, *Director*
Jeanne Marie Teutonico, *Associate Director, Field Projects and Sciences*

The Getty Conservation Institute works internationally to advance conservation and
to enhance and encourage the preservation and understanding of the visual arts in all
of their dimensions—objects, collections, architecture, and sites. The Institute serves
the conservation community through scientific research; education and training; field
projects; and the dissemination of the results of both its work and the work of others
in the field. In all its endeavors, the Institute is committed to addressing unanswered
questions and promoting the highest possible standards of conservation practice.

© 2005 J. Paul Getty Trust
Getty Publications
1200 Getty Center Drive, Suite 500
Los Angeles, California 90049–1682
www.getty.edu

Christopher Hudson, *Publisher*
Mark Greenberg, *Editor in Chief*

Patrick Pardo, *Project Editor*
Abby Sider, *Copy Editor*
Pamela Heath, *Production Coordinator*
Hespenheide Design, *Designer and Compositor*

The individual case studies were originally designed by Joe Molloy and copyedited by
Sylvia Tidwell and Dianne Woo. The book cover is based on a design by Joe Molloy.

Photographs in the Grosse Île case study are courtesy of Margaret G. H. MacLean.
Photographs for all other case studies have been provided as indicated.

The accompanying CD-ROM contains copyrighted materials that have been used with
permission. See last page for full credit information.

Printed in Canada by Friesens

Library of Congress Cataloging-in-Publication Data
Heritage values in site management : four case studies / Marta de la Torre
.. [et al.] ; edited by Marta de la Torre.
        p. cm.
   Includes bibliographical references and index.
   ISBN-13: 978-0-89236-797-0 (pbk.)
   ISBN-10: 0-89236-797-0 (pbk.)
   1. Historic sites–Management–Case studies. 2. Cultural
property–Protection–Case studies. I. De la Torre, Marta, 1946– II. Getty
Conservation Institute.
   CC135.H46525 2005
   363.6′9–dc22

2004017483

Contents

Contents of Supporting Documents on CD-ROM

Foreword

I am pleased to write this foreword to *Heritage Values in Site Management: Four Case Studies*, the result of research carried out by both the staff of the Getty Conservation Institute (GCI) and our colleagues in heritage organizations around the world. The book presents the results of the work of a group of dedicated professionals, who came together over a period of two years to discuss values-based management of cultural heritage sites.

The case studies presented in this volume are the result of a collaborative project of the Australian Heritage Commission (now the Australian Heritage Council), English Heritage, the United States National Park Service, Parks Canada, and the GCI. The individuals representing these organizations—Jane Lennon, Christopher Young, Kate Clarke, Francis McManamon, Dwight Pitcaithley, Christina Cameron, Gordon Bennett, and François LeBlanc—steered the development of the case studies and worked closely with the quartet who coordinated the work and wrote the text: Marta de la Torre and David Myers of the GCI and Margaret G. H. MacLean and Randall Mason. I am grateful to all of them for their time and expertise, and this volume owes a great deal to their insights and experience. In particular, I would like to recognize and thank Marta de la Torre, whose vision and leadership guided both the research project and the case studies team.

The case studies project brought together two areas in which the GCI has done considerable work: site management, and research in significance and values in the conservation of cultural heritage sites. These case studies continue this work, presenting an in-depth analysis of how four important organizations in different hemispheres identify, understand, and protect the values attributed to cultural heritage sites when considering the preservation, care, and management of those sites.

The sites in these case studies are diverse and include a variety of elements, ranging from buildings, archaeological remains, and views and landscapes, to towns and agricultural lands. Focusing on these four sites and their unique characteristics and challenges, the case studies bridge a gap in the conservation literature between international guidance documents and technical intervention guidelines. It is our hope that the case studies provide the reader with a new and different viewpoint over the landscape of managing and preserving complex heritage sites.

The case studies themselves are available on the GCI Web site at www.getty.edu/conservation. However, this publication of the case studies also includes a comparison of the management policies implemented at the different sites and an explanation of the methodologies and process followed in the development of the case studies. It is our expectation that these methods, when used by others in the conservation field, might provide a critical mass of information to create guidelines and evaluation standards for best practice.

I hope that this volume will provide unconventional insights into the challenges of preserving the unique, ever-changing, and often-conflicting values of cultural heritage sites to both students and practitioners in the field.

Timothy P. Whalen
Director
The Getty Conservation Institute

PART ONE Project Background

Marta de la Torre

Introduction

Presentation of the Project

This publication presents four case studies developed in a collaborative project of the Getty Conservation Institute, the Australian Heritage Commission (as of January 2004, the Australian Heritage Council), English Heritage, the U.S. National Park Service, and Parks Canada. Each case focuses on a specific cultural site and analyzes its management through the lens of the site's values and significance. These materials have a didactic intent, and it is anticipated that they will be used by institutions and individuals engaged in the study or practice of site management, conservation planning, and historic preservation. The case studies are preceded by a discussion of site management concepts used in the case analyses. They are followed by a summary of some of the more important points that emerged in the studies, comparing, in some instances, how a particular issue developed at the different sites.

The heritage literature contains a large number of charters and guidance documents intended to assist the practitioners in planning and management.[1] More recently, many international documents have started to advocate new comprehensive management approaches focused on the values of a place. The organizations participating in this project share a belief in the usefulness of values-based management in a broad range of local, regional, national, and international contexts. They also recognized that there is little information about the application of theoretical guidelines to specific cases and critical analyses of actual management practices. These cases are intended to fill some of that gap by illustrating how values and significance are understood and used in actual management practices.

The case studies in this publication deal with sites that are unique, and thus each one emphasizes the issues that were considered to be important in that place and its circumstances. Operational activities generally target specific problems and rarely allow the time to consider broad implications. The case studies step back to look at the impact of the operational decisions on the essential qualities of the site. They provide detailed analyses of the processes that connect policy statements and management guidelines with on-site planning and operational decisions by looking at all the values attributed to the sites, and examine how these values influence management. One of the clearest insights emerging from this study is the complexity of the relationships of a site's values and the many implications that most routine management decisions have for them. Looking at the ramifications of such decisions and their impact on the various aspects of the place, it becomes evident that heritage management will benefit from approaches that promote holistic thinking, that go beyond the prescriptions issued in charters and guidelines, and that can sustain activities to monitor the integrity of values and significance.

The cases do not measure the success of a given management model against some set standard. Rather, they are intended to illustrate and explain how four different groups have dealt with the protection of values in the management of four specific sites, and how they are helped or hindered in these efforts by legislation, regulations, and other policies.

It must be said from the start that the responses that an organization can give to a specific situation are not unlimited. Limitations are created by the legal and administrative context. The managing authorities involved in the cases are governmental agencies, in three cases national ones. In practical terms this means that the approaches used and the decisions made in these sites are governed as much by the national policies and regulations as by the specific situations of the sites. Balancing higher authorities with local needs is a challenge faced by most managers. If negative impacts of policies or actions have been pointed out in the case studies, it has been done to illustrate the complexity of managing sites with multiple values. These comments should not be taken as an evaluation of the actions of the site authorities.

THE SITES AND THEIR GOVERNING AGENCIES

The four sites studied as part of this project—Grosse Île and the Irish Memorial National Historic Site in Canada, Chaco Culture National Historical Park in the U.S., Port Arthur Historic Site in Australia, and Hadrian's Wall World Heritage Site in the United Kingdom—were put forth by their governing agencies as examples of how values issues have been addressed. The sites were chosen to present a variety of resources and circumstances that affect management.[2] The administrative environment of each is different, determined by its legal status, applicable legislation, and policies of governing agencies. The sites also vary in their history as a heritage place, and those that have enjoyed heritage status the longest have seen a more thorough transformation of their values and significance.

Site Management

THE CHANGING MANAGEMENT ENVIRONMENT

The management of cultural sites has become a topic of much interest in recent years. Heritage management, however, is not a new enterprise. Sites have been managed in one way or another since the moment they came to be considered "heritage." Some of the recent attention can be attributed to important changes that have occurred in the environment in which sites are managed and the need to find ways of doing an old task under new conditions.

Heritage management used to be the concern of small groups of experts who defined and controlled what constituted heritage and determined how it was conserved and interpreted. Conservation of physical resources was the central concern, since value was defined in terms of material "authenticity" and "integrity."[3] All the other activities that occurred at a site were generally measured against the impact they had on the fabric. (This does not mean that decisions that had a negative impact were never taken; but they were seen initially as "necessary compromises" and later as "bad decisions.")

As a result of years of work, the care and conservation of materials have been greatly advanced, and today there are many effective—albeit often expensive and complex—solutions. However, in spite of technical solutions, the preservation and management of heritage have become more difficult and complex. Among the factors contributing to this complexity are the expansion of the concept and scope of heritage, the trend to look for solutions in market approaches, and the growing participation of new groups in heritage decisions.

The idea of what constitutes heritage has extended from individual buildings and monuments to much greater ensembles of human creations, such as cities and landscapes—many now protected as World Heritage Sites. Heritage professionals have had to make the transition from managing and conserving one building, where the protection of the monument was the principal objective, to dealing with places in which the heritage is only one among many elements of a living and evolving environment. None of the cases presented here are concerned exclusively with a single structure. The sites vary in degree of complexity, but all include buildings, archaeological remains, and important views and landscapes, and in the case of Hadrian's Wall, towns and agricultural lands.

Market (or business) approaches have been applied in the heritage world in recent decades. This is a logical move if viewed as turning for solutions to a discipline with experience in allocating resources and resolving conflicts in complex and dynamic environments. At the same time, the global trend toward privatization of activities and functions traditionally in the public domain has also encouraged this shift.

However, while the application of market concepts and business approaches can be useful for heritage management, it also has dangers. A good example of efforts to adapt business methods to the cultural field is cost-benefit analysis. As one of the most frequently used tools in business decision-making processes, it was applied early on to the heritage field. In an attempt to bring heritage into the economic arena, the benefits of heritage decisions were justified by economic outcomes, such as generation of employment or increased revenues from visitors. However, it was soon evident that monetary measurements never account for the totality of either benefits or costs of heritage decisions. There are intangible benefits of preserving heritage and costs in its loss that cannot be assigned a monetary or quantitative value. This has led the heritage field to use these quantitative tools with reservations, and more important, to seek measurement methods that are more suitable to cultural resources.[4]

Basically, the benefits of heritage are defined by the values that society attributes to it. There are many sources of information that can be tapped to establish the values of a heritage place. Historical records and research findings have been used most in the past, and generally are consulted first. The values that generally emerge from these sources are the traditional ones: historic, scientific, and aesthetic.

More recently, the various groups who have a stake in the place, be they experts, politicians, ethnic or religious groups, or neighborhood communities, have been recognized as an important source of knowledge about values. Social benefits such as ethnic dignity, economic development, spiritual life, and social stability have started to be recognized. No doubt, many groups and individuals derive economic benefits from the heritage.

And, as new values emerge, there are questions as to whether the new ones are as "valuable" as the more traditional ones or those that can be measured in monetary terms. A greater interest in heritage is a good thing indeed, but it also creates complex and sometimes difficult management situations.

VALUES-BASED MANAGEMENT

Heritage resource management can be defined simply as "the way that those responsible choose to use it, exploit it, or conserve it."[5] However, as more people feel responsibility for heritage, authorities can seldom make management choices solely on their own. New interested groups come with opinions about the values of their heritage and how it is to be conserved and managed—opinions that do not always coincide with the views of experts. People have come to anticipate benefits from these resources, and authorities must take into consideration these expectations. Sometimes, the values of different groups are incompatible and can result in serious conflicts. Heritage professionals have been looking for ways to bring forth the views of all stakeholders and to resolve the conflicts that inevitably arise. In this changed environment, decisions about heritage need to be negotiated. The search is on for an approach that assures equity, avoiding those in which the values that prevail belong to the group with the most political power.

The approaches most often favored are those called "values-based," in which the main management goal is the preservation of the significance and values of a place. Understanding all the values attributed to cultural resources is fundamental to these methods. Only after this happens can one consider how these values are to be effectively protected. This systematic analysis of values distinguishes these approaches from more traditional ones, which are more likely to focus on resolving specific problems or issues without formal consideration of the impact of solutions on the totality of the site or its values, or to focus on the conservation of the tangible resources.[6]

These new management methods are seen to have a number of advantages. They require awareness of all the values of a site; they rely on consultation and therefore involve more of society in the conservation process; and they create a deeper understanding of the resource. Most importantly, they are seen as means of achieving sustainability for the heritage, by promoting the participation and involvement of all those who care.

Values and Significance

Values-based site management is the coordinated and structured operation of a heritage site with the primary purpose of protecting the significance of the place as defined by designation criteria, government authorities or other owners, experts of various stripes, and other citizens with legitimate interests in the place.

"Value" and "significance" are terms used in cultural management with increasing frequency but with various definitions. They are also central concepts to values-based management and to the case studies of this publication.[1]

In this project, "value" has been used to mean positive characteristics attributed to heritage objects and places by legislation, governing authorities, and other stakeholders.[2] These characteristics are what make a heritage site significant and are the reason why stakeholders and authorities are interested in it. The benefits of heritage are inextricably linked to these values.

"Significance" has been used to mean the overall importance of a site, determined through an analysis of the totality of the values attributed to it. Significance also reflects the importance a place has with respect to one or several of its values, and in relation to other comparable sites.

Notes

1. See, for example, R. Mason and E. Avrami, "Heritage Values and Challenges of Conservation Planning," in J. M. Teutonico and G. Palumbo, *Management Planning for Archaeological Sites,* Los Angeles: The Getty Conservation Institute, 2000, 13.

2. As will become evident in the cases, each of the organizations involved in the study defines values in slightly, but not significantly, different ways.

Nevertheless, values-based management is a new approach with many aspects remaining to be explored. The report of a recent meeting of experts brings out advantages and challenges of managing multiple values in a participatory process when it says "[T]raditional absolute values are replaced by relative, pluralistic value systems, which in turn allow the bridging of large cultural differences. The methods of decision-making and the determination of policies have moved away both from over-regulated, state-dominated process and the simplistic use of optimization models . . . to partially chaotic, not foreseeable social processes."[7] This publication attempts to shed new light on some of the less known aspects of these new approaches.

Values

One of the most important steps in values-based management is the identification of the values of the place through an elicitation process involving stakeholders. Only after this has been done, and in conjunction with a thorough understanding of the physical resources, is management in a position to establish the significance of the place and the appropriate policies and strategies.

In reality, however, planners and managers almost always deal with sites whose primary significance has been established earlier, usually at the time of designation. The significance of the sites included in this study was established by legislation or as part of the designation process. This significance can be called different things: "purpose of the park" in the National Park System; criteria for listing, in the case of Hadrian's Wall's World Heritage Site status; and "commemorative intent" in Parks Canada. All heritage designation schemes are based on specific criteria that favor certain values. For example, national heritage systems consider only those values— generally historic ones—that are important to the nation as a whole. World Heritage listing is based on criteria that consider so-called universal values. Official designations address the values that make sites significant at the national or international level, but in almost all instances exclude other important values held by legitimate stakeholders. In general, the higher the designation level, the narrower the values that are recognized as significant. Since heritage places have a multiplicity of values, favoring certain ones at the time of designation can create interesting challenges for management, and these issues are explored in each of the case studies. All the agencies involved in this study use management approaches that attempt to recognize and protect values that go beyond those identified by designation or listing processes. The ability of each organization to recognize additional values varies, and depends on the broader legal and administrative framework in which the governing authority exists.

It is important to recognize that in all cases the governing agencies consider the protection of the physical resources to be paramount. As expressed by English Heritage: "significance involves a detailed understanding of the historic fabric of the site and how it has changed through time, and then an assessment of the values—both historic and contemporary—ascribed to that fabric."[8]

ELICITING VALUES

Governing authorities deal differently with the identification of stakeholders and the elicitation of values. The involvement of stakeholder groups can happen in several ways. In many instances, interested groups make their views known and demand involvement in the decision-making process. Less frequently, authorities may request the participation of legitimate stakeholders. Often, eliciting information about values is not a simple process, and the recognition of this challenge by the heritage field has led to some important recent work on values-elicitation and assessment tools.[9]

Traditional stakeholders of cultural sites have been professionals in various disciplines, such as history, archaeology, architecture, ecology, biology, and so forth, who simultaneously express and create value through their research or expert opinions. Every site has a group of people who are considered to be the principal stakeholders. Often, they are the ones who were involved with the place when its significance was first recognized. Their long-term interest and strong association with the original values have often earned them a privileged relationship with the managing agencies, and they are the "experts" who are consulted in major decisions.

More recently, groups who value heritage sites for different reasons have come forth and demanded to be involved. These new stakeholder groups can range from communities living close by, to groups with traditional ties or interests in particular aspects of the site. New values often surface as a result of the involvement of these groups. Broad involvement of public groups provides legitimacy to the results of the planning process and can assist management in the implementation of the plans. However, the involvement of new groups is not always an easy process. Most of the values articulated in a values-elicitation or consultation process are legitimate and merit serious consideration and protection as the site is

managed. But, as stakeholders multiply, heritage managers face wide-ranging and sometimes conflicting interests. In practice, involving different groups in the planning and management processes creates new challenges to identify legitimate spokespersons, choose appropriate elicitation methods, and consider all the values of a place.

In more traditional approaches, authorities still take it upon themselves to articulate what they believe to be the views of the different groups, or selected informant-stakeholders are consulted in the early stages of the planning process. The involvement of stakeholders in the planning process or the recognition of their values is not a guarantee that they will be involved in management decisions. In many instances, "experts" or the authorities interpret the values of a wide spectrum of stakeholders as needed in the management process, or consult only those groups whose values they consider would be most directly affected by a decision. This is necessary since any management approach requiring constant consultations with many groups would be extremely inefficient. In this situation, what becomes important is that those with the power of decision have sufficient interaction with stakeholders so that they may truly take their views into consideration.

Finding the right spokespersons for a group is critical. Only groups with formal structures, such as tribes or religious sects, can easily designate representatives who speak for the group as a whole. In all other instances, authorities must rely on their knowledge of the groups or on informants to identify legitimate representatives. If those representing a group are not considered to have the authority to do so, the information they provide is likely to be contested later on.

Heritage places might be seen to remain fairly unchanged over time, but like stakeholder groups, values also evolve and new ones emerge. There are many ways in which a site changes, even after its designation as "heritage" guarantees its preservation. Archaeological work can bring to light additional resources; research and new information can generate value for objects; events can give new significance to a place; and, alas, deterioration can diminish values.

ECONOMIC VALUE

Heritage management tends to assess the cultural and social values of sites separately from their economic dimension. This happens in spite of the fact that in many instances, economic value is significant and a large number of individuals benefit from it. This situation seems to be created by two separate factors: first, the field's traditional aversion to assigning "a price" to heritage, insisting that the value of "heritage"—something that is unique and irreplaceable—cannot be measured in monetary terms; and second, the real difficulties that exist in comparing economic and cultural values.

Considerable effort has been devoted in recent years to researching the economic value of heritage and to finding the means of integrating it with other values. This is an important problem requiring solution. As heritage becomes ubiquitous, the amount of resources needed for its care becomes significant and has to be considered in the context of other possible investment. In order for this to be done responsibly, there need to be tools that measure the full value of heritage, and not only monetary contributions.

Overemphasis of any value can be detrimental to heritage, and this is most true of economic considerations. Playing up to the economic value of heritage has generally meant increasing the number of visitors, generally tourists. Visitor access and preservation have always been recognized as a potential source of conflict. More recently, the economic benefits generated by tourism have come to be seen as the means of assuring preservation.

While tourism can be either a positive or a negative factor in cultural sites, there are other "economic values" that are without a doubt detrimental. Such a case is where the cultural resource sits on land that has alternative uses that could generate significant economic benefits, such as mining or development. Unless the cultural resource enjoys a very strong legal protection, this is a dangerous situation because the realization of the potential economic benefits could bring about its destruction.

Consideration of economic values will continue to gain importance in the future as heritage encompasses larger areas and more "working" environments, with the privatization trends, and the emphasis on public-private partnerships. Many in the world of heritage have already noted that the narrow view of conservation as the care of the material cultural property must yield to a wider concept of conservation as an economically sustainable practice that involves society at large.

PROTECTION OF VALUES

The purpose of knowing and understanding the ways a place is valued is to protect the significance attributed to it by different groups in society and create a sustainable preservation environment. However, because cultural heritage has a multitude of values, it is not always possible to protect all of them equally. Values are sometimes in conflict, and managers must make decisions that favor some but not others. This involves setting priorities among the values. Some priorities are mandated by law, usually favoring those values that uphold the heritage designation.

Each of the case studies in this publication discusses conflicts that have been faced by site authorities. The source of conflict can be the uses that different stakeholders want to make of the site in accordance with their values, and others can surface when the protection of a certain value has a negative impact on another.

The priority given to certain values often depends on the system that labels cultural heritage. In World Heritage Sites, for example, national authorities are committed to protecting those values that make the sites significant at a universal level. The choice of justification for inscription in the list is left to the country nominating the site, but the site must meet the criterion or criteria selected beyond the local or national level. This restriction, by definition, will not allow all values of a site to be part of the World Heritage Nomination and affects all other values not meeting the "universal" criterion.

THE IMPORTANCE OF FABRIC

While the values and significance of a place ought to be the touchstone of management decisions, day-to-day operations are most often concerned with the use and care of the physical resources. Thus, to protect values and significance, it is critical to determine the relationship of values to fabric. In its most literal sense this can mean mapping the values on the features of the site and answering questions such as, which features capture the essence of a given value? What about them must be guarded in order to retain that value? If a view is seen to be important to the value of the place, what are its essential elements? What amount of change is possible without compromising the value? Clear understanding of where values reside allows site managers to protect what makes a site significant. This is somewhat different from the rationale behind the protection of the fabric in traditional conservation. In that perspective, the original materials were the only essential elements of significance and sustained the concepts of "integrity" and "authenticity." Values-based management does not diminish the value of the physical materials, but the conservation of other elements—some tangible, others not—is also important, such as the conservation of landscape views and traditional uses.

Heritage agencies use different means to determine where values reside. Traditionally, work was conducted as if values resided in any material that was "authentic" and any structure that had "integrity." The values-based planning process calls for two steps—documentation of the site and assessment of the conditions of the resources—that provide a clear understanding of the place, which is fundamental to the connection between values and fabric.[10]

Conclusions

VALUES-BASED MANAGEMENT: A FRAMEWORK FOR CONSERVATION

The evolution from a vision of identifying and caring for specific resources to one that focuses on the benefits to be obtained from these activities has transformed the heritage field in recent years. Nevertheless, one of the major challenges in this new vision has been making a clear statement of the objectives to be achieved and finding ways of measuring success.

Monitoring continues to be one of the weakest areas of professional heritage practice in spite of recent efforts to establish indicators or new tools to assist in this task. Members of the Steering Committee of the Case Study Project have suggested that values-based management could provide a new framework for heritage care. This would occur when the protection and preservation of significance are accepted as the principal objective of management, which in turn would require that heritage management focus on the intangible values of the place while at the same time protecting the physical and tangible embodiment of those values. With this new perspective, the effectiveness of management can be monitored by identifying appropriate indicators.

The cases that follow illustrate the reality of many of the issues discussed in this introduction. The final chapter of this publication looks across the four cases to compare how the local administrative and legal environments affected specific issues.

Notes

1. A list of charters and other international standards is available on the Web sites of the International Council on Monuments and Sites (http://www.icomos.org); a more comprehensive list of cultural heritage documents is available at http://www.getty.edu/conservation/resources.

2. The rationale and methodology used in the development of the cases are presented in the next section of this publication.

3. The concept of authenticity was the focus of considerable international debate in recent years. These debates brought into evidence that "authenticity" is difficult to define and

means different things in different cultures. If "authenticity" is seen as a surrogate for "value," it is easier to understand why it can have such different meanings across cultures. For more details on authenticity, see K. E. Larsen, ed., *Nara Conference on Authenticity, Japan 1994*, Paris: UNESCO, ICOMOS & ICCROM, 1995, and G. Araoz and M. MacLean, eds., *Authenticity in the Conservation and Management of the Cultural Heritage of the Americas*, Washington, D.C.: US/ICOMOS & The Getty Conservation Institute, 1999.

4. See, for example, D. Throsby, *Economics and Culture*, Cambridge: Cambridge University Press, 2001.

5. M. Pearson and S. Sullivan, *Looking After Heritage Places: The Basics of Heritage Planning for Managers, Landowners*, Melbourne: Melbourne University Press, 1995, 7.

6. Values-based heritage management has been most thoroughly formalized in Australia, where the Burra Charter guides practitioners. Faced with the technical and philosophical challenges posed by aboriginal places, nonarchitectural sites, and vernacular heritage, Australian heritage professionals found that the existing guidance in the field failed to provide adequate language and sensitivities. Building on the basic ethics and principles of the Venice Charter, they devised guidelines for heritage management—a site-specific approach that calls for an examination of the values ascribed to the place by all its stakeholders, and the precise articulation of what constitutes the site's particular significance. While it is officially endorsed only in Australia, the Burra Charter has become an adaptable model for culturally tailored approaches to site management in other parts of the world.

7. R. Nanda, "Group Report: Values and Society," in N. S. Baer and F. Snickars, *Rational Decision-Making in the Preservation of Cultural Property*, Berlin: Dahlem University Press, 2001, 76.

8. English Heritage, "Policy Statement on Restoration, Reconstruction, and Speculative Recreation of Archaeological Sites Including Ruins," Feb. 2001: para. 32.

9. For more information, see M. de la Torre, *Assessing the Values of Cultural Heritage Research Report 2002*, Los Angeles: The Getty Conservation Institute.

10. For a step-by-step explanation of this process, see M. Demas, "Planning for Conservation and Management of Archaeological Sites: A Values-Based Approach," in J. M. Teutonico and G. Palumbo, *Management Planning for Archaeological Sites*, Los Angeles: The Getty Conservation Institute, 2000, 27–54.

About the Case Studies: Purpose, Design, and Methods

The five partners involved in this project hope that these case studies will motivate other groups or agencies to create examples of values-based site management. As soon as the first case was made available on the Web, the GCI received inquiries as to the methodology followed for its development. This section explains the process that was followed and the reasons for some of the choices made as part of that process.

Representatives of all five organizations—the Australian Heritage Commission, English Heritage, the GCI, Parks Canada, and the U.S. National Park Service—met in Los Angeles in February 2001 at the invitation of the GCI and agreed to work together to create four case studies. In this first meeting it was established that this newly constituted group would determine the final objectives of the project, identify the sites, and generally steer the project as the cases were developed.

While the idea of the project was conceived at the GCI, it was only with the spirited guidance of all the experienced and thoughtful members of the project team that this broad idea was challenged and refined, becoming the case studies here: the systematic analyses of actual planning and management efforts, of the interpretation of principles and guidelines in unique situations, and of the intended and unintended outcomes of operational decisions.

The Partnership and Purpose of the Project

SELECTION OF PARTNERS

The choice of partners for this project was in large part a practical decision of the GCI. For an effort with no real precedent, the potential for finding a common set of goals and objectives was likely to be higher in a collaboration among organizations whose policies were broadly known and well established. It was also helpful to start with organizations with which the Institute had some prior association. Additionally, the use of a common language would help ease the process, given the number of documents that would need to be found, read, written, and circulated. The willingness of the U.S. National Park Service, Parks Canada, the Australian Heritage Commission, and English Heritage to commit to a time- and labor-intensive project like this was the final and essential factor, allowing the creation of a good working team.

From the start the project had a didactic intent. The objective set early on by the members of the Steering Committee of the Case Study Project was to create cases focused on the management of values in heritage sites with the intention of filling a gap they perceived in the conservation and heritage management literature between publications dealing with guiding principles—whether in the form of charters or policy documents—and those of management plans for specific sites. It was felt case studies focusing on analyses of the processes of planning and management for specific sites, the application of principles and guidelines to unique situations, and the results of operational decisions would provide much-needed information on planning and management.

AUDIENCES FOR, AND USES OF, THE CASES

The organizations participating in this project share a belief in the potential usefulness of values-based management in a broad range of international contexts. The cases were written for use by people engaged in the study and/or practice of site management, conservation planning, and historic preservation. They are teachers, researchers, and/or site managers, or studying to do one or more of these things. The reader is assumed to be familiar with heritage management concepts and terminology, international charters and guidance, and general conservation principles.

Heritage professionals in the target audience may represent many disciplines, all of which have a role in the management of cultural sites. In fact, one of the objectives of the project is to present values-based approaches as a common framework that can bring together a diverse and broadly representative group of people who must work together in managing cultural sites.

SELECTION OF SITES

One important task of the Steering Committee was to identify one site to be studied from each of the four participating countries. While the final decision fell to the respective officials from each organization, the group suggested the following criteria:

• Significance at a national level

• Not overly difficult to travel to or visit

• Accessibility and completeness of documentation on the site and its history

• Access to organizations and stakeholders involved

• A published management plan and information on the process used to develop it

• Demonstrated consultation with stakeholders

• Strong interest of site staff in participating in this project

• Examples of conflicts and their resolutions

• Evidence of consideration of the relationship of values to fabric

• Presence of political sensitivities

• Strong didactic potential

The sites selected were Grosse Île and the Irish Memorial National Historic Site (Parks Canada), the Chaco Culture National Historical Park (U.S. National Park Service), Port Arthur Historic Site (The Australian Heritage Commission and Port Arthur Site Management Authority), and Hadrian's Wall World Heritage Site (English Heritage). Together, these sites represent a range of situations with diverse stakeholders and values; interesting differences among the management plans in terms of date, style, and implementation; and an assortment of planning processes that presented specific challenges with obvious potential for use in teaching/learning contexts.

The Design and Methods of the Project

THE INTELLECTUAL CONSTRUCT

At the first meeting in 2001, the broad outlines of the project were defined, and the Steering Committee members began to focus on the issues and questions that would guide the research. While each successive meeting refined the issues further, three central questions were agreed to early on:

• How are the values associated with the site understood and articulated?

• How are these values taken into account in the site's management policies and strategies?

• How do management decisions and actions on-site affect the values?

Once the central questions were established, the group focused on the most appropriate scope and tone for the finished cases. They agreed that each site would be examined through its own lens, and the analysis would exclude any comparison of the relative success of its management against an external or arbitrary standard. Also, each case would present only that site and not assume that the steward agency handles all its sites in the same way. Given the high level of interest and experience of the individuals involved, it remained a challenge throughout the project to steer clear of judgment, while at the same time maintaining a constructively critical and rigorous tone.

In order to provide a context for the discussion of values, policies, and actions, each case first needed to include a history of the place as a heritage site. Second, it was important to examine the administrative and legal environment within which management planning was done, with a view toward how site authorities were helped or hindered in their tasks by legislation, regulations, and other policies. Third, it was crucial to study the actual place, in order to see the impact of particular management decisions.

THE PROCESS OF CREATING THE CASES

A five-step process was used to create each case study:

1. *Research and document collection*

The case-writing team first conducted a thorough review of the relevant heritage statutes and policies and became familiar with the history of each site. They conducted a LEXIS-NEXIS search for relevant news articles and obtained copies of, and became familiar with, other pertinent site-management documents. They wrote summaries of the key documents and generated a time line of key dates in the history of the site. The governing agency and the staff of the site provided pertinent documents, including the management plan, which were then assembled with other information and sent to each member of the team in advance of the site visit.

2. *Site visit*

The entire project team traveled to the site. During the four- or five-day visit, the group toured the site, heard staff presentations, and met with site staff and representatives of other agencies or partners. These meetings took the form of group discussions as well as one-on-one interviews. (In two cases, return visits were made by case writers for additional interviews or to use the site archives.)

On the last half-day of the visit, the project team met to review the main issues that had surfaced during the visit and to discuss how they might be addressed in the case.

3. Drafting

Four people associated with the GCI were responsible for writing the cases. The decision to assign responsibility for the writing to these people instead of employees of the respective agencies associated with the sites was based on the need to have consistency among the cases, to maintain objectivity, and to avoid burdening the partner agencies with additional work.

Starting with the outline and the three questions (noted above) that had been established, the case writers set to work. They studied the official management documents for the site, the legislation that established the site, planning guidelines used by the operating agencies, news stories, professional journals, personal observations, historic photographs, their own photographs, and their extensive notes from the project team meetings as well as field interviews. As questions arose, the writers consulted with one another, other project team members, site staff, and stakeholders for clarification.

4. Review of drafts

Each case was subjected to at least three revisions following reviews by all members of the project team, the relevant site staff, and representatives of the governing agency. The purpose for such extensive review was to ensure that the many issues, interests, and sensitivities were presented in an accurate and balanced way. Also, while the final texts might reflect the perspectives of the project team more than those of the site staff, it was very important to eliminate errors of fact through this vetting. In each case, the governing agency provided a sign-off on the study of its site.

5. Production

Photographs were chosen to support the content of the case studies, and maps were created to orient the reader. The texts were given a final editorial review and made available in PDF format on the GCI's Web site.

It is important to remember that all four case studies present situations that were already found during the time of the project, and some management policies and decisions have already started to change in the short time elapsed since its conclusion. The same holds true of the guidance and management documents used at the sites. Because of the importance that these documents played in the development of the cases, the main ones for each site are made available in the CD-ROM that accompanies this publication. A list of these documents is provided on page iv.

Although the four cases follow the content outline established at the beginning of the project, each one has unique features corresponding to the issues found at each site. The studies are presented here as a set, but they are also intended to be used as separate units for analysis or teaching.

Steering Committee of the Case Study Project

Members' affiliations are given as of the time of the project.

Gordon Bennett
Director
Policy and Government Relations
National Historic Sites Directorate
Parks Canada

Christina Cameron
Director General
National Historic Sites Directorate
Parks Canada

Kate Clarke
Head of Historic Environment Management
English Heritage

Marta de la Torre
Principal Project Specialist
The Getty Conservation Institute

François LeBlanc
Head
Field Projects
The Getty Conservation Institute

Jane Lennon
Commissioner
Australian Heritage Commission

Margaret G. H. MacLean
Heritage Consultant
Los Angeles

Francis P. McManamon
Departmental Consulting Archaeologist
Archaeology and Ethnography
U.S. National Park Service

Randall Mason
Assistant Professor and Director
Graduate Program in Historic Preservation
University of Maryland

David Myers
Research Associate
The Getty Conservation Institute

Dwight Pitcaithley
Chief Historian
U.S. National Park Service

Christopher Young
Head of World Heritage and International Policy
English Heritage

PART TWO **The Case Studies**

Grosse Île and the Irish Memorial National Historic Site

Margaret G. H. MacLean and David Myers

About This Case Study

This case study examines Grosse Île and the Irish Memorial National Historic Site, which is managed by Parks Canada. The small island of Grosse Île is located in the St. Lawrence River, near the city of Quebec. Largely because of its strategic location, it began to play an important role in Canadian history in 1832, functioning as a quarantine station that received newly arriving immigrants from Europe and the British Isles before they reached the mainland. For 150 years it was a place of intense activity; as of 1984, it was recognized as a place of memory by Parks Canada. Its management is still evolving, and the eventful first phases of planning are still fresh in the minds of staff.

This section consists of a brief orientation to the site itself and a preview of issues that are discussed in the rest of the case study.

The next section, "Management Context and History of Grosse Île," describes Parks Canada, including its place in the government, its organization, and the guidance it provides for the resources under its stewardship. This background is meant to aid the reader in understanding the evolution of Parks Canada and the current environment in which decisions are made. This section continues with a description of the strategic location of Grosse Île, the history of its use, and its evolution as a heritage site.

The following section, "Understanding and Protecting the Values of Grosse Île and the Irish Memorial National Historic Site," focuses on the identification and management of the values of the site and takes as its structure the three questions highlighted on page 11: the identification of the values associated with the site, their place in management policies and strategies, and the impact that the actual management of the site is having on the values.

The final section, "Conclusions," reviews the principal issues and questions that have emerged in the discussion of this case. Some of these may also be applicable to other cases in this series, as well as to management situations at other sites with which the reader may be familiar.

This study of the management of Grosse Île and the Irish Memorial National Historic Site draws on extensive consultation among the members of the project steering committee, staff of the site, and Parks Canada authorities. The authors have consulted many reports, plans, and statutory and guidance documents relating to this site, to other Level I heritage sites in Canada, and to Parks Canada in general. They have relied on the staff of the site and of the regional Parks Canada office in Quebec for the interpretation of this documentation and the rationale for many decisions made on-site.

The situation studied in this case existed between June 2001 and June 2002, when the case was developed and written. Parks Canada is a dynamic organization, and certain changes have taken place in the interim, including policy reviews and adjustments; also, certain activities have been completed on-site that had been in the planning stages during the research for this study. The analysis focuses on the situation as it was, not on the recent changes.

Digital reproductions of the following supplementary documents are contained within the accompanying CD-ROM: Grosse Île National Historic Site—Development Concept (1992); Grosse Île National Historic Site—Report on the Public Consultation Program (1994); Part III (Cultural Resource Management Policy) of Parks Canada Guiding Principles and Operational Policies (1994); Commemorative Integrity Statement for Grosse Île and the Irish Memorial National Historic Site (1998); Grosse Île and the Irish Memorial National Historic Site Management Plan (2001); and Guide to the Preparation of Commemorative Integrity Statements (2002).

Issues Addressed in This Case Study

Many of the challenges of managing a heritage site designated as having national significance are very similar from one site to another: defining what is important and determining what is fragile, what requires vigilant protection, and what merits interpretation for the public on whose behalf it is held in trust. The three questions that anchor the discussion testify to these similarities. The difficulties faced by those who plan for and manage heritage sites quite often arise when policies conflict or when the balance among social, administrative, or other components is upset. These problems and their resolutions are opportunities—or "learning points"—from which others involved in heritage site maintenance can learn.

In this case study, four main learning points emerge:

1. As practiced by the planners and stewards of Grosse Île and the Irish Memorial National Historic Site, values-based site management places significant weight on the role and voice of stakeholders. Initial assumptions about categories of stakeholders differed somewhat from the actual stakeholders who stepped forward. The process was designed to be flexible and inclusive, and it expanded and worked effectively, even in ways that were not always anticipated.

2. With regard to a national historic site like Grosse Île, the mission of Parks Canada is to foster appreciation of Canada's past by protecting and presenting the site for the benefit, education, and enjoyment of current and future generations. The stewards are responsible for focusing on aspects of the site that define its value to the nation. Thus, local values and interest in the site are secondary to values that are meaningful at the national level.

3. Parks Canada has developed two pivotal concepts—commemorative intent and commemorative integrity—that define the principal objectives for the protection and presentation of a national-level site and describe in detail what constitutes the site in its optimal condition. These two concepts serve to anchor policy discussions about objectives and limits of acceptable change.

4. At Grosse Île, one of the most interesting challenges in the development of the interpretive scheme is how to tell one of the principal stories of the site when much of the historic fabric associated with that story has been destroyed and overlaid with later additions. Interpretive programming that enables visitors to see past the visual confusion created by the existing physical conditions is difficult but necessary. Moreover, choices regarding treatment interventions (which affect the appearance of the built resources) must balance historical accuracy with physical durability while maintaining the hierarchy of messages mandated by authorities.

Management Context and History of Grosse Île

This section looks first at Parks Canada, the agency responsible for Grosse Île and the Irish Memorial, as an administrative entity and as a keeper of heritage sites on behalf of the Canadian people. The organization has evolved over time, and its purpose and mission are reflected in the way in which its holdings have been and are valued and managed. Following this account of the management context is a fuller description of Grosse Île itself, of its location in the St. Lawrence River, and of how it came to occupy a position of significance.

Parks Canada

The Parks Canada Agency was established on 1 April 1999 by an Act of the Parliament of Canada.[1]

The Chief Executive Office of Parks Canada reports directly to the minister of Canadian heritage. This minister "is responsible for national policies and programs relating to broadcasting, cultural industries, arts, heritage, official languages, Canadian identity, Canadian symbols, exchanges, multiculturalism, and sport."[2]

Prior to the passage of the *Agency Act*, Parks Canada had been part of three different departments during the period of time covered in this case study. For each of these three departments, the official responsible for Parks Canada was an assistant deputy minister. From 1974 to 1979, Parks Canada was part of the Department of Indian and Northern Affairs; from 1979 to 1993, it was part of the Department of the Environment; and from 1993 to 1999, it was part of the Department of Canadian Heritage.

The mandate of Parks Canada is "to protect and present nationally significant examples of Canada's natural and cultural heritage, and foster public understanding, appreciation and enjoyment in ways that ensure their ecological and commemorative integrity for present and future generations."[3]

The agency administers three systems—national parks, national historic sites, and national marine conservation areas—and other programs concerned with Canada's heritage.

The national historic sites directorate of Parks Canada "is responsible for Canada's program of historical commemoration, which recognizes nationally significant places, persons and events."[4] It comprises not only the historic sites but also the more than five hundred persons and three hundred events deemed to be of national significance. Parks Canada has direct responsibility for 145 of the 849 designated national historic sites across the country. The agency contributes to the conservation and/or presentation of an additional seventy-one sites through cost-sharing agreements.

Parks Canada has a broad range of responsibilities in the management of national historic sites. These include developing policies for conserving and presenting each site's cultural resources, for conserving natural resources, and for providing infrastructure for public visitation. These activities often involve consultation with interested members of the Canadian public. The agency also reviews existing heritage legislation in order to propose enhancements to federal law for the protection of national historic sites.

The federally appointed Historic Sites and Monuments Board of Canada (HSMBC, or "the Board") advises the minister of Canadian heritage on various aspects of the work of the historic sites program. The Board is made up of individuals representing all of the Canadian provinces and territories and some of the national heritage agencies. Their duties and functions are described in the *Historic Sites and Monuments Act*, and the Board develops its own policies and procedures, which are then approved by the minister. With the administrative support of staff from the national historic sites program, the Board examines new site or monument nominations, commissions research as needed, balances stakeholder claims, and formulates recommendations to the minister regarding designation and the most appropriate form of commemoration of a given subject.

The criteria for national significance (as stated by the HSMBC) are as follows:

A place may be designated of national historic significance by virtue of a direct association with a nationally significant aspect of Canadian history. An archaeological site, structure, building, group of buildings, district, or

Peopling the Land
Canada's earliest inhabitants
Migration and immigration
Settlement
People and the environment

Governing Canada
Politics and political processes
Government institutions
Security and law
Military and defense
Canada and the world

Expressing Intellectual and Cultural Life
Learning and the arts
Architecture and design
Science
Sports and leisure
Philosophy and spirituality

Developing Economies
Hunting and gathering
Extraction and production
Trade and commerce
Communications and transportation
Technology and engineering
Labor

Building Social and Community Life
Community organizations
Religious institutions
Education and social well-being
Social movements

Figure 1.1. National Historic Sites of Canada thematic framework.

cultural landscape of potential national historic significance will:

a. illustrate an exceptional creative achievement in concept and design, technology, and/or planning, or a significant stage in the development of Canada; or

b. illustrate or symbolize in whole or in part a cultural tradition, a way of life, or ideas important in the development of Canada; or

c. be most explicitly and meaningfully associated or identified with persons who are deemed of national historic importance; or

d. be most explicitly and meaningfully associated or identified with events that are deemed of national historic importance.[5]

Since 1981 the work of the Board in the identification of subjects for commemoration has also been guided by the National Historic Sites of Canada System Plan,[6] which provides a framework to ensure that the National Historic Sites System adequately represents each of the important historic themes in Canadian history. The system plan uses a thematic construct to organize history, classify sites, and provide a comprehensive view of Canadian history; the themes of the current plan are presented in figure 1.1. Today, Grosse Île and the Irish Memorial National Historic Site is associated with the "Peopling the Land" theme, under the subtheme "Migration and immigration."

Geography and History of Grosse Île

BEFORE 1832

Human habitation on Grosse Île prior to European contact appears to have been occasional and seasonal, probably attracted by the fish and game resources that still draw hunters to this area.[7] When the Europeans arrived in the sixteenth century, they quickly recognized the value of the St. Lawrence River, which gave their ships access well into the North American interior.

The first record of a land concession on Grosse Île dates to 1662, only fifty-four years after the city of Quebec was founded on the site of the indigenous settlement of Stadacona. For the next 150 years, Grosse Île was used primarily for hunting and fishing by nonresident colonial landowners. By 1816, records indicate the presence of homesteads and agriculture; farming continued on Grosse Île until 1832, when the island was expropriated by the government for use as an immigrant quarantine station.

1832 TO 1937

After the end of the Napoleonic wars in 1815, emigration to North America from Ireland, Scotland, and England surged. By 1830, Quebec had become by far Canada's largest immigrant port, accepting some thirty thousand entrants annually, two-thirds of whom came from Ireland. With these new arrivals came the cholera epidemic that was then raging in the British Isles; about thirty-eight hundred people died of cholera in 1832 in Quebec City,

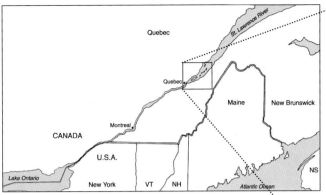

Figure 1.2. Map of the region. This map shows the Canadian Maritime Provinces, just north of the New England states, and the waterway that leads from the North Atlantic Ocean into the Gulf of St. Lawrence and continues as the St. Lawrence River past Quebec and into the interior. Grosse Île, shown on the map, sits at a transitional position in the river where freshwater meets seawater; it is therefore home to a distinctive array of flora and fauna. The towns shown on the south shore are those from which ferry service carries visitors to the island.

and half that number died in Montreal. With this, and with their experience with outbreaks of typhus among immigrants in the 1820s, the British authorities recognized the need for an immigrant quarantine station for the port of Quebec to check the spread of disease. They chose Grosse Île for its size, its harbor, its proximity to Quebec City, and its isolated position in the river.

The Great Famine raked over Ireland from 1845 to 1849; during its peak years of 1847–48, about 100,000 European emigrants came to Quebec City, most of them Irish. Already weakened by malnutrition, many contracted typhus and dysentery during the six-week sea voyage. Waves of gravely ill passengers overwhelmed the quarantine station's staff and facilities—there were only 200 beds for sick immigrants and about 800 for the healthy; yet, by the spring of 1847, more than 12,000 individuals were detained at Grosse Île.

Colonial authorities scrambled to build hospitals and shelters. When the station's facilities were finally adequate, the end of the sailing season stopped the seemingly endless stream of immigrant ships. During the course of 1847, more than 5,000 immigrants had perished at sea, and 5,424 more had died and were buried on Grosse Île. Thousands more perished in Quebec, Montreal, and other cities in eastern Canada.[8]

After a less-devastating epidemic of cholera hit in 1854, the function of Grosse Île began to change. From 1861 to 1900, while the average annual number of immi-

grants to Quebec City remained between 25,000 and 26,800, they were coming from different places. During this period the Irish became the minority; English emigrants were most numerous, and more Scandinavians and other western Europeans were joining them. They all were leaving considerably less-desperate conditions in Europe and Great Britain. They arrived in Canada in much better health, having been far better accommodated and fed on board than earlier immigrants. The replacement of sailing vessels with steamships cut the crossing time from Great Britain to twelve days—one-quarter of the previous passage. And, toward the end of the nineteenth century, St. John and Halifax, better connected to the country's interior by railroad, began to compete with Quebec as immigration ports.

During the economic boom from 1900 to 1915, annual arrivals to Quebec surged to 92,000. While emigrants from Great Britain still dominated and many still came from Scandinavia and western Europe, joining them now were people from the Middle East, Australia, North and South Africa, Asia, and the Caribbean.

During World War I and continuing through the Depression, immigration numbers dropped markedly. Between 1932 and 1941, Quebec received only a quarter of those arriving in Canada, reflecting the opening of new ports of entry, some on the Pacific coast. In February 1937, the Canadian government finally closed the Grosse Île quarantine station; it was no longer needed.

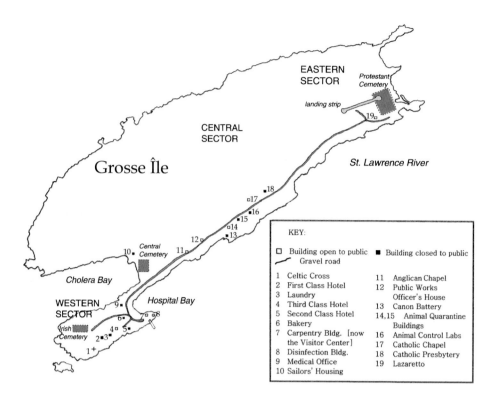

Figure 1.3. Map of Grosse Île. Grosse Île is one of the twenty-one islands in the Îles-aux-Grues archipelago in the St. Lawrence River, about 48 kilometers (30 miles) northeast (downstream) from the city of Quebec. The island is 2.5 kilometers (1½ miles) long and 800 meters (roughly half a mile) wide at its broadest point, with a land surface of approximately 185 hectares (457 acres). The shoreline includes beaches (at Cholera Bay), cliffs (on the southern edge of the Western and Central Sectors), tidal wetlands (Hospital Bay), and tide pools. Pine trees and other woodland plants cover much of the island north of the gravel road. Access to the island is largely by ferry from the south shore of the St. Lawrence River; staff and visitors are ferried to the wharf, which is located at the northeast end of the Western Sector. (Numbered and named features are discussed in the text and/or shown in photographs.)

1937 TO 1988

During World War II, under the Canadian Department of National Defense, Grosse Île became the War Disease Control Station. Taking advantage of the site's isolation, scientists experimented with viruses and vaccines to prevent the deliberate introduction of animal diseases to North America. Although this work ended in 1945, similar scientific work was performed there from 1951 to 1956 in response to the Korean War and the Cold War.

In 1957 animal disease research on the island shifted to the Canadian Department of Agriculture, whose work continued there until 1988. In 1965 Agriculture Canada's contagious disease division also started using the island as a quarantine station for imported livestock. Although there have been no animal quarantine activities on Grosse Île since 1986, lands and facilities used by Agriculture Canada are still subject to sectoral agreements between Parks Canada and Agriculture Canada.[9]

Grosse Île Becomes a Heritage Site

This section traces the evolution of the status of Grosse Île as a heritage site and discusses how ideas and contributions leading to an understanding of the site's values and significance emerged during this process and coalesced.

1897: THE FIRST PILGRIMAGE

Grosse Île was first recognized as a place of significance in 1897, when a group from the Ancient Order of Hibernians, an Irish Catholic fraternal organization whose members were Canadians of Irish descent, visited Grosse Île to commemorate the fiftieth anniversary of the terrible year of 1847. It is important to note that the Great Famine of the mid-1840s in Ireland was not a simple natural disaster; rather, it was a tragic coincidence of failed agricultural methods, harsh social policies, unrelenting poverty, and inadequate medical practices, the legacies of which still haunt English-Irish relations. At only fifty years after the fact, some who made the Hibernian pilgrimage to Grosse Île in 1897 were themselves likely to have been survivors of that traumatic time; others may have been relatives or friends of those who perished. For them and for many others, Grosse Île had the powerful and poignant quality of a cemetery of innocents.

1909: DEDICATION OF THE CELTIC CROSS

In 1909 the Ancient Order of Hibernians dedicated a Celtic Cross on a high promontory on the southwestern end of the island as a memorial to the lost immigrants. Inscriptions on the base of the monument testify particularly to residual bitterness about the conditions that forced

Figure 1.4. The Celtic Cross. Erected in 1909 by the Ancient Order of Hibernians to commemorate the Irish emigration, it stands on a south-facing cliff in the Western Sector of Grosse Île; cut from Irish stone, it is about 15 meters (49 feet) high.

the flight of so many Irish to the New World. The English inscription reads, "Sacred to the memory of thousands of Irish emigrants who, to preserve the faith, suffered hunger and exile in 1847–48, and stricken with fever, ended here their sorrowful pilgrimage." The translation of the Gaelic inscription reads rather differently: "Children of the Gael died in the thousands on this island, having fled from the laws of foreign tyrants and artificial famine in the years 1847–48. God's blessing on them. Let this monument be a token to their name and honor from the Gaels of America. God Save Ireland."

From 1909 on, the Ancient Order of Hibernians organized a nearly annual pilgrimage from Quebec City to the great stone cross, a tradition that continues to the present.[10] To go there as a pilgrim was to retrace the steps of one's forebears and to acknowledge the courage and pathos of the immigrants' journeys. The isolated location of the island and its minimal development easily evoked earlier times and surely added to the emotional power of the experience.

1974: HSMBC RECOMMENDS NATIONAL HISTORIC SITE DESIGNATION

In 1974, long after Grosse Île had finished its work as an immigrant quarantine station and had seen service as a biological testing station, an agricultural research station, and a livestock quarantine station, the HSMBC made its recommendation to place a commemorative plaque on Grosse Île. With the acceptance of this recom-mendation by the minister, Grosse Île became a national historic site. The plaque, unveiled in 1980, bore the following inscription:[11]

> In 1832, a quarantine station was established here on Grosse Île in an attempt to prevent the introduction of cholera from Europe. The station's medical and quarantine facilities proved inadequate in the face of the cholera and typhus which periodically accompanied immigrant ships; conse-quently, epidemics spread through the Canadas on a number of occasions in the course of the nineteenth century. Origi-nally designed as a temporary establishment under military command, the station was later operated as a regular service by the Canadian government until superseded in 1937 by new facilities at Québec.[12]

1981: NATIONAL HISTORIC SITES OF CANADA SYSTEM PLAN

With the introduction of the National Historic Sites of Canada System Plan, all of the national historic sites were concatenated into a thematic framework, described ear-lier.[13] By categorizing sites according to themes and sub-themes, the system plan aids the HSMBC and Parks Canada to see the strengths and gaps in the commemora-tive programs they oversee and to identify needs or opportunities for education programs or strategic planning.

1984: THE BOARD REAFFIRMS THE SIGNIFICANCE OF GROSSE ÎLE IN CANADIAN HISTORY

In 1983 and 1984, the HSMBC discussed at length the theme of immigration. The minutes of its meetings record that "the Board once more stated its opinion that the theme of Immigration is among the most significant in Canadian history." In the same meeting, the Board "reaffirmed its statement of June 1974 that the Quarantine Stations at Grosse Île and Partridge Island are of national historic significance" and recommended that "in light of the number and quality of the in situ resources on Grosse Île related to the theme of immigration, the Minister should consider acquiring the island, or portions of it, and there developing a national historic park."[14]

1988: GROSSE ÎLE COMES UNDER THE JURISDICTION OF PARKS CANADA

Following the recommendations of the Board, the envi-ronment minister (then responsible for Parks Canada) reached an understanding with the agriculture minister, and in August 1988 a formal agreement was reached between the two departments to transfer the buildings and sites of historical interest to Parks Canada.[15]

Figure 1.5. Two of the ferries that operate out of the private marina at Berthier-sur-Mer. The one on the left can carry 140 passengers; the one on the right, 50.

Figure 1.6. A view toward the east, showing the Disinfection Building and the Carpentry and Plumbing Building (now the Visitor Center and gift shop) at the left. Built in 1892 on the north end of the western wharf, the Disinfection Building housed three disinfection chambers and, eventually, showers. The south wing was erected in 1915; the north, in 1927. The Disinfection Building has been restored to its 1927 appearance; it is the first place modern visitors enter.

Beginning in the late 1980s and extending into the mid-1990s, the period covered by planning for the management of Grosse Île, there were significant policy changes and related developments in Parks Canada. These included the development and approval of the cultural resource management policy and of commemorative integrity, both of which were much more explicitly values-based than Parks Canada's previous policy documents. While it was a challenge for people involved in planning (and management) to integrate the latest thinking, there was, overall, surprisingly little lag between new policy direction and other activities.

Facilities and Services Today

Grosse Île and the Irish Memorial National Historic Site is open to the public May through October. High season for visitation generally lasts from mid-June through the beginning of September. All visitors to the island arrive by private ferry service from either the south shore of the St. Lawrence or from the port of Quebec. Ferries from the south shore depart from the ports of Berthier-sur-Mer and Montmagny (fig. 1.2). Most visitors depart from Berthier-sur-Mer for the thirty-minute boat ride to the island. This schedule allows visitors to stay at the site from two to four hours. In 2001, adult tickets from Berthier-sur-Mer were about $34 each, and a child's ticket (ages 6–12) was about $17.[16] Admission to the site is included in ticket prices (all

quoted in U.S. dollars). The ferry service from Montmagny mainly transports site staff. The journey takes some forty-five minutes, depending on the tides. Two round-trip ferries depart from this small dock—early each morning and in the late afternoon.

Ferries from the port of Quebec are marketed as cruises offering sightseeing along the river rather than as transportation exclusively to Grosse Île. They are available by reservation only. The boat trip takes approximately three hours each way, thus allowing visitors to stay at the site for about three hours. Tickets for this service from Quebec are about $48 for adults and about $24 for children.

Upon arrival at the wharf on the south shore of Grosse Île, which is situated in the island's Western Sector, visitors are met by trained guides. Guided tours are divided into three parts. They begin with a visit to the Disinfection Building (location 8, fig. 1.3), where several exhibits explain the history and workings of the quarantine station. This building was fitted with bathing facilities for new arrivals and with a steam chamber for disinfecting their clothing and carried items.

Visitors can then take a sixty-minute hike around the Western Sector, to see the hotels and other facilities (locations 2–6, fig. 1.3), the Celtic Cross (location 1, fig. 1.4), and the Irish Memorial at the Irish Cemetery. This loop takes the visitors back around to a point at the head of Hospital Bay, where a tram takes visitors out to the Central and Eastern Sectors.

Figure 1.7. The Catholic Presbytery and the chapel next door, built in 1848 and 1874, respectively. The presbytery was remodeled in 1913, when a wraparound porch was removed and a second story was expanded. In the backyard of this structure, archaeological work, shown in figure 1.8, was done in summer 2001.

Figure 1.8. A small excavation in the back of the Catholic Presbytery. Opened in autumn 2001 as part of a water piping project, the dig revealed wooden piers on which a small outbuilding stood. While no traces of the building remained above ground, this find substantiates records and photographs of the time.

Figure 1.9. The Public Works Officer's House (location 12, fig. 1.3). It was an important building, judging from the quality of its decoration. The exterior has recently been restored, and the interior has been conserved.

This approximately sixty-minute tour includes a stop at the Catholic Chapel and Presbytery (locations 17 and 18, fig. 1.7) and the Lazaretto (location 19, fig. 1.3), where the interpretive scheme focuses on the tragedy of 1847. Fifteen of the buildings surviving from the quarantine station will eventually be accessible to visitors.[17] Several are undergoing conservation work and will be open to the public in the near future, such as the Public Works Officer's House, the Anglican Chapel, and the Marconi Station. The other historic buildings, as well as those from the Canadian Army and Agriculture Canada's occupation of the island, are not open to the public.

Some of the historic structures are used by visitors and staff for other purposes. The old Carpentry and Plumbing Building (location 7, fig. 1.3) houses the Visitor Center and its gift shop. The second floor holds the administrative offices of the site. The Disinfection Building (location 8) and the Third Class Hotel (location 4) house public washrooms. The Third Class Hotel also accommodates the cafeteria that serves visitors as well as site staff and others working on the island.[18] Rooms on the upper floors of this building are used as short-term sleeping accommodations for staff and others working on site. The Medical Examination Office (location 9) as well as some buildings in the Central Sector are also used as seasonal residences for staff.[19]

More-modern facilities on the island include an aircraft landing strip in the Eastern Sector, used exclusively by Parks Canada; a wastewater treatment plant; an underground water storage tank; and heating oil tanks.

Figure 1.10. The Anglican Chapel (location 11, fig. 1.3). Built in 1877–78, the Anglican Chapel was made of wood and set on masonry pillars. It was intended for the use of the staff and residents of the island, not for the immigrants. In order to preserve the structure's largely original appearance and to stop leaks, the pillars are being reinforced; a moisture barrier is being placed between the interior walls and the board-and-batten exterior skin; and the tin roof is being repaired.

Figure 1.11. The gift shop interior.

Figure 1.12. Built in 1912 of concrete with some wooden cladding and other details, the First Class Hotel accommodated arriving passengers who were placed under medical observation. By the second half of the nineteenth century, the shipping companies had made it clear to the authorities that facilities for passengers being detained for medical reasons needed to correspond to their classes of passage, to avoid uncomfortable mixing of passengers.

Figure 1.13. Now called the Second Class Hotel, this building served as the first-class hotel from its construction in 1893 until 1912. This two-story wooden building is 46 meters (150 feet) long and had room for 152 cabin passengers; there was a dining room, a sitting room, and washrooms.

Figure 1.14. The Third Class Hotel, built in 1914, is the largest of the three hotels, designed to hold 140 beds in its fifty-two rooms. Built of concrete, it included kitchens and dining areas at either end of each floor of the building, with living quarters in the center. While it offered close quarters and little privacy, it was fitted with electricity and central heating. Today this building houses the cafeteria that caters to visitors to Grosse Île. Also seen here is the square-plan Bakery, built between 1902 and 1910. Inside the wooden building are many of the original specialized features used for making and baking bread.

Understanding and Protecting the Values of Grosse Île and the Irish Memorial National Historic Site

Values Associated with Grosse Île

In essence, the values associated with Grosse Île emerge in three categories: the role played by this island in Canada's history; the good condition and representative character of the buildings and other features relating to its various roles over the period of a century; and the potential for effective communication of its importance. Even though all of the elements of value that are currently recognized and captured in the management policies and principles for the site were present in the earliest discussions, they were articulated and prioritized slightly differently by the stakeholders as the process detailed below unfolded.

PARKS CANADA BEGINS TO FORMULATE ITS PERSPECTIVE

For Grosse Île, as with most historic sites of national or international interest, perspectives on the value of the place emerged gradually from several directions. Following the 1988 agreement to transfer historic resources on the island to Parks Canada, the staff launched the process of planning for the preservation and presentation of the new national historic site.[20] The products required of this planning process are described in detail in Parks Canada management directives.[21] They were:

1. *Themes and objectives*—based on the commemorative intent established by the HSMBC when the site was designated, which articulates the historical rationale and national context for planning, management, and development of the site.

2. *Terms of reference*—provide direction on essential protection and site operation measures, pending the approval of a management plan.

3. *Interim management guidelines*—provide direction on the priorities, roles, responsibilities, and implementation of the planning program.

4. *Management plan concepts*—identify a range of possible options that would direct the future management of the site.

5. *Management plan*—articulates long-range direction for the protection, presentation, and use of resources of the site, and the proposed means and strategies for achieving statement management objectives. The management plan provides a framework within which subsequent decision making and detailed planning could take place.

The Quebec regional staff of Parks Canada undertook and reported on their work on items 1 through 3 in 1989 in a public information paper.[22] The information paper became the basis of the development concept discussed below,[23] and it represented the first official proposal of Parks Canada regarding the values of Grosse Île. It considered how the site might best be presented to the public and elaborated on the themes that would frame the interpretive program.[24]

The general theme was "Canada: Land of Welcome and Hope," to be expressed through two themes. The main theme, "Immigration to Canada via Quebec City (1830–1939)," would be conveyed by six concepts:
- the national and international context surrounding the arrival of immigrants in Canada
- government policy
- risks and perils of the Atlantic crossing
- profiles of immigrants
- public opinion about new arrivals
- contributions of immigrants to Canadian society

The second theme, "Grosse Île Quarantine Station (1832–1937)," would be conveyed by five concepts:
- selecting the site of Grosse Île
- the station as it dealt with people and their illnesses
- operation of the station (authorities, legislation, reception of immigrants, the tragic years of 1832, 1834, and 1847)
- daily life
- geographical and environmental features

This last subtheme dealing with the geographical setting seemingly recognizes the natural value of the site and "will try to evoke the natural environment as it may have been at the time . . . and will consider the natural environment as it appears today."[25]

In effect, Parks Canada was devising an approach to presenting the stories of a small island and attempting to connect them to the expansive concepts that framed the national experience. It had worked to present Grosse Île in the proposal documents as a national historic site and endeavored to reveal the values recognized for the place by means of research and expert testimony. The HSMBC had stipulated that interpretation should focus on the national significance of the immigration theme and not exclusively on immigration from Ireland, although particular emphasis would be placed on Irish immigration.[26] In what can be seen as an early version of a statement of significance, the public information paper states:

> The Grosse Île quarantine station played a major role in the process of immigration to central Canada for more than a century. The contribution of immigration to the formation of the Canadian population was substantial. Immigrants arriving from every corner of Europe, from every class, helped to build the country by bringing their courage, toil, and culture. Some of them settled in Québec, while others traveled onward to various regions of Canada and the United States. The least fortunate, no doubt several thousand strong, saw their adventures end before their new lives began.[27]

While this perspective shaped the research and its outcome to a considerable extent, other values were also recognized and described in this early document. The information paper also incorporates the results of a marketing study conducted on behalf of Parks Canada.[28] Perhaps as a result of this market orientation, the information paper recognizes the economic value placed on the site by the authorities, interest groups, and communities on the south shore of the St. Lawrence River, who saw the development of Grosse Île as a potential engine for regional tourism and economic development. The information paper also identified actual and potential stakeholders of the national historic site, such as some ethnic and cultural communities (mentioning the Irish specifically), which it recognized would attribute spiritual and associative values to the site. And, while it is not discussed in the paper, an interesting challenge taking shape was that of presenting a national story with an Irish connection within a long-established local society that was French speaking and not particularly enthusiastic about all aspects of immigration.

Many of the buildings and structures dating from 1847 onward still stood, and identifiable ruins and sub-surface remains of historic features were located all over the island. These historic features—housing, kitchens, disinfection facilities, isolation wards, hospitals, residences, piers, roads, churches, and so on—were found to be remarkably authentic, as few major changes were ever made. They were witness to all chapters in the history of Grosse Île.

Furniture, fittings, personal items, and even vehicles from all phases of the island's use were also found in good condition, evoking the quality of life for the various kinds of residents, patients, and visitors who passed through. Moreover, the unique character of the island in its riverine location gave rise to a great variety of habitats, flora, and fauna.

The paper concludes with a summary of reasons why Parks Canada predicted that Grosse Île would become a significant site in the national system: the continuing importance of immigration in Canada's history; the number, diversity, and representative quality of the cultural resources; the emotional power of the place for thousands of descendants of immigrants (particularly the Irish); and its geographic location and favorable position on the tourism market.

PARKS CANADA PRESENTS ITS IDEAS AND PLANS TO THE PUBLIC

The Parks Canada guidance available at the time states that

> management planning is based on consensus, both internally through team work and functional review, and externally, through public participation. . . . A comprehensive public consultation strategy should be developed early in the planning program to ensure that operationally relevant information is sought, obtained and used proactively, and to facilitate consensus building with stakeholders and with the public at large.[29]

In early 1982, the public consultation effort was launched by Parks Canada to present its plans for the protection and interpretation of the site. In advance of the public meetings, copies of the development concept document were made available to interest groups and the press in areas where the meetings would be held.

In spite of the extensive research and preparation of thorough and comprehensive internal documents relating to all aspects of the history of Grosse Île, the development concept was subject to fairly broad and, in some cases, quite negative interpretation by certain groups. The development concept carried forth the themes of immigration and quarantine identified in the information paper, but it did not reflect the sensitivity to the Irish tragedy that was evident in other preliminary documents.

Throughout, from descriptions of the status and condition of individual features and classes of resources on the island through a detailed section about the government's objectives for the site,[30] there is no mention of the experience of the Irish in 1847. The main point of contention during the public debate was that some groups felt significance was being taken away from the Irish tragedy of 1847. In a discussion of how the site should be promoted, the topic arises:

> As for the "image" of the site to be promoted, both current and potential clienteles clearly stated that the theme of immigration has little impact. In that respect, the image must be modeled on clientele expectations, interests, and motivations, using the thematic context primarily as a backdrop. . . . It is also felt that there should not be too much emphasis on the tragic aspects of the history of Grosse Île. *On the contrary, the painful events of 1832 to 1847, which have often been overemphasized in the past, need to be put back into perspective, without robbing them of their importance* [emphasis added].[31]

The unfortunate last sentence of this statement would be quoted often in the next phase of the process.

After a lengthy exploration of the local commercial development interests and logistical considerations relating to transportation and infrastructure, the report returned to the subject of values and themes, stating that one of the three development principles should be respect for the emotions felt by visitors who are connected to those who died on the island and the fact that the island is seen as a "place of pilgrimage, remembrance, and contemplation." The second principle was that the interpretive program should cover the full range of historical themes chosen for the site. The third principle was that the development of Grosse Île would follow an integrated approach, "drawing on both the natural and cultural facets of the site."[32]

THE PUBLIC RESPONDS

17 March–8 April 1992
Several information sessions were held in Montmagny, Quebec, L'Île-aux-Grues, St. Malachie, and Montreal, attended by approximately two hundred people.

22 April–20 May 1992
A series of three formal public meetings were held in Montmagny, Quebec, and Montreal.

Two hundred Irish Canadians who attended the final meeting in this series insisted that additional meetings be held outside Quebec in order to give more people from across Canada the chance to be heard, adding that the development concept did not do justice to, or was otherwise deficient with, respect to the "Irish dimension" of the site. This point of view was echoed in statements from across the country. The minister directed Parks Canada to organize a second round of public meetings in spring 1993.

16 February 1993
The *Grosse Île National Historic Site—Development Concept Supplement*[33] was issued in response to the clearly unexpected reactions of many Irish Canadians to the original development concept document. This supplement was intended to "expand upon and clarify certain points before continuing with the public exercise."[34] The document acknowledges the inappropriateness of the emphasis of the development concept:

> Based on this passage [*quoted above*], representatives of the Irish community have generally attributed to the Canadian Parks Service the intention of minimizing the importance of the tragedy that Irish immigrants experienced in 1832 and 1847. Such is not the case. The passage in question expresses the personal opinion of individuals who participated in the market study; that is, that *promotion of the site* for future tourists—which was the specific issue they were addressing—should not be based solely on the tragic events of 1832 and 1847.[35]

Correcting what had become—and would continue to be—an emotionally charged situation promised to be a test for those who would manage the next phase of the process. In this document, Parks Canada acknowledges that clarification is needed when it states, "in light of the reactions and comments received, the Canadian Parks Service has concluded that the March 1992 document did not fulfill its mission of informing the public. It is indeed somewhat vague on certain points, particularly those of specific concern to the Irish community."[36] The last page of this document attempts to correct the vagueness of the development concept by stating clearly and forcefully the intentions of the Canadian Parks Service with regard to the site, which include utmost respect for the Irish events on the island. It further recommends that "the expression of the immigration theme as 'Canada: Land of Welcome and Hope' should be dropped; the tragic dimensions of events on the island make it inappropriate. The story told, and the theme, is *immigration*; simply that."[37]

22 March–15 April 1993

In this second round, seven public meetings were convened in Vancouver; Fredericton, N.B.; Charlottetown, P.E.I.; and Toronto. Participants at these meetings made statements and submitted briefs; people who did not attend were invited to submit formal statements as well. A toll-free telephone number was set up to take statements from callers. Written statements were received from 228 people, most of Irish descent. Some 920 people sent letters to Prime Minister Brian Mulroney, whose Irish heritage did not escape the writers' notice. About two-thirds of the writers used boilerplate text that had been suggested for this purpose. The letters and the written briefs demonstrate the deep emotion stirred by reaction to the perceived shortcomings of the development plan, but most convey concern without accusations. Three petitions were also received bearing signatures of 23,855 additional people.[38]

The content of the responses relating to the significance of the site stressed the importance of Grosse Île as a memorial to the dead and as a reminder of a bitter chapter in Irish history. Present in many of the statements was the appreciation that many immigrants recovered from illnesses and went on to thrive; even so, this was not considered sufficient reason to forget the tragedy. Some note that the immigrant experience of the 1840s was not a simple, joyful arrival on the fertile shores of Canada as much as it was the end to a treacherous crossing through hell and high water.

Apart from the occasional inflammatory missives, these were genuine sentiments, put forth in good faith during this uncomfortable episode. Some difficulty was probably inevitable at this point, as the site was, in effect, converted from a shrine of significance to a specific group to a national historic site. And while the former memorializes a tragedy, the latter was intended to celebrate the arrival and contributions of thousands of immigrants to Canada. The National Historic Sites of Canada System Plan[39] had not been in force for very long, and it seemed to some that these efforts to convey the story of immigration—at one of the few sites with the historic fabric to support the story—were taking over the long-established significance of the site. The task ahead for Parks Canada would be to recognize and shelter the spiritual qualities of the place as the development of the national historic site went forward.

RESULTS OF THE PUBLIC CONSULTATION PROGRAM

Although the public consultation program had a strong confrontational edge, Parks Canada published its experience of this pivotal phase of planning at Grosse Île. The staff transcribed all the audiotaped verbal presentations at the public meetings as well as the messages left at the toll-free telephone number. They collected all the briefs presented and all the letters received by the government. Each one had its own computer file, and the topics covered were classified and charted. This documentation now constitutes an important resource for those in search of models for heritage preservation.

March 1994

Parks Canada published *Grosse Île National Historic Site— Report on the Public Consultation Program* (Parks Canada 1994c), which presents passages quoted from these files, organized under five topic areas.[40] It also lists the names of people and organizations present at each of the public meetings.

The report contains only minimal analysis or judgment of the commentaries, and no attempt was made to react to the issues. It is remarkably free of defensiveness and, in fact, encourages still more feedback. The final page in the report text informs the reader that the HSMBC would be responsible for the analysis of the findings from the consultation phase and would submit its recommendations to the minister. The government would then formulate and announce its position regarding the "orientation of the project."

10 August 1994

Minister of Canadian Heritage Michel Dupuy announced that he had accepted the new advice of the HSMBC regarding the future development of Grosse Île, and thus he would direct Parks Canada to tell "the full story of the Canadian immigrant experience at Grosse Île. The Irish experience on the island, especially during the tragic epidemic years of the first half of the nineteenth century, is to be a particular focus of the commemoration. . . . [He] also announced the establishment of a panel of prominent Canadians reporting to him to assist Parks Canada in the implementation of his decision on Grosse Île."[41]

The members of the panel, together with eight ranking Parks Canada staff, analyzed all the responses and requests received during the public consultation program, and they formulated and justified a set of recommendations for submission to Dupuy.

August 1995

Parks Canada published the report of the advisory panel,[42] which contains eleven recommendations on matters of interpretation, use of specific historic buildings, ranking of the island's resources with regard to their care, themes for development, tone of presentations, ambience and atmosphere, financing, and access. Each recommendation is accompanied by specific operational suggestions as to how it might best be realized.

One dependable fact in the heritage field is that values evolve with time and with the involvement of new stakeholders. In the case of Grosse Île, however, it was becoming clear that the values of the original Irish stakeholders had not changed to permit a broad acceptance of the proposals as stated in the development concept. It appeared that an optimistic, thematic construct that knitted together Canada's national historic sites had, in Grosse Île, collided with memories of suffering and injustice that still remain profoundly important to some people of Irish nationality or descent. It also became evident that both positions represent legitimate values of Grosse Île and that they needed to be preserved and presented in the new national site.

In recounting events whose resolution is now known, one risks the trap of "present-ism"—judging a past situation through present sensibilities. Contextualizing and explaining the reasoning of Parks Canada is done not to stanch discussion but, rather, to inform it. Toward this end, then, the question can be posed: Who were the Irish? This may seem to be a curious question, but it is an important one given recent scholarship on the Irish in Canada.

Traditionally it has been presumed that the Irish in Canada were primarily Roman Catholic and largely urban dwellers (and probably anti-British and republican as well), much as was the case in the United States. But recent scholarship, particularly on nineteenth-century Irish immigration to Canada, has challenged that view. In fact, based on quantitative data, approximately two-thirds of Irish immigration to Canada was Protestant; the immigrants more typically settled initially in rural areas and in smaller towns; and they may well have chosen Canada (which before 1867 was commonly referred to as British North America) rather than the United States because it was British.

In the case of Grosse Île, references to "the Irish" (including to the "Irish Memorial") generally indicate the Irish Catholic community, but this narrower use needs to be understood in context, because Canadians of Irish origin constitute a much broader group, and the group as a whole does not necessarily have the same concerns or share the same views.[43]

Therefore, the strength of the public reaction to the perceived underemphasis on the "Irish tragedy"

was somewhat surprising for the Parks Canada staff working on this project. It seemed to be out of proportion and based on a misreading of imperfect materials—and possibly related to the political events of the moment in Ireland.

An important point one may glean from this case is that stakeholders' divergent views on values are subject to a broad range of influences not confined to official histories or even to facts. Anticipating potential sources of influence in a planning situation can prepare participants for effective public consultations; retrospective analysis of consultations can shed new light on how values have emerged and how they may have changed.

NEW STATEMENT OF COMMEMORATIVE INTENT AND ITS IMPACTS

A statement of commemorative intent is the concise declaration of the reasons and purpose for which a national historic site has been so designated. Following extensive research and deliberations, the HSMBC writes this statement for the approval of the minister of Canadian heritage. Once approved, it becomes the touchstone for the management planning at the site. The statement of commemorative intent delimits and prioritizes the main interests of Parks Canada regarding the stewardship and presentation of a site under its jurisdiction. In March 1996 the Minister of Canadian Heritage clarified the commemorative intent of Grosse Île by modifying the name of the national historic site, which became "Grosse Île and the Irish Memorial,"[44] thereby bringing the fateful year of 1847 into sharper focus than was proposed by the development concept four years earlier. The statement of commemorative intent became:

> The Grosse Île and the Irish Memorial National Historic Site commemorates the significance of immigration to Canada, especially via the gateway of Quebec City, from the beginning of the 19th century up to the First World War.
>
> Grosse Île also commemorates the tragic events suffered by Irish immigrants on the island mainly during the typhus epidemic of 1847.
>
> Finally, the site commemorates the role played by the island, from 1832 to 1937, as the quarantine station for the port of Quebec, for years the principal point of entry for immigrants to Canada.[45]

When compared to the wording in the development concept, this statement demonstrates that while the recognized facts are the same and no new values have been added, an important shift in emphasis has taken place. Instead of shying away from putting the "Irish tragedy" in a position of prominence that (it had been thought) might overshadow the other aspects and interpretive opportunities of the site, this statement reflects the voices of the stakeholders by promoting the tragedy to prominence along with the recognition of the role of immigration and of this island in the establishment of modern Canada.

In 1998, a new HSMBC plaque replaced the one dedicated in 1980; the new text referred to the role of Grosse Île as a quarantine station, stressed the phenomenon of immigration, and gave special attention to the Irish experience of 1847.

The three elements most closely associated with the tragic events are located in the Western Sector of the island. The Celtic Cross, erected in 1909, stands above the southeastern cliff of Grosse Île (fig. 1.4) and is reached only by a rustic woodland trail, seen in figure 1.15. The other two elements are the Doctors' Memorial and the Irish Cemetery (figs. 1.16, 1.17).

Figure 1.15. A woodland trail, which leads to the cliff-top location of the Celtic Cross.

Figure 1.16. The Doctors' Memorial. The trail shown in figure 1.15 continues over the top of the crag; on the other side, a small marble monument stands in a birch grove next to the Irish Cemetery. This stele is a memorial to the physicians who sacrificed their lives in the 1830s and 1840s for the sick immigrants. It was placed here in about 1853 by Dr. Douglas, the first superintendent of the quarantine station.

Figure 1.17. The Irish Cemetery was laid out in 1832 between two crags located southwest of Cholera Bay. This view looks east across the cemetery, with Hospital Bay in the distance. Until 1847 individual burials were performed here. That year, because of the high rate of mortality from typhus, long trenches were used as mass graves. The cemetery's topography shows evidence of the trenches. This cemetery is believed to hold over 6,000 of Grosse Île's 7,553 dead.

A new element was planned as an enhancement to the spiritual aspect of Grosse Île—a new Irish Memorial. A design competition was held, and, from the winning design, an expressive earthwork and surround were built to commemorate those who had died and been buried in unmarked graves on Grosse Île. The new memorial, a few meters south of the Irish Cemetery, evokes an ancient barrow tomb. It consists of paths in the shape of a Celtic cross cut through an earthen mound, which is topped by native shale. It is framed on the north by an arc of glass panels that bear the engraved names of those who died on the island. In August 1998, Parks Canada inaugurated this memorial in the presence of Ireland's president, Mary McAleese.

At the end of a difficult but successful process that was best understood in retrospect, the values cited in the commemorative intent of the historic site of Grosse Île and the Irish Memorial are a poignant blend of optimism and sadness that captures the full character of the place.

Consideration of Values in Management Policies and Strategies

Once discovered and stated, how would the values expressed in the statement of commemorative intent be framed within a management plan? How are they connected to, and incorporated into, the guidance regarding actions recommended on the site?

Figure 1.18. The new Irish Memorial is tucked against the hillside, just southwest of the Doctors' Memorial and above the Irish Cemetery. The stone structure in the center is framed by glass panels etched with the names of the dead from the epidemic years.

Figure 1.19. Glass panels at the Irish Memorial on which visitors may read the names of those who died either en route to or at Grosse Île.

COMMEMORATIVE INTENT AND COMMEMORATIVE INTEGRITY

As of 1994, Parks Canada has employed a powerful normative approach to establishing the management and interpretive framework for the sites under its stewardship. Two core concepts help to maintain the focus of management decisions: commemorative intent (described above) and commemorative integrity.[46] Each of these concepts is operationalized by a document that defines in detail the concept as it applies to a specific site.

Commemorative integrity is a term used to describe the health or wholeness of a national historic site. A state of commemorative integrity can be said to exist when:

• the resources that symbolize or represent a site's importance are not impaired or under threat;

• the reasons for the site's national historic significance are effectively communicated to the public;

• the site's heritage values (including those not related to national significance) are respected by all whose decisions and actions affect the site.[47]

The commemorative integrity statement is a detailed document written as part of the management planning process for a site. It ties the commemorative intent to the physical features where value resides, and expands on the specific characteristics of that value. It also emphasizes the obligation of the site managers to ensure that the site retains its commemorative integrity. The statement serves as a guide for the management of the site and as a means of assessing its state and determining the necessary measures to be taken.

The first part of the statement identifies and evaluates the cultural resources with reference to the historic values that prompted the national designation of the site. Included are specific goals and objectives regarding the desired state of these resources as well as work that may be necessary to achieve these goals. The second part is the articulation of the key messages, any secondary messages, and any context or tone that is seen as important to associate with the messages that are to be communicated to the public about the site. Included in this part is the mention of any challenges that are already anticipated in the area of communication. The third part of the statement describes resources and other values that are not of national significance but that carry historic significance for the site, and it identifies messages regarding these resources that are important to communicate through the interpretive program.

CULTURAL RESOURCE MANAGEMENT POLICY AND VALUES PRESERVATION

For Parks Canada, historic value—rather than social, cultural, scientific, economic, use, program, or other values—determines whether a resource is a cultural resource and, hence, whether it should be managed under the policy. The seminal guidance contained in the cultural resource management policy, part of the *Guiding Principles and Operational Policies*,[48] ensures a values-based approach to heritage management through its definition of its principles, practice, and activities. Throughout, all the principles deal in one way or another with values, even when the word *value* is not specifically used. The following excerpts demonstrate this fundamental commitment:

1.1   PRINCIPLES[49]

1.1.2   While all cultural resources are valued, some cultural resources are deemed to be of the highest possible value and will be protected and presented accordingly. Parks Canada will value most highly those cultural resources of national historic significance.

1.1.4   Cultural resources will be valued not only for their physical or material properties, but also for the associative and symbolic attributes with which they are imbued, and which frequently form the basis of their historic value.

1.1.5   A cultural resource whose historic value derives from its witness to many periods in history will be respected for that evolution, not just for its existence at a single moment in time. Parks Canada will reveal an underlying or previous physical state of an object, structure, or site at the expense of later forms and material only with great caution; when historic value is clearly related to an earlier form, and when knowledge and existing material of that earlier form allow.

1.2   PRACTICE

1.2.2   To understand and appreciate cultural resources and the sometimes complex themes they illustrate, the public will be provided with information and services that effectively communicate the importance and value of those resources and their themes.

1.2.3   Appropriate uses of cultural resources will be those uses and activities that respect the historic value and physical integrity of the resource, and that promote public understanding and appreciation.

1.4   RESPECT

1.4.1   Cultural resources will be managed with continuous care and with respect for their historic character; that is, for the qualities for which they are valued.

The cultural resource management policy describes the "practice" of cultural resource management as providing a "framework for decision-making rather than a set of predetermined answers. Its aim is to ensure that the historic character for which resources are valued is identified, recognized, considered, and communicated." In the same vein, it provides the principles for decision making in conservation and other interventions. This is an important document, as it is at the same time clear about the important relationship between value and resource and concerned more with process than with outcome.

SAFETY FROM IMPAIRMENT OR THREAT

The first task in ensuring the protection of physical resources from impairment is to identify and characterize all the resources in the Level I category. Brief passages extracted from the cultural resource management policy define Level I and Level II resources:

2.2.1   Level I:

National historic significance is the highest level assigned to a cultural resource in the custody of Parks Canada. National historic significance will be determined in accordance with the National Historic Sites Policy.

2.2.1.1   Evaluation to determine national historic significance is undertaken by the Historic Sites and Monuments Board of Canada. Its recommendation to the Minister, and any subsequent Ministerial designation, may specify which resources within a designated national historic site are themselves of national historic significance.

2.2.1.2   Where a Ministerial designation is not specific with respect to the national historic significance of resources at a national historic site, the program will apply the commemorative intent of the designation to determine which resources are to be specifically considered of national historic significance.

2.2.2   Level II:

A resource that is not of national historic significance may have historic value and thus be considered a cultural resource.

2.2.2.1   Parks Canada will establish and apply criteria to determine which resources under its jurisdiction are Level II. A resource may be included in this category by virtue of its historical, aesthetic, or environmental qualities. Criteria will also give consideration to such factors as regional or local association; or provincial, territorial or municipal designations.

2.2.2.2   Buildings that are designated "classified" or "recognized" in accordance with the Federal Heritage Buildings Policy will automatically be considered as Level II cultural resources, unless they meet the requirements that have been described for Level I cultural resources. Buildings may also be considered Level II cultural resources in accordance with criteria described . . . above.[50]

The commemorative integrity statement catalogs all the features and characteristics that symbolize the importance of Grosse Île and draws on historical and archaeological research to explain and interpret these elements.[51] The Level I features are cultural landscapes, architectural and archaeological vestiges, and movable cultural resources. The cultural landscapes include the geographic location as well as the natural features and characteristics of the island that were so well suited to its uses—and that are in ways still largely unchanged since 1832. Also included are the roads, wharfs, views, and cemeteries as well as the strategic separation of activity sectors employed for health purposes.[52] Taken together, all these resources are valued for their authenticity, for the fact that they represent the periods in Canadian history being commemorated, and for their ability to help convey the themes to the public.

The integrity statement also sets the stage for defining the management strategies. For each class of feature, the text includes objectives for securing the linkages between the feature and the communication of its significance, in the form of statements of a desired outcome: "Presentation of the landscape reinforces the expression of landscape components in such a way as to support the historic nature of significant sites from the human quarantine period; . . . a maintenance program to control vegetation, notably in the heritage areas, has been elaborated and implemented; . . . the various maintenance and presentation facilities take into account the fact that the fences are among the dominant and significant elements of the island's historic landscape."[53]

This approach is also used in describing the structures, proceeding building by building; reestablishing connections of historic fabric with the historic uses of the buildings; and delineating their respective relevance to the larger site's commemorative intent. Key messages associated with Level I features are also gathered and presented in a summary supporting the themes of immigration, quarantine, and the Irish dimension.

The second component of protecting the significant resources from damage or threat is the identification of risks, of their sources, and of their potential impacts. Attention to this is ensured through the guidance available in the site management plan. The physical condition of each of the three classes of Level I resources is described, with examples of some of the principal risks; these include inherent characteristics of materials or context, weather and the deterioration of previous protective measures (such as paint), impacts caused by vehicles, or changes in vegetation.[54]

The third component in protecting these resources is developing and/or employing management strategies—including conservation interventions—that have as their objective the mitigation or avoidance of threats to the integrity of the physical resources. There are two main sources of guidance for decision making, covering prevention and intervention. The first is the cultural resource management policy section of the document *Parks Canada Guiding Principles and Operational Policies*.[55] The chapter on conservation begins by stating, "Conservation encompasses the activities that are aimed at the safeguarding of a cultural resource so as to retain its historic value and extend its physical life."[56] The guidelines that follow cover the steps to be taken by site managers as they formulate approaches for the general care of cultural resources or formulate the detailed plans leading to a conservation intervention. They refer the user to site management plans and to the resources available from the Federal Heritage Buildings Review Office (FHBRO)[57] for more specific guidance.

Section 4 of the management plan[58] supplies direction for actions being considered for landscapes, buildings, and other Level I resources, as well as for Level II resources.[59] The guidance provided for these actions indicates the importance attributed to the presentation of the resources. The plan offers the most specific guidance on ensuring that decisions are made according to established policies, taking account of concerns for the physical safety of Level I resources when presentation is also a requirement. The quality of this guidance is demonstrated by summaries offered for two resource types:

Landscapes and Environment
Actions should seek to protect significant views recognized as Level I; restore and maintain the divisions and character of the three-sector organization of the station; and accentuate the landscapes that highlight the areas associated with the quarantine activities. The plan favors subtle indicators over explicit text panels at every turn, such as using vegetation to locate features or limit views or access.

Buildings
Action or inaction is proscribed that will directly or indirectly damage the appearance, architectural detail, or structural integrity of a historic building. For each building, an architectural intervention plan is to be produced that describes problems anticipated in preserving, using, and presenting the structure. The plan requires the use of best practices in planning and implementing interventions and points the staff toward additional guidance, such as the FHBRO Code of Practice, which specifically governs federally owned structures.[60]

EFFECTIVE COMMUNICATION OF THE REASONS FOR THE SITE'S IMPORTANCE

As eloquent as a dilapidated but intact nineteenth-century laundry house might be to an architectural historian, it may stand mute before a nuclear physicist on vacation with her family. As is recognized fully in all the pertinent Parks Canada guidance, the meaning of cultural resources such as those at Grosse Île is revealed through effective communication of the values held therein. Furthermore, the site is actually seen to lose its commemorative integrity if the messages authored for the site are not effectively communicated to visitors.

The interpretive scheme for Grosse Île is not yet fully in place. In keeping with its responsibilities, Parks Canada has divided its attention between the stabilization of the physical resources and the phased development of the interpretive plans. Therefore, while it is not yet possible to experience a completed presentation, it is possible to review the ideas and principles that will help shape the interpretive scheme and to see how they reflect the values identified for the site. The *Plan of the Visit Experience*[61] of Grosse Île defines the experience that the visitor will have at the site, through the activities and services to be offered. This document identifies three dimensions of the visitor's encounter with the site: associative, educational,

and spiritual. These dimensions are values related to the solemn, serene atmosphere of the place. The first dimension of the encounter relates to the sense of place, defined as the emotions evoked in the visitor by the site. A second dimension is the knowledge that can be transmitted to visitors through the resources of the island. The final dimension or value is a spiritual one, consisting of visitors' insights about themselves that they might obtain through their visit to the site.

An important contribution of this document is that it analyzes and ties the various elements of the site— buildings, layout, patterns of land use, landscapes, and views—to the three statements of the commemorative intent and other heritage values. It also elaborates on the topics to be presented to communicate the three elements of the commemorative intent and indicates which resources will be used to do so. For example, under the theme of the Irish Memorial, the information about Irish immigration during the first half of the nineteenth century is to be mentioned first in the Disinfection Building, although this structure did not exist during the period being discussed. Later, guides will present information about the Irish Famine and the tragedy of 1847 during the visit to the Celtic Cross, the Irish Cemetery, the new Irish Memorial, and the Lazaretto. Finally, the topic of the symbolic value of Grosse Île to the Irish is to be "communicated" through visits to the cemetery and the Irish Memorial. Similar analyses and plans are presented for each of the themes and their topics.

The *Plan of the Visit Experience* also examines the potential for, and constraints relating to, expanding the audiences for Grosse Île, including the logistics of getting to and from the island. The plan proposes a range of selective tours, each targeting a particular audience or concept, to be developed and tested over time. The various tours recognize the constraints imposed by the short duration of visits to the site, a result of the transportation schedule.

Both the management plan and the integrity statement acknowledge other issues that promise to complicate the presentation of messages regarding the significance of Grosse Île in several areas: periodization, survival of features from all phases, and uneven representativeness of the cultural resources, among others.

The one-hundred-year span of time being commemorated saw dramatic changes in the operation of Grosse Île as a quarantine station. Public health, science, medicine, and transportation all went through important developments that left an impact on the island; these changes form part of the significance of the landscape and built environment. As the integrity statement reports, "The initial installations at the quarantine station were marked by improvisation (hurried planning) and ignorance (forms of transmission of epidemic diseases). This phase was followed by a rationalisation of reception infrastructures for immigrants that went beyond Grosse Île, improving the complementary facilities at the port of Quebec, Levis, and Pointe au Père. In this manner, the history of quarantine is in many ways marked by the evolution of the phenomenon of immigration in the world and especially at Quebec."[62]

The traces of these events can be difficult to maintain, but they are important to the story. To realize the commemorative intent of the site, the story of a particular period must be told in the physical context of buildings and other features that were not present during that time. Without some thoughtful interpretive cues, the visitor would have a difficult time distinguishing the features of one period from those of the next.

In fact, most of the historic resources on the island date to the final phase of use of the quarantine station. Very little standing architecture survives from the time when the station's most dramatic events transpired—and for which the site is, in part, commemorated. This situation challenges the interpretive program to address the history in other ways.

Communicating the principal themes and the stories that convey them through the physical remains requires a sophisticated program of interpretation. While it might be possible to dismantle some of the very recent structures (such as storage buildings from the 1960s) in order to simplify the landscape, it may not be appropriate. Requirements inherent in the statement of commemorative intent require an innovative approach that does not sacrifice any of the resources. Thus the statement affords strong, holistic protection that calls for creative and conscientious management.

The management plan echoes these protectionist concepts and offers guidance on methods for realizing these objectives by folding them into three workable principles: respecting the spirit of the place, employing a comprehensive and specific view of history, and using an approach that emphasizes the important connections between the natural environment and the cultural resources.

In light of these principles, the intention expressed in the management plan is to present the historic and natural features in an informative and engaging way while maintaining a dignified and relatively somber image for the site. A low-key tone is preferred on-site, and off-island interpretive panels and brochures about Grosse Île and the Irish Memorial will be only sparsely used.

> ### Objectives for Messages of National Historic Significance from the Commemorative Integrity Statement
>
> - The presentation of Grosse Île is tied in with commemorative intent, linking the resources that symbolize the site's national significance with messages of national historic significance.
> - The messages elaborated in pursuing the commemorative intent ease the interaction between the visitor and the resources of the national historic site, for which the values are communicated.
> - The resources are presented as a coherent and significant whole.
> - The messages are communicated to the public in a clear fashion, taking into account the needs of different clienteles and using appropriate means.
> - Evaluation methods and tools are established to determine the efficiency of message transmission.[63]

> ### Quality of the Visitor's Experience
>
> The quality of the visitor's experience is a concept that is used in the management of many cultural resources and that generally summarizes what the staff has identified as the key values or aspects of the place. For Grosse Île and the Irish Memorial, this is done in the *Plan of the Visit Experience*,[64] which identifies the factors that contribute to this positive experience and ties it to specific resources on the site. The elements identified as contributing to a quality experience are
> - historic landscapes and views that evoke the past
> - visible archaeological remains
> - important buildings with public access
> - competent guides
> - interpretation routes and paths that allow the visitor to experience the site firsthand
> - a cultural and natural experience
> - the presence of partners of Parks Canada who can enrich the experience of the visitor

PROTECTION OF THE SECONDARY HERITAGE VALUES OF THE SITE

All management documents touch on the secondary heritage values of the site, which include historic, archaeological, or other evidence of paleohistoric dimension; the early land-grant settlements; the army presence during periods of war; and use by Agriculture Canada. The exceptional natural environment of the island also falls in this category.[65] Assignment of these diverse and interesting kinds of resources to this second level does not imply that they are not important or delicate or worthy of attention. The principle of commemorative integrity of Parks Canada requires that the heritage values of the site—represented by Level II resources—be respected in management decisions. These resources, however, are not the focus of intensive interpretive or protective activity.

In some instances, buildings of the postwar era are in conflict with some of the Level I landscapes, particularly in the Central Sector of the island. While the commemorative integrity principle requires that these structures be respected, site management staff has considered removing or relocating some of them to free some significant vistas. None of the buildings have yet been removed, and there is serious discussion as to the impact that actions of this type would have on the commemorative integrity of the site.

In the management plan, strategic direction with regard to infrastructure notes that all new facilities will be designed and located to have the least possible impact on cultural and natural resources. The environmental values of Grosse Île, while they are seen as Level II, have their own set of protections under federal law. The *Canadian Environmental Assessment Act,* passed in 1992, provides powerful support for environmental protection at nationally managed sites, among other places. The act established a federal environmental assessment process that requires that any action that may have an effect on resources of natural or cultural significance must be preceded by an assessment of potential risks or damaging impacts. An effect is considered to be "any change that the project may cause in the environment, including any effect of any such change on health and socio-economic conditions, on physical and cultural heritage, on the current use of lands and resources for traditional purposes by aboriginal persons, or on any structure, site or thing that is of historical, archaeological, paleontological or architectural significance."[66]

The act calls for the redesign with appropriate risk mitigation, or for the withdrawal of any project having an effect, in order to ensure a proactive protective approach. Again, all management documents encourage avoiding solutions that require dramatic decisions regarding the environment in order to save an important historic feature.

The management plan contains a summary of the environmental assessment that examined the potential impacts of the activities of visitation and management

at Grosse Île. The report found that the strategic guidelines in the plan that relate to protecting and presenting the natural resources of the site are enhancing the vision of the site and fostering sound management.[67] Nevertheless, some areas of potential conflict are singled out for monitoring, including the possible impact on the shoreline of new or expanded visitor facilities, difficult choices relating to the effect of vegetation (rare or typical) on historic structures, and impact on bat colonies of conservation interventions on buildings. These areas will be discussed further below.

At Grosse Île, two specific management policies are aimed directly at protecting the environmental values, and they have an interesting effect on an important objective of the site. The first is that visitors are not allowed to go into the backcountry, away from the areas near the gravel road, the buildings, and the public spaces. Second, they are not allowed to come ashore from private transport or from anywhere except the main wharf. These policies both protect the natural environment and limit access to the site to the commercial carriers. While managers would welcome more visitors and would like to have visitors stay for longer periods, they are not willing to put even the Level II resources at risk to accomplish these goals.

Impact of Management Policies on the Site's Values and Their Preservation

How do management decisions and actions on-site affect the values? This question may also be posed in terms of the integrity statement: How are management decisions affecting the protection of the Level I resources or the effective communication of the site's significance or the management of the other heritage values?

This question can be addressed from at least two directions. First, Parks Canada has several procedures to track its own effectiveness in achieving the objectives defined during the planning process. Second, specific situations and their resolutions can shed light on how well plans are being implemented and whether they are producing the desired effects. This discussion will look at each of the areas of value at Grosse Île and the means used by Parks Canada staff to assess effectiveness. Particular situations in each of the areas will be used to illustrate decisions made on-site.

PROTECTING LEVEL I RESOURCES
A number of operational controls help Parks Canada staff ensure the protection of the resources for which Grosse Île is recognized at the national level. Each year, the crew

of skilled technicians and the site managers define a work program of urgent remedial actions, normal maintenance, infrastructure improvements, and the occasional research activity. Various factors affect the design of this program, including opportunity, importance, and available resources. In the discussions regarding these decisions, the staff depends on a relational database in which specific resources have individual files, and their physical histories are tracked. Having detailed records of this kind helps maintain objective priorities when there are literally hundreds of conservation challenges awaiting attention. A team-based approach used in planning situations— combining architects, archaeologists, technicians, ethnographers, and interpreters—and in the field also helps the site staff maintain a balanced approach to ensuring the health of the resources. While each specialty has its own concerns, the team is united by the institutional commitment to Grosse Île's commemorative integrity. The fact that the buildings are important because they have stories to tell makes it all the more important that the architects, the technicians, and the interpretive experts all participate in decisions about their care.

One of the reasons the HSMBC recommended the designation of Grosse Île as a national historic site was the presence of many structures on the site that represented its quarantine functions. Today those buildings constitute one of the most eloquent elements of the site; they also present a challenge in terms of conservation. The number of structures and their condition call for a long period of conservation activities until all of them have been stabilized and made sound. Maintenance of any building in this climate is always a challenge, even when there are no requirements apart from pure physical preservation. However, when the building is considered to have value in part because of its age, its bleak location, and its fragile status, the job becomes rather more demanding. Parks Canada has developed approaches to the conservation and presentation of the individual buildings, something that has been discussed at various points in this case. The *Grosse Île National Historic Site— Development Concept* of 1992 states in this regard that:

> the treatment of visible archaeological remains, structures and buildings would remain discreet and non-invasive . . . work would be performed on the buildings with the aim, primarily, of maintaining the features they have generally retained since their relative abandonment, while protecting them against further deterioration. Care would be taken, in particular, to preserve the marks left by the passing years,

[continued on page 46]

The Lazaretto

*lazaretto [or **lazaret** or **lazarette**]* — 1. A hospital treating contagious diseases. 2. A building or ship used as a quarantine station. 3. A storage space between the decks of a ship.[1]

Significance of the Building

The Lazaretto is a Level I structure located near the eastern tip of Grosse Île (location 19, fig. 1.3). It is one of only four structures on the island that dates from the early years of the quarantine station, and it is the single one remaining from the tragic year of 1847. It is also the only remaining intact building that served as a hospital during the period commemorated at Grosse Île. Because of its unique significance, it was designated a Federal Heritage Building and singled out for commemoration by the Historic Sites and Monuments Board.[2]

The Lazaretto was built as one of a set of similar buildings in a complex dedicated to the care of the ill and convalescing immigrants. The complex included kitchens, residences for cooks and nurses, a police station, washhouses, outbuildings, and latrines built in response to the vast number of immigrants who reached the island in 1847.

Most of the structures from this complex have since disappeared, and any remaining vestiges are underground or overgrown with vegetation; even the Protestant Cemetery, nearby,

The Lazaretto seen from the southwest.

The west end and rear of the Lazaretto, showing some of the windows and doors in the back wall of the building, as well as the bead-board skirt that covers the replaced piers that support the building.

was partly obliterated in the construction of the landing strip. As a result, it is hard to visualize the original spatial organization of this special zone.[3] Thus, the survival of the remaining Lazaretto takes on great importance in communicating the commemorative intent of the site.

History

Although Grosse Île began operating as a quarantine station in 1832, its early role was largely limited to cursory examinations of immigrants on their way to the port of Quebec.[4] It was not until the great epidemics of the 1840s that passengers, both healthy and sick, were detained on the island. A historian describes the situation vividly: "Conditions were chaotic at GI throughout 1847. Both the facilities and staff

were inadequate. . . . All the buildings intended for the general use of emigrants were converted into hospitals. By 1848, the quarantine station, which could accommodate at the opening of navigation in 1847 only 200 hospital patients and 800 healthy immigrants, possessed facilities sufficient for 2,000 sick, 300 convalescent and 3,500 immigrants in detention. There were two convalescent hospitals in the end of the island, 'containing 150 beds each, together with sheds capable of lodging 3,500 immigrants.'"[5]

The Lazaretto is one of a dozen of the quickly assembled sheds erected that year to handle the large numbers of arriving immigrants. By the following year, all the accommodations in the Eastern Sector of the island had been designated as sick bay, keeping the sick and

The interior of the east end of the Lazaretto, showing one of the diagonal braces as well as one of the windows modified for a late use of the building.

The Marconi Station in September 2001. Built in 1919, the Marconi Station is a small building with a double-sided roof. It is set back from the road, close to the river, and not far from the physicians' residence. The utilitarian role of the building is reflected in its interior arrangement: the console and its operator were in the western half, and the generator and washroom were in the eastern half. The Marconi Station replaced the old telegraph office between 1885 and 1892. The building demonstrated the technological advance in communications as well as the daily operations of a human quarantine station such as Gross Île.

convalescing immigrants away from their healthy travel companions, who were housed in the Western Sector in the First, Second, and Third Class Hotels.

By 1878, all the 1847 sheds had disappeared except for this one. Over the years, this remaining shed was repurposed several times and altered many more. The first transformation was done quickly in 1848, to change the shed's use from passenger accommodations to hospital quarters. At that time the interior was divided into four separate areas, evidence for which survives to some extent today. Floors, ceilings, paneling, and exterior siding were changed several times over the years. Documents indicate that during its years as a hospital, the interior and exterior walls were limewashed regularly as a means of disinfection. From the 1850s until it ceased being used as a hospital in the 1920s, it housed mainly smallpox patients, and it became known as the *Shed des picotés*. Plumbing for toilets and baths was installed around the turn of the twentieth century. In line with the contemporary practice of shielding smallpox patients from daylight, a project was started in 1904 to cover the interior walls of the rooms with red paneling—and possibly to install red glass in the windows. This measure appears to have been achieved only in the westernmost room.

Around 1942 the island was used by the

The Laundry. Built in 1855, at the shoreline, the Laundry facilitated the washing of the immigrants' clothing. Inside are some of the original features, including three of the four original chimneys and fireplaces used for heating water and disinfecting clothing. It is the only remaining structure that attests to one of the important steps in disinfection as practiced in the mid-nineteenth century.

Canadian Army for experimental research on animals. At that time, the Lazaretto was converted into a chicken coop, with significant modifications that closed several of the doors on the facade and cut new windows into the walls to improve air circulation. The easternmost of the four interior rooms was not altered much, keeping its old paneling, ceiling, and windows.

Conservation Treatment

The Lazaretto is one of the few buildings on the island that saw continuous use from the 1840s until it was restored in 1997 and 1998. As recorded in the Cultural Resources Registry of Quebec, it had been modified several times: walls were paneled, the interior was partitioned into four zones, and a three-section ceil-ing and then a flat ceiling were added. Nevertheless, the structure has retained a number of original features in addition to its volume: French casement windows with many small glass panes, ventilation outlets, and traces of the original interior, including graffiti from patients housed in the building over the years.

In the first condition assessment of the built resources done by Parks Canada staff when the island became a national historic site, this building was found to be in precarious condition. Perhaps most alarming was the fact that it was sagging badly, because its foundation footings had shifted and settled. While the structure was supported on jacks awaiting the new footings, a brief salvage archaeology project was undertaken, yielding objects that came across on the ships with the Irish in those early years.[6] Today a small glass display case in the eastern room contains objects found during this work.

The challenge before the technical team was to employ all the requisite guidelines, retain (or reinstate) the historic aspect and value of this unique structure, and make it safe for visitors and guides to use. This team—as is standard for historic sites in Quebec—included representatives from the fields of architecture, engineering, history, archaeology, and historic preservation. They examined and analyzed the structure and the site and concluded that the "as-found" form of the Lazaretto allowed for a complete presentation and "reading" of its evolution, described briefly above. They proposed that the interior of the building be divided into three sections, each presenting one phase of the building. The eastern room would represent the building during the 1847 epidemic; the central section would correspond to its service as a hospital; and the western section would evoke the 1850–1927 period of the smallpox quarantine.[7]

As it now stands, the building sits on new foundations, so the sagging floors and slightly leaning walls are not very exaggerated or precarious. Some early graffiti on the interior whitewashed wood is protected behind clear plastic sheets. The westernmost room has its red-painted walls and ceiling restored from the 1920s.[8] Much of the interior space retains its original fabric, and the windows opened during its period as a chicken coop can be closed in the easternmost room to show how the room looked originally. Any new elements that have been added in the interior are immediately recognizable, distinguished by their different paint treatment.

The interior of the Lazaretto now reads like a historic narrative of the life cycle of the building, from 1847 to 1950. Restoring a building to a single phase of a multiphase history (a process referred to as "periodization") has been recognized as an undesirable management option, but in previous generations, it was often the option chosen. Parks Canada planners anticipated the potential for periodization during the planning phases and were able to avoid oversimplifying this unique building.[9] The technical and philosophical decisions followed the normative guidance, which states that cultural resources should be valued in their context and that a cultural resource "whose historic value derives from its witness to many periods in history will be respected for that evolution, not just for its existence at a single moment in time."[10]

By comparison, the current appearance of the Lazaretto's exterior seems to tell quite a different story. Certainly it is the result of decisions that required juggling a number of considerations, and the difference between the interior and the exterior demonstrates visibly how management decisions can affect how a place expresses its own history. Below are listed some of the considerations that were part of the discussions about how best to protect this particular building.

- The general objectives for protecting in situ cultural resources, which include protecting the structure and all external characteristics of the buildings and ensuring that all maintenance respects the range of interior finishes.[11]
- The objective of preserving the "spirit of the

place" and of maintaining in the structures some of the character they have acquired over years of neglect.[12]

- Where material (or artifactual values) are preeminent, prolonging the life of surviving historic fabric becomes the primary concern; generally speaking, a preservation approach focused on stabilization/consolidation and supported by a concern for caution in the conservation principles applied will provide the best means to respect these values.[13]

- Interventions respectful of heritage character should be guided by the principles of fit (or compatibility)—for example, harmonizing proportions, color, texture, forms, materials, or structural characteristics of added elements, when contextual values are dealt with. Where contextual values are concerned with physical relationships, the primary concern may be preserving or reestablishing important relationships between and among building elements and the whole; where these values are concerned with functional context, reestablishing proper fit between a building and its use would become important.[14]

- The cost-effectiveness of long-wearing surface finishes for protecting the wooden shell, as well as the more fragile and fully authentic features inside, requires no long explanation. One needs only to witness one nor'easter to see how violent the weather can be, especially up on this exposed promontory. Normal exposure to weather at this latitude is unquestionably stressful on clapboard buildings, particularly one set on pilings instead of on full foundations.

From the outside, the Lazaretto today can be read as a handsome building in an antique style, covered not with whitewash but, rather, with robust butter-colored latex paint, with green trim. The same finishes are used for the Marconi Station, which was built seventy-eight years later. For a visitor who expects an approximation of authenticity in the appearance of the sole survivor from the crisis years, the Lazaretto's pristine appearance is a visual surprise. The unique importance of the building and of the events it represents are obscured by what can be seen as a mask—protective, perhaps, but inscrutable. The external appearance could be said to diminish the associative value of this building by making it more difficult for the visitor to make associations with the times and events being commemorated. This strong contrast with the as-yet-unrestored historical buildings on the island, such as the Laundry, might lessen as the other structures are restored or as the Lazaretto weathers over time.

Notes

1. *American Heritage College Dictionary*, 3rd ed. (New York: Houghton Mifflin, 1993).

2. HSMBC 1993; Federal Heritage Buildings Review Office 1995.

3. Parks Canada 1998a, 7.

4. A considerable amount of information regarding the history of use and transformation of this building is found in the *Registre des ressources culturelles du Québec*.

5. Anick 1984.

6. Informal comparisons done to date with object assemblies of the time in Ireland suggest the potential for extraordinary research in this particular area of the island; they also suggest a rich information resource for the interpretive program (Monique Elie, Parks Canada, personal communication).

7. From Fortier 1997.

8. The dark red environment was thought to reduce damage to patients' eyesight as they recovered.

9. Parks Canada 1998a, 45.

10. Parks Canada 1994a, 103.

11. Parks Canada 1998a, 10.

12. Environment Canada, Canadian Parks Service 1992a, 27.

13. FHBRO 1996, 23.

14. Ibid., 24.

which heighten the authenticity of resources. No building would be restored to a former state and none would be rebuilt.[68]

To be consistent with this directive, decisions regarding how best to protect and present such buildings must address and balance considerations of protection from weather and exposure, the authenticity of the materials, and the visual presentation. These are not simple decisions. In a few cases at Grosse Île, recent treatment projects reflect decisions that appear to be in conflict with these principles. Three buildings—the Marconi Station, the Public Works Officer's House, and the Lazaretto—now have a pristine appearance, in stark contrast to other historic structures that surround them. The restoration of the Public Works Officer's House has recently been completed. The funding for this work was provided by the Ministry of Public Works, which supplemented the budget available to Parks Canada. The participation of another government department made possible the conservation of this Level I building, which up to that point had not been among the ones identified for priority attention.

The case of the Lazaretto is examined in more detail in the sidebar (see p. 40). Topics addressed include the treatment process for that building and its impact on the values associated with the building as well as a possible missed opportunity to develop an innovative approach to treatment for an important building.

The conflict created by the existence of postwar structures in the central part of the island remains to be resolved. While there are plans to rehabilitate some of the animal quarantine stations for new uses after moving them to remote areas of the island, no action has been taken. There is no doubt that these newer structures stand where significant structures (such as the Medical Superintendent's House) once stood and that they block what would have been the historic views of the eastern and western wharfs. While these are Level II structures, the principle of commemorative integrity requires that they be "respected" in all decisions. It remains to be seen how the site staff will interpret this guidance.

EFFECTIVE COMMUNICATION OF THE SITE'S NATIONAL SIGNIFICANCE

Effective communication requires that both the speakers and the listeners are able to do their respective jobs. First, Parks Canada and the site staff have the responsibility to express the messages crafted for the site. There are also some interpretive panels in locations around the island that offer information on particular features. However, there is currently a preference for the more personal approach to interpretation that depends on guides.

The quality of the guides' presentation, the style of their delivery, their ability to respond to questions, and their own knowledge of, and interest in, the subjects can determine to a great extent the quality of the visitors' experience. Parks Canada pays a great deal of attention to this indicator of the commemorative integrity of the site.

Grosse Île and the Irish Memorial is open May through October. After the close of the season, an assessment of the experience of the guides is undertaken by means of a survey. This gives the guides the opportunity to report on the relative success of the content of their presentations; on the levels of interest demonstrated by visitors; and on the ways in which content is calibrated to the particular interests, ages, nationalities, ethnicities, and so on of people to whom they spoke. They can report on their difficulties in conveying certain issues or on their views of the need to expand on particular topics. At some point before the start of a new season, site staff studies the surveys, and adjustments may be made to the interpretive presentations for the coming season.

Before the site opens again in the spring, the guides who will work on Grosse Île during the season are brought together for seventy-five hours of classroom training. Training materials are prepared and given to each member of the group; specialists from Parks Canada, other agencies, and academic institutions in the region serve as lecturers on Irish history, medical history, Canadian history, Parks Canada policy, and other topics.

The content of the interpretive scheme is subject to constant change and refinement, depending on the findings from surveys and on new ideas that come from staff and partners. Other sources for new content are the HSMBC and additions to the system plan that the Board and Canadian Heritage might recommend. Two recent additions will have an impact on the presentation of Grosse Île: the commitment to tell the stories of women in Canadian history, and the commitment to tell the stories of cultural and ethnic diversity. This new emphasis reiterates the point, made earlier in this discussion, that when a place becomes a national historic site in Canada (as in many other countries), it becomes part of a system that exists for all the citizens. Its stories become larger when presented on a national, rather than local, stage. There is the risk of losing some of the specific meaning of the place, and decisions about this are in the hands of the national authority. It is interesting to see that in the case of Grosse Île, a preponderance of visitors to the site is, in fact, native to the province.

AUDIENCE AND ACCESS

The second element in effective communication is the ability of the audience to receive and understand the messages being delivered. Part of the reason why so much historic fabric survived on Grosse Île relates to the fact that this is a protected island in the middle of a river that has been off limits to the public for many generations. While the benefits of this isolation are obvious, the difficulties it poses in presenting the site to the public are considerable. Briefly stated, transport to Grosse Île is limited and expensive. A visit to the island ranges between 1.5 and 4.5 hours. Taken together, these factors significantly constrain the potential for access to the site and for a thorough presentation of the commemorative intent messages.

The earliest planning documents for the site stipulate that Parks Canada "will operate no marine or air transportation services to Grosse Île. Responsibility for the marine transportation service may be assumed by the service provider or by independent carrier."[69] As described earlier, visitor transportation is provided mainly by one boat company operating from the south shore town of Berthier-sur-Mer. The crossing lasts approximately thirty minutes, and there are only three trips to the island per day during the high season (each trip can transport approximately 150 passengers). The captain gives a brief river tour along the way as the ferry passes other islands on the way to the Grosse Île dock.

The business partnership between this boat company and Parks Canada can be construed as vital to Grosse Île and the Irish Memorial, but not necessarily to the company. Their other business comes from whale-watching trips in the St. Lawrence, and from charter trips arranged for hunters during the October and November hunting season. This situation has made it difficult for Parks Canada staff to negotiate different arrangements or longer stays on the island for visitors. The situation may soon change, as other transport companies seem to be interested in providing access to Grosse Île from Quebec City. Discussions are also under way about the possibility of large cruise ships sending passengers to the island on small launches. No private boats are presently allowed to dock or anchor to bring visitors to the island, and there are no plans to change this policy. While transportation to the island was being provided only by boat companies based on the south shore, the economic benefits that the site might bring were limited to this area. The transportation now being provided directly from Quebec, although potentially increasing the number of visitors to the site, might diminish the number of those who travel through the south shore towns.

All means of access must take into consideration their impact on the resources of the national historic site. In 2001, a firm in Quebec approached Parks Canada with interest in delivering visitors to Grosse Île by hovercraft, but this scheme posed several problems. First, the craft would need a floating dock to be constructed at a cost of Canadian $100,000, as it would be unable to use the existing fixed, multilevel dock. Second, the noise made by the compressed air engines would interfere with the quiet ambience of the island. In addition, the impact of this type of vessel on the flora and fauna of the shore would need to be evaluated.

Wind or rain can make the crossing from the mainland difficult and unpleasant for visitors unaccustomed to rough seas. Getting around on the island is relatively easy if one is ambulatory. An uphill hike with stairs and rough terrain prohibit wheelchair access to the Celtic Cross, although a level road is available to the cemetery and the new Irish Memorial. Trolleys carry visitors through the village and out to the island's Eastern Sector.

Although Grosse Île and the Irish Memorial is a national historic site, it has not been actively promoted for long, and it is not yet well known to travelers from other provinces or from outside Canada. Its interpretive programs are not fully deployed, and the carrying capacity of this site is still below the projections. Various aspects of the infrastructure are still being improved, with the possibility in view of larger numbers of visitors. The water system has recently been upgraded; expanded sewage facilities are in the works; and overnight accommodations on a modest scale are being contemplated. It is up to the local and regional Parks Canada staff to undertake marketing efforts; they attend tourism fairs to seek publicity for the site and to identify channels through which they can encourage interested visitors.

While the "success" of Grosse Île and the Irish Memorial is not judged on the basis of the numbers of visitors attracted annually, the development of the site (and the enhancement of the interpretive programs) does hinge partly on its attendance and income. The success of the site is, however, evaluated on the basis of how effectively its heritage values are conveyed to its visitors. The current situation has visitors on the island for three to four hours at most. There are a dozen historic features spread out over the 3.45-km (2.14-mile) length of the island that are open to the public, numerous others that can be visited from the outside only, and many opportunities for taking in the scenery from various vantage points. Leaving time for lunch—either a picnic or a meal in the cafeteria—there

is little chance the visitor can see the whole site. If the guides have only 1.5 hours in which to present a four-hour interpretive program, they cannot be as effective as they are trained to be.[70]

The content of the interpretive program is still in development. Success in this area is tracked by periodic reporting. The 1999 report on the state of protected heritage areas[71] includes a commemorative integrity reporting table, covering several national historic sites, including Grosse Île and the Irish Memorial. The table assigns a grade to several items listed under the categories of "Resource Condition," "Effectiveness of Communications," and "Selected Management Practices." All indicators at Grosse Île had improved since the previous evaluation two years earlier, except in the area of "Communication," which includes overall communication, communication of national significance and of the national historic site general values, and communication of the range and complexity of perspectives presented. Grosse Île was given poor marks in this category, indicating shortcomings in the presentation of the site and an absence of programming on the general subject of "Immigration."

Another way to visit Grosse Île is through its Web site.[72] Interestingly, the Web site reflects some of the problems in communication seen on the island. In the medium that allows the creative revisualization of the site, its buildings, and its landscapes, the Web site designers chose to present the site in its three geographical sectors, exactly the way one sees it on the ground. In the "Grosse Île at a glance" part of the Web site, the Western Sector is explained building by building, illustrated by individual photographs. Elsewhere on the Web site, a very abbreviated history is given that does not connect the physical remains to the stories of the place.

There is an intertwined set of issues that will continue to challenge the managers of Grosse Île. Constraints on access to the island allow the continued protection of the natural environment and ensure that all visitors enter the site at the main wharf. The conservation priorities for the natural resources of the island include the shoreline as a Priority I sector; Priority I elements are considered unique or highly sensitive, and limited access is recommended, since "all human activity . . . runs the risk of ultimately extinguishing the element in question."[73] The current arrangement with transport companies may be limiting the number of visitors to a level lower than the actual demand; the arrangement also keeps their visits short. The apparent exclusivity of the transport arrangement has economic benefits for the south shore and for the business partnerships in force, but these benefits might be shared between several companies in the near future.

RESPECT FOR, AND PROTECTION OF, OTHER HERITAGE VALUES

This category of values includes most notably the cultural remains and built environment dating from before 1832 and after 1937, discussed earlier, as well as the natural environment. Cultural remains predating 1832 are scant, but their protection is addressed through strict controls over any activity involving excavation or disturbance of subsurface remains. When archaeology is undertaken, it is usually in the context of some inevitable works project, or when it can be justified as crucial for some other reason. Cultural features postdating 1937 include a number of structures built for storage, quarantine-related uses, or scientific activity by the military or agricultural sectors of the Canadian government. While these structures seem less romantic to the visitor keen to see vestiges of the nineteenth century, the buildings and their contents represent parts of the multilayered history of Grosse Île, and they are likely to grow in interest as they age, within the context of the larger story.

The natural environment is central to the condition of commemorative integrity of Grosse Île, as the environment is so much a part of the spirit of the place. In addition, there is a significant set of ecozones and habitats in this riverine context. As has been noted, the delicate nature of the littoral zone encircling the island is probably one of the key features of the protective plan in this area. The protection of this fragile shore system is part of the reason why Parks Canada has prohibited the docking or anchoring of private boats. But, as mentioned above, this restriction limits the modes of access and the number of visitors who can experience the site or become familiar with the commemorative message in situ. At this point, the protection of the "other cultural value" of the natural environment appears to be taking priority over creating opportunities for greater communication of the significance of Grosse Île and the Irish Memorial. Managing the conflict between dual responsibilities—protecting a fragile area and making an important site available—is a classic challenge for a site manager.

One interesting situation demonstrates the delicate balance of historic structures and the local wildlife population. For many years, a number of historic buildings on the island were home to large bat colonies—including the Lazaretto. Here, bats entered under the eaves and nested in the rafters, above the drop ceiling. When Parks Canada took over the site and began its systematic examination and evaluation of buildings, it became obvious that the bats were compromising a number of significant structures. Parks Canada also recognized that the bats needed somewhere to live, as they require considerable heat and enclosed spaces to survive the island's weather.

Possible options for dealing with the bats included allowing them to remain in the buildings, eliminating the bats altogether, or offering them alternative housing. The option chosen was the third. Several specially designed structures were built close to the historic structures where bats had become a serious problem. These new dwellings were high off the ground, with extended eaves and internal baffling that retained the body heat of the crowding bats. They were also built on skids, rather than set into the ground, so that as the bats came to prefer these structures to the restored historic buildings, the new structures could be gradually moved away from the historic buildings.

It is important to note that one of the most important mechanisms for ensuring the continued protection of all of a site's values and resources is the Canadian federal law that requires Parks Canada to review the management plans of its sites every five years. In this way, the values of the site and the way in which they are articulated, presented, and protected are continually monitored.

The review begins with staff assessing progress made on implementing the plan in force; this is done through the production of a State of the Park Report (now called the State of Protected Heritage Area Report). This report evaluates the state of commemorative integrity of the site under review. It can shed light on the effectiveness of the management plan and can indicate to the managers certain adjustments that may be necessary. In some cases, public consultation is undertaken as part of this review if it is felt that the plan (or the work that it recommends) does not fully support the commemorative integrity, if policy or legal shifts provide new information or considerations relating to the plan's objectives, if significant new information becomes available about risk or damage, if substantial changes are noted in visitation, or if other changes affect the management context.[74]

Conclusions

The Parks Canada guidelines provide a structured and systematic approach to the planning and management of historic sites. In most national heritage systems, the designation of a national site attributes a particular value or significance to a site, often prior to an analysis of the full range of values that the site might embody. The Canadian system is no exception. The official declaration of a site's values—the commemorative intent in the case of Canadian national historic sites—acquires primacy in all decisions on-site, and in some cases it can overshadow other values associated with a place before it was recognized at the national level. In the case of Grosse Île as a national historic site, the values that were initially deemed to be important were those that told a story about the development of the nation, and those that were already important to a particular group of stakeholders were initially downplayed. However, when the prescribed process of public consultation and review was undertaken, the conflicts over values were resolved.

One of the interesting issues that emerged in the public consultation phase was the possibility of unexpected stakeholders stepping forward and demanding inclusion. While this process involved some stress and expense, it reminds us that heritage touches human emotions, and it is advisable to allow their expression. Also, it offered further evidence that places can have stakeholders who may never see the place itself. A year after an affecting visit to Grosse Île, Mary Robinson, then president of Ireland, gave a speech to the Irish legislature entitled "Cherishing the Irish Diaspora," in which she talked about the important connections between contemporary Ireland and its people to those who emigrated during the dark famine years.

Parks Canada's concept of commemorative integrity, with its three indicators of the health and wholeness of the resource, advocates an approach that takes into consideration the totality of the site and its values. By requiring not only that the physical elements be conserved but also that the significance of the site be effectively communicated, commemorative integrity effectively places equal value on the protection of the physical materials and of their meanings, ensuring the preservation of both for present and future generations. The practice of devising a statement of commemorative intent and then building a commemorative integrity statement seems to be an enormously useful process that encourages focus on the principles and values that are most important and allows the technical and statutory compliance to follow behind.

The technical issues are not any simpler here than at other historic sites. Site managers need to be vigilant as they make treatment and management decisions that have impacts on Level I buildings—balancing historical integrity and physical survival. The protection of a unique building such as the Lazaretto as an artifact and as a museum is a complex challenge, an interesting didactic case in itself.

The isolated location of Grosse Île and the accompanying logistical constraints on use, access policies, and environmental protections have in some respects limited the ability of those who value the site to experience it. Creative means will be necessary in order to implement the commemorative intent fully.

The third indicator of the health of a historic site is that the heritage values of the site are respected by all whose decisions or actions affect the site. The purpose of this requirement is to avoid harm to values attributed to a site that are not included in the statement of commemorative intent. The ambiguity of the phrase "respected by all whose decisions or actions affect the site" does not provide much guidance in cases where the protection of the heritage values of some of the Level II resources is seen to diminish the commemorative intent of the site. As the site and its interpretive program continue to be developed and as the place becomes better known, the balance of perspectives regarding messages, preservation, access, and other currently dynamic issues is likely to become steadier.

Notes

1. Referred to as the *Agency Act*, its purpose was "to establish the Parks Canada Agency and to amend other Acts as a consequence." Statutes of Canada 1998, chap. 31 (assented to 3 Dec. 1998). First Session, Thirty-sixth Parliament, 46–47 Elizabeth II, 1997–98.

2. From the Web site of Canadian Heritage: A Report on Plans and Priorities 2001–2002: http://www.pch.gc.ca/pc-ch/pubs/rpp2001/vue-ens_eng.htm (Jan. 2003).

3. Parks Canada, n.d, 1.

4. Home page of the National Historic Sites of Canada Web site: http://www.parkscanada.gc.ca/lhnnhs/index1_e.asp (Jan. 2003).

5. The HSMBC Web site provides a thorough discussion of the Board's history, activities, and procedures, including the criteria as cited in the text at: http://www2.parkscanada.gc.ca/hsmbc/english/criteria_e.htm (Feb. 2003).

6. The first version was published in 1981. The version in force today is Parks Canada 2000a; http://www2.parkscanada.gc.ca/Nhs/sysplan/english/comp_e.pdf. In 1974, when Grosse Île became a National Historic Site, it was associated with the theme of immigration under the heading "Demography/Population."

7. This section summarizes information included in several documents, including the *Grosse Île and the Irish Memorial National Historic Site Management Plan* (Parks Canada 2001).

8. Parks Canada 2001.

9. Ibid., 63.

10. The August 2001 pilgrimage included about two hundred people, from the Ancient Order of Hibernians, Irish Heritage (Quebec), and Action Grosse-Île (Toronto).

11. One of the guiding documents in considering the site for commemoration at this level would have been the 1968 version of the *National Historic Sites Policy*, which states that historic sites could be designated on the basis of five criteria, which related to a site's association with events that shaped Canadian history, or with the life of a great Canadian, or with an important movement in Canadian history (Department of Indian Affairs and Northern Development 1968, 5).

12. From Parks Canada 1998a, annex 1, Deliberations of the Historic Sites and Monuments Board of Canada.

13. Parks Canada 1981.

14. Minutes of the HSMBC meeting, June 1984 (HSMBC 1984), presented in Parks Canada 1998a, annex 1, 55–56.

15. Parks Canada 2001, 2.

16. All prices in this section are in U.S. dollars, quoted from the Web site of Grosse Île and the Irish Memorial National Historic Site: http://www2.parkscanada.gc.ca/parks/quebec/grosseile/en/schedule_e.html (Feb. 2003).

17. Parks Canada 2001, 50.

18. The cafeteria and special events are catered by Le Manoir des Erables, one of Parks Canada's business partnerships.

19. Parks Canada 2001, 40.

20. Their point of departure was the 1984 recommendation that Parks Canada acquire the site, which followed on the recognition by the HSMBC of two important components: a commitment to the element of immigration as part of the national story, and the surviving historic resources that would support the telling of the story of immigration and its pivotal role in the building of the nation. The other nineteenth- and twentieth-century ports of entry for immigrants had long since, and repeatedly, been redeveloped.

21. Environment Canada 1986; earlier and later versions of this directive are also available.

22. Environment Canada 1989.

23. Environment Canada 1992a, 5.

24. Ibid., 47.

25. Ibid., 54–55.

26. HSMBC 1984.

27. Environment Canada 1989, 9.

28. As has been noted, Parks Canada is entrusted with the stewardship of significant sites with the trust of the government and the faith of the citizenry. With this mandate, it must present a view derived from its best efforts to gather accurate and comprehensive information and perspectives from all appropriate sources. In the case of Grosse Île, this was effected through commissioned research, consultation with experts, and a marketing study.

29. Environment Canada 1991, app. A, p. 4.

30. Environment Canada 1992a, 46.

31. Ibid., 62.

32. Ibid., 69.

33. Environment Canada 1993.

34. Ibid., 3.

35. Ibid., 21.

36. Ibid., 3.

37. Ibid., 23.

38. Two texts were used: (1) "We, the undersigned, are dismayed that the tragic truth of the death of 15,000 Irish men, women, and children whose mortal remains are buried in mass graves on Grosse Île is ignored in Environment Canada's plan to develop the island as a theme park celebrating Canada: Land of Welcome & Hope. We therefore urge the Government of Canada to ensure that the Irish graves of Grosse Île are perpetuated as the main theme of the National Historic Park, and as a reminder of the Irish role in the building of Canada"; and (2) "The Federal Government of Canada has stated the remains of 20,000 Irish people who tried to escape the Famine lie buried in Grosse Île. Yet, they

plan to turn this National Historic Site into a playground for the boaters of the St. Lawrence. They wish to forget the tragic events of 1847 stating the story of those who lie there has been over-emphasized. Action Grosse-Île has been formed to ensure that the mass graves on the island are protected and to ensure that the revisionists do not distort or bury the story of those who rest at Grosse Île and those who managed to survive the island. Action Grosse-Île plans to ensure that Grosse Île maintains a prominent place in both Canadian and Irish history and that the graves and the story of those buried there are protected and preserved. Show your support by lending your signature to this petition." (Parks Canada 1994c, 70–72).

39. Parks Canada 1981.

40. The five topic areas are: historical significance, development objectives and principles, commemoration themes, cultural resources, and public participation. Parks Canada 1994c.

41. *Canadian Heritage News Release Communiqué P-07/94–84.*

42. Parks Canada 1995.

43. Gordon Bennett, Parks Canada, personal communication, 2002.

44. Parks Canada, 1998a, 3.

45. Ibid.

46. See appendix A for further discussion of commemorative intent and commemorative integrity.

47. Parks Canada, 2002.

48. Parks Canada 1994a.

49. Ibid., sec. 1, Principles of Cultural Resource Management, subsecs. 1.1.2–1.4.1: http://www2.parkscanada.gc.ca/Library/PC_Guiding_Principles/Park146_e.htm.

50. Ibid., sec. 2.2, also found at the Web site cited in note 49.

51. Parks Canada 1998a. This statement is also summarized in Parks Canada 2001, 13–18.

52. The more-modern elements from later occupations are classified as Level II resources, discussed later in this section.

53. Parks Canada 1998a, 8.

54. Parks Canada 2001, 27ff.

55. Parks Canada 1994a, sec. 3, Activities of Cultural Resource Management, subsec. 3.4: http://www2.parkscanada.gc.ca/Library/PC_Guiding_Principles/Park157_e.htm#3.4.

56. Ibid., sec. 3.4.

57. Specifically, FHBRO 1996, found at: http://www2.parkscanada.gc.ca/Library/DownloadDocuments/DocumentsArchive/CodeOfPractice_e.pdf (Feb. 2003).

58. Parks Canada 2001, 43ff.

59. In the case of Grosse Île, Level II resources are those associated with the "other heritage values" discussed below.

60. FHBRO 1996.

61. This document is available only in French (Parks Canada 1998b).

62. Parks Canada 1998a, 52.

63. Parks Canada 1998a.

64. Parks Canada 1998b.

65. Parks Canada 1998a gives particular emphasis to issues related to the management of natural resources in appendix 2, "Conservation Priorities for Grosse Île Natural Resources." This section discusses management decisions through the assignment of four levels of conservation priority to particular natural resources on the island.

66. This passage is quoted from *Canadian Environmental Assessment Act 1992, c. 37,* found at: http://laws.justice.gc.ca/en/C-15.2/26791.html#rid-26830 (Feb. 2003).

67. Summary of the environmental assessment in Parks Canada 2001, 68.

68. Environment Canada 1992a, 72.

69. Environment Canada 1989, 46.

70. First raised in Environment Canada 1989, 19.

71. Parks Canada 2000b, 49, 51.

72. The official Web site for Grosse Île is found at: http://www2.parkscanada.gc.ca/parks/quebec/grosseile/en/index.html (Feb. 2003).

73. Parks Canada 2001, 83.

74. Parks Canada 2000c, secs. 4.4, 7.4.

Appendix A: Commemorative Integrity—A Short History of a Central Concept in Heritage Management in Parks Canada

Gordon Bennett
Director, Policy and Government Relations
National Historic Sites Directorate
Parks Canada

The concept of commemorative integrity was originally developed by Parks Canada in 1989 for purposes of reporting on the state of national historic sites in the 1990 State of the Parks Report. In the course of preparing this report, it became apparent that Parks Canada had information on many of the individual features and program activities that existed at individual national historic sites but that it lacked a conceptual framework to report on the overall state of health and wholeness of its national historic sites. In other words, we had information about the parts but not about the whole. And it became apparent to us that we could not simply aggregate the parts and equate the resulting sum with the state of the whole (the site). Thus was born the concept of commemorative integrity.

Simply stated, commemorative integrity describes the health and wholeness of a national historic site. A national historic site possesses commemorative integrity when:

- the resources that symbolize or represent the site's importance are not impaired or under threat;
- the reasons for the site's national historic significance are effectively communicated to the public; and
- the site's heritage values (including those not related to national significance) are respected by all whose decisions and actions affect the site.

What began as a framework to monitor and report systematically on the state of the national historic sites quickly evolved into something much broader. Indeed, by 1994, when *Parks Canada Guiding Principles and Operational Policies*[1] was issued, and when new approaches to management and business planning had been introduced, commemorative integrity had evolved into:

- a fundamental program objective (ensure the commemorative integrity of national historic sites);

- a statement of results to be achieved (health and wholeness of national historic sites, i.e., commemorative integrity); and

- a primary organizational accountability.

Over the next few years, the concept was rapidly elaborated. One of the most important advances was the introduction of Commemorative Integrity Statements. The purpose of these statements is to provide a site-specific description of what commemorative integrity means for a particular national historic site (how can we try to ensure commemorative integrity if we do not know what it means in the context of a specific site?). As is the case with commemorative integrity itself, the Commemorative Integrity Statement (referred to as a CIS) is rooted in Parks Canada's Cultural Resource Management Policy. The CIS identifies the historic/heritage values—associative as well as physical—relating to the site (including those not directly related to the formal reasons for designation) and provides guidance or indicators for determining when these values might be impaired or under threat, not adequately communicated or respected. Stakeholder and public participation in the development of the CIS is encouraged. Along with the Cultural Resource Management Policy, the CISs were critical components in Parks Canada's move to values-based management. They responded to the question posed by former ICOMOS secretary-general Herb Stovel: "Where does value lie?" As stated in the 1995 draft Guidelines for the Preparation of Commemorative Integrity Statements, knowing where value lies (i.e., what the values are) is essential to stewardship, because knowing where value lies fundamentally informs:

- what we need to do (i.e., manage);
- how we should do/manage it (i.e., adopt management strategies appropriate to the specific case based on the values); and
- what one should be accountable for (i.e., the nature of management accountability).

The draft guidelines were superseded by a considerably more detailed *Guide to the Preparation of Commemorative Integrity Statements* in 2002[2] to provide clarification and direction on issues that had not been addressed or adequately addressed in the 1995 version, to codify best practice that had developed after 1995, and to provide guidance to a wide range of historic site managers and stakeholders—not simply those in Parks Canada—who might wish to prepare such statements. Commemorative integrity and Commemorative Integrity Statements require the input of experts, but they are not the private preserve of experts. The new guide also made some minor editorial changes to the definition of commemorative integrity, which now reads as follows:

> A national historic site possesses commemorative integrity (health and wholeness) when:
>
> > • the resources directly related to the reasons for designation as a national historic site are not impaired or under threat;
> >
> > • the reasons for designation as a national historic site are effectively communicated to the public; and
> >
> > • the site's heritage values (including those not related to the reasons for designation as a national historic site) are respected in all decisions and actions affecting the site.

The new guide is available on the Parks Canada Web site at http://www.pc.gc.ca/docs/pc/guide/guide/commemorative_1_0_e.asp.

On the monitoring front, it was not until 1997 that Parks Canada began to explicitly report on the state of commemorative integrity of national historic sites. In that year, eight sites were reported on. One of the most interesting findings was that the greatest impairment to these eight sites was in the communication of national significance. Beginning in 2001–02, Parks Canada committed to evaluating the state of commemorative integrity for fifteen national historic sites a year. The Commemorative Integrity Statements serve as the basis for these evaluations.

Within a Parks Canada context, commemorative integrity has become the key component in planning, managing, operating, evaluating, and taking remedial action in national historic sites. The Commemorative Integrity Statement provides the core for national historic site management plans and annual business plans. Commemorative integrity evaluations point to where remedial management action is required, and, for an increasing number of managers, they are considered to be a prerequisite to any new management planning activity (how can you plan if there is not a sound understanding of the state of the place for which the plan is being done?).

Commemorative integrity will also be the centerpiece of new legislation planned for Canada's national historic sites, including sites not owned by Parks Canada. In little more than a decade, the values-based management approach inherent in commemorative integrity has

gone from a conceptual construct to a way of describing our business. How could this have happened, given all the interests (managers, operations people, professional disciplines, stakeholders, etc.) affected and/or involved? A number of reasons can be suggested to explain this:

- the simplicity of the concept
- the emphasis on values and on a systematic and comprehensive articulation of values
- the focus on the site, rather than on an organization or specific activities or functions
- its usefulness as a management, planning, and evaluation tool
- its clear relationship to what we (should) do at historic sites
- the involvement and engagement of a broad range of people
- it's not exclusionary
- it's a unifying concept

Notes

1. Parks Canada 1994b.
2. Parks Canada 2002.

References

Anick, N. 1984. *Grosse Île and Partridge Island, Quarantine Stations.* Historic Sites and Monuments Board of Canada Agenda Paper No. 1983–19. Ottawa: HSMBC.

Canadian Heritage. 1994. *Canadian Heritage News Release Communiqué P-07/94–84.* Quebec: Canadian Heritage.

Department of Indian Affairs and Northern Development, National Historic Parks Branch. 1968. *National Historic Sites Policy.* Ottawa: Department of Indian Affairs and Northern Development, National Historic Parks Branch.

Environment Canada, Canadian Parks Service. 1986. *Management Directive 4.2.1: Management Planning Process for National Historic Sites.* Ottawa: Canadian Parks Service.

———. 1989. *Grosse Île National Historic Site Project Orientation—Public Information Paper.* Quebec: Canadian Parks Service.

———. 1991. *Management Directive 3.2.1: Management Planning Process for National Historic Sites.* Ottawa: Canadian Parks Service.

———. 1992a. *Grosse Île National Historic Site—Development Concept.* Quebec: Canadian Parks Service.

———. 1992b. *Grosse Île National Historic Site—Development Concept Supplement.* Quebec: Canadian Parks Service.

———. 1993. *Grosse Île National Historic Site—Development Concept Supplement.* Ottawa: Canadian Parks Service.

Federal Heritage Buildings Review Office (FHBRO). 1995. *Énoncé de la valeur patrimoniale: Le Lazaret (no. 100) Grosse-Île, Québec.* Rapport BEEFP No. 90-31.

———. 1996. *Federal Heritage Buildings Review Office (FHBRO) Code of Practice.* Ottawa: FHBRO.

Fortier, Y. 1997. *Le Lazaret de Grosse-Île: Synthèse et conclusion préliminaires.* Unpublished report.

Historic Sites and Monuments Board of Canada (HSMBC). 1984. Minutes, June.

———. 1993. Minutes, Nov.

Parks Canada. 1981. *National Historic Sites of Canada System Plan.* Ottawa: Parks Canada.

———. 1994a. Cultural resource management policy. In *Parks Canada Guiding Principles and Operational Policies.* Ottawa: Parks Canada.

———. 1994b. *Parks Canada Guiding Principles and Operational Policies.* Ottawa: Parks Canada.

———. 1994c. *Grosse Île National Historic Site—Report on the Public Consultation Program.* Quebec: Canadian Heritage/Parks Canada.

———. 1995. *Grosse Île and the Irish Quarantine Tragedy: Report of the Advisory Panel on Grosse Île.* Quebec: Parks Canada.

———. 1998a. *Commemorative Integrity Statement: Grosse Île and the Irish Memorial National Historic Site.* Quebec: Parks Canada.

———. 1998b. *Plan d'expérience de visite [Plan of the Visit Experience]—Lieu Historique National de la Grosse-Île-et-le-Mémorial-des-Irlandais.* Quebec: Parks Canada.

———. 2000a. *National Historic Sites of Canada: System Plan.* Ottawa: Parks Canada.

———. 2000b. *Parks Canada Agency State of Protected Heritage Areas—1999 Report.* Ottawa: Parks Canada.

———. 2000c. *Parks Canada Guide to Management Planning.* Ottawa: Parks Canada.

———. 2001. *Grosse Île and the Irish Memorial National Historic Site Management Plan.* Quebec: Parks Canada.

———. 2002. *Guide to the Preparation of Commemorative Integrity Statements.* Quebec: Parks Canada. http://www.pc.gc.ca/docs/pc/guide/guide/commemorative_1_0_e.asp

———. N.d. *Parks Canada Agency 2001–2002 Estimates: A Report on Plans and Priorities.* Ottawa: Parks Canada.

Statutes of Canada. 1998. *Parks Canada Agency Act.*

Persons Contacted during the Development of the Case

Jean Barry
Site Management Specialist
Quebec Service Center
Parks Canada

Pierre Beaudet
Chief
Cultural Heritage
Quebec Service Center
Parks Canada Heritage

Denis Belleau
Chief of Technical Services
Quebec District
Parks Canada

Marie-Josée Bissonette
Parks Canada administration

Jeanne Boulanger
Corporation for Heritage

Monique Élie
Archaeologist
Quebec Service Center
Parks Canada Heritage

Jean-François Lachance
Parks Canada transportation partners
Croisiers Lachance

Daniel Villeneuve
Site Manager
Grosse Île and the Irish Memorial
National Historic Site

Chaco Culture National Historical Park

Marta de la Torre, Margaret G. H. MacLean,

and David Myers

About This Case Study

This case study looks at the management of Chaco Culture National Historical Park (CCNHP) by the U.S. National Park Service (NPS). This site was declared a national monument in 1907 and became one of the original units of the NPS when the agency was created in 1916. The long history of CCNHP as a heritage site provides an excellent illustration of how values emerge and evolve with new knowledge as well as how they are influenced by changes of values in society. This case also explores how the specific values and circumstances of a site can be respected within the very specific management guidance provided by a complex national agency with responsibility for a large number of sites. Both the emergence and evolution of values and the management of a site as part of a large system provide opportunities to analyze the resolution of conflicts and the impact of management decisions.

The case is presented in two parts. First, "Management Context and History of CCNHP" provides general background information about the NPS and the site. It first describes the management context of the NPS, including its place in the government, its organization, and the administrative guidance it provides for managers of the resources under its stewardship. The discussion then narrows its focus to CCNHP itself, addressing the geographic location of the Park, its history of habitation, and its evolution as a heritage site. The final section of this part describes the Park's features, partnerships, infrastructure, and facilities.

The archaeological remains of the Chacoan civilization protected by the Park are recognized to have national and international significance. The significance assigned to this site has always been based on these archaeological resources, but the values attributed to them have changed and expanded over time. The initial section of the next part, "understanding and Protecting the values," examines how the values of CCNHP have emerged and evolved over its history. The following section analyzes how these values are reflected in the policies that guide the operations of the site. The final section explores the impact that these policies—and other management actions—have had on the values of the site and

includes examples of how some specific situations were handled by the site authorities.

This study of the management of CCNHP draws on extensive consultation among the authors, the members of the project steering committee, staff of the site, and NPS authorities, in interviews and frank discussions. The authors have consulted an extensive range of reports, plans, and statutory and guidance documents relating to this Park, to related park units, and to the NPS in general. The staff of the Park and of NPS headquarters in Washington, D.C., have provided interpretation of this documentation and the rationale for many decisions made on site.

The situation studied in this case existed between October 2001 and June 2002, when the case was developed and written. Since then, there have been changes in management personnel, and certain policies are being reviewed and modified. The analysis focuses on the situation as it was then, not on the recent changes. Management is a continuous process, and the case presents a snapshot taken at a particular moment in time. A similar study done in a few years would likely capture a different picture.

Digital reproductions of the following supplementary documents are contained within the accompanying CD-ROM: Chaco Culture General Management Plan / Development Concept Plan (1985); Chaco Culture Statement for Interpretation and Interim Interpretive Prospectus (1991); and National Park Service Management Policies 2001.

Management Context and History of CCNHP

Management Context

DEPARTMENT OF THE INTERIOR

The National Park Service (NPS) is a federal agency within the United States Department of the Interior. This department, through its various agencies, is responsible for the management of most federal public lands in the United States, which constitute one-third of the total acreage of the country. The agencies that make up the department cover a great deal of ground, literally and figuratively; in addition to the NPS, they include, among others, the Bureau of Land Management, the Fish and Wildlife Service, the Office of Surface Mining Reclamation and Enforcement, and the Bureau of Indian Affairs. The secretary of the interior and the agencies' directors manage the inevitable conflicts resulting from the overlapping mandates and resources for which they are accountable. The secretary and the agency directors are appointed by the U.S. president and generally represent the particular views and philosophy of a political party.

NATIONAL PARK SERVICE

The U.S. Congress created the NPS in 1916 with the mandate to preserve natural and cultural resources of national significance. The founding legislation states that

> the Service shall promote and regulate the use of Federal areas known as national parks, monuments and reservations by such means and measures as conform to the fundamental purpose of the said parks, monuments and reservations, which purpose is to conserve the scenery and the natural and historic objects and the wild life therein, and to provide for the enjoyment of the same in such manner and by such means as will leave them unimpaired for the enjoyment of future generations.[1]

At its founding, the NPS assumed responsibility for twelve existing national parks, nineteen monuments (including Chaco Canyon National Monument), and two reservations. Its mission specified the dual obligation of conserving unimpaired the scenery and the cultural and natural resources, and providing access for their enjoy-

ment. Interpretations of what constitutes conservation, access, and unimpaired resources have created tensions between these obligations at various times during the history of the NPS. Over the years, however, the unimpairment imperative from the NPS mandate has been interpreted by NPS directors and sometimes by secretaries of the interior as giving conservation primacy over access.[2] This position is strongly supported in current NPS management policies.[3]

Located in the States, the District of Columbia, American Samoa, Guam, Puerto Rico, Saipan, and the Virgin Islands, the NPS properties include 56 national parks, 39 national historical parks, 75 national monuments, 19 national reserves and preserves, 78 national historic sites, and 25 national battlefields. More than half of the units of the system are considered to be of cultural or historic significance.

The NPS presently has responsibility for 385 units or places of national significance—natural, historical, and recreational areas—the diversity of which is demonstrated by citing a few examples: Yellowstone National Park, Independence National Historical Park, Mesa Verde National Park, the Vietnam Veterans Memorial, Abraham Lincoln's Birthplace National Historic Site, the Blue Ridge Parkway, Cape Cod National Seashore, and the White House.

In addition to these sites, the NPS oversees programs that serve broad conservation and recreation needs. Examples include the National Register of Historic Places; the National Historic Landmarks Program; the Land and Water Conservation Fund Grants Program; the Historic American Building Survey; the Historic American Engineering Record; the American Battlefield Protection Program; the National Maritime Heritage Grants Program; the Rivers, Trails and Conservation Assistance Program; and the Tribal Heritage Preservation Grants Program.

Over its eighty-six years, the NPS administration has expanded and contracted, as the times have required and as resources have allowed. In the mid-1990s, as part of an effort to streamline the federal government, the NPS underwent a decentralizing reorganization that reassigned twelve hundred jobs from the headquarters in Washington, D.C., and regional offices to individual parks and specialized service centers.

The mission of the NPS to preserve unimpaired the natural and cultural resources and values of the national park system for the enjoyment, education, and inspiration of this and future generations represents a great deal of responsibility.[4] But, as with many large U.S. government bureaucracies, the actual authority for selecting and implementing management strategies resides in legislation and related procedural documents written to ensure compliance. As NPS policy clarifies, "the management of the national park system and NPS programs is guided by the Constitution [of the United States], public laws, treaties, proclamations, Executive Orders, regulations, and directives of the Secretary of the Interior and the Assistant Secretary for Fish and Wildlife and Parks."[5]

In the current organization, each park or site has a management team headed by a superintendent, who is the principal authority in most decisions regarding that unit. Superintendents report to their respective regional directors, but outside the issuing of certain permits, most park operations are handled locally once the annual budget and activity plans are approved. Superintendents have been compared to ship captains: "others might own the property and determine the cargo, but once away from the dock (or in the field), the captain (or superintendent) makes the decisions."[6]

Description of CCNHP and Its Context

NATURAL CONTEXT

CCNHP is situated in the northwestern part of the state of New Mexico, near the center of the 6.47-million-hectare (25,000-square-mile) San Juan Basin, within the much larger Colorado Plateau. The basin is generally semiarid, typically receiving only 21.6 centimeters (8.5 inches) of precipitation annually, which accounts for the region's sparse vegetation. Summers bring intense but brief thunderstorms with flash floods. Annual temperatures vary widely, with winter lows well below freezing and summer peaks around 38°C (100°F). Year-round, daily temperatures at Chaco Canyon also tend to range widely, rising and falling with the sun, due to an elevation in excess of 1,829 meters (6,000 feet).

The Park today covers approximately 13,760 hectares (34,000 acres). Chaco Canyon itself, which cuts east-west through the Park, is some 91 meters (300 feet)

Figure 2.1. North Mesa. The limited vegetation, temperature extremes, occasional flooding, and gusting winds contribute to active erosion patterns in the landscape. Horizontal sedimentary layers have been carved into colorful plateaus, mesas, buttes, and canyons. Photo: David Myers

deep and 2.5 kilometers (1.5 miles) wide, bordered by sandstone cliffs to the north and south. Above these cliffs lie mesas dotted with piñon and juniper trees. Grasses and shrubs cover the alluvial canyon bottom, drained by the ephemeral Chaco Wash. At the west end of the Park, Chaco Wash and Escavada Wash join to form the Chaco River.

From the tops of the mesas, the natural boundaries of the San Juan Basin may be viewed in all directions: Colorado's San Juan and La Plata Mountains to the north, the Chuska Mountains to the west, the Jemez Mountains to the east, and Mount Taylor to the south. Throughout the basin, vast deposits of uranium, coal, natural gas, and oil lie beneath the surface.

CULTURAL CONTEXT

CCNHP is located in a relatively poor and lightly populated area of New Mexico. Native Americans, primarily Navajo, constitute the majority of the residents immediately surrounding the Park. The Pueblo tribes live in areas further east, west, and south. The lands around the Park are used primarily for grazing sheep, cattle, and horses and for industrial extraction and processing of the region's abundant deposits of energy resources.

Intertribal, as well as non-Indian, relations in the Southwest are shaped significantly by the extent of federal and tribal governments' control of land in this area—and by the complexities of land interests in general. Nuances in legalities of land use are often complicated by the opposition of surface and subsurface interests, which are in many cases divided between different parties for one land parcel.[7] Many residents of the Southwest question the extent of government involvement in land management in the region. In part, they feel that federal control reflects the interests of distant bureaucrats in Washington, D.C., rather than local interests, and that local revenues lost due to the exemption of government land from property taxes are not made up by federal payments and subsidies. In addition, setting aside lands as national parks and under the *Wilderness Act of 1964* is seen as preventing viable economic activities in those areas. Nevertheless, grazing and the industrial extraction of various types of natural resources have long been allowed in other federal lands in the region.

The presence in the region of many Native American reservations, which are among the nation's largest, complicates local and federal land issues. The lands in and around several of these reservations are the subject of long-standing controversies over sovereignty due to sometimes-conflicting treaties between the U.S. government and the tribes. A case in point is a century-old dispute between the Hopi tribe and Navajo Nation over approximately 248,000 hectares (1.8 million acres) of land in the Four Corners region—the meeting point of the states of Arizona, Colorado, New Mexico, and Utah. Complicating and occasionally fueling the land dispute is the unresolved issue of legal control over coal reserves, valued in the billions of dollars. Not surprisingly, this conflict reverberates in management issues at CCNHP.

History of Settlement and Use

Current evidence indicates a broad and relatively continuous habitation of the San Juan Basin during the Paleo-Indian period, roughly between 8,000 and 10,000 years ago.[8] The earliest remains of human habitation in Chaco Canyon date to 7,000 to 2,000 years ago. These early inhabitants apparently were seminomadic hunter-gatherers. Between two and three thousand years ago, inhabitants of the canyon began to establish more-permanent settlements, facilitated by their increasingly sophisticated use of domesticated strains of squash, beans, and corn.

During the 1,300 years of Anasazi,[9] or ancestral Puebloan, culture, architecture, technology, social organization and population distribution continued to evolve. A period of increased precipitation between A.D. 400 and 500 provided for greater ease in growing crops, allowing for the first permanent occupation of Chaco Canyon and a significant population growth in the area. Settlement patterns, including subterranean pit houses and accompanying storage structures, eventually coa-

lesced into small villages. By about A.D. 500, the canyon's inhabitants were building one-story masonry dwellings above ground, organized around central pit houses.

The period from A.D. 700 to 1300, also called the Pueblo period, is associated with what is known as the "Chaco Phenomenon." The core area of Chaco Canyon appears to have served as an administrative, economic, and ceremonial nexus of a culture that dominated what today is known as the Four Corners.

The phases of occupation in Chaco Canyon left behind complex masonry structures known as "great houses," containing hundreds of rooms and dozens of kivas (round structures of varying size) that were much larger in scale than anything previously built in the region (fig. 2.2); their appearance is unique in the Americas. Other features of the Chaco Phenomenon include road alignments (some segments are more than 64 kilometers—40 miles—long) with cut stairways and masonry ramps that lead to more than 150 outlying great houses and settlements. The Chacoans also created and depended on their water control and distribution structures to manage the scant seasonal rains, and they depended on their astronomical knowledge to anticipate calendric cycles. They left petroglyphs that marked solar events, and they appear to have used road and architectural alignments to reflect lunar and stellar events. Excavations of the great houses have revealed seashells, copper bells, and remains of macaws, suggesting trade with peoples of the Pacific Coast and the Gulf of California as

Figure 2.2. Pueblo Bonito seen from the air. Great houses, such as Pueblo Bonito, are unique to Chaco culture. They have large numbers of rectangular and irregular rooms as well as round structures of different sizes, called kivas. The purpose of the kivas is not known with certainty, although it is assumed that they were communal gathering places, perhaps used for ceremonies. Photo: Courtesy National Park Service, Chaco Culture NHP Collection Archives.

well as of Mesoamerica. The Chacoans also traded their intricately decorated coiled pottery and fine turquoise jewelry.

By A.D. 1130, new construction at Chaco had ceased, and by A.D. 1300 most of the population of the canyon had moved away. Over time, Chacoan people migrated to other areas of the region, including, to the north, the Mesa Verde area; to the west and southwest, the Hopi Mesas, the Zuni Mountain area, and the Chuska Mountains; and to the east and southeast, along the Rio Grande.

Archaeologists generally believe that Chaco Canyon was not resettled until the Navajo migrated into the region from the north in the late 1500s or 1600s, although Native American groups assert that the canyon has been in continuous use since Anasazi times.[10] Archaeological evidence shows that Chaco Canyon was used by both Rio Grande Pueblo and Navajo groups, from just before the Pueblo Revolt of 1680 against the Spanish through the mid-nineteenth century. From the end of that period through the first part of the twentieth century, Navajo populated the canyon, establishing seasonal camps, permanent dwellings, plant and mineral gathering areas, and ceremonial sites. After the establishment of Chaco Canyon National Monument in 1907, Navajo families continued to farm and graze there until the NPS initiated a resettlement program in the mid 1930s.

Evolution of Chaco Canyon as a Heritage Site

The first documented interest in Chaco Canyon by European Americans as a place of archaeological significance came in 1849, when the Washington Expedition, a U.S. Army Topographical Engineers reconnaissance detachment, encountered and wrote descriptions of Chacoan sites.[11] Like the earlier Spanish military expeditions of the 1820s, the U.S. Army engineers were met by Navajo who had inhabited the area for almost four hundred years. When first "discovered," the ruins of Chaco Canyon were seen as the abandoned vestiges of a vanished civilization. In spite of this perception, affiliated clans and religious societies of the Hopi of Arizona and the Pueblos of New Mexico claim to have visited the site to honor their ancestral homelands since the time of the emigration of its prehistoric inhabitants in the thirteenth century.[12]

In 1877, the U.S. government's Geological and Geographical Survey of the Territories produced extensive descriptions and maps of the Chacoan sites. The next important documentation of the site came in 1888, when the Bureau of American Ethnology surveyed and photographed the major Chacoan sites for a study of Pueblo architecture. These photographs provide evidence that looting and vandalism of prehistoric remains were already occurring at this early date.

In 1896, relic hunter Richard Wetherill arrived at Chaco after excavating several ancestral Puebloan sites, including some at Mesa Verde, in search of "antiquities." His successes attracted the interest of the wealthy Hyde brothers of New York, who over the next five years collaborated with Wetherill to conduct full-scale excavations at Pueblo Bonito, one of the most prominent of the site's great houses. George H. Pepper of the American Museum of Natural History supervised the excavation work of the Hyde Exploring Expedition, while Wetherill directed a Navajo crew. The primary purpose of the expedition was to gather artifacts for the Hydes, who later donated their collections to the American Museum of Natural History in New York, where they are found today.

By this time, the proliferation of treasure-hunting excavations throughout the Southwest had created great concern among the scientific establishment of the country. Early attempts to protect archaeological sites met strong resistance from western settlers who saw these efforts as one more initiative by the federal government to regulate the use of the land. However, a 1901 federal investigation of the Hyde Exploring Expedition's excavations and the land claims of Richard Wetherill at Chaco Canyon strongly recommended that the U.S. government create a national park to preserve the archaeological sites in the area. The General Land Office responded by putting a stop to the Hyde Expedition's excavations at Pueblo Bonito and by rejecting Wetherill's land claim. Despite these decisions, Wetherill continued to homestead at Chaco Canyon, and he operated a trading post at Pueblo Bonito until his death in 1910.

Eventually, after twenty-five years of concern over damage to the archaeological record, the *Antiquities Act* was signed into law in 1906. The act was designed to protect and regulate the use and care of "historic landmarks, historic and prehistoric structures, and other objects of historic or scientific interest"[13] and "to preserve [their] historic, scientific, commemorative, and cultural values."[14] The new law authorized the creation of national monuments on lands owned or controlled by the federal government by presidential proclamation, without congressional approval, as was (and still is) required for the creation of national parks. The act stipulates that the extension of national monuments is to "be confined to the

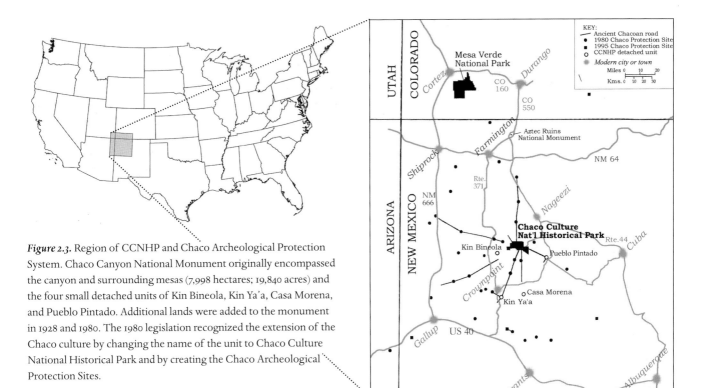

Figure 2.3. Region of CCNHP and Chaco Archeological Protection System. Chaco Canyon National Monument originally encompassed the canyon and surrounding mesas (7,998 hectares; 19,840 acres) and the four small detached units of Kin Bineola, Kin Ya'a, Casa Morena, and Pueblo Pintado. Additional lands were added to the monument in 1928 and 1980. The 1980 legislation recognized the extension of the Chaco culture by changing the name of the unit to Chaco Culture National Historical Park and by creating the Chaco Archeological Protection Sites.

smallest area compatible with the proper care and management of the objects to be protected."[15] In March 1907, President Theodore Roosevelt issued Presidential Proclamation No. 740, establishing Chaco Canyon National Monument.

The new national monument was administered by the General Land Office of the Department of the Interior until 1916, when it came under the administration of the newly founded NPS. In 1920, 461 hectares (1,140 acres) within the Park were technically the property of Navajo families. Over time, some of that land has been acquired by the NPS; today, title to some of these parcels, called *in-holdings*, may be divided among more than 100 descendants of the original titleholder. It is estimated that just over 120 hectares (300 acres) of these lands in the western part of the Park are still grazed and could be mined or developed by their titleholders. About 650 hectares (1,620 acres) of land inside the Park are still held by private individuals. Complicated titles and ownership transactions over time have made it difficult for the NPS to say with any degree of certainty the extent of grazed or privately owned land.[16] While the NPS has an obvious interest in acquiring these lands, it recognizes the challenge involved: "Recent efforts to acquire allotments having only one owner have failed, and acquiring these small tracts will require decades of negotiations for each estate."[17]

During the first eighty years of the Park, both governmental and nongovernmental archaeologists excavated various locations at the site. From 1933 to 1937, Gordon Vivian carried out extensive conservation work at Pueblo Bonito, Chetro Ketl, and Casa Rinconada. A Civilian Conservation Corps (CCC)[18] crew of local Navajo stonemasons initiated repairs in 1937 to many of the large Chacoan structures that were deteriorating after years of exposure to rain, wind, and freeze-thaw cycles as well as years of archaeological excavations. The CCC project planted approximately 100,000 trees throughout the canyon to forestall soil erosion, constructed earthen berms for the purpose of soil conservation, and improved many roads and trails. It began construction of a road to the top of the cliff overlooking Pueblo Bonito, but World War II interrupted the project, which was abandoned in 1941 and never resumed. The conservation unit eventually left the CCC but continued work on the stabilization of ruins as park personnel.

Between 1971 and 1986, the comprehensive and interdisciplinary Chaco Center Project undertook a broad survey of the monument, the examination of previous documentation, and the excavation of a number of sites. Publication of the findings was a key component of the project. The information that resulted has allowed scholars to examine the Chaco Phenomenon from a much

Figure 2.4. Early view of Pueblo Bonito, with Threatening Rock still standing. For almost half a century, Pueblo Bonito was excavated under the shadow of Threatening Rock. Finally, in 1941, the enormous boulder separated from the crumbling mesa and fell onto the great house, destroying some thirty rooms excavated during the two previous decades. Photo: Courtesy Southwest Museum, Los Angeles, Photo # P23826

broader perspective, and their conclusions have greatly influenced the interpretation of the site.[19]

Motivated by new knowledge about the extension of the remains of Chaco culture and by threats from increased exploitation of natural resources in the region, Congress enacted legislation in 1980 adding 5,060 hectares (12,500 acres) to the monument and changing its name to Chaco Culture National Historical Park.[20] The law affirmed the Park's mandate of preservation, interpretation, and research. The legislation also designated thirty-three other sites in the San Juan Basin as Chaco Culture Archeological Protection Sites and provided for the addition of more sites in the future. More than two-thirds of these newly protected sites, which are not part of CCNHP, are in Navajo tribal lands, allotments, or lands used by the tribe for grazing. Subsequently, the *Chacoan Outliers Protection Act of 1995* added nine new and removed four formerly designated Chaco Culture Archeological Protection Sites, resulting in a total of thirty-nine outliers, extending the area of protected sites beyond the San Juan Basin.

In 1987, the UNESCO World Heritage Committee formally recognized the international importance of CCNHP when it inscribed it in the World Heritage List. The nominating documents present the site as containing "the physical remains of the Chacoans; a unique population of a culture that has been extinct for hundreds of years."[21] Chaco was inscribed in the list under criterion

C(iii) of the 1984 World Heritage Convention, which covers properties that "bear a unique or at least exceptional testimony to a civilization which has disappeared" and that meet requirements of authenticity.[22] Five other Chacoan sites—Aztec Ruins National Monument, Casamero, Halfway House, Twin Angels, and Kin Nizhoni—were also included in the World Heritage inscription, highlighting the extension of the Chaco culture.

PARK OPERATIONS AND FACILITIES

Today, CCNHP is managed by a superintendent who reports to the director of the NPS Intermountain Regional Office in Denver.[23] The NPS alone is responsible and accountable for the management of the Park, and under law, other stakeholders or groups can only become involved in a consultation capacity. Currently, the Park has a staff of 21 permanent employees and 16 seasonal hires, organized in six operational divisions: the superintendent's office (2 full-time employees [FTEs]), cultural resources (the largest group, with 14 FTEs in preservation and 3 in museum curatorial), natural resources (1 FTE), law enforcement and emergency services (2 FTEs); visitor services and interpretation (4.5 FTEs), and maintenance (5.5 FTEs). The Park's base budget in 2002 was approximately US$1.6 million, of which US$300,000 was transferred to an agency of the Navajo Tribe for the Navajo site protection project.[24]

The main access to the Park is from the northeast through a road that starts at New Mexico 44/U.S. 550, the main east-west highway from the Four Corners region to Santa Fe and Albuquerque. The distance from this highway to the Park entrance is 33.6 km (21 miles), of which 25.5 kilometers (16 miles) is unpaved road. A second road approaches the site from the south from U.S. 40 via Crownpoint; the last 30.4 km (19 miles) of this road are also unpaved. In order to encourage access to the Park from the northeast, for a long time maps and brochures of CCNHP issued by the NPS did not indicate the existence of the south road. A third unpaved road that provided access to the site from the northwest was closed several years ago.

The Park is open all year from sunrise to sunset, although the unpaved roads can be impassable during inclement weather. The Park charges an entrance fee of US$8 per car or US$4 per motorcycle, which is collected at the Visitor Center.

Of the approximately four thousand archaeological sites that have been identified within Park boundaries, thirty-seven are open to visitors. These are located on the

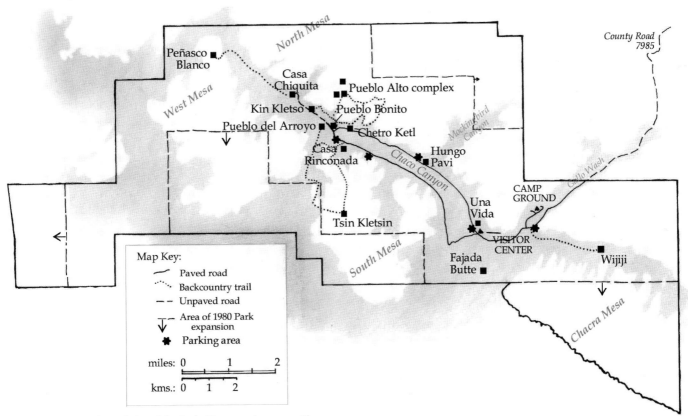

Figure 2.5. Current boundaries of the Park. The areas demarcated by arrows are those added in 1980, when legislation changed the status of the site from a national monument to a national historical park. The paved road inside the Park passes by the Visitor Center and makes a 14.5-km (9-mile) loop on the floor of the canyon. Visitors have easy access to over a dozen important sites from this loop road. CCNHP has some facilities for visitors, such as the Visitor Center, a small campground, and picnic areas.

Figure 2.6. CCNHP visitation characteristics. (Source: National Park Service Public Use Statistics Office, 29 May 2002, http://www.aqd.nps.gov/stats.)

loop road and on some of the backcountry trails. Walking trails with interpretive signage that lead visitors through the major ruin sites are surfaced with compacted gravel. The 30.4 kilometers (19 miles) of trails in the backcountry areas and the mesa tops are rougher and are not easily discerned. Access to the backcountry sites is allowed individually or with ranger-led tours. Visitors to those areas must obtain permits so that rangers can keep track of off-trail hikers. The detached Park units are connected to the Park by paved and unpaved roads passing through private land. Thus, the construction of gates to limit access is precluded.

Starting in the 1970s, the number of visitors to the Park declined from an estimated 90,000 annually to approximately 74,000 in 2001. Park staff attribute the decline in recent years in part to the appearance of hantavirus in the region.[25] According to a 1994 study, the great majority of visitors to CCNHP are of European ancestry and have had several years of higher education.[26] Only 20 percent of visitors are accompanied by children or teenagers. Almost half of them spend between two and six hours on-site, and one-fourth stay in the Park overnight.

The Visitor Center, built in 1957, is open daily except Christmas and New Year's Day. The center has a small exhibition focused on Chaco culture and on Navajo and Pueblo history; three films about Chaco, the Anasazi, and Fajada Butte are shown in a small projection room. The Center also houses a bookstore, administrative offices, restrooms, and drinking fountains.

There are four picnic areas in the Park with a total of nine picnic tables; camping sites have their own eating areas. Parking areas along the interpretive loop road can accommodate sixty-two vehicles. Off the main entrance road are a forty-five-site campground and a small-group camping area with comfort stations. Minimal overflow camping space is available during peak visitation season. The site is 96 kilometers (60 miles) from the nearest town that provides accommodations. There are no lodgings, automobile services, or food facilities inside the Park.

Because of its relative remoteness, all maintenance facilities, water treatment systems, and employee housing are located within the Park in an area not far from the Visitor Center. These facilities consists of six maintenance and ten housing structures, a water well and storage tanks, water and sewage pipelines, and 0.8 hectares (2 acres) of sewage discharge lagoons.[27]

Understanding and Protecting the Values of the Park

This part of the Chaco case study examines the values of CCNHP—how they were and are identified and recognized and how they are considered in the management of the site. It then analyzes the impact of operational decisions and actions on the values attributed to the site.

Three questions focus the discussions of the sections that follow:

- How are the values associated with the site understood and articulated?
- How are these values taken into account in the site's management policies and strategies?
- How do management decisions and actions on site affect the values?

In these discussions, it is important to keep in mind that CCNHP cannot operate independently; as a unit of the NPS it must follow the directives established for the system as a whole. The NPS is a federal agency that bases the management of its holdings on the U.S. Constitution, federal laws, executive orders, federal regulations that have the force of law, and policy directives from the secretary of the interior and the secretary's deputies. Within the NPS, policies and guidance make operational these laws and directives. At the park level, memoranda of agreement establish specific relationships with other institutions, and planning documents of various kinds specify the work to be done and the means by which it is to be implemented.

At times, conflicts arise between what is expected from all NPS units and what may be best for, or reasonable to expect from, a particular site. Each unit came into the system under different circumstances, and each brings its own unique resources, history, and potential into one vast administrative structure that is accountable to Congress and the American people. The NPS management structure and guidelines focus on the overarching needs and issues of the properties of the system. Superintendents must address the unique values and needs of their parks through decisions made with the broad powers and discretion that they are given in the system.

Current NPS policies clearly state that the fundamental purpose of the national park system is to "conserve Park resources and values," and they further explain that this fundamental purpose "also includes providing for the enjoyment of Park resources and values by the people of the United States."[28] The NPS management policies and the various directors' orders provide a framework of compliance with laws, executive orders, and other regulations. In addition, CCNHP management is guided by the mission and purpose of the Park.

Most of the management documents available for CCNHP predate the current NPS management policies,[29] and in general, they do not analyze values or carry clear statements of the Park's values and significance.[30] This does not mean that the values attributed to CCNHP have not been recognized or protected over time. Some values (scientific) were well articulated and protected from the start; other values fall under constitutional provisions that were designed to protect a broad range of civil liberties (e.g., freedom of religion, Native American rights); and others have been promoted mainly through national (as opposed to site-specific) legislation (e.g., environmental). Nevertheless, the absence, until recently, of a formal statement of values means that in order to understand what values have been recognized at CCNHP and how they have evolved, this study has had to take an indirect approach, relying on reviews of federal and site-specific legislation, presidential proclamations, regulations, the guidance provided by NPS, and, at the park level, priorities, allocation of resources, and actions.

Values Associated with CCNHP

When Chaco Canyon National Monument was created in 1907, the presidential proclamation cited "the extraordinary interest [of Pueblo ruins], because of their number and their great size, and because of the innumerable and valuable relics of a prehistoric people which they contain."[31] This proclamation was made possible by the *Antiquities Act* passed in June 1906, which provides for the creation of national monuments that include "historic landmarks, historic and prehistoric structures, and other objects of historic or scientific interest."

VALUES OF CHACO

When President Theodore Roosevelt created Chaco Canyon National Monument to protect the collection of ruins and materials that survived from an ancient civilization, their potential for generating knowledge about the past was being recognized as a principal value. Among the most prominent stakeholders of the monument were anthropologists and other scholars who feared the possibility of loss of information if the archaeological remains were not protected.

At the same time, the ruins inspired awe and a new respect for earlier inhabitants of the land, considered then as a vanished race. An early description of Chaco Canyon illustrates these sentiments when it says, "the most remarkable ruins yet discovered are those standing in New Mexico. They put to shame the primitive log-hut of our forefathers; the frame shanty of the prairie town; the dug-out of the mining regions; the adobe shelter of the Pacific slope. In size and grandeur of conception, they equal any of the present buildings of the United States, if we except the Capitol at Washington, and may without discredit be compared to the Pantheon and the Colosseum of the Old World."[32] From this perspective, the early stakeholder groups of the national monument extended beyond the scientific community to include all those with an interest in the past, who also saw in these ruins the validation of a new nation.

Since then, the archaeological resources have remained the central focus and purpose of the Park, and other values have come to be ascribed to them and their surroundings over time. The present mission statement reflects the ways in which the values as formally recognized have expanded: "Chaco Culture National Historical Park provides for the preservation, public enjoyment, study, and interpretation of the internationally significant cultural features and natural ecosystem processes within the Park, and of the associated cultural features found throughout the surrounding Four Corners Region."[33] The statement declares the obligation of the NPS to preserve these features; to provide opportunities for the public to experience and appreciate them; to study them; and to present and make available information about them.

The current version of the Resource Management Plan[34] identifies the four thousand sites and 1.5 million artifacts and archival documents, which hold ten thousand years of evidence of human cultural development, as having a significance that consists of:

• Evidence of a civilization that flourished between the ninth and the eleventh centuries and had high achievements in architecture, agriculture, social complexity, engineering, astronomy, and economic organization

• Chaco "great houses"—the largest, best preserved, and most complex prehistoric architectural structures in North America. . . .

• A regional system of communities centered in Chaco Canyon and linked by roads and trade networks throughout the San Juan Basin

• 120 years of archaeological and anthropological research in the Park . . . and . . . more than 1.5 million artifacts and archival documents. . . .

• Other links to the past and to the natural landscape through contemporary American Indian descendants of Chaco Canyon, who value it today for its spiritual connection with their past

• A remote location offering opportunities to enjoy solitude, natural quiet, clear air, starlit skies, and panoramic vistas. . . .

• The largest long-term protected area in northwestern New Mexico, which encompasses relatively undisturbed examples of floral and faunal communities within the Colorado Plateau ecosystem, and offers opportunities to conserve the region's biodiversity and monitor its environmental quality.[35]

These statements present a more detailed and expanded set of values than those mentioned in the 1907 proclamation. Values have deepened and expanded as a result of research, new perspectives, and the passage of time. The number of archaeological sites recognized as being of interest and worthy of protection has increased substantially. The Park is known to include a particular kind of feature—the great houses—that has been revealed to be unique to this culture. The thousands of known Chacoan sites constitute an interrelated system of communication and trade. Known, but not officially recognized at the time of designation, was the survival and continuation linking contemporary tribes with the ancient builders and subsequent inhabitants of what is now Park land. The communities of flora and fauna possess a recognized interest, and they have increased in rarity and importance because they have been protected for nearly sixty years within the Park, while surrounding areas have been grazed and subject to other uses over the same period.

This section examines the values detected in the Park's mission and the statements of significance in the latest Resource Management Plan.[36] The emergence and evolution of these values are discussed under the headings of information value (scientific and educational), aesthetic value, spiritual value, social value, historic value, environmental value, associative/symbolic value, and economic value.

Information Value—Scientific and Educational
The earliest descriptions of what is now CCNHP refer almost exclusively to the importance of the Chacoan architectural sites. The emphasis was on the potential of these remains to provide information about their creators and early inhabitants. The passage of the *Antiquities Act* in 1906 was the result of twenty-five years of efforts on the part of a group of dedicated citizens and members of the emerging anthropological profession to save the relics of the past. Fascination with Native American antiquities started when European travelers got their first glimpses of the magnificent ruins of the Southwest. However, it was in the late nineteenth century, shortly after the conclusion of the Civil War and following the heyday of the western expansion, that these antiquities captured the interest of the scientific community on the eastern seaboard. The professionals' curiosity was continuously fueled by reports and descriptions of new sites; by the creation of collections exhibited in museums in Washington, New York, Philadelphia, and Boston; and by their presentation to even wider publics at the World's Columbian Exposition in Chicago in 1893 and the Louisiana Purchase Exposition in Saint Louis in 1904.[37]

As research was conducted and the extent of the Chacoan culture started to be understood, the information value of the archaeological resources of Chaco expanded to encompass features other than the architectural ruins. It was obvious even in the early years of scientific archaeology that these places were evidence of a sophisticated culture, with capacities for labor organization and large-scale food production. With new techniques and sensitivities to certain kinds of data being increasingly available to archaeologists, the field moved toward research into systems in the Southwest. Once the general cultural sequences in architecture and pottery had been mapped out, the evidence from the Chacoan sites began to emerge, and it demonstrated that trade goods from great distances were moving around the region. More recently, the astronomical associations among Chacoan sites and roads, their orientations to the move-

ment of the sun and moon and to other heavenly events, have drawn the attention of researchers.

The information value attributed to the Park resides in the remains of the architecture, the associated material culture, the ways in which materials were deposited in antiquity, the evidence of ancient lifeways, the subtle imprints of activity still visible in the landscape, and the spatial relationships among all these elements. Information value provides the most benefit when professional research methods are used to study the resource. *Scientific value* is the term often given to this information value by stakeholders involved in academic research. This value is particularly fragile, and, paradoxically, its preservation depends to a great extent on nonintervention. Excavation or exposure of physical remains inevitably diminishes future information value, so disturbance of any kind must be carefully considered. As new technical advances become available to archaeologists and technicians, they are able to extract far more information from physical evidence than in times past; thus, the value of pristine sites, authentic materials, soils, and more ephemeral subtleties increases with time. Logically, then, the value of reliable, early narrative and graphic documentation of these sites and their environments increases over time as well, as a record of change in condition or physical status.

The value of archaeological materials has been supported over the years by national legislation. The *Antiquities Act of 1906*—the first general legal protection afforded to the remains of the past in the United States—clearly states that archaeological and historic resources were valued at the federal level for their importance to science, education, and other national interests and that the government took seriously its responsibility to ensure their proper investigation, interpretation, and preservation. Scientific and educational values are reaffirmed by the *Historic Sites Act of 1935*, the *National Historic Preservation Act of 1966*, and the *Archaeological and Historic Preservation Act of 1974*, a more sophisticated law that underscores the importance of the information potential of archaeological and historic resources. The *Archaeological Resources Protection Act of 1979* further strengthens the government's position supporting the value of archaeological resources on federal and Indian lands to scholars, the public, and native peoples. By reaffirming the value of cultural remains, these acts support and validate the efforts of the NPS to protect the resources of CCNHP.

CCNHP is rich in archaeological and cultural materials created and left behind over a period of many centuries. These materials bear witness not only to the Anasazi people but also to other inhabitants over time. The 1985 General Management Plan, in an attempt to facilitate the prioritization of protection initiatives and the determination of appropriate uses of the land, presented a rating system to establish the importance of the different types of vestiges found in the Park.[38] Although Park staff indicate that this ranking has never had any practical application, it still provides a good indication of the relative value assigned by the NPS to the various types of cultural resources. Anasazi remains are given the highest score, as befits those that constitute the primary purpose of the Park. Within the Anasazi category, habitation and kiva sites are ranked higher than roads and trails, and higher than shrines and ceremonial sites. Artifact scatters or hearths and baking pits are at the lower end of the value scale. Remains of earlier and later habitations received lower rankings.

The educational value of CCNHP is realized when the information obtained through the research of experts and the knowledge of traditional users is communicated to a broader audience. Visitors to the site are informed or educated through observation and through the information and interpretation provided on site. Other members of the public may gain access to information through reports and publications, the World Wide Web, objects on display at museums in the United States and abroad, academic courses, television programs, and so on. The educational value ascribed to the Park today goes beyond the archaeological remains to encompass all aspects of the site, such as Native American ties and natural resources and habitats.

Aesthetic Value

The aesthetic value of Chaco Canyon was recognized early on, and it is codified in the mandate of the *NPS Organic Act*[39] to protect "the scenery" unimpaired. Although the original designation of Chaco as a national monument (rather than a national park) placed the emphasis on the protection of the archaeological ruins and their scientific and educational values, when the site became part of the national park system in 1916, it assumed a number of values held by the new agency.

There are a number of intangible elements that contribute to the aesthetic quality of the place, such as clean air, silence, and solitude. Taken together, they are a powerful value of the Park and more than the simple sum of the parts. The evocative qualities of the landscape have

Figure 2.7. Pueblo Bonito ruins. The notion of "scenery" in national parks was associated early on with the aesthetic experience of visitors. This is still the case today at CCNHP, where aesthetic considerations hold a place of prominence in Park management. The qualities that make the place so appealing to the visiting public do not lend themselves easily to objective description, but they are recognized to include the desert landscape, the panoramic vistas, and the architectural remains. Photo: Marta de la Torre

changed little since 1907, but they have become more valuable because of the increasing rarity of such places in a more crowded, more mobile world.

In recent decades, the aesthetic value created by the conditions mentioned above has been bundled with other elements and is referred to by Park managers as "the quality of the visitor experience." This quality is seen to depend on a number of elements that include:

- sweeping, unimpaired views
- an uncrowded park
- appreciation of ancient sites with minimal distractions
- clear air
- no intrusions of man-made noise or light (at night)
- clean water and adequate facilities
- access to a ranger for personal interpretation

This "quality of experience" has become a prominent value articulated by the managers of CCNHP over time, and it is specifically mentioned as such in the Resource Management Plan of 1995[40] and the 2002 draft.[41] Its protection has become one of the top priorities of Park management, second only to the conservation of the ruins. The importance attached to it is supported by the results of a 1994 visitor study that ranked scenery, solitude, natural setting, and calm atmosphere as the most appreciated values of the Park, after its educational value.[42]

Some of the items in the list above have importance beyond the aesthetic experience. For example, sweeping, unimpaired vistas are inextricably tied to ancient Chacoan roads in lands outside the Park and to the traditional Native American views from the top of the mesas that encompass the four sacred mountains of the Navajos. The loss of these vistas (whether from development or pollution) would impinge not only on Chaco's aesthetic value but also on the spiritual value of the site for some stakeholders, as well as on the educational value of the CCNHP to provide visual evidence of the Chaco Phenomenon.

Spiritual Value

Native American interest in the sites of CCNHP is reported to have been present for generations. Chaco Canyon is claimed as a sacred place for members of clans and religious societies of the Hopi of Arizona and the Pueblos of New Mexico. While they descend from a different language group and cultural tradition from the Puebloans, Navajo moved into the area in the late sixteenth or seventeenth century and thus claim attachment as well. Studies commissioned by the Park have recorded that Chaco is a place important to Native American groups for a range of ceremonial activities, including the offering of prayers, the gathering of plants and minerals, and the collection of Anasazi potsherds for use as tempering material by pottery makers. Paintings and carvings in the rock walls of the Chaco Canyon show modern Pueblo religious symbols and Navajo healing ceremonies.[43]

Federal appreciation of contemporary Native American groups' interest in these ancient sites is very recent. While the *American Indian Religious Freedom Act of 1978* did not create additional rights or change existing authorities, it made it a requirement that federal agencies develop means for managers to become informed about Native American religious culture, consult with them about the impact of proposed actions, and avoid unnecessary interference with traditional practices. This act provided a legal framework within which consultation and negotiation could take place among the federal stewards and Native American stakeholders regarding activities being considered by either side that might affect places, animals, plants, and other federal resources of religious significance to Native Americans. It served to signal the formal acknowledgment of an ongoing traditional culture

and the need for respectful consultation to ensure the protection of the interests of all stakeholders involved.

Park staff have recognized the importance of considering Native American perspectives in the management of Chacoan sites for years. However, formal cooperation with tribes came about with the creation in the early 1980s of the Interagency Management Group (IMG) to provide direction for the management of thirty-three Chaco Archeological Protection Sites (see map, fig 2.3). In 1990, the Joint Management Plan created by the IMG was amended to make the NPS "responsible for administration of archaeological protection sites on Navajo lands, and for requesting and distributing funds to the Navajo Tribe for the management of Navajo-related sites."[44] These arrangements were codified in the *Chacoan Outliers Protection Act of 1995*.[45] The NPS was represented in the IMG initially by the NPS Regional Office in Santa Fe, but this responsibility was transferred to CCNHP in the mid 1990s. This change expanded the relationship between the Navajo and the Park administration, which had existed for decades through the Navajo conservation crews of the Park.

In 1990 the position of Native Americans was strengthened by the passing of the *Native American Graves Protection and Repatriation Act (NAGPRA)*,[46] mandating consultation with tribes prior to any disturbance of burial sites, as well as the return of burial objects or human remains to the appropriate culturally affiliated tribe. Cultural affiliation to human and material remains existing or originating from within the boundaries of the Park was formally established in 2000, when CCNHP assigned this status to the Navajo Nation; the Hopi; the Zuni; and the Pueblos of Acoma, Cochiti, Isleta, Laguna, Nambe, Picuris, Pojoaque, San Felipe, San Ildefonso, San Juan, Sandia, Santa Ana, Santa Clara, Santo Domingo, Taos, Tesuque, and Zia.[47] The issues relating to cultural affiliation remain contentious, so work continues on assessing specific aspects of the claims by some groups. These discussions have gained an importance that goes beyond the concerns of *NAGPRA* since they indirectly affect civil, land, and water rights outside the Park.[48]

Shortly before the enactment of *NAGPRA*, the superintendent of CCNHP formed the American Indian Consultation Committee, the first one of its kind in the country. Tribal participation was kept informal, and all New Mexico and Arizona Pueblo governments, the Navajo Nation, and the All Indian Pueblo Council were invited to send representatives to the meetings. Without a clear mandate, the early times of the committee are reported to have been difficult, with the NPS advocating an informal approach of "let's get together and talk about things of mutual importance."[49] From the Native American perspective, the message is reported to have been interpreted to mean that "the purpose of this committee in real Park planning efforts is unclear. The committee seems to have devolved into a kind of nominal body that makes the Parks' efforts look good without really doing anything of substance."[50] Over the years, some tribal groups have participated consistently in the committee's deliberations, the consultations have become regular, and the advice from the tribes is given serious consideration by Park management.

Laws protecting religious freedom also cover the interests of groups and individual practitioners of what have been called New Age spiritual rites and activities. A number of ancient sites around the world have attracted people wishing to experience and interact with these places in new and nontraditional ways that often blend aspects of various religions and cultures. CCNHP, to which they ascribe spiritual value, has become a favorite place for these groups. The emergence of new stakeholders often complicates the management tasks of authorities, since they sometimes bring values that are different from others of longer standing. The recognition, respect, and eventual integration of these new values in the management of the site can give rise to conflicts, as has been the case in CCNHP. These issues are explored in more detail in the last section of this study.

Social Value

In addition to the spiritual connection many Native American groups have to the site, the lands of CCNHP were home to the Navajo for several centuries, during which time they forged cultural and historical ties to the place. During the first forty years of the monument, Navajo "traversed the trails, ran livestock, conducted sings, and occupied scattered hogans along the wash."[51] By the early 1930s, NPS administrators had determined that the grazing of sheep was damaging the ruins, and they started to evict the Navajo from the monument. In 1947, the NPS finished fencing the perimeter of the monument, and in 1949 the last Navajo family living in the site moved away, although the use of small portions of the land still continues today.[52] Scholars as well as Navajo recognize that, in addition to the religious values discussed above, "Navajos retain an emotional tie to many places [within the Park],

Figure 2.8. Navajo cornfield. In the late sixteenth or early seventeenth century, Navajo groups arrived in the area now occupied by the Park, where they established camps and lived from farming and herding. A few decades after the creation of the national monument in the early twentieth century, NPS authorities considered that the protection of the ruins required the cessation of these activities. Although no longer living within the boundaries of the Park, many Navajo retain family and cultural ties to the place. Photo: # 44-297. Chaco Canyon: Willy George's Corn Patch, Mocking Bird Canyon. Archives, Laboratory of Anthropology, Museum of Indian Arts & Culture, Santa Fe, New Mexico.

such as former homes, burial places of relatives, and places of importance in their religious traditions."[53]

While most of the history used in this case study is that constructed by historians and archaeologists, it is important to note that the Navajo and the Pueblo groups see the history of the region in a very different way. Since many aspects and details of these histories—as well as religious and cultural beliefs—are not shared with outsiders, this study can only hint at the numerous values attributed by Native Americans to the lands occupied by the Park.

Historic Value

As one of the earliest national monuments and later as a founding unit of the national parks system, Chaco occupies a place of importance in the history of the NPS. By virtue of its status as a national monument until 1980, the site developed in a path that was different from that followed by national parks. The significance of the monument was clearly understood to reside in its archaeological ruins, and the main management objectives always focused on them. The emphasis on access and visitation of some other NPS units of comparable resources, such as Mesa Verde National Park nearby in Colorado, was absent from Chaco Canyon National Monument. Today these two national parks present a marked contrast in the quality of experience they provide for visitors, much of which is the result of decisions made over the years.

CCNHP also bears witness to a century of evolution of the practices of archaeology and preservation. The research activities carried out on site have reflected the practices of archaeologists and conservators at the time they were conducted. These activities have left their mark in excavated sites and reconstructed structures. This history of the Park as a heritage site is part of the information provided to visitors.

Environmental Value

The environmental qualities of the Park can be seen to have two components. The first is composed of the landforms and water resources in their relatively unimpaired condition, and the plants and wildlife native to this ecological zone, along with relict natural communities of cultivars and other species that were introduced or used in ancient or historic times. As such, this constellation of features and elements creates an environment that exists in only a few places in the world. The second important quality resides in rarity. These kinds of microenvironments are becoming less common over time, and one exists at CCNHP today because it has been protected for decades from the damage caused by grazing, mining, air and water pollution, and the introduction of exotic species.

Early in the twentieth century, environmental degradation was not a significant worry for the NPS at Chaco Canyon. Livestock were grazed in areas of the national monument for years without their impact on the landscape ever becoming a concern. The eventual banishment of herds and flocks from the site was motivated by the damage they were causing to the ruins. Ecological concerns did, however, eventually reach the Park from the outside world. Public awareness of the fragile nature of the ecology of the planet began to flower in the 1960s, as a reaction to the damaging effects of population growth and little regulation of large-scale industry, mining, or agriculture. The U.S. Congress began to respond to the groundswell of public concern for the environment with piecemeal legislation, and Congress eventually passed the comprehensive *National Environmental Policy Act (NEPA)* of 1969. This act, and later its amendments,[54] converted into federal policy the growing recognition of the responsibility of the federal government to protect the quality of the environment.[55] Regulations for all NPS units to comply with this legislation came in the form of management guidelines protecting the environment.[56] As was the case for the information value of the archaeological resources, the natural values of the Park were also enhanced as a result of national legislation.

The regeneration of the ecosystem of CCNHP—as a result of the almost complete elimination of grazing and other damaging uses—has transformed the Park into a reservoir for the Navajo of medical and ceremonial plants and into an important source for scientific research. Some of the conflicts that have arisen as a result of this situation are discussed in the next section.

Associative (Symbolic) Value

Many individuals attribute great value to the experiencing of a site physically and through the senses. This value has been well explored in relation with natural sites, where it has been called *naturalistic value*, defined as the direct experience and exploration of nature that satisfies curiosity, discovery, and recreation.[57] In the cultural world, this value has been called associative or symbolic.[58] The quantity and importance of the archaeological elements found in Chaco Canyon and the surrounding area, as well as the undeveloped character of the site, give the place a strong associative value. In the modern world, this value can be experienced virtually, but without doubt, it is strongest when visitors are able to experience the reality of the tangible remains of the past. This value comes out very strongly in the 1994 visitors study, which found that "visitors at Chaco desire a physical environment where independence and access to ruins are achievable, Park facilities are few and primitive, and an interpretative approach is self guided. This is necessary for them to experience the physical and interpretative aspect of the history depicted at Chaco on a more personal, introspective level."[59]

This value closely depends on the authenticity of the ruins and the vistas and terrains that have remained relatively unchanged over centuries. It is also a key element of the "quality of the experience" mentioned above.

Although the existence of this value is not articulated in any CCNHP document, the mention made often of the Park as a "special place," as well as the preoccupation with the conservation of the authentic remains and with maintaining a certain "atmosphere" in the Park, can be interpreted as a tacit recognition of a strong associative value.

Economic Value

One of the first values associated with the Chacoan ruins was the artifacts found in them. While a big part of the interest was motivated by scientific curiosity, there was an economic value implicit in the gathering of artifacts to be sold to museums and collectors. This economic value is still upheld by those involved in the trade of Native American antiquities, who often derive significant financial benefits from their endeavors. This economic value is seen to be negative and detrimental in many heritage quarters, since the pursuit of its benefits results in the looting of sites.

In addition to the monetary value of artifacts, one of the strongest sources of economic value of sites depends on the use of the land. In general, this aspect of economic value is the area where the interests of stakeholders create the most serious—and most public—conflicts. At CCNHP, as in many other heritage sites, the most significant economic value lies in alternative or additional uses that can be made of the Park and the surrounding land. The economic benefits that become unrealizable from lands protected as national parks or wildlife sanctuaries have always been a concern of farmers and ranchers of the western U.S. These groups presented the strongest opposition to the preservation movement, since "preserving the unique but obscure heritage of the region required the withdrawal of lands that contained tangible ruins. More often than not, these lands also included resources that had commercial value."[60]

The San Juan Basin is known to contain significant underground resources of coal, uranium, natural gas, and oil, and there are active coal and uranium mines in the lands neighboring the Park. The subsurface rights in certain areas of the Park are not held by the NPS, and, theoretically, mineral, oil, and gas exploration and exploitation could take place there. In the 1970s and 1980s, the threats posed by the exploitation of these resources were so immediate that they prompted legislation expanding the surface of the Park and creating additional protected zones that contain archaeological remains. The 1985 General Management Plan for CCNHP has a strong focus on the challenges that would emerge if industrial concerns became interested in exploiting the resources within the Park and if there were a rapid development of the surrounding areas.[61] Some of these issues have receded into the background, since the price of these resources in recent times has made their exploitation uneconomic. This has brought about a decrease in this type of activity, but circumstances could well change in the future.

Other alternative uses of the land that would bring economic benefits to some stakeholder groups include cattle and sheep grazing. The Navajo used Park lands for their herds and flocks for centuries, and it is only in recent years that this practice has started to be phased out. Today, approximately 121 hectares (300 acres) in the western sector of the Park are privately owned allocations on which sheep and cattle are still grazed.

The Park also has an economic value for the surrounding communities. At present, some local families derive their livelihood from employment in the Park, mainly as part of the conservation crews. The Park also has a potential economic value for the surrounding communities if they were to develop services for visitors, such as accommodations and food. While this has not yet happened, a project to build a hotel overlooking the Park—with serious potential of having an impact on many of the values of the site—was canceled, not because of concerns about the Park, but because of a shift in the priorities of the Navajo Nation.

World Heritage Value

When CCNHP was nominated to the World Heritage List in 1984, the NPS had to consider which of the values attributed to the Park had an outstanding universal, rather than a national or local, dimension. In the context of the World Heritage Convention, *outstanding universal value* is "taken to mean cultural and/or natural significance which is so exceptional as to transcend national boundaries and to be of common importance for present and future generations of all humanity."[62] The site was proposed as meeting a criterion that recognizes sites that bear a unique testimony to a civilization that has disappeared. The 1984 documents described the site as preserving "the physical remains of the Chacoans; a unique population of a culture that has been extinct for hundreds of years."[63] The nomination underwent an important modification that led to the inclusion of several other neighboring Chacoan sites as part of the World Heritage Site. This expansion, suggested by the World Heritage Committee, recognized that the Chacoan civilization and its remains are not confined to the area covered by CCNHP.[64]

In considering the values of individual sites, the criteria of the World Heritage Convention have also evolved over time. In 1992 the World Heritage Operational Guidelines were modified to allow the inscription of Cultural Landscapes. The United States could request that the inscription of CCNHP in the World Heritage List be reexamined under the new category of relict and associative cultural landscapes.[65] This would recognize the universal value of the more-intangible elements of the site, such as viewsheds and spatial relationships.

The management documents of CCNHP do not address specifically the values of the site as specified in the World Heritage nomination materials, although they mention its international significance. This does not imply that the universal values are not being protected; rather, it seems to mean that the values associated with Chaco, according to the criterion under which it was inscribed in 1987, are encompassed within the values already recognized and protected.

STAKEHOLDERS

CCNHP authorities identify "professional archaeologists and cultural anthropologists; Native American tribes; state, county, city and tribal governments; and 'New Age' religious followers" as the Park's principal constituencies.[66] Defining stakeholders as any group with legitimate interest in the Park, and based on the previous analysis of the values ascribed to it, the list could be expanded to include other professionals and researchers, such as environmentalists, zoologists, and botanists; Congress and some government agencies, such as the Bureau of Land Management, the Bureau of Indian Affairs, and the U.S. Forest Service; other NPS units with Puebloan and Chacoan sites; neighbors, local landowners, and their business communities; tourism agencies; visitors, campers, and other recreational travelers; the general U.S. public; and the international community, as represented by the World Heritage Committee and UNESCO.

CCNHP's stakeholders certainly never gather at the same table, nor do they speak with equal force. Some of the stakeholders do not visit, or have any contact with, the Park. Some are only interested in the economic value of the land for alternative uses and hold this value higher than any of the others. In some cases, the values of stakeholders are irreconcilable.

Some conflicts between stakeholders' values at CCNHP have been resolved (or at least simplified) outside the arena of the Park by the introduction of new legislation or regulations, shifts in authority, or changes in priorities. In some instances, the values are simply ignored, so as not to raise interest (and therefore potential conflict) from any quarter. Conflicts over subsurface mineral rights, for example, can pit legal ownership and development rights against the need to safeguard air and water quality and against the requirement to protect ruins from damage. However, the conflict may be dormant until another energy crisis emerges or until some other issue changes the current situation.

Consultations with Native American groups, particularly those culturally affiliated with the Park, are supported, and to some extent mandated, by *NAGPRA*. CCNHP created its American Indian Consultation Committee in anticipation of *NAGPRA*, and it continues to consult it extensively on matters related to the use and conservation of the site.

Although the only official consultative group associated with the Park is that of Native Americans, the superintendent and staff of CCNHP maintain a complex network of stakeholder relationships. A great deal of effort is given to cultivating contacts with local stakeholders and decision makers in neighboring towns.

The Park superintendent and staff also adhere to a good-neighbor policy toward other Chacoan sites in the region. This policy leads to close collaboration with other NPS units, tribal cultural resource officers, and state park authorities.

EVOLUTION OF VALUES

From a comparison of the values of the Park when it was first established with those attributed to it now, it is clear that time has brought about evolution and expansion through new knowledge and through enhanced appreciation of cultural traditions and the benefits of protecting a fragile landscape. As this evolution has happened, the original information and associative values have become stronger. Some of the other values, such as the spiritual and social ones held by Native American groups, were always present, but they had to wait until quite recently for formal recognition from federal authorities. The spiritual value of the site for some New Age adherents has emerged more recently on this ancient site, and it is rather more difficult to integrate into a management strategy, given the conflict between their practices and those of the longer-term Native American stakeholders. Others, such as the natural or ecological values, have emerged as society as a whole recognized the importance of these values, in national parks and elsewhere. In all, then, the enrichment and deepening of the values of the site have also increased the site's significance.

Consideration of Values in Management Policies and Strategies

This section examines how the values ascribed to the Park or established through national laws and other federal provisions having the force of law figure in current management policies, strategies, and objectives at CCNHP. Answers to the question of how values are taken into consideration in the management policies, strategies, and objectives have been gleaned from existing documentation, conversations with NPS and Park staff, and observations on-site.

CURRENT GUIDANCE

The NPS has an impressive body of policies, regulations, and guidelines that attempt to standardize, if not the decisions in the parks, certainly the criteria and the processes used to reach them. The purpose of this guidance is to ensure fulfillment of the agency's mandate to protect and manage the great variety of nationally significant areas under its care without "derogation of the values and purposes for which these various areas have been established"[67] and to comply with federal laws and regulations relevant to park operations. This weighty policy framework must still allow field personnel the flexibility needed to make decisions appropriate to the conditions of the individual parks.

The new NPS Management Policies 2001 requires four planning processes at park level: general management planning, strategic planning, implementation planning, and annual performance planning.[68] Within this framework, planning proceeds from broad management concerns to specific implementation programs. Each part of the process is set to result in written plans. However, these new policies will be implemented gradually, and not all parks are in compliance with the planning requirements yet. In the case of CCNHP, the main management documents currently in force are the General Management Plan of 1985, the Strategic Plan for 2001–05, the Resource Management Plan of 1995, and the Chaco Archeological Protection Site System Joint Management Plan of 1983 (with its 1990 amendment).[69]

The seventeen-year-old General Management Plan is not regarded as obsolete by staff, but it is used principally as a list of actions from which the superintendent can select some for implementation.[70] This plan cannot be characterized as a strategic document. Rather, it focuses on certain matters that were considered problematic at the time and identifies specific actions to be undertaken. Some of the issues that were critical in 1985—such as the exploitation of natural resources around the Park and a possible exponential growth in population in the area and in the number of Park visitors—have failed to materialize or have faded into the background. For these reasons, the usefulness of the 1985 General Management Plan for the purposes of this study is limited, since it no longer reflects the main preoccupations of Park staff. In terms of day-to-day operations and the actions that most directly affect and reflect values, the most relevant documents are the Resource Management Plan of 1995 and the more recent one in draft form.[71]

The research undertaken for this study identified three management priorities at CCNHP:

- protection of the archaeological resources
- provision of a high-quality experience for visitors
- compliance with legal, statutory, and operational requirements[72]

The restoration of the natural ecosystems is also a concern, but to a lesser degree than the other three, as indicated in the 2002 draft of the Resource Management Plan, which states, "while both cultural and natural preservation efforts are compatible, conflicts may arise. In these instances, given the legislative purpose of the Park, management of cultural resources will be favored over management of natural resources."[73]

The mission statement of CCNHP also speaks of four main areas of activity—preservation, public enjoyment, research, and interpretation. These four areas have been used in this study to organize the discussion in this and the next sections. It should be noted that, in most instances, all policies have an impact on many, if not all, values of a place. Some impacts are intentional and anticipated; others are not. A policy can also have a positive effect on a given aspect of a value, while at the same time negatively affecting some of its other dimensions. One of the benefits of values-based management is that it increases the awareness of these impacts through the monitoring of values. The discussions that follow attempt to identify both positive and negative results of policies, in order to illustrate the reality and complexity of management decisions; these discussions should not be construed as a criticism of CCNHP management.

PRESERVATION POLICIES

Conservation of Cultural Resources
In accordance with the founding purpose of the Park and with subsequent legislation, the conservation of cultural resources is the first priority of CCNHP. The main policy in this area seeks to avoid impairment of the archaeological resources by disturbing them as little as possible. Three strategies are being employed: minimizing physical intervention and favoring noninvasive actions; avoiding exposure to the elements; and limiting access.

Although reconstruction of architectural ruins was carried out during the early years of the Park, this approach was abandoned decades ago. Most of the current conservation work on-site consists of stabilization of the ruins, backfilling, drainage control, and erosion management. Other passive conservation measures are

Figure 2.9. Reburial teams working in the field. Over the last decade, the Park's cultural resource management team has implemented a program of reburial and backfilling of excavated structures. While these methods have proved to be effective in terms of conservation, they hide from view the totality or parts of the archaeological resources. The criteria used to select the sites for backfilling look at the interpretation strategies of the Park, the materials under consideration, the fragility of the structures, and the degree of maintenance that the sites would require if left exposed. Reburied sites are regularly monitored. Photo: Guillermo Aldana

also employed and consist of barriers that prevent access, of documentation, and of monitoring. This minimal intervention approach, together with the policy of allowing archaeological excavations only in extreme cases, protects both the physical remains and the information they contain.

There are approximately 1,250 sites in the Park classified as Active Preservation Sites. These include several hundred of the largest and most exposed structures, all excavated sites, sites where research and analysis are going on, sites that require routine or cyclical treatment, and sites actively threatened by erosion. The condition of 150 of these sites is assessed on a regular basis, and about forty sites that are considered very sensitive are examined every year. All other sites are considered Passive Preservation Sites, and characteristically they are low-maintenance sites that are partially exposed or buried, relatively stable, unexcavated or pristine, and not actively interpreted.[74]

Restricting public access to the ruins is a preservation strategy that has been used in CCNHP for decades. This strategy is also manifested in attempts made to limit the number of visitors coming to the Park (discussed below under "Public Enjoyment Policies") and the resources that are accessible to those who do arrive. With over four thousand known archaeological sites in the Park, most of those that have been excavated are now reburied. Approximately fifty sites are being interpreted

and are open to visitors. The rest of the exposed ruins are in what is classified as backcountry, an area that can be visited with permission from Park management.

Limiting excavations to those that are absolutely essential is also a part of the preservation strategy at Chaco, as it is in most other national parks. As part of the policy of minimizing interventions to the site, CCNHP has pointed scholarly research requests to the materials that are already excavated. This policy is supported by work designed to enhance access to the 1.5 million objects yielded over the years from excavations at Chaco and surrounding sites. A few objects are exhibited at the Visitor Center, but most of the collections are held at the University of New Mexico in Albuquerque. NPS policies support this strategy, and additional funds have been allocated for the construction of improved storage and study facilities at the university, as well as to improve databases, which will facilitate access by scholars.

Chacoan Resources outside the Park

The involvement of CCNHP in the protection of resources outside its boundaries has come about as a result of legislation, rather than Park policy. In 1980, legislation[75] established the Chaco Culture Archeological Protection Site program to manage and protect thirty-three Chacoan sites located on tribal or federal lands, outside the jurisdiction of the NPS. There are, however, thousands of other sites, many of them in privately held lands that remain without any protection, and over which NPS has no influence or jurisdiction.

Amendments to the Chaco Culture Archeological Protection Site System Joint Management Plan[76] have made CCNHP responsible for the administration of sites located in Navajo lands, and for requesting and distributing funds to the Navajo Nation for the management of these sites. These arrangements have brought about a close working relationship between the Park staff and Navajo cultural specialists. As with the conservation of resources inside the Park, the objectives of the management of these external resources are to maintain their integrity as remains from the past and to preserve the informational value they embody. Conservation policies and strategies of minimal disturbance have been adopted for sites located in Navajo lands. In contrast to Park resources, these sites are seldom open to visitors.

Conservation of Natural Resources

Natural resources have recently started to receive more attention from Park staff as a result of legislation, directives from NPS administration and executive orders, and the availability of funds for their study and protection. The stated long-term objective is to allow natural processes to take over, with full knowledge that this will not restore the land to Chaco-era conditions. As mentioned before, the protection of these resources can never be the top priority of the Park, and it is recognized that if conflicts were to arise between their preservation and that of cultural resources, the latter would be favored.[77]

At this time, much of the activity in natural resource management is directed at complying with legal or NPS policy requirements. It consists of species inventories and mapping, baseline data collection, and various kinds of impact studies. Erosion control work could be considered as environmental protection efforts; nevertheless, the principal purpose of such work is the preservation of the ruins. Other actions are directed at the protection of water and air quality, as mandated by legislation and NPS directives.

At first glance, the impact of pollution on the resources of the Park does not appear to be as serious as other threats. However, any deterioration of air quality would affect the viewsheds of the Park and, if extreme, could contribute to the physical degradation of archaeological materials. By limiting the number of vehicles and visitors, Park managers are ensuring a low level of ambient contamination in the immediate environment. For areas outside NPS jurisdiction, there is protective legislation that may be employed whenever problems threaten to encroach on the integrity of the site. The Park has several monitoring efforts under way to collect data on air quality, water quality, and other indicators, so that any changes will be immediately evident and managers may take appropriate action. These kinds of activities, including fire management planning, are largely preventive conservation on a large scale and are aimed toward preparation for dealing with problems before they affect the archaeological resources or the quality of the visitor experience, as discussed below.

PUBLIC ENJOYMENT POLICIES

Policies in the area of public enjoyment fall into two main categories: those directed at the conditions found by visitors in the Park and those related to access to the site. Some of the elements that guarantee the quality of the visitors' experience are covered by legislation and by broad NPS directives, such as those concerned with air quality, extraneous sounds, and so on. Others, such as the choice of having interpretation delivered by Park rangers rather than by descriptive panels, or limitations on the

development of the Park, are the result of CCNHP policy decisions.

The quality of the visitor experience sought by CCNHP staff can only be achieved if the number of visitors is kept relatively low, and this aim has become a driving preoccupation over the years. Perhaps the most obvious manifestations of this concern are the efforts made to isolate the site by limiting access from several existing county roads and by keeping the main road to the Park unpaved. This unpaved entrance road could be said to have become a symbol of protection in Park lore. Although this rough 25.5-kilometer (16-mile) ride can be a partial deterrent, particularly in winter and during the rainy season, other factors can be said to be as important in keeping visitor numbers down, such as the distance from overnight accommodations and the lack of facilities on-site.[78]

The low level of development on-site has been a long-standing policy of CCNHP. In the opinion of some NPS staff, this policy came about, and has been maintained, as a result of the national monument status that the site had for many decades. The "undeveloped" quality of the Park is seen as a great asset, by both Park staff and visitors.[79] The emphasis on visitor access found in the national parks seems to have been absent from the national monuments, where the primary concern has been the protection of the cultural, historic, or scientific resources of the units.

In most cultural sites, values are affected and often brought into conflict over issues of conservation, access, and the quality of the visitor experience. CCNHP is no exception, as is illustrated by decisions regarding the Park's campground. The 1985 General Management Plan calls for the creation of a new and larger campground closer to the entrance of the Park, in the Gallo Wash.[80] The justifications for moving the campground from the old location were conservation (campgrounds were too close to unique cliff dwellings) and the safety and enjoyment of visitors (camping facilities were located within the one-hundred-year floodplain and too close to the access road). Seventeen years later, the campground remains in its original place. Park management explains that more-detailed studies invalidated some of the 1985 rationale, since the move to Gallo Wash implied development of a pristine area, rich in archaeological remains, while the cliff dwellings close to the old campsite are seen to have already been subjected to many decades of contact with visitors. The campsite move would also have required a considerable investment and ground disturbance to bring water and electricity to the new site. In this particular case, the information and scientific values of the pristine Gallo Wash area, as well as practical considerations, prevailed over visitor convenience and comfort.

The majority of Park visitors are tourists who come mainly for educational or recreational reasons.[81] There are other groups whose interest is of a different nature, and they would like to use the site in different ways. Some Native American groups fall into this category. However, the overarching goal of protection of the cultural and natural resources has precluded certain activities that Native Americans consider to be their right and obligation, such as the gathering of plants and the performance of certain rituals.

The social and spiritual values of CCNHP to Native Americans, New Agers, and other interest groups are vested to a considerable extent in the protected setting of the Park. The General Management Plan states, "a key element is the concept of maintaining the existing scene—the canyon ambience—so that the major ruins can be experienced and interpreted in a setting much like the environment that supported the daily existence of the Chacoan inhabitants."[82] Leaving aside discussion as to whether the original environment of the Chacoan age can, in fact, be recaptured, in effect, the management strategies protect the possibility of spiritual experience at the site by keeping distractions to a minimum. While forbidden by law to favor the practice of one religion over another, the stance of the Park protects the interests of those with a spiritual interest in the Park by excluding activities that could compromise the integrity of the setting. Paradoxically, regulations designed to protect the ruins limit access to certain places and can prevent stakeholders from using the Park for their ceremonies or rituals.

RESEARCH POLICIES

In line with its mandate to "facilitate research activities on the unique archaeological resources," CCNHP has a research policy based on collaboration with other NPS units, educational institutions, independent scholars, and tribal and state governments. The research priorities of the Park are developed in accordance with the Chaco Research Planning Strategy. The projects currently identified are intended to fill information gaps needed for interpretation, management, and preservation, or to comply with cultural resources and environmental laws and NPS policies.[83]

The Park's long-standing collaborative research strategy has partnered CCNHP with other institutions

and academic groups, such as the School of American Research in Santa Fe and the Smithsonian Institution. Of particular importance was the Chaco Center Project (1969–81), a joint endeavor of the NPS and the University of New Mexico, and one of the largest archaeological research projects ever undertaken in the U.S. The Chaco Center Project consisted mainly of fieldwork and the publication of results of this and other research activities. Starting in 1971, the project located and appraised the archaeological remains in the Park and adjacent lands. Over one thousand sites were identified, and twenty-five sites were excavated as part of the work. The project's pioneering use of remote sensing aided in identifying the prehistoric road system that radiated outward from Chaco Canyon to connect numerous outlying Chacoan communities in the region.[84] The Chaco Center Project had a strong influence during the 1980s on the interpretation presented at the Park. More recently, a new effort of the University of Colorado–Boulder and the NPS aims to synthesize the findings of the earlier project and make them more available.

At the conclusion of the Chaco Center Project in 1981, CCNHP adopted a policy of limited archaeological excavations. All excavation proposals are reviewed by Park staff and presented to the American Indian Consultation Committee; almost without exception, requests are denied. Park personnel support this position because it avoids exposing new structures and sites that require active conservation. Native Americans tend to oppose excavation because of concerns about disturbing human remains and sacred sites. This policy gives priority to the values of Native Americans and to the protection of future potential information value over the value of information in the present.

INTERPRETATION AND
DISSEMINATION POLICIES

Interpretation at CCNHP is done according to the main lines of a program established by the 1991 Statement for Interpretation and Interim Interpretive Prospectus.[85] This document identifies seven primary concerns regarding interpretation: "promoting safety, lessening impact to resources due to increasing visitation by explaining to the public internal and external threats to the resources, telling a complete Park story, fostering sensitivity toward American Indian views of Chaco and archaeology, developing better community relations through outreach services, responding to interpretive needs of special populations, and interpreting Chaco Culture as a designated World Heritage Site."[86]

In addition, current interpretation priorities[87] emphasize consultation with Native American stakeholders and the incorporation of their views and beliefs in the stories told. The interpretation available at the site includes information about the conservation of the archaeological resources. The topics and perspectives presented in the interpretation of the site acknowledge the multiplicity of values attached to the Park.

At the site, interpretation and information are available at the Visitor Center (through a small exhibition, interpretive videos, literature for sale, or human contact at the information desk) or from regularly offered tours with Park rangers. Interpretive panels and other information in situ are limited to signs stating the sacredness of the place and to small booklets sold at some of the major sites. Some of the important sites of the Park that are not open to visitors, like Fajada Butte, are made accessible by other means—publications and audiovisual presentations in the Visitor Center.

The policy of relying on human interpreters onsite is considered by Park management to be well suited to the telling of the very complex Chaco story. The contact of visitors with Park rangers and the absence of signs or interpretative panels in the ruins are believed to contribute to the quality of the experience, in particular by enhancing the associative value of the place. In addition, the presence of rangers around the site is believed to discourage vandalism and inappropriate visitor behavior. However, the majority of Chaco visitors interviewed for the 1994 visitor survey strongly preferred the freedom to visit the site independently and to rely on brochures and site panels for interpretation.[88]

Despite the emphasis on quality of experience, certain circumstances—some of them outside the Park's control and others created by policy—have an impact on interpretation. In general, the biggest limiting factors are the very short time that visitors are usually able to spend in the Park and the lack of access to some critical areas of the Park. With the nearest overnight accommodations (except for the Park's campground) located an hour and a half away, travel time to and from the Park consumes at least three hours of most visitors' day—and often as much as five. Almost half the visitors spend between two and six hours visiting the Park.[89] The exhibition and the audiovisual presentations at the Visitor Center provide a good introduction to the site, but they can occupy another hour or more, shortening further the time the visitor has for direct contact with Park resources.

The area encompassed by the Park is extensive, but the majority of open archaeological sites are located around the loop road. Access to the top of the north mesa and to the views afforded by that vantage point can give visitors a clearer understanding of the Chaco Phenomenon, including the system of roads. The Chaco Center Project included extensive research and work at Pueblo Alto, a great house on top of the north mesa. This site was selected, among other reasons, because many of the roads linking Chaco Canyon with sites to the north converged there, and "it was felt that the excavated and restored site could play an important part in the interpretative story presented to visitors by the National Park Service."[90] Today only a small percentage of visitors have that experience, since the mesa tops can only be reached through a difficult climb up the rock face, challenging even for able-bodied visitors.

Like all other parks in the NPS system, CCNHP uses the Internet to provide information to the public. The Park's Web site is less developed than that of other parks in the system, but it contains practical as well as historical information. Currently, interpretative priorities include expanding educational outreach opportunities and developing a Chaco-based curriculum. Although information about the Park appears in every NPS map of the system and is listed in the National Park Foundation's *Passport to the Parks*, recent Park management has followed a strategy of discouraging publicity locally and nationally. This has been viewed as an important factor in controlling the number of visitors, and thus the conservation of the resources and the quality of the visit. The impact of these policies and strategies is discussed in the next section, on the quality of the visitors' experience.

The interpretation policies of the Park emphasize the educational value of the site. Interpretation is seen as an opportunity to communicate the story of Chaco to the public (actual visitors to the site, potential visitors and the interested public through written and other media, and virtual visitors on the World Wide Web). The topics for interpretation, however, extend beyond the factual information or communication about the Chaco stories. At CCNHP, interpretation opportunities are seized to communicate most of the values of the Park: scientific, educational, aesthetic, historic, natural, and spiritual.

Impact of Management Policies on the Site's Values and Their Preservation

This final section of the case looks at the impact on the site of the policies identified earlier. It also examines three specific issues—the closing of Fajada Butte, access to Casa Rinconada, and the quality of visitors' experience—as illustrations of management decisions.

The NPS provides guidance to field personnel through its strategic plans, management policies, and director's orders. Nevertheless, these directives leave considerable discretion to the superintendents, so that their actions and responses can be appropriate to their parks' specific conditions. In addition to these regulations, superintendents must take into consideration the resources—both human and financial—available to them, and they must set priorities consistent with the spirit of the mission and mandate of the park.

Management decisions have impact on areas or issues that are beyond those of immediate consideration. Although values-based management seeks to protect, to the largest extent possible, all the values of a site, the total protection of all values—or of all aspects of a given value—is seldom possible. These are inevitable consequences of decision making, and they are the reason why it is extremely important to understand how values are affected by specific decisions.

This section is organized according to the type of policy being discussed. However, the interrelation among values and the multiple effects of decisions will be clearly evident, as the same issues are sometimes raised in relation to several policies. The discussions raise positive and negative effects of decisions in order to illustrate the realities and complexity of management.

IMPACT OF PRESERVATION AND RESEARCH POLICIES

As has been established, the legislative purpose of CCNHP gives undisputed priority to the preservation of the cultural features of the Park—more specifically, to the Anasazi archaeological remains. But as also seen earlier, the values attributed to these resources are varied and evolving. Since most of the preservation policies of CCNHP are meant to protect—physically—the archaeological materials and structures, their impact on other values can vary.

The conservation policy of minimal intervention on the fabric—mainly reburial and stabilization—meets with the approval of most Native American groups. From their perspective, this conservation approach limits the

[continued on page 87]

Fajada Butte

Fajada Butte is a prominent geological formation on the eastern end of the Park. Near its top, on the eastern cliff, there are three large, shaped stone slabs positioned vertically against two spiral petroglyphs. This "Sun Dagger" engraving was unknown to the NPS until its discovery by Anna Sofaer and her colleagues in 1977.[1] Sofaer interpreted her timed observations of the position of the sun and moon relative to the assemblage to indicate that it marked solstices and equinoxes and other astronomical events; some challenged her claims.[2] In the late 1980s, Sofaer and her colleagues reevaluated and reaffirmed their earlier interpretation of the Sun Dagger as a calendrical marker and also noted the existence of a total of thirteen astronomical glyphs at three different locations on the butte.[3]

Despite the controversy over the significance of the Fajada Butte petroglyphs and other assemblages to Chaco's prehistoric inhabitants, Sofaer's findings immediately drew the interest of contemporary Native Americans as well as non–Native Americans. This interest in turn increased visitation to the butte. When Park managers became concerned about the site's stability, the superintendent prohibited access to the butte in 1982 except for visits authorized by permit.

The 1985 CCNHP General Management Plan specifies that "use of Fajada Butte will be by permit only and will be restricted to Native Americans using the site for religious purposes (requests for access to be supported by tribal leaders, including religious leaders); researchers with antiquities permits or with research proposals approved by the superintendent, after consultation with the Division of Anthropology, Southwest Cultural Resources Center, and cleared only when the proposed research is nondestructive; and, National Park Service personnel on well-justified official business approved by the superintendent."[4] The document also recognizes potential safety hazards to visitors in its reasons for limiting visitor access.

In 1989 Park staff discovered that even these limited activities were causing damage. On the summer solstice of that year, Park staff became aware that two of the three vertical slabs had shifted. This movement prevented the petroglyph spirals from accurately marking astronomical events. An NPS study to evaluate the causes and extent of the damage concluded that the site is extremely fragile and that even

limited access accelerates normal erosion processes. The study also recommended stabilization of the site and reevaluation of the site's use policy. In 1990 access to the site was closed to everyone, including researchers and traditional users, pending completion of a management plan for the area and stabilization of the Sun Dagger solstice marker.[5] Since then, the only access allowed has been by NPS employees to monitor conditions. A 1994 ethnographic study[6] questioned whether the site should be closed to all Native Americans or whether it should be open to the ceremonial activities of

Sun Dagger. As a geological formation, Fajada Butte has always been a striking feature of Chaco Canyon. It was not until 1977, however, that the existence of a Native American marker on top of the butte became known. Today several Native American groups claim the Sun Dagger, as well as other areas on and around the butte, as culturally significant. A slight shift in the position of the stones of the Sun Dagger has skewed its alignment with astronomical events. Currently, access to the butte is limited to monitoring visits by NPS personnel. Photo: Courtesy National Park Service, Chaco Culture NHP Collection Archives.

some approved members of tribes determined to be traditionally associated with the site. Important questions in allowing privileged use of Fajada Butte by Native Americans would be whether these groups traditionally used the butte for ceremonial and other purposes, or whether use began after the 1977 "discovery" of the Sun Dagger. Those questions are difficult to answer, since Native Americans have tended to keep information about their sacred places and ceremonies secret.[7]

Many of the representatives interviewed for the 1994 study offered interpretations, which some-times varied, of Anasazi use of prehistoric cultural features, as well as information about the vegetation and minerals on and around the butte, based upon knowledge of their own cultural systems. However, an ethnohistorical literature review found no evidence of historical use of any Chaco Canyon resource by Rio Grande Pueblos prior to the mid-1980s, although some of these tribes have visited the Park for ceremonial purposes since then. Nor have contemporary Zuni ceremonial or other uses at Fajada Butte been identified. The research also indicated that the Navajo have important historical and traditional associations with Fajada Butte (including having a story in their oral traditions explaining the origin of the butte), and revealed a 1974 account of the butte as a place where Navajo gathered plants. In general, though, this one instance from the Navajo is the only precise

example of historic ceremonial use of the butte prior to 1977.[8]

Other questions raised by the 1994 study are whether all of Fajada Butte should be off limits to visitors, or whether some parts should be accessible to some groups. Officially, the Park has only closed access to the upper part of the butte, as indicated by the *Federal Register* notice of closure, which specifies that the butte will be closed "from the top of the talus slope, i.e., contour interval 6400,"[9] and the crevice on the south face, providing access to the top has been blocked with a metal grate. However, visitors are turned away well before they reach this point; signs on the access path and at the base of the butte indicate that the site is off limits. This situation gave rise to the request that as part of the 1994 study, Native Americans be asked to define the boundaries of Fajada Butte to see how that boundary compares with the Park administration's perception of what is or should be closed.[10]

NPS's concern started with damage to the Sun Dagger. There are other cultural features that are currently within the inaccessible areas. The 1994 study, in part through interviews with Native American residents of the area, identified the following cultural components important to Native Americans today, listed in the order they appear when the butte is ascended:[11]

- plants used by Native Americans
- historical family living quarters, both north and south of Fajada Butte
- petroglyph panel away from the base of Fajada Butte
- historic hogan on flank of Fajada Butte
- minerals
- calendars and symbols near roofs of astronomers' rooms
- rooms where astronomers are believed to have lived
- Sun Dagger
- eagle's nest
- contemporary ceremonial area
- prayer shrine

It should be noted that the value of all of these features to Native Americans contrasts sharply with the perceptions held by non–Native Americans concerning Fajada Butte, which essentially define its significance in terms of the Sun Dagger.[12]

In the Park's examination of how to proceed in managing Fajada Butte, it requested input from Native Americans to gain their views on the subject. Stoffle and colleagues report that "most Indian representatives would define all of Fajada Butte off limits to all non-Indian activity."[13] They recommended boundaries to protect the areas of value to them, which coincide with the measures taken by Park management. The irony is that the area defined by Native Americans has become off limits to them too.

This case raises the difficult question of dealing with social values attributed to heritage sites by traditional culture groups. Should—or, more to the point, could—NPS grant special access to Native Americans to Fajada Butte while excluding other groups, such as New Age adherents? The issues raised in relation to the decisions on Casa Rinconada indicated that NPS considers that any special-access arrangements that exclude other groups would be not only against policy but also unconstitutional. If this is a position that is accepted without further analysis, it puts into question whether the NPS can respect and protect the values of all stakeholders of a site.

Notes

1. For an in-depth discussion of the significance of Fajada Butte, see Stoffle et al. 1994.
2. Sofaer et al. 1982a.
3. Ibid.
4. NPS 1985, 54.
5. NPS 1990b.
6. Stoffle et al. 1994.
7. It is common for only certain members of clans or tribes to possess knowledge concerning sacred sites and ceremonies. Secrecy with respect to non–Native Americans has also arisen because of a history of non–Native Americans intentionally desecrating sacred sites.
8. Wozniak, Brugge, and Lange 1993, 18–21; Stoffle et al. 1994, 26–32.
9. NPS 1999.
10. Stoffle et al. 1994, 37.
11. Ibid., 38–39.
12. Ibid., 38.
13. Ibid., 48.

efforts to preserve the ancestral heritage that some believe should be left to follow a natural course of decay. Some archaeologists also support the use of these conservation methods, which they see as protecting the information value of the archaeological record. The current policy that allows excavation only on very rare occasions also reflects the approach of minimal disturbance of the archaeological remains. Native American groups support limiting excavations, since this stance concords with cultural beliefs that these sites should remain undisturbed. The Society for American Archaeology also takes the position that "modern archaeology, in fact, frequently requires no excavation but depends upon the study of existing collections and information reported in scientific publications. Instead of digging, archaeologists bring new technologies and methods to bear upon materials excavated earlier."[91] Individual archaeologists, however, are more reluctant to accept this policy, as evidenced by the ongoing requests for permissions to excavate.

The excavation policy protects the potential for information valued by academics and the integrity valued by Native Americans. It reserves the resources for future investigation, limiting the information value to that which can be realized from nondestructive research activities. The emphasis on the survival of the physical remains addresses the associative value of the Park by protecting the integrity and authenticity of the remains.

The conservation policies of CCNHP also protect many other values attributed to the site. The protection that has been given to plant and animal communities in the Park has created a sanctuary with unusual or rare conditions of interest to the scholarly community and to Native American groups. The statutory and operational constraints on unnecessary disturbance of the environment—such as the Park policy of control over grazing and mineral exploration—can increase the value given to the resources' information potential, while at the same time impinging on other values, such as the spiritual and cultural values of Native Americans, as well as the economic value to those who would prefer to exploit Park lands for alternative uses.

There are a number of laws and NPS directives for the protection and management of natural resources that could be said to work against some of the cultural values of CCNHP. For example, the executive order that restricts the introduction of "exotic" (nonnative) species into natural ecosystems in federal lands, if interpreted literally or enforced strictly, will limit the options of plants

that could be used in erosion control strategies to protect the archaeological remains.[92]

In other instances, strict enforcement of the regulations against removing any resources—cultural or natural—from the parks impinges on Native American practices of gathering plants and other materials for medicinal and ritual purposes and creates an interesting conflict between values. The importance of the Park's resources for these purposes is heightened by the depletion of many of these species from nearby lands by grazing and other uses.[93]

The 1985 General Management Plan[94] allows nondestructive uses of the site and establishes that permission is required for anyone, including Native Americans, to gather materials. During the period of consultation of the plan, the Navajo Nation objected to these provisions as "an intrusion on the privacy and independence of Navajo ceremonial life," but the permission requirement stood.[95] CCNHP strictly follows the NPS policy that collecting materials on-site is not allowed; unofficially, staff recognize that some collecting is likely to be taking place. In this particular situation, the conflict goes beyond an issue of different values. There is a contradiction between stipulations in the Native American Relations Policy requiring respect of religious ceremonies and traditions; the General Management Plan; and the *American Indian Religious Freedom Act* on one side; and, on the other side, the prohibitions of removing anything from national parks found in federal regulations[96] and the *Archaeological Resources Protection Act of 1979*. The NPS Management Policies 2001 recognize the conflict and indicate that "these regulations are under review, and NPS policy is evolving in this area."[97]

CULTURAL LANDSCAPES

NPS has recently proposed a study of the cultural landscape of CCNHP. The NPS defines a cultural landscape as "a geographic area, including both cultural and natural resources and the wildlife or domestic animals therein, associated with a historic event, activity, or person or exhibiting other cultural or aesthetic values."[98]

Early studies of the Park's resources tended to view them as a static grouping of ruins. However, in the 1970s, the Chaco Center Project brought a greater understanding of other prehistoric landscape features, such as roads and water-control devices. More-recent studies have considered the astronomical alignments of prehistoric structures and natural features. A new cultural landscape study could be an important effort, since there is evidence of a sophisticated understanding of environmental dynamics and astronomical events that demonstrates a strong connection between the ancient inhabitants and their natural environment. Chaco scholars have reached these conclusions based upon a careful examination of the physical remains of Anasazi habitation of the region, which include evidence of lifeways adapted to provide food and water in an arid environment as well as structures, roads, and astronomical markers. Their conclusions have also been supported by the prominence of landscape features in the oral traditions of the descendants of the Puebloan culture who live in the region today.

The archaeological and environmental elements of the Park are already the focus of preservation, research, and interpretation. Seeing a place from a more-traditional, reifying perspective that singles out easily definable objects (artifacts, structures, sites, etc.), as has occurred to date at Chaco, limits the attribution of value—and, therefore, explicit protection and monitoring—to those types of objects.[99] A cultural landscape perspective will look at these elements together with natural features, documenting and understanding the relationship between them and identifying other significant geographical elements. The results of cultural landscape studies will be important for management purposes: they will bring a different perception of what is valuable in CCNHP and allow the development of a preservation policy in this area.

IMPACT OF RESTRICTING ACCESS

The policies of CCNHP intended to restrict access—by visitors, researchers, or stakeholders—are very successful in preserving the resources and the information they contain. However, shielding the resources from physical damage does not mean that all the values attributed to those resources are being protected. Limitations of access can have a negative impact on some values; in this case, by restricting the number of visitors to the site, the benefits of the site's associative value are enjoyed by fewer people. The limitations of access to many areas of the Park have reduced the number of places and vistas that visitors can see and the ways in which they can experience the values of the Park. However, the policies increase the quality of the visit by fostering a quiet and reflective atmosphere. These restrictions, combined with limited interpretation around the site, do not facilitate the communication of the importance and extension of Chaco Culture beyond the lands of the Park. A visitor who stays on the canyon floor misses the views of the Chaco roads, views of the mountains sacred to Native Americans, and a panoramic view of the great and small houses seen from above.

[continued on page 91]

Casa Rinconada

Casa Rinconada is the largest known great kiva in the Park, and it is among the largest in the Chacoan sphere of influence. Excavated in the 1930s, it now stands open to the elements, with its circular walls in relatively good condition. Because of its enormous size, its impressive engineering and position, its interesting interior details, and its association with ancient religious ceremonies, it has always attracted the attention of visitors. Until recently it was the only kiva where entrance was permitted.

In 1987, a New Age event—the "Harmonic Convergence"—was planned and was expected to attract about five thousand people to the Park for two days for ceremonies, dancing, chanting, bonfires, and meditation in and around some of the major ruins. Casa Rinconada was to be an important venue for the festivities.

The Park's cultural resource specialists feared that irreparable damage would be done to the structure and to the archaeological integrity of the floors and other features, given the numbers of people and the kinds of activities planned. However, Park management felt that it needed to allow some access by this group to the kiva.[1] Refusing access to the petitioners might have resulted in legal action alleging discrimination. The superintendent and his staff faced the conflicting values of the mandate—

on the one hand to protect the integrity of the ruins, and on the other hand to uphold the right of access to the site, religious freedom, and the mandate to provide for enjoyment by the public. In keeping with the available guidelines, the staff put together a mitigation plan establishing behavioral and geographical boundaries for all proposed activities for this event and recommended preventive measures to protect Casa Rinconada. These included laying down a protective floor over the exposed archaeological levels. Contingency plans for problems were prepared.

The event took place, attracting only about half of the anticipated crowd, and the impact on the physical resources was negligible. After the event, however, staff started to find "offerings" that were being left in some areas of the Park, principally in Casa Rinconada.[2] In 1991 cremated human remains started to be left in the kiva, and although the scattering of ashes from cremations may be permitted by Park superintendents,[3] no permits had been granted in these cases. Perhaps more important, both the offerings and the deposit of human remains violated the sensitivities of Native American groups affiliated with the Park. Members of the American Indian Consultation Committee recommended to Park staff that access to the kiva be forbidden. According to Park staff, there was disagreement among the tribal representatives as to which Native American groups

Casa Rinconada viewed from above. For several years during the time that Casa Rinconada—the largest kiva in the Park—was open to visitors, a shallow layer of dirt protected the floor features. Recently, the features were uncovered after access to the interior was prohibited. Both Native American sensitivities and conservation concerns influenced this decision. Photo: Guillermo Aldana

had a legitimate right to use the kiva, and they also had concerns about the impact that inappropriate access would have on visitors.

In 1996, heeding the advice of the committee and concerned with visitor-induced damage and the new practices, CCNHP proposed the closure of Casa Rinconada and conducted the required environmental impact study,[4] followed by a period of public consultation. The study expressed particular concern over the practice of leaving ashes, since their removal required the scraping of the surface where they were deposited. Although the removal of the ashes left on the kiva floor disturbed only the layer of fill that had been added in 1991 as a protective buffer, it was felt that this fill should be removed since it obscured the original floor and its features. The documents make no mention of Native American concerns.

Gate blocking the entrance to Casa Rinconada. Today access to the interior of the kiva is blocked by these barriers. From the rim above, visitors can see the kiva, including the floor features, which were obscured in the past. The uncovering of all the architectural features can contribute to the understanding of the visitor. However, the ban on access required for the protection of the ruins prevents visitors from experiencing the space of the kiva. Photo: Marta de la Torre

Shortly after the public consultations, it was announced that Casa Rinconada would be closed to all.[5] At present, visitors can view the interior from the doorways or the rim above, and access is possible only with special permission of the superintendent. Some Native Americans perceive the cause of the closure to be the acts of groups who had no cultural claim to the place. In their view, the actions were violating the sacredness of "their" place, and only these new rituals should have been banned. The official reason given for closing the kiva was the protection of the physical resource.[6] Any decision to allow use by Native Americans but not by other groups would have violated the establishment clause of the U.S. Constitution, which pertains to the separation of religion and the state.

This decision is consistent with the priority given by Park management to the conservation of the archaeological remains. Continued access by visitors and the leaving of offerings and the deposit of human ashes were seen to be detrimental mainly to the physical conservation of the site. At the same time, the obscuring of flooring elements was seen to have a negative impact on the educational value of the place, not on its spiritual values. Since backfilling and reburial are conservation strategies widely used in the Park, one can assume that the value of maintaining the visibility of floor elements—even if from a distance—was seen as critical in this case.

The values favored by the decision to close Casa Rinconada were the scientific importance of the site—the unique, fragile, and unrestorable qualities of its original features, and the potential for yielding further information if these qualities are not disturbed. Affected by the decision were the spiritual values held by Native Americans and New Agers and the benefits to the general public from entering the kiva and experiencing the interior space.

The conflict brought about by the introduction of New Age practices in a heritage place was not an issue explored during the decision making process. However, the emergence of stakeholder groups ascribing new values or appropriating existing ones and the need to determine legitimacy for their claims are difficult issues that many heritage managers confront. In this particular case, denying access to a new spiritual group would have been seen as religious discrimination and thus unconstitutional. The resolution of the conflict did not have to be reached through negotiations, since NPS management was able to find a "conservation" justification for the closure and thus sidestep the difficult matters of determining the legitimacy of new stakeholder groups and prioritizing values.

Notes

1. The Cultural Resource Management Guidelines (NPS 28) (NPS 1994) was the primary reference for staff as they considered the request for this use of the site. NPS 28, which was supplanted in 1998 by Director's Order No. 28 and the updated Cultural Resource Management Guidelines (NPS 1997a), contains a procedure to be followed whenever any intervention is contemplated.

2. Although depositing materials on-site is prohibited by federal and NPS regulations, offerings found in the Park are gathered by staff and curated according to the practices established by the NPS for items left at the Vietnam Veterans Memorial in Washington, D.C.

3. In accordance with NPS general regulations and applicable state laws.

4. NPS 1996.

5. NPS 1997b.

6. Loe 1996, B-04.

Preservation reasons have been given for closing some important sites in the Park to visitors. Fajada Butte and Casa Rinconada, for example, hold particular significance for certain tribal members. While keeping visitors away from these sites can protect Native American spiritual values, the no-access rule, which also applies to those who hold the place sacred, prevents them from enjoying the benefits of this value.

IMPACT OF LIMITING THE NUMBER OF VISITORS

The policy of restricting contact with the resources is based on the Park's estimation that this is the best way to protect the sites given the available resources. This policy requires a strategy to maintain a low number of visitors, but the optimal number is not known. Park staff recognize that they would have difficulty establishing the maximum number of visitors the Park could sustain at any given time from the point of view of conservation and safety; nevertheless, they feel that peak visitation days in the summer months come close to maximum carrying capacity of the site. A small number of visitors is seen as being preferable both for the sake of the physical condition of the ruins and the landscape and for the sake of the quality of the experience.

Geographical isolation and few facilities and services inside the Park support efforts to limit the number of visitors. The "primitive" nature of the site is seen as positive by many visitors, who consider their stay in the Park as an opportunity to get back to nature and away from the annoyances of civilization.[100] The lack of services and facilities, however, limits the amount of time that those who visit can spend. Short visits obviously present a challenge to the staff in providing a meaningful interpretation of such a complex site.

IMPACT OF STAKEHOLDER RELATIONSHIPS

CCNHP has a considerable number of stakeholders at the local, national, and international levels. The values that they ascribe to the Park vary, and Park staff recognize the balance of power that exists among stakeholders as well as the potential for serious conflict. The fact that CCNHP is administered by a federal agency gives the strongest weight to the voice of the NPS and its cabinet-level parent, the Department of the Interior. While these authorities are the voice of the citizenry on one level, their specific institutional requirements and priorities can sometimes relegate the interests of other stakeholders to lesser positions. Compliance with higher authorities obliges the NPS to certain priorities and actions that favor the values that underlie these mandates over what might be important to the local or nonfederal interests.

Over the years, heritage professionals—archaeologists in particular—held a privileged position among stakeholder groups. Today, Native Americans might have moved to that position, and their stake in the site is broadly recognized in the management of the Park. Although concerned only with the repatriation of objects and human remains, *NAGPRA* has indirectly reinforced the importance of these stakeholders and their values. The participation of Navajo, Zuni, and Hopi tribes and Pueblo groups in the Park's American Indian Consultation Committee has given them an important advisory role in the management of the site. The superintendent brings to this group most issues that impact the conservation and use of the site—fostering a consultation that goes well beyond that mandated by *NAGPRA*. While Park management recognizes that officially this group has only a "consultative" role, it admits that opinions expressed by this group are given very serious consideration. The most recent Resource Management Plan draft[101] acknowledges the shift in the stakeholders' power map: "over the past ten years, the Park's American Indian Consultation Committee has gradually taken the lead role in shaping Park policy and practice. This has created a certain tension between the Native American and archaeological constituencies. Resolving this tension is the current challenge for the [Cultural Resource] division."[102]

The opinions of the members of this consultative committee are not always unanimous, nor are they always in agreement with those of Park management. The closing of Casa Rinconada seems to be one instance in which Native American groups feel that their cultural right to enter the ruins has been curtailed by a NPS decision requiring their asking for permission to do so, even though they were the first to suggest the closure. Conversely, however, the change in attitudes of some Native Americans toward the preservation of resources could be attributed to contacts and discussions in this committee. Some members of the group now support "conservation" of the ruins, recognizing that some of the non–Native American values of the site can enhance and protect their own values.

There are stakeholders who have a passive relationship with the site and will continue to have one—until such time as they wish to highlight the values they ascribe to the site or until they consider those values threatened. As a hypothetical example, the stakeholder group represented by the international community (not very active under normal circumstances) could be stirred into action if it saw a threat to the values that placed the site on the World Heritage List. Another example of a stakeholder group, at a more-local level, is the neighbors of the Park. Park staff report that this group, in general, is not very involved or interested in Park-related issues. However, if the authorities decided to pave the road leading into the Park, some members would side with the Park against the paving project, but others would come out in favor of it. The difference in their positions would probably be based upon whether they thought a paved road created a danger to their herds from speeding vehicles, or whether they would like to facilitate access to their homes.

Park management recognizes that the position of a stakeholder group will depend upon the matter being considered. There are not many stakeholder groups who would be on the side of the Park on all issues. Thus, the Park has no unconditional allies, and the importance of maintaining good relations and open lines of communication with all stakeholders is critical.

Quality of Visitors' Experience

The superintendent and staff of CCNHP are committed to providing a high-quality experience for visitors. Management strategies are established and decisions are made with awareness of their impact on the protection of this quality. Although not explained or analyzed in detail in any official document, the quality of a visitor's experience is believed to depend on direct contact with the archaeological and natural resources, a peaceful atmosphere, and a pristine environment. Those responsible for the Park carefully manage all three factors.

CCNHP's mandate to maintain the archaeological resources of the Park in "unimpaired" condition requires that direct contact of visitors with the ruins be carefully controlled. The strategy employed by Park management has been to restrict access to a sufficient but relatively small number of ruins and to require special permission for venturing into the backcountry.[1]

The Park's peaceful environment is maintained by limiting the number of visitors. This strategy also favors the protection and regeneration of the natural environment. Visitor numbers at CCNHP in 2001 are variously reported to be between 61,000 and 74,000, and both figures represent a decline over totals of recent years. Other national parks in the region have visitation numbers that are several times those of CCNHP.[2]

CCNHP is able to maintain this isolation through a combination of factors—some circumstantial, others resulting from policy decisions. The geographic location of the Park and the relatively few accommodations for travelers in the surrounding towns play an important role in maintaining low visitor numbers. Other contributing factors are a direct result of the strategy of little development that the Park has followed for decades. These factors include not paving the access roads, offering minimal services for visitors on-site, limiting the number of campgrounds, and discouraging publicity about the Park.

The efforts to maintain the low profile of the Park are easily justified in terms of legislation and managerial discretion, in the sense that it is undeniable that sooner or later any policy encouraging visitation is likely to have a negative impact on the conservation of the resources. However, other national parks—Yosemite in California, for example—have encountered great resistance from stakeholders to curtailing visitation for conservation reasons. The acceptance of CCNHP's policies designed to discourage public access could be attributed to a combination of factors. At the local level, the Park's stakeholders are relatively small groups of Native Americans or others who do not benefit much from the Park (neighboring communities). A large stakeholder group—the scientific community—can derive benefit without visiting the Park on a regular basis. And finally, there seems to be a general lack of appreciation of the values of the Park among the public at large.

The paving of the main road leading into the Park has been discussed for many years. Thus far, Park management has been able to hold its position, one that is fueled by fear of increased numbers of visitors. A memorandum dated July 1989 from the superintendent at CCNHP to the director of the Southwest Regional Office presents a hypothetical scenario in which visitation to CCNHP would double within three years if the entry road were paved. Using the 1989 visitor number of 91,000 and estimating an annual increase of approximately 11 percent, the scenario envisaged a possible visitor load of over 200,000 by the year 2000. Park authorities considered that these new conditions would require a larger visitor center; more parking areas; new comfort stations; a larger campground; and expansion of waste treatment facilities, food services, and other amenities. It would also demand additional funds for staffing, including guides, law enforcement rangers, resource management professionals, and conservation technicians. The prospect was overwhelming, and it was considered certain that the quality of the visit would diminish. Chaco would become a crowded national park like others in the region. Two years after this memorandum was issued, the first cases of hantavirus were reported in the region, and

tourism in the Southwest decreased dramatically. The anticipated population growth from regional development of the energy and fuel industries never materialized either. Current visitation is well below 1989 levels. Park management is not making any efforts to increase it, and the quality of the experience for Park visitors remains very high.

One of the management objectives stated in NPS's 1995 Resource Management Plan is to "prevent development in the primary visitor-use areas [no additional roads, no expansion or addition of parking areas, and no further support facilities] that would adversely impact the historic landscape and setting."[3]

The almost pristine natural environment, another factor of a quality visitor experience, has resulted from the absence of damaging activities such as high visitation, grazing, and mining over a long period of time. This quality appreciates as Park lands continue to be protected. However, in the setting of CCNHP, the characteristics of the lands outside its boundaries can influence the experience of the visitor. While the region has not experienced the development that was anticipated a few years back, any eventual new uses of the surrounding lands—whether habitation or mining—are likely to have a significant impact on the quality of the air and views from the Park. While this is an area that is technically outside the responsibility and control of NPS management, the good-neighbor relationship with local stakeholders that Park staff maintain could influence decisions in the future.

Some of the qualities identified with a good visitor experience are apparently supported by the results of a visitor study carried out in three national park units in 1994.[4] As part of the study, visitors at CCNHP were asked their reasons for visiting the Park and asked to identify "aspects of the Park settings, which are composed of the managerial, physical, and social aspects of a Park, that were important to the realization of their desired experiences."[5] The researchers found that the main reason visitors came to Chaco was to learn about history; the desire to experience the natural environment came second.[6]

Another element contributing to the quality of the visit is related to the educational value of the Park and considered very important by CCNHP management. This element is the opportunity to offer ranger-led tours and presentations. However, the 1994 study found that visitors were not as interested in the personal contact available in ranger-led tours as they were in the freedom to walk independently through the ruins with self-guided booklets or be helped with informational signs in the ruins and elsewhere in the Park.[7]

The undeveloped nature of the Park was considered a positive attribute by the majority of visitors interviewed, and the study goes so far as to recommend that "future proposals to add facilities or upgrade existing ones at Chaco seriously consider their potential impact on the present experience environment. Modifications that would significantly increase the number of visitors or severely restrict visitor independence and mobility would probably have the greatest influence in detracting from the present conditions."[8]

This last quotation from the visitor study summarizes most of the conflicts and issues raised by the focus on the quality of the experience. Visitors to CCNHP constitute a relatively small group that recognizes the ruins' educational and symbolic value and seeks contact with nature in a tranquil environment away from crowds. The study points out, however, that the conditions that exist in the Park are the result of a series of decisions and circumstances, as discussed above. Changes in some of these conditions—such as the paving of the road or construction of overnight accommodations on-site—could attract a much larger number of visitors and change the atmosphere of the place.

As always, choices are to be made between access and protection: in this case, access by many or by few, and the physical protection of the resources as well as protection of a certain quality of visit that can exist only if it is limited to a relatively small number of people. All the values attributed to the Park are affected by decisions in this area—in both positive and negative ways.

Notes

1. Most of the regulations governing access to the resources of the Park are left to the discretion of the superintendent, as authorized by the *Code of Federal Regulations* (36 *CFR* 1.5). These regulations can be found in NPS 2001c. Site-specific regulations include the closure of certain areas (Fajada Butte, Atlatl Cave, and the interior chamber of Casa Rinconada), the restriction of access to the ruins and frontcountry and backcountry areas, and the requirement that permissions be requested for special uses.

2. While each park is unique in its facilities and carrying capacity, the following figures are given as indicators (from: http://www.nps.gov):

	Gross Park Surface (FY2001)	Visitors (FY2001)
CCNHP, New Mexico	13,750 hectares (33,974 acres)	61,602
Mesa Verde National Park, Colorado	21,093 hectares (52,122 acres)	511,764
Wupatki National Park, Arizona	17,013 hectares (42,042 acres)	537,851
Bandelier National Park, New Mexico	13,628 hectares (33,677 acres)	293,548

3. NPS 1995, objective page.

4. The two other parks included in the study were Mesa Verde National Park and Wupatki National Monument; see Lee and Stephens 1994.

5. Lee and Stephens 1994, 2–3.

6. Ibid., 33–36.

7. Ibid., 39.

8. Ibid., 46–47.

Conclusions

The NPS mandate to preserve "unimpaired the natural and cultural resources and values of the national park system for the enjoyment, education, and inspiration of this and future generations"[103] carries with it a great deal of responsibility. As with many large government bureaucracies, the actual authority for selecting and implementing management strategies resides in legislation and related procedural documents written to ensure compliance.

One of the overarching issues explored by this study is the possibility that the individual parks—supported by the NPS management environment—can recognize, take into consideration, and protect all the values ascribed to a place. The information gathered indicates that, while there are certain constraints, this is possible within limits. The case of CCNHP indicates that regardless of any number of values that are ascribed to a national park, the preponderant and primary ones will always be those that were the reason for the creation of the Park. In the case of

Figure 2.10. Meditating in Casa Rinconada. CCNHP is considered a place of spiritual significance by several Native American groups. More recently, New Agers have also come to view Chaco as a special place. Some of the practices of this new group of stakeholders offend the sensitivities of stakeholders of longer standing. The NPS has found itself having to decide whether all stakeholder claims are legitimate and whether some groups have rights that take priority. So far, the NPS has sidestepped a direct decision on these matters by resolving the conflict in the arena of "conservation." Photo: Courtesy National Park Service, Chaco Culture NHP Collection Archives.

CCNHP, the purpose of the Park lies in the archaeological ruins, but the value seen in those resources has grown and changed over time. However, the focus on the physical conservation of the archaeological materials is at times an obstacle to the recognition and protection of some of the values ascribed to those materials. In addition, the force of law, not policy, appears to be the main factor in the recognition and protection of values in national parks.

In the long history of Chaco Canyon as a heritage site, the evolution and emergence of values over time have been fueled by new knowledge and by changing societal mores and professional practices. The evolution in values brought about by professional practices is best reflected in the information and associative values, protected by policies related to excavation and conservation. The fate of Native American spiritual values and the natural values of the site illustrates how, in the case of the NPS, legislation plays a major role in the creation of new values and in the recognition of stakeholders' interests.

Other questions explored in this case have been the amount of latitude Park superintendents have, within this very structured national system, to establish policies and objectives that address the specific situation of the Park, as well as whether compliance with higher-level authorities limited their choices of action. The answers do not clearly fall on one side or the other. There are certainly many activities at the site, particularly at the level of reports and justification, intended to address issues of compliance. However, at a more-pragmatic level, the case has shown that the superintendent has a surprising amount of latitude to interpret the national policies and directives. In addition, an examination of Chaco Canyon as a heritage place illustrates how this site is the result of its history and the decisions that have been made in the past. In theory, policies at the national and local levels could change drastically—with emphasis shifting, for example, between conservation and access. In fact, while policies have changed over the Park's history, the priorities and conditions on-site have remained fairly constant.

A simple comparison of CCNHP with another nearby national park can illustrate this point. This study has repeatedly pointed out the primacy of the conservation of the cultural resources in all management decisions at CCNHP. This emphasis is justified at the NPS system level by its mandate to maintain resources unimpaired, and justified at the park level by its legislative purpose. At the same time, other parks in the system were created with similar purposes and today are very different from CCNHP, with its undeveloped and tranquil setting.

Mesa Verde National Park, in the neighboring state of Colorado, provides an interesting contrast to CCNHP with regard to its management policies and its approach to visitors and access. Mesa Verde became a national park (rather than a national monument) in 1906, and almost immediately it became one of the national sites featured in efforts to develop tourism and visitation. Decisions were made to harden the front-country areas of the site to make them accessible to as many people who wanted to see them, and to make them relatively impervious to damage through the paving of pathways and the permanent consolidation of ruins, while forbidding all visitor access to the backcountry. Today more than 500,000 people visit a small part of Mesa Verde National Park every year, where a paved road delivers them to the edge of a few archaeological sites. There they are encouraged to explore inside the ruins, eat in the restaurant, and sleep at the inn. At Mesa Verde, it could be said that a choice was made to sacrifice some sites for the sake of access and in exchange for the protection of others in the backcountry. The archaeological remains were the reason for the creation of both parks, but Mesa Verde and Chaco protect these resources through very different strategies.

The ever-present dilemma in heritage sites of access versus conservation appears to be handled at CCNHP with less conflict than in other parks in the system that have tried to limit the number of visitors. The geographic location of CCNHP and its surroundings has supported the isolation policy. In 1985 there was considerable concern about the impact that a change in these conditions would bring to the Park. Although the anticipated threats never materialized, the development of the region remains not a possibility but a certainty at some point in the future. As the region evolves, the long-term protection of CCNHP depends substantially on the ability of its superintendent and staff to understand and balance the interests of all the stakeholders, to meet its compliance obligations, and to find acceptable solutions when these forces conflict. The specific threats that might emerge in the future are unpredictable. However, they are likely to originate principally from development and its corollaries of alternative land uses, pollution, increased population (and visitors). The battles to be fought will require strong Park coalitions with some of the stakeholder groups. The groups that will be the needed allies will depend on the battle to be fought. The good-relations approach with all the stakeholders (rather than strong-and-fast alliances with some of them), which is followed at this time, seems wise. As in the past, the critical element of management in the Park will be the ability of the superintendent to maintain focus on the core values of the Park, on behalf of its constituents, present and future.

Notes

1. *U.S. Code 1916.*

2. For a discussion of these evolving definitions and conflict among them, see Sellars 1997 and Winks 1997.

3. NPS 2000a, sec. 1.4.4.

4. See NPS 2000a, sec. 1.4, for the interpretation of the *National Organic Act of 1916,* the *General Authorities Act of 1970,* as amended (*U.S. Code,* vol. 16, secs. 1, 1a–1).

5. NPS 2000a, 5.

6. Lowry 1994, 29.

7. Birdsall and Florin 1992, 349–52.

8. The information here has been gathered from Lister and Lister 1981; Lekson et al. 1988; and Strutin and Huey 1994. For a more comprehensive bibliography of Chaco Canyon, see "Bibliography of Chaco Resources" maintained by Dan Meyer, Department of Anthropology, University of Calgary: http://www.ucalgary.ca/~dameyer/chacbib.html (12 Feb. 2003).

9. *Anasazi,* a Navajo word usually translated as "ancient enemies," was introduced in 1936 to replace Basket Maker–Pueblo as the archaeological label for the prehistoric ancestors of the historical Pueblo people of northern Arizona and New Mexico. The Navajo are not descendants of the Anasazi, and some Pueblo people prefer to use a term from their own language, such as the Hopi *Hisatsinom,* to refer to their prehistoric ancestors.

10. It should be noted that in many cases, Native American histories differ from what could be called "academic" history. Attempts are made throughout this study to state Native American views if they have been made known to the authors of the study and if they differ from those presented by the NPS or academic sources.

11. A more-complete time line of Chaco Canyon and CCNHP in historical times is presented in appendix A. Unless otherwise noted, the information provided in this section has come from Lee 1971; Lister and Lister 1981; and Strutin and Huey 1994.

12. Wozniak, Brugge, and Lange 1993; Stoffle et al. 1994.

13. *U.S. Code* 1906, sec. 2.

14. McManamon 2001, 257.

15. *U.S. Code* 1906, sec. 2.

16. CCNHP staff, private communication, April 2002.

17. NPS 2002b, pt. 1, 4–5.

18. The Civilian Conservation Corps was established in 1933 by the *Act for the Relief of Unemployment through the Performance of Useful Public Work, and for Other Purposes* during the Great Depression years. Originally intended to deal with the conservation of natural resources, its work later extended to the construction and repair of paths, campsites, and so on and, in some cases, as in Chaco, to the stabilization of archaeological structures.

19. NPS 1991, 19.

20. *U.S. Code* 1980.

21. NPS 1984, 27.

22. UNESCO World Heritage Committee 1984, 7–8.

23. The official Web site of the park (www.nps.gov / chcu) provides more information on facilities and visits to the site.

24. NPS 2002a.

25. Hantavirus, a disease carried by rodents, is potentially deadly to humans.

26. Lee and Stephens 1994, 14–28.

27. Park infrastructure information is taken from NPS 2002a.

28. NPS 2000a, 1.4.3.

29. NPS 2000a.

30. NPS 2002b contains a statement of the Park's significance (to be discussed below). The 1995 Resource Management Plan (NPS 1995) and the 1985 General Management Plan (NPS 1985) mention the importance of only the archaeological remains, which constitute the purpose of the Park.

31. U.S. President 1907.

32. Hardacre 1879, 274.

33. NPS 2002b, 1.

34. NPS 2002b.

35. Ibid., 3–4.

36. NPS 2002b.

37. For an extensive description of the interest in Native American antiquities in the late nineteenth and early twentieth centuries, see Lee 1971.

38. NPS 1985, 119–29. Appendix B summarizes the various categories and their "scoring" value.

39. *U.S. Code* 1916.

40. NPS 1995.

41. NPS 2002b.

42. Lee and Stephens 1994, 33–36.

43. Wozniak, Brugge, and Lange 1993; Stoffle et al. 1994.

44. NPS 1990a.

45. *U.S. Code* 1995.

46. *U.S. Code* 1990.

47. *Federal Register*, 12 March 1999 (vol. 64, no. 48).

48. See Hoover 2001, 34–37.

49. Stoffle et al. 1994, 81.

50. Begay et al. 1993, quoted in Stoffle et al. 1994, 81.

51. Keller and Turek 1998, 190.

52. Ibid., 191.

53. Brugge 1993, 12.

54. *U.S. Code* 1969, as amended by Public Law 94-52, 3 July 1975; Public Law 94-83, 9 Aug. 1975; and Public Law 97-258, 4(b), 13 Sept. 1982.

55. Sec. 101 (*U.S. Code*, vol. 42, sec. 4331) (a): "The Congress, recognizing the profound impact of man's activity on the interrelations of all components of the natural environment, particularly the profound influences of population growth, high-density urbanization, industrial expansion, resource exploitation, and new and expanding technological advances and recognizing further the critical importance of restoring and maintaining environmental quality to the overall welfare and development of man, declares that it is the continuing policy of the Federal Government . . . to create and maintain conditions under which man and nature can exist in productive harmony, and fulfill the social, economic, and other requirements of present and future generations of Americans."

56. NPS 1982 was superseded and replaced by NPS Director's Order No. 12: Conservation Planning, Environmental Impact Analysis, and Decision Making (NPS 2001b), effective 8 Jan. 2001.

57. See Satterfield 2002.

58. For a discussion of the associative / symbolic value of heritage, see Lipe 1984, 1–11.

59. Lee and Stephens 1994, 135.

60. Rothman 1989, 17.

61. NPS 1985.

62. UNESCO World Heritage Committee 2002, I.C.3.

63. NPS 1984, 28.

64. UNESCO World Heritage Committee 1985.

65. UNESCO World Heritage Committee 1999.

66. NPS 2002b, III.

67. *U.S. Code*, vol. 16, sec. 1a–1.

68. NPS 2000a, sec. 2.3.

69. Respectively, NPS 1985; NPS 2000b; NPS 1995, currently being revised and existing in draft form, NPS 2002b; and NPS 1983, with its 1990 amendment, NPS 1990a. These and other

documents consulted for the preparation of this case are listed in the references.

70. A new general management plan is required by the new NPS management policies, but no time has yet been specified for its development.

71. NPS 2002b.

72. A list of the more-specific management priorities or actions identified in the 2002 draft of the Resource Management Plan (NPS 2002b) is presented in appendix C.

73. NPS 2002b, 4.

74. Ibid., 11–12.

75. Public Law 96-550 (*U.S. Code* 1980).

76. NPS 1990a.

77. NPS 2002b, pt. 2, 1.

78. The closest towns with tourist accommodations are Bloomfield, Aztec, and Farmington. Santa Fe and Albuquerque, the two major cities in the area, are two and a half to three hours away by car. There has been talk in the Navajo Nation of building a hotel in Crownpoint, south of the site, but there has been no follow-up. Some local families allow camping on their lands during the high season.

79. Lee and Stephens 1994, 37–40.

80. NPS 1985.

81. Lee and Stephens 1994, 38.

82. NPS 1985, 46.

83. NPS 2002b, 7.

84. For details of the work done by the Chaco Center Project, see Lister and Lister 1981.

85. NPS 1991.

86. Ibid., 6.

87. Information provided by CCNHP staff.

88. Lee and Stephens 1994, 127.

89. Ibid.

90. Lister and Lister 1981, 157.

91. Stuart and McManamon, n.d., 8.

92. Public Law 90-583 (*U.S. Code* 1968) provides for the control of noxious plants on federal lands, and Executive Order 11987 (U.S. President 1977), "Exotic Organisms," calls for restrictions on the introduction of exotic species into natural ecosystems on federal lands. NPS policy also states that control or eradication of an exotic species will be implemented when that species threatens resources (such as native species, rare or endangered species, or natural ecological communities or processes) on park lands (NPS 1988). Priority is placed on control programs for exotic species having a high impact on park resources and for which there is a reasonable expectation for successful control.

93. *Code of Federal Regulations*, title 36, chapter 1, sec. 2.1 (Parks, Forests, and Public Property), 2002. Although current regulations provide some latitude to park superintendents to designate that certain fruits, berries, or nuts may be gathered if this has no adverse effect on park resources, no other gathering or consumptive use of resources is allowed unless authorized by federal statute or treaty rights.

94. NPS 1985.

95. CCNHP N-5.

96. *Code of Federal Regulations*, title 36, chapter 1, sec. 2.1, 2002.

97. NPS 2000a, sec. 8.5, 90.

98. Birnbaum 1994, 1.

99. For a discussion of limiting versus more-holistic perspectives toward cultural heritage, see Byrne et al. 2001, 55–72.

100. Lee and Stephens 1994, 46.

101. NPS 2002b.

102. Ibid., pt. 2, 1.

103. Ibid., 10.

Appendix A:
Time Line during Heritage Status

1250–present
Members of affiliated clans and religious societies of the Hopi and the Pueblos of New Mexico have visited Chaco on pilgrimages to honor their ancestral homelands.

1823
The Spanish military expedition led by José Antonio Vizcarra passed through Chaco Canyon and produced the first written account identifying the ruins there.

1849
While in the area of Chaco Canyon, the Washington Expedition, a U.S. Army Topographical Engineers reconnaissance detachment headed by Lt. James H. Simpson, encountered and wrote descriptions of Chacoan sites. The resulting government report included detailed illustrations. This was the first substantial written and graphic report concerning the cultural heritage at Chaco Canyon.

1877
William Henry Jackson, a photographer who was part of the U.S. government's Geological and Geographical Survey of the Territories, led by F. V. Haydn, produced more-extensive descriptions and maps of the Chacoan sites.

1888
Victor and Cosmos Mindeleff of the Bureau of American Ethnology surveyed and photographed the major Chacoan sites for a study of Pueblo architecture. Their photographs included the documentation of looting and vandalism. As the oldest-known photographs, they provide a baseline for measuring the subsequent effects of looting, vandalism, visitation, and natural collapse at the sites.

1896–1901
After excavating several ancestral Puebloan sites in the Four Corners region, including sites at Mesa Verde in 1888, amateur archaeologist and relic hunter Richard Wetherill came to excavate at Chaco Canyon. Wetherill drew the interest of the Hyde brothers of New York to the site. Over the next five years, the Hyde Exploring Expedition conducted full-scale excavations at Pueblo Bonito. George H. Pepper of the American Museum of Natural History in New York supervised the excavations, while Wetherill "led a band

of Navajo laborers who did much of the actual digging."[1] Their primary purpose was to accumulate artifacts for the museum's collection. Numerous artifacts were shipped to the museum, where they are located today.

1901
Following an investigation of the Hyde Expedition's excavations at Chaco Canyon, as well as the land claim of Richard Wetherill there, which included Pueblo Bonito, Chetro Ketl, and Pueblo del Arroyo, General Land Office special agent S. J. Holsinger strongly recommended that the U.S. government create a national park to preserve Chacoan sites, and he compiled a report documenting many ruins. The General Land Office responded by suspending the Hyde expedition's excavations at Pueblo Bonito. The Hyde expedition never resumed its archaeological work at Chaco.

1902–10
Despite the denial of Richard Wetherill's land claim in 1902, he continued to homestead at Chaco Canyon and operated a trading post at Pueblo Bonito until his controversial murder in 1910.

1906
As a direct result of controversy over Wetherill's excavations at Chaco Canyon and claims by professionally trained archaeologists that they did not properly account for the site's scientific significance, Congress enacted the *Antiquities Act*. The law—the nation's first to protect antiquities—granted the president the power to establish national monuments.

1907
President Theodore Roosevelt set aside approximately 20,630 acres at Chaco Canyon as Chaco Canyon National Monument under the authority of the *Antiquities Act*. Until 1916, when the National Park Service (NPS) was created, the monument was administered by the federal agencies that had jurisdiction over the land.

1916
Congress passed the *Organic Act*, which provided for the creation of the NPS, which has administered Chaco Canyon National Monument and Chaco Culture National Historical Park since that time.

1921–27
Neil Judd of the National Geographic Society led the excavation of several hundred rooms at Pueblo Bonito, as well as parts of Pueblo del

Arroyo and several smaller sites, for the Smithsonian Institution. A goal of this expedition was to preserve the excavated Pueblo Bonito; extensive conservation treatments were conducted at the site.

1928   After a resurvey of the monument property indicated that the lands mentioned in the original proclamation did not contain all of the described ruins, President Calvin Coolidge issued a second proclamation, Presidential Proclamation 1826, to correct these errors.

1929–41   Edgar Lee Hewett of the School of American Research and Donald D. Brand of the University of New Mexico led excavations at Chetro Ketl and many small Chacoan sites.

1931   Congress enacted legislation (*U.S. Statutes at Large* 46: 1165) that related to several aspects of interest in lands at Chaco. First, it authorized the exchange of private lands within the monument for federal lands elsewhere in New Mexico. In addition, it authorized the driving of livestock across monument lands for owners (and their successors in interest) of certain lands in and adjoining the monument. The act also specified means by which the University of New Mexico and the Museum of New Mexico and/or the School of American Research (located in Santa Fe) could continue to conduct research on their former lands within the monument or, at the discretion of the secretary of the interior, on other lands within the monument.

1933–37   Gordon Vivian carried out extensive conservation work at Pueblo Bonito, Chetro Ketl, and Casa Rinconada.

1937   A Civilian Conservation Corps (CCC) crew of all-Navajo stonemasons initiated repairs to many large excavated Chacoan structures that were deteriorating due to years of exposure to rain, wind, and freeze-thaw cycles. In addition, the CCC built a two-hundred-person camp near Fajada Butte to house workers to provide improvements to the monument.

1941   After a year of heavy rains, Threatening Rock fell onto and destroyed approximately thirty rooms at Pueblo Bonito that had been excavated in the 1920s.

1947   After the last Navajo resident at the monument moved away, the NPS erected fences at its boundaries to exclude livestock and thereby to restore rangeland vegetation.

1949   The University of New Mexico deeded lands in Chaco Canyon National Monument to the NPS in return for continued rights to conduct scientific research at the monument.

1959   As part of the NPS's Mission 66 construction campaign, which extended from 1956 to the agency's 50th anniversary in 1966, the NPS created the monument's Visitor Center, staff housing, and campgrounds.

1969–81   The NPS and the University of New Mexico run the Chaco Center Project, a multidisciplinary research unit established to enhance the understanding of prehistoric Native American cultures of the San Juan Basin. The center carried out fieldwork and publication and experimented with the application of new technologies to research. The center's work identified and appraised over one thousand sites in the Park and adjacent lands and used remote sensing to identify the prehistoric road system that radiates outward from Chaco Canyon to connect numerous outlying Chacoan communities in the region.

1979   The NPS approved the document Chaco Canyon National Monument: General Management Plan/Development Concept Plan (NPS 1979).

1980   Congress enacted Public Law 96-550, which created Chaco Culture National Historical Park, taking the place of Chaco Canyon National Monument. This law contained three general provisions: (1) it added approximately 12,500 acres to the Park; (2) it designated thirty-three outlying sites in the San Juan Basin as Chaco Culture Archeological Protection Sites and provided for the addition of other sites in the future; in addition, it created the Chaco Culture Archeological Protection Site program to jointly manage and protect Chacoan sites located on lands not under the jurisdiction of the NPS; and (3) it authorized a continuing program of archaeological research in the San Juan Basin.

1981   The Chaco Culture Interagency Management Group—composed of the NPS, the Bureau of Land Management, the Bureau of Indian Affairs, the Navajo Nation, the State of New Mexico, and the U.S. Forest Service—was created to provide for development of a joint management plan for formally designated Chacoan outlying sites, as required under Public Law 96-550. The agencies involved in the development of the plan had either jurisdiction over, or interest in, lands containing outlying sites.

1982   The Park superintendent closed access to Fajada Butte, a Native American sacred site, to all visitors except those authorized by permit.

1983   The Chaco Culture Interagency Management Group issued the document Chaco Archeological Protection Site System: Joint Management Plan, which contained guidelines for the identification, preservation, protection, and research of designated Chacoan outlying sites.

1984   Based on public comments and planning and management discussions that followed, the NPS prepared the document Draft General Management Plan / Development Concept Plan / Environmental Assessment, Chaco Culture National Historical Park, New Mexico. The document included a description of proposed actions (general management plan) as well as alternatives for major proposals contained in the plan. In October, this document was released for public and agency consideration. On November 1, a public meeting to receive comments was held in Albuquerque. According to the NPS, "the majority response was in favor of the general management plan proposals as described in the draft document."[2] In the fall of the same year, the NPS also held meetings with federal, state, and local agencies; the Navajo Nation; energy companies; and individuals to review the most important land management and protection proposals contained in the Draft Land Protection Plan, Chaco Culture National Historical Park.

1985   In September, the Southwest Region approved the document General Management Plan / Development Concept Plan / Chaco Culture National Historical Park, New Mexico.

1987   The World Heritage Committee of the United Nations Educational, Scientific, and Cultural Organization (UNESCO) designated Chaco Culture National Historical Park as a World Heritage Site.

1991   Chaco Culture National Historical Park instituted the Chaco American Indian Consultation Committee.

1993   The NPS created the Vanishing Treasures Initiative, which is aimed at providing additional funding for ruins conservation at agency sites in the Southwest, including CCNHP. Since that time, the program has provided significant funding to the Park for carrying out conservation-related work and for hiring conservation-related staff.

1995   Congress enacted the Chacoan Outliers Protection Act of 1995 (Public Law 104-11). The act added nine new outlying sites and removed four formerly designated outlier sites as Chaco Culture Archeological Protection Sites. These changes increased the total number of outliers to thirty-nine and extended their geographic scope outside the San Juan Basin.

1996   World Monuments Fund named CCNHP and associated archaeological sites in New Mexico to its list of the 100 most endangered monuments.

In response to the urgings of affiliated Native American tribes, the NPS closed both entrances to the great kiva known as Casa Rinconada.

1997   The Natural Resources Defense Council and the National Trust for Historic Preservation issued the report Reclaiming Our Heritage: What We Need to Do to Preserve America's National Parks, which included CCNHP as one of several case studies of threatened parks.

The NPS and the University of Colorado—Boulder formed a collaboration aimed at creating a synthesis of the work done by the Chaco Center Project (1969–81) through a series of conferences.

1999   The National Parks Conservation Association named CCNHP to its annual list of the ten most endangered national parks in the United States—citing damage to the resources caused by environmental conditions; insufficient preservation and maintenance; looting; and potential development of surrounding lands.

As part of its required activities under the *Native American Graves Protection and Repatriation Act of 1990 (NAGPRA)*, CCNHP determined that the Navajo Nation should be included in its list of Native American tribes deemed to be culturally affiliated with the prehistoric inhabitants of Chacoan sites. This determination meant that the Navajo, like the Pueblo and Hopi tribes of the region who had already been considered descendants, can legally claim possession of human remains and artifacts within the Park. This finding has produced a series of protests from the Hopi and most of the Pueblo tribes, as well as criticism from the Society for American Archaeology.

Notes

1. Rothman 1989, 23.
2. NPS 1985, 4.

Appendix B:
Resource Classification

This scoring system was developed to determine the relative importance of resources after the addition of new lands to the Park as a result of the 1980 legislation. Although it was not intended to be used as a ranking of resources, it does seem to indicate the relative value attributed to resources on the basis of cultural affiliations, site type, and date. The information was taken from NPS 1985, 119–29.

Cultural Affiliation

Score 5: Anasazi

Score 4: Archaic, Paleo-Indian, and unknown (probably Anasazi or Archaic)

Score 3: Navajo and unknown (probably Anasazi or Navajo)

Score 2: Historic and unknown (Navajo or historic)

Score 1: Unknown

Site Type

Score 5: Habitation, kiva

Score 4: Hogan, Anasazi road or trail, signaling site, shrine or other ceremonial feature, Anasazi ledge unit, field house, water control feature, Archaic or Paleo-Indian camp

Score 3: Artifact scatter; other—Archaic or Paleo-Indian; camp—Anasazi, Navajo, historic, or unknown; rock art; storage site

Score 2: Baking pit; Anasazi or unknown hearth; Navajo or historic ledge unit; burial; ranch complex

Score 1: Road or trail—Navajo or historic; animal husbandry feature; sweathouse; oven; quarry; cairn; other—Navajo or historic; other—unknown; unknown

Period of Occupation

Score 5: Anasazi

Score 4: Paleo-Indian, Archaic, and Navajo 1750–1900; unknown—Anasazi or Archaic

Score 2: Navajo 1900–45 and unknown; historic pre-1900; unknown—Navajo or historic

Score 1: Unknown

Appendix C:
Management Priorities of CCNHP in 2001

Source: NPS 2002b, pt. 4, 3–5.

Summary of Cultural Resources Priorities

- Updating all site records and maps to provide accurate information on the resources managed by the Park

- Developing and managing NPS and GIS databases to monitor Park natural and cultural resources

- Conducting NPS-required cultural resources studies to improve understanding and management of the resources

- Complying with all laws regulating activities on federal lands and consulting with culturally affiliated tribes on Park management issues

- Publishing final reports on past archaeological projects to make the data available to the general public

- Continuing the site preservation backfilling program to protect archaeological sites for the future

- Developing preventative maintenance plans to conduct regular, cyclic preservation treatments to prevent catastrophic site loss

- Conducting baseline site condition assessments and completing architectural documentation as required

- Compiling the backlog of preservation records and preparing annual reports documenting site preservation treatments

- Gaining museum collection accountability through the development and implementation of museum management plans and through reducing the backlog of uncataloged objects and archives

- Preserving museum collections by properly conserving and storing objects and archives and housing them in facilities that meet federal and NPS standards

- Making museum collections more accessible to researchers by providing information on museum holdings in a variety of formats

- Updating museum exhibits to provide more accurate information to visitors about the current understanding of the Park's cultural resources

Summary of Natural Resources Priorities

- Initiating studies and monitoring to gather data for use in developing a management plan for the Park's pioneering elk herd

- Continuing studies of Park vegetation and wildlife to understand Park resources and their long-term recovery from poor range management prior to 1990

- Conducting studies to understand the Park's ecological significance and its role in conserving regional biodiversity

- Implementing and monitoring recommendations from research studies to effectively manage natural resources

- Continuing development of the night sky monitoring program

- Developing hydrology data as needed to manage erosion threats to cultural sites and to preserve riparian habitats and biodiversity

Appendix D:
Summary of Legislation
Pertinent to CCNHP

Antiquities Act of 1906 (U.S. Code, vol. 16, secs. 431–33)—1906

This act was passed to protect archaeological resources from damage or destruction at the hands of looters, amateur archaeologists, and curious visitors. The act specified that unauthorized excavation of any historic or prehistoric ruin may be punishable by fine and/or jail. It gave the president the authority to proclaim as national monuments landmarks of historic or prehistoric interest. It named the federal departments that might issue permits for proper research on federal lands and allowed that further constraints on such activity could be issued by these departments.

National Park Service Organic Act (U.S. Code, vol. 16, secs. 1–4)—1916

This act established the NPS and provided its mandate, stating that it "shall promote and regulate the use of the federal areas known as national parks, monuments, and reservations hereinafter specified by such means and measures as conform to the fundamental purposes of the said parks, monuments, and reservations, which purpose is to conserve the scenery and the natural and historic objects and the wildlife therein, and to provide for the enjoyment of the same in such manner and by such means as will leave them unimpaired for the enjoyment of future generations."

The director of the NPS is given considerable latitude in this legislation for granting privileges, leases, and permits to use the land or its resources, provided that the grantees are satisfactorily qualified.

Historic Sites Act of 1935 (U.S. Code, vol. 16, secs. 461–67)—1935

This law declares the national policy to preserve for public use historic sites, buildings, and objects of national significance for the inspiration and benefit of the people of the United States. The NPS director, on behalf of the secretary of the interior, shall ensure that the following functions are undertaken:

• Make, organize, and preserve graphic, photographic, and narrative data on historic and archaeological sites, buildings, and objects;

• Survey these resources to determine which possess exceptional value as commemorating or illustrating the history of the United States;

• Conduct the research necessary to get accurate information on these resources;

• Enter into contracts, associations, partnerships, etc., with appropriate organizations or individuals (bonded) to protect, preserve, maintain, etc., any historic or ancient building, site, etc., used in connection with public use.

Further, it establishes the NPS Advisory Board and Advisory Council to assist the director in identifying sites for NPS nomination, in managing those sites, and in gathering information from the most qualified experts on the matters within their purview.

National Historic Preservation Act of 1966 (NHPA), as Amended (U.S. Code, vol. 16, secs. 470ff.)—1966

This act declares the recognition of the federal government of the importance of historic places to the quality of life in the United States and declares a commitment to the preservation of the historical and cultural foundations of the nation as a living part of its community life and development, in order to give a sense of orientation to the American people. It states that "Although the major burdens of historic preservation have been borne and major efforts initiated by private agencies and individuals, and both should continue to play a vital role, it is nevertheless necessary and appropriate for the Federal Government to accelerate its historic preservation programs and activities, to give maximum encouragement to agencies and individuals undertaking preservation by private means, and to assist State and local governments and the National Trust for Historic Preservation in the United States to expand and accelerate their historic preservation programs and activities." Further, it makes clear that the federal government has a strong interest to provide leadership in the preservation of the prehistoric and historic resources of the United States and of the international community of nations and in the administration of the national preservation program in partnership with states, Indian tribes, Native Hawaiians, and local governments. Two sections are particularly pertinent to archaeological resources such as those at CCNHP:

SECTION 106 REGULATIONS

This section requires federal agencies to take into account the effects of their undertakings on historic properties and afford the Advisory Council a reasonable opportunity to comment on such undertakings. The procedures define how agencies meet these statutory responsibilities. The "106 Process" seeks to accommodate historic preservation concerns with the needs of federal undertakings, through consultation early in the planning process with the agency official and other parties with an interest in the effects of the undertaking on historic properties. The goal of consultation is to identify historic properties potentially affected by the undertaking; assess its effects; and seek ways to avoid, minimize, or mitigate any adverse effects on historic properties. The agency official must complete this process prior to approving the expenditure of federal funds on the work or before any permits are issued.

The regulations that implement section 106 define the appropriate participants and the professional and practical standards they must meet; they also describe the components of the process necessary to comply with the *National Historic Protection Act*, including the identification and recording of historic properties; an assessment of threats, potentially adverse effects, and readiness for emergencies; consequences of failure to resolve such threats; and the appropriate kinds of consultation required.

SECTION 110 REGULATIONS

Section 110 sets out the historic preservation responsibilities of federal agencies; it is intended to ensure that historic preservation is fully integrated into the ongoing programs of all federal agencies.

The guidelines that accompany this act show how federal agencies should address the various other requirements and guidelines in carrying out their responsibilities under the act. The head of each federal agency, acting through its preservation officer, should become familiar with the statutes, regulations, and guidelines that bear upon the agency's historic preservation program required by section 110.

The section also requires that all federal agencies establish a preservation program for the identification, evaluation, nomination to the national register, and protection of historic properties. Each federal agency must consult with the secretary of the interior (through the director of the NPS) in establishing its preservation programs. Each must use historic properties available to it in carrying out its responsibilities. Benchmarks in this respect include the following:

• An agency's historic properties are to be managed and maintained in a way that considers the preservation of their historic, archaeological, architectural, and cultural values;

• Properties not under agency jurisdiction but potentially affected by agency actions are to be fully considered in agency planning;

• Preservation-related activities must be carried out in consultation with other federal or state agencies, Native American tribes, and the private sector;

• Procedures for compliance with section 106 of the same act are to be consistent with regulations issued by the Advisory Council.

Agencies may not grant assistance or a license to an applicant who damages or destroys historic property with the intent of avoiding the requirements of section 106.

Archaeological and Historic Preservation Act of 1974 (U.S. Code, vol. 16, secs. 469ff.)—1974

Supporting earlier legislation, this act specified that it was federal policy to require the preservation, to the extent possible, of historical and archaeological data threatened by dam construction or alterations of terrain. It includes the preservation of data, relics, and specimens that might be lost or destroyed as the result of flooding, road construction, or construction-related activity, by any U.S. agency or by someone licensed by such an agency, or by any alteration of the terrain caused by a federal construction project or federally licensed activity.

It requires the notification of the secretary of the interior if any such damage is possible, in advance of the start of such a project, so that the appropriate mitigating action could be initiated (research, salvage, recovery, documentation, etc.). To reduce the burden on contractors, landowners, and other citizens, this law requires the secretary of the interior to initiate such work within sixty days of notification and to compensate the owner for the temporary loss of use of the land, if necessary. It also specifies the reporting procedures to be used, disposition of recovered materials, and the coordination of such work at the national level, and recommends follow-up procedures in order to assess the need for and success of this program.

American Indian Religious Freedom Act of 1978 (U.S. Code, vol. 42, sec. 1996)—1978

This act states that "it shall be the policy of the U.S. to protect and preserve for American Indians their inherent right of freedom to believe, express, and exercise the traditional religions of the American Indian, Eskimo, Aleut, and Native Hawaiians, including but not limited to access to sites, use, and possession of sacred objects and the freedom to worship through ceremonials and traditional rites."

The Archaeological Resources Protection Act of 1979 (U.S. Code, vol. 16, sec. 470aa–mm)—1979

This act secures the protection of archaeological resources and sites on public lands and Indian lands, and fosters increased cooperation and exchange of information between governmental authorities, the professional archaeological community, and private individuals having collections of archaeological resources and data obtained before 31 October 1979.

It requires that any investigation and/or removal of archaeological resources on public or Indian lands be contingent on a qualified applicant obtaining a permit. The successful application must demonstrate that the work is in the public interest, that recovered materials will remain U.S. property (curated by an appropriate institution), and that the work proposed is consistent with the larger management goals of the lands in question. Other requirements include tribal notification, reporting, oversight, deadlines, prohibited acts, and confidentiality, among others.

Government Performance and Results Act of 1993 (U.S. Statutes at Large 107 [1993]: 285; Public Law 103-62)

This act requires federally funded agencies to develop and implement accountability systems based on goal setting and performance measurement and to report on their progress in both planning and results in the budgetary process. The act was created to address a broad range of concerns about government accountability and performance, with the goal of improving citizens' confidence in the government by forcing accountability in the managerial and internal workings of federal agencies. All participating agencies must complete three documents: a strategic plan, a performance plan, and a performance report.

Strategic plans, issued every three to five years, must include a comprehensive mission statement, a description of general goals and objectives and how these will be achieved, identification of key factors that could affect achievement of the general goals and objectives, and a description and schedule of program evaluations.

Agencies are required to consult with Congress and to solicit and consider the views and suggestions of other stakeholders and customers who are potentially affected by the plan.

Performance plans are done on a yearly basis, covering the agency's fiscal year. Linked with the strategic plan currently in effect, performance plans must include the goals for the fiscal year; a description of the processes and skills and of the technology, human, capital, and information resources needed to meet the goals; and a description of how the results will be verified and validated.

Performance reports, prepared at the end of each year, detail the agency's achievements toward the accomplishment of the annual goals set out in the performance plan.

References

Birdsall, S., and J. W. Florin. 1992. *Regional Landscapes of the United States and Canada*. 4th ed. New York: John Wiley and Sons.

Birnbaum, C. A. 1994. *Protecting Cultural Landscapes: Planning, Treatment, and Management of Historical Landscapes*. Preservation Briefs 36. NPS. http://www2.cr.nps.gov/hps/tps/briefs/brief36.htm (12 Feb. 2003).

Brugge, D. 1993. "Navajo Interests at Chaco Culture National Historical Park." In Wozniak, Brugge, and Lange 1993.

Byrne, D., et al. 2001. *Social Significance: A Discussion Paper*. Hurstville, New South Wales, Australia: New South Wales National Parks and Wildlife Service.

Chaco Culture Interagency Management Group. 1983. Chaco Culture Interagency Management Group. Chaco Archeological Protection Site System: Joint Management Plan. Chaco Culture Interagency Management Group.

Code of Federal Regulations. 2002. Title 36, chapter 1, sec 2.1.

Hardacre, E. C. 1879. "The cliff-dwellers." *Scribners Monthly, an Illustrated Magazine for the People* 17 (1879), pt. 2: 266–76.

Hoover, J. 2001. "A cultural affiliation controversy." *American Archaeology* 4 (4) (Winter 2000–01): 34–37.

Keller, R., and M. F. Turek. 1998. *American Indians and National Parks*. Tucson: University of Arizona Press.

Lee, M. E., and D. Stephens. 1994. Anasazi Cultural Parks Study Assessment of Visitor Experiences at Three Cultural Parks. Northern Arizona University, Flagstaff.

Lee, R. F. 1971. *The Antiquities Act of 1906*. Reprinted in *An Old Reliable Authority: An Act for the Preservation of American Antiquities*, ed. R. H. Thompson. A special issue of *Journal of the Southwest* 4 (2) (Summer 2000): 198–269.

Lekson, S. H., et al. 1988. "The Chaco Canyon community." *Scientific American* 259 (1): 100–109.

Lipe, W. D. 1984. "Value and meaning in cultural resources." In *Approaches to the Archaeological Heritage: A Comparative Study of World Archaeological Resource Management*, ed. H. Cleere. Cambridge: Cambridge University Press.

Lister, R. H., and F. C. Lister. 1981. *Chaco Canyon: Archaeology and Archaeologists*. Albuquerque: University of New Mexico Press.

Loe, V. 1996. "Entering Anasazi ruin prohibited: Chaco Canyon kiva doors closed to prevent further desecration." *Dallas Morning News*, 17 Nov., B-04. *Note*: This article discusses the practices of New Age adherents at Chaco Culture National Historical Park, how these acts are deemed to be a desecration of places held sacred there by Native Americans who claim cultural affiliation to the site, and how the U.S.

National Park Service closed Casa Rinconada, a great kiva at Chaco, as a result.

Lowry, W. 1994. *The Capacity for Wonder: Preserving National Parks*. Washington, D.C.: Brookings Institution.

McManamon, F. P. 2001. "Cultural resources and protection under United States law." *Connecticut Journal of International Law* 16 (2): 247–82.

Mason, R., ed. 1999. *Economics and Heritage Conservation*. Los Angeles: Getty Conservation Institute. http://www.getty.edu/conservation/publications/pdf_publications/econrpt.pdf (12 Feb. 2003).

National Park Service (NPS).
See U.S. National Park Service.

Pearson, M., and S. Sullivan. 1995. *Looking after Heritage Places*. Carlton, Victoria: Melbourne University Press.

Public Broadcasting System. 1980. *The Chaco Legacy* [film]. Odyssey Films.

Rothman, H. 1989. *Preserving Different Pasts: The American National Monuments*. Urbana: University of Illinois Press.

Satterfield, T. 2002. "Numbness and sensitivity in the elicitation of environmental values." In *Assessing the Values of Cultural Heritage: Research Report*, ed. M. de la Torre. Los Angeles: Getty Conservation Institute.

Sellars, R. W. 1997. *Preserving Nature in the National Park: A History*. New Haven: Yale University Press.

Sofaer, A., et al. 1982a. "Lunar marking on Fajada Butte." In *Archaeoastronomy in the New World*, ed. A. Aveni, 169–81. Cambridge: Cambridge University Press.

——. 1982b. *The Sun Dagger* [film]. Washington, D.C.: Solstice Project, Bullfrog Productions.

Stoffle, R. W., et al. 1994. American Indians and Fajada Butte: Ethnographic Overview and Assessment for Fajada Butte and Traditional (Ethnobotanical) Use Study for Chaco Culture National Historical Park, New Mexico-Final Report. BARA, University of Arizona, Tucson.

Strutin, M., and G. H. Huey. 1994. *Chaco: A Cultural Legacy*. Tucson: Southwest Parks and Monuments Association.

Stuart, G. E., and F. P. McManamon. N.d. "Archaeology and you." Society for American Archaeology. http://www.saa.org/publications/ArchAndYou (25 May 2004).

United Nations Educational, Scientific and Cultural Organization (UNESCO) World Heritage Committee. 1984. *Operational Guidelines for the Implementation of the World Heritage Convention*. Paris: UNESCO.

——. 1985. Report of the rapporteur. Ninth Session, SC-85/Conf. 007/9.

——. 1999. *Operational Guidelines for the Implementation of the World*

Heritage Convention. Paris: UNESCO. http://whc.unesco.org/opgutoc.htm (25 May 2004).

———. 2002. Revision of the "Operational Guidelines for the Implementation of the World Heritage Convention": Third Draft Annotated Revised "Operational Guidelines" by the March 2002 Drafting Group. 26 COM WHC-02/Conf. 202/14B, Twenty-sixth Session, 24–29 June. http://whc.unesco.org/archive/2002/whc-02-conf202-14be.pdf (12 Feb. 2003).

U.S. Code. 1906. *An Act for the Preservation of American Antiquities.* Vol. 16, secs. 431–33. http://www.cr.nps.gov/local-law/anti1906.htm (12 Feb. 2003).

———. 1916. *The National Park Service Organic Act.* Vol. 16, secs. 1–4. http://www.nps.gov/legacy/organic-act.htm (12 Feb. 2003).

———. 1931. *An Act to Authorize Exchange of Lands with Owners of Private-Land Holdings within the Chaco Canyon National Monument, New Mexico, and for Other Purposes.* U.S. *Statutes at Large* 46: 1165. *Note*: This act passed by the U.S. Congress provided means to the U.S. secretary of the interior to eliminate private holdings of land within Chaco Canyon National Monument. The act also provided that if certain lands within the monument owned by the University of New Mexico, the Museum of New Mexico, and the School of American Research were conveyed to the U.S. government, then those institutions would be permitted to continue scientific research within those specified parcels. This statute is superseded by *U.S. Statutes at Large* 94 (1980): 3227.

———. 1968. *Carlson-Foley Act of 1968* (noxious plant control), sec. 1241; Public Law 90-583.

———. 1969. *National Environmental Policy Act of 1969 (NEPA).* Vol. 42, secs. 4321–47. http://ceq.eh.doe.gov/nepa/regs/nepa/nepaeqia.htm (12 Feb. 2003).

———. 1979. *Archaeological Resources Protection Act (ARPA).* Vol. 16, sec. 470aa–mm.

———. 1980. *U.S. Statutes at Large* 94: 3228; Public Law 96-550, title v, sec. 503. *Note*: This act passed by the U.S. Congress provides for the establishment of Chaco Culture National Historical Park as well as for thirty Chaco Culture Archeological Protection Sites and the abolishment of Chaco Canyon National Monument. http://www4.law.cornell.edu/uscode/16/410ii-5.html (12 Feb. 2003).

———. 1990. *Native American Graves Protection and Repatriation Act (NAGPRA).* Vol. 25, sec. 32; Public Law 101-601. http://www.cr.nps.gov/nagpra/index.htm (as of 12 Feb. 2003) and http://www.cast.uark.edu/other/nps/nagpra/nagpra.dat/lgm003.html (12 Feb. 2003).

———. 1995. *Chacoan Outliers Protection Act of 1995. U.S. Statutes at Large* 109 (1995): 158; Public Law 104-11. *Note*: The act added nine new outlying sites and removed four formerly designated outlier sites as Chaco Culture Archeological Protection Sites. These changes increased the total number of outliers to thirty-nine, totaling 14,372 acres, and extended their geographic scope outside the San Juan Basin. http://www.nps.gov/legal/laws/104th/104-11.pdf (12 Feb. 2003).

U.S. National Park Service (NPS). 1979. Chaco Canyon National Monument: General Management Plan/Development Concept Plan. NPS.

———. 1982. NPS 12: National Environmental Policy Act Guidelines. NPS.

———. 1983. Chaco Archeological Protection Site System: Joint Management Plan. NPS.

———. 1984. World Heritage List Nomination Submitted by the United States of America, Chaco Culture National Historical Park. NPS.

———. 1985. General Management Plan/Development Concept Plan, Chaco Culture National Historical Park, New Mexico. NPS.

———. 1988. Resource Management Plan: Chaco Culture National Historical Park. NPS.

———. 1990a. Chaco Culture Archeological Protection Site System Joint Management Plan: Plan Amendment. NPS.

———. 1990b. Chaco Culture National Historical Park temporarily closes Fajada Butte. News release, 19 March. NPS. *Note*: A copy of this news release is contained in app. B of Stoffle et al. 1994.

———. 1991. Statement for Interpretation and Interim Interpretive Prospectus: Chaco Culture National Historical Park, Chaco Canyon, New Mexico. NPS.

———. 1994. NPS 28: Cultural Resource Management Guidelines. Release No. 4. NPS.

———. 1995. Resource Management Plan: Chaco Culture National Historical Park. NPS.

———. 1996. Protection of Casa Rinconada Interior: Environmental Assessment: Chaco Culture National Historical Park. NPS.

———. 1997a. Director's Order No. 28: Cultural Resource Management Guidelines. Release No. 5. NPS.

———. 1997b. Finding of No Significant Impact: Protection of Casa Rinconada Interior: Chaco Culture National Historical Park. NPS, 30 June.

———. 1999. Chaco Culture National Historical Park, San Juan County, New Mexico; Fajada Butte closure. *Federal Register* 64 (48). Washington, D.C.: U.S. Government Printing Office, 12 March.

———. 2000a. Management Policies 2001. NPS. *Note*: The report's introduction states that "this volume is the basic service-wide policy document of the National Park Service." It includes sections concerning park system planning, land protection, natural resource management, cultural resource management, wilderness preservation and management, and interpretation and education. The document also includes a glossary and appendices containing references to laws cited in the text and relevant executive orders, memoranda, and director's orders. http://www.nps.gov/policy/mp/policies.pdf (12 Feb. 2003).

———. 2000b. National Park Service Strategic Plan, FY2001–FY2005. NPS. http://planning.nps.gov/document/NPS%5Fstrategic%5Fplan%2Epdf (12 Feb. 2003).

———. 2001a. Chaco Culture National Historical Park Annual Performance Plan: Fiscal Year 2002. NPS.

———. 2001b. Director's Order No. 12: Conservation Planning, Environmental Impact Analysis, and Decision-Making. NPS. http://www.nps.gov/policy/DOrders/DOrder12.html (12 Feb. 2003).

———. 2001c. Chaco Culture National Historical Park. Superintendent's Compendium (Site Specific Rules and Regulations). NPS.

———. 2002a. Chaco Culture National Historical Park Annual Performance Plan, Fiscal Year 2002. NPS.

————. 2002b. Chaco Culture National Historical Park Resource Management Plan (Draft). NPS, 10 Jan.

U.S. President. 1907. Proclamation 740. *U.S. Statutes at Large* 35: 2119, 11 March. *Note*: This proclamation by U.S. President Theodore Roosevelt created Chaco Canyon National Monument.

————. 1928. Proclamation 1826. *U.S. Statutes at Large* 45: 2937, 10 Jan. *Note*: This presidential proclamation by U.S. President Calvin Coolidge extended the boundaries of Chaco Canyon National Monument.

————. 1977. Executive Order 11987, "Exotic Organisms." 24 May. http://envirotext.eh.doe.gov/data/eos/carter/19770524.html (12 Feb. 2003).

Winks, R. W. 1997. *The National Park Service Act of 1916*: "A contradictory mandate"? *Denver University Law Review* 74 (3): 575–620.

Wozniak, F. E., D. Brugge, and C. Lange, eds. 1993. An Ethnohistorical Summary of Ceremonial and Other Traditional Uses of Fajada Butte and Related Sites at Chaco Culture National Historical Park. New Mexico Historic Preservation Division, Santa Fe. *Note*: This document was prepared for the New Mexico Historic Preservation Division under an intergovernmental agreement with the Southwest Regional Office of the U.S. National Park Service, which funded the study.

Persons Contacted during the Development of the Case

Rachael Anderson
Vanishing Treasures Archaeologist
Chaco Culture National Historical Park
National Park Service

Taft Blackhorse
Navajo Nation Chaco Sites Protection Program
Navajo Nation Historic Preservation Department

Russell Bodnar
Chief of Interpretations
Chaco Culture National Historical Park
National Park Service

Wendy Bustard
Museum Curator
Chaco Culture National Historical Park
National Park Service

G. B. Cornucopia
Park Guide
Chaco Culture National Historical Park
National Park Service

Jill Cowley
Historical Landscape Architect
Intermountain Support Office–Santa Fe
National Park Service

Dabney Ford
Chief of Cultural Resources Management
Chaco Culture National Historical Park
National Park Service

Richard Friedman
McKinley County GIS Center
New Mexico

Petuuche Gilbert
Tribal Councilman
Acoma Pueblo

Joyce Raab
Archivist
Chaco Culture National Historical Park
National Park Service

James Ramakka
Chief of Natural Resources Management
Chaco Culture National Historical Park
National Park Service

Virginia Salazar
Regional Curator
Intermountain Support Office–Santa Fe
National Park Service

Richard Sellars
Historian
Intermountain Support Office–Santa Fe
National Park Service

Brad Shattuck
Natural Resources Program Manager
Chaco Culture National Historical Park
National Park Service

C. T. Wilson
Superintendent
Chaco Culture National Historical Park
National Park Service

Port Arthur Historic Site

Randall Mason, David Myers,

and Marta de la Torre

About This Case Study

This case study looks at the management of Port Arthur Historic Site in Australia. Since 1987 the governing body has been the Port Arthur Historic Site Management Authority (PAHSMA), a government business enterprise created by the Tasmanian State government. Conservation and stewardship of Port Arthur as a heritage site are the primary objective of PAHSMA, which in managing the site also must take into consideration financial viability.

The following section describes the site of Port Arthur itself—its geographic situation, history, and evolution as a heritage site—as well as its contemporary features, partnerships, infrastructure, and facilities. It then discusses the management context in which PAHSMA operates, including its relationship to state and commonwealth governments and heritage organizations.

The next section examines the identification and management of the values of the site and is structured around the three research questions established for the case studies: (1) How are the values associated with the site identified?; (2) What is their place in management policies?; and (3) What impact is the actual management of the site having in the values?

In the concluding section, several didactic themes are addressed, including the balancing of cultural and economic values, the implications of PAHSMA's particular institutional arrangements, and the impact of its Burra Charter–based conservation planning process on site values.

This case study is the result of many hours of research, interviews, site visits, extensive consultation, and frank discussion. The staff and board of PAHSMA have been extremely helpful in the research, production, and refinement of this study. They have been forthcoming and generous and have participated energetically in the discussions that took place during the Steering Committee's visit to Port Arthur in January 2002, and later by correspondence.

In preparing this case study, the authors consulted the extensive documentation produced by PAHSMA and previous managing authorities as well as sources from elsewhere in Australia.

We sincerely thank all those who have patiently and generously contributed their time and ideas, those who have helped us focus our interpretations, and those who otherwise assisted us in our fieldwork and research.

Digital reproductions of the following supplementary documents are contained within the accompanying CD-ROM: Broad Arrow Café Conservation Study (1998); Port Arthur Historic Site Conservation Plan, volumes 1 and 2 (2000); and PAHSMA Annual Report 2001.

Management Context and History of Port Arthur Historic Site

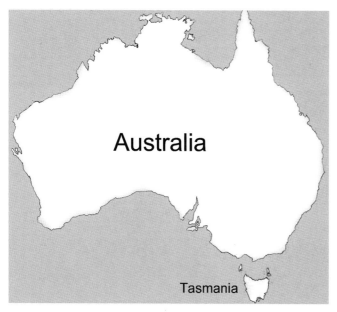

Figure 3.1. Map of Australia. Port Arthur is located on the island of Tasmania, south of the Australian mainland.

Geographic Description[1]

In the seventeenth and eighteenth centuries, England implemented a policy under which convicted criminals were sent to Australia to serve out their sentences and be reformed through work. Prisons, support communities, and small industries were established in Australia to punish, employ, and equip the incoming convict population. Port Arthur was to be the center of this new convict system, organized in the remote area now known as the Tasman Peninsula. There, repeat offenders and the recalcitrant served out their terms—often life sentences at hard labor.

Now in a ruined state, Port Arthur is of great significance to contemporary Australians, particularly Tasmanians. The site is one of the best-known symbols of the era of "convictism," which played such a formative role in Australia's history and identity.

Australia's only island state, Tasmania is located south of Australia, separated from the mainland by Bass Strait. In designating a site for its penal colony, England chose the Tasman Peninsula for its remoteness and isolation. The peninsula is connected to mainland Tasmania

Figure 3.2. The Tasman Peninsula, located at the southeast end of Tasmania.

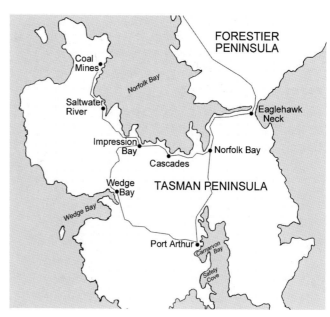

Figure 3.3. The location of Port Arthur and seven other prominent convict heritage sites.

by a slender isthmus known as Eaglehawk Neck, which is less than 30 meters (33 yards) wide. Aside from this narrow land link, the Tasman Peninsula is surrounded entirely by water. Directly to the south is the southern Pacific Ocean, and to the east is the Tasman Sea. To the west and north is a series of bays, some sheltered from the open ocean. One of these protected, deep harbors was dubbed Port Arthur. Its location on the peninsula made it ideal for the construction of a penal settlement in large part because it would provide a port for oceangoing vessels traveling across Storm Bay to and from Hobart, the center of colonial government in Tasmania. Today, Hobart is Tasmania's capital and remains an important port in its own right. By road, Port Arthur is approximately 100 kilometers (62 miles) from Hobart; by modern boat, the trip takes between three and four hours.

Port Arthur has a temperate and wet climate. The area's plentiful rain once supported lush vegetation, including forests dominated by various species of native eucalypt. Today, much of this native vegetation has been cleared and replaced by grass and European deciduous trees.

History of Settlement and Use[2]

Port Arthur is a complex and rich heritage site. Dozens of buildings occupy the site, some in ruins, some restored as museums, others adapted for reuse in a variety of ways. Some structures date from the convict period (1830–77), and others represent later eras. The site is also rich in archaeological resources.

PRE-CONVICT PERIOD

Aboriginal peoples are believed to have inhabited the island of Tasmania for at least 36,000 years prior to the arrival of the first Europeans in the mid-seventeenth century. Dutch navigator Abel Tasman led the first European expedition to Tasmania in 1642 and named the island Van Diemen's Land after his sponsor, the governor-general of the Dutch East India Company.[3]

CONVICT PERIOD AND CONVICTISM[4]

Under the British Empire, the convict system was formally initiated through the *Transportation Act* of 1717, which stated that the "labor of criminals in the colonies would benefit the nation." Convicts were once auctioned to British colonists in North America, but the American Revolution put an end to this practice. In December 1786, Orders in Council identified, among other territories, the

east coast of New Holland (Australia) and its adjacent islands as the colonies that would receive transported criminals. The first fleet that sailed from England the following year to settle the Australian state of New South Wales carried a significant number of convicts. In 1790, Governor Phillip of New South Wales introduced the policy of assigning convicts as indentured laborers or

Figure 3.4. View of the church and Mason Cove, 1873. Photo: Courtesy W. L. Crowther Library, State Library of Tasmania.

Figure 3.5. View of the church and Mason Cove, 2002. Photo: David Myers

Figure 3.6. The penitentiary building, the largest and most prominent structure from the convict period. Photo: Marta de la Torre

servants to free settlers. Phillip believed that providing convict labor for a period of two years at the expense of the Crown would encourage settlers to the area. The practice soon spread throughout the colony and became known as the assignment system.

In 1803, Governor King of New South Wales sent a fleet, which included convicts, to establish the first British settlement in Van Diemen's Land (Tasmania) near the present city of Hobart. King had chosen the island to ward off the threat of French settlement and to monitor American whaling ships. Hobart soon became an important port and the seat of government for the island. Van Diemen's Land, which originally was not a separate colony but an outpost of New South Wales, and its isolated location were viewed as suitable for the containment of hard-core convicts. The island's first penal settlement was established at Macquarie Harbour, on the island's west coast, in 1821. A second station was created at Maria Island in 1825. Both facilities were secondary penal stations that held prisoners who had committed new offenses since their transport to Australia.

Demand in Hobart for wood was high, particularly for shipbuilding, and in September 1830 the first convicts were sent to Port Arthur to cut timber. Soon thereafter, the island's third secondary penal station was constructed at Port Arthur.

Following the closure of the penal settlements at Maria Island in September 1832 and at Macquarie Harbour a month later, Port Arthur's population, infrastructure, and importance grew rapidly. The following year, a small island within sight of Port Arthur was selected for burials. The island, which would over time receive approximately one thousand interments, was then known as Dead Island. In 1834, prisoners' barracks were built and the first juvenile prison in the British Empire was constructed at Point Puer, across the bay from Port Arthur. Its purpose was to separate young male convicts from the "bad company and example" of the adult convict population. Construction began on the settlement's first permanent buildings, which included a church. By 1836, the settlement contained almost one thousand convicts and Point Puer nearly three hundred boys. Port Arthur had become an important industrial center, the site of ship and shoe manufacturing, lime making, saw milling, stone quarrying, coal mining, brick and pottery manufacturing, leather tanning, and agricultural production.

An 1838 British House of Commons Select Committee on transportation severely criticized the arbitrariness of the assignment system. Consequently, convictism in Australia changed markedly. The committee proposed replacing the assignment system with a new approach known as the probation system. Committee members believed new convicts should complete various stages of incarceration and labor and eventually earn their freedom through good behavior. Under the new system, newly transported prisoners would initially spend a portion of their sentences working at a probation station. They then would be organized into gangs to work on roads, to clear land, and to provide agricultural labor in remote areas. To incorporate the probation system, housing for the convict gangs had to be constructed quickly.

Immediately following the adoption of the probation system in 1841, Van Diemen's Land was chosen as the location of several probation stations to be administered from Port Arthur. These stations were established at Saltwater River, the Coal Mines, Cascades, and Impression Bay. Additional stations were set up on the adjacent Forestier Peninsula. When criminal transport to New South Wales ceased after 1842, the number of convicts sent to Van Diemen's Land increased significantly.

By this time, Port Arthur had entered a significant period of development, marked by construction of a hospital (1842), flour mill and granary (1842–44), and houses for administrators. The start of construction of the Model Prison (later known as the Separate Prison) in 1848 signaled a shift in the settlement's approach to the administration of prisoners. The new approach was based on ideas from Britain and the United States at the end of the eighteenth century and the beginning of the nineteenth century that prisoners should be reformed through a regime of total silence and anonymity. In the 1820s, experiments in separate and silent incarceration were carried out in the United States, most notably at Eastern State Penitentiary in Philadelphia, Pennsylvania. The Philadelphia system was refined in Britain and later at Pentonville Prison in London, which served as the model for the design of the Separate Prison at Port Arthur. Among the system's more prominent components were its solitary cells used to isolate prisoners from the corrupting influences of other prisoners, and its "dumb cells," wherein problem inmates were deprived of light and sound. These prisoners were allowed outside their cells only once a day. They were forced to wear hoods to avoid being recognized by other convicts and felt slippers to muffle the sound of their footsteps. Other changes at the settlement during this period included the closure of the Point Puer boys' prison in 1849 and the conversion of the flour mill and granary into a penitentiary from 1854 to 1857.

The number of transported convicts to Van Diemen's Land decreased over the years, and the practice finally ceased in 1853. Three years later, Van Diemen's Land was renamed Tasmania. Although probation stations on the island gradually were shuttered as the last convicts passed through them, Port Arthur and its outstations continued to operate for some time. The settlement evolved into a welfare establishment, housing paupers, invalids, and the mentally ill, as evidenced by the construction of a Paupers' Mess in 1864 and the asylum in 1868. In 1871, control over Port Arthur was transferred from the British imperial to the Tasmanian State government. The cessation of imperial funds signaled the impending decay of Port Arthur's structures. Six years later, the Port Arthur penal colony was finally closed down. This event signaled the end of the free labor supply that Tasmania had relied on since the beginning of the nineteenth century. From 1830 to 1877, more than 12,000 sentences were served out at the settlement.

THE COMMUNITY, OR "CARNARVON," PERIOD[5]

After the end of convictism in Tasmania, the physical remains of the convict system were often referred to as "blots on the landscape." Reminders of the island's sordid past, they were routinely demolished and their materials reused. In 1877, the newly dubbed Tasman Peninsula was opened to private settlement, the former prison site was renamed Carnarvon, and the government attempted to auction the land lots and buildings to the public. At first, local residents resisted buying property at Carnarvon, but by the early 1880s a small community with a school and post office had been established. Some of the penal buildings were demolished and sold as salvage, and others were converted to serve new purposes. Carnarvon became the center of the Tasman Peninsula community, functioning as a gathering spot for sporting events and other functions. Tourism grew, benefiting the local economy.

Although the establishment of the Carnarvon community was slow to take hold, both local and outside interest in the former penal site had grown, nurtured by curiosity about its dark past. Many locals wished the remains of the penal settlement would crumble into oblivion; at the same time, they realized its potential for income. Thus began Carnarvon's evolution into a tourist town.

The first concerted effort to benefit financially from the site's tourist potential came in 1881—only four years after the closing of the penal colony—when the Whitehouse brothers launched a biweekly steamer service between Hobart and Norfolk Bay to transport visitors to Carnarvon. Two years later, the brothers opened the first hotel at the site of the former Commissariat Store. In 1893, the volunteer Tasmanian Tourist Association was formed to promote and develop Tasmania as a tourist destination. The association prepared and distributed leaflets about Carnarvon, focusing on the scenic qualities of the region. The site's sordid past was rarely mentioned, an omission that became a recurring pattern in the promotion of Carnarvon and the rest of Tasmania. The 1890s also witnessed the opening of the Port Arthur Museum in Hobart at the photography studio of J. W. Beattie, which exhibited numerous period photographs of the site as well as convict-era relics.

A series of fires in 1884, 1895, and 1897 destroyed and damaged several structures. Many of the remaining convict-era buildings were gutted, including the church, asylum, hospital, prison, and penitentiary. Concurrently, however, many new buildings were being constructed, as the community around Carnarvon grew.

In 1913, the Tasmanian Tourist Association submitted the first proposal to the Tasmanian State government for the management of the ruins at the site. Later that year, the government drafted the first set of recommendations for the site's management, including physical repairs to the church, and began to implement them the following year. This move marked the first effort of the Tasmanian State government to actively preserve a historic site.

The government then established the Scenery Preservation Board (SPB) in 1915 to manage parks and reserves across the state, including the Port Arthur site. The following year, the SPB laid the groundwork for the first formal protection of the ruins at Port Arthur through the creation of five reserves: the church, the penitentiary, the Model Prison, Point Puer, and Dead Island. The SPB was directly responsible for Port Arthur's management, but its secretary and field staff—all state employees—were based in Hobart. It is worth noting that the board's main function was to protect the site's natural environment and scenery rather than its cultural heritage.

These reserves were Australia's first gazetted historic sites—a measure of Port Arthur's long-standing importance in Australian culture. Gradually, the SPB acquired land at the site, appointed guides, and conducted a few small-scale preservation projects. Over the next two decades, Carnarvon was widely publicized, and its notoriety spread quickly. By 1925, the SPB, its financial resources running low, accepted the Tasman Municipal Council's offer to assume management of the reserves, subject to certain conditions set by the SPB.

In 1926, a remake of the 1908 film *For the Term of His Natural Life* was shot at the site, despite protests that it would result in negative publicity for Tasmania. Released in 1927, the film was a box-office success and had a significant impact in promoting tourism to the site. That same year, Carnarvon was renamed Port Arthur in an effort to help outsiders identify the site's convict history. The Port Arthur Tourist and Progress Association was also formed for the purpose of further developing the site into a tourist center.

The Tasman Municipal Council managed the site until 1938, when control was turned over to the Port Arthur and Eaglehawk Neck Board, a new group within the SPB, as a result of the Tasmanian State government's renewed financial support for the SPB. Over the next two years, the government acquired the Powder Magazine, the Government Cottage, the Commandant's House, and the cottage in which Irish political prisoner William Smith O'Brien was held in 1850. As before, the justification for purchasing the properties was their economic earning potential from tourism. However, during World War II, visitation to the site plunged. The SPB had its budget slashed at the same time it was assigned the task of managing sixteen new reserves. As a result, the buildings at Port Arthur were allowed to decay even further, and losses due to theft and vandalism only added to the toll.

Following the recommendations of a document known as the McGowan Plan, the Tasmanian State government took a bold step in 1946, purchasing the town of Port Arthur for the sum of £21,000. In a stark change from the past, the plan called for valuing the history and architecture of the site rather than focusing primarily on its economic value. Tourist visitation to the site grew rapidly once again after the end of World War II. Access to the site remained free, however, and the SPB had difficulty developing and managing the site with the small amounts of income generated from guide fees and building rentals. Nevertheless, some conservation and ground beautification projects moved forward. In the 1950s, the SPB managed to purchase the town hall / asylum building and leased it to the Tasman Municipal Council, which had been using the building as its chambers. Encountering licensing problems at Hotel Arthur, located in the former Medical Officer's House, the SPB approved construction of a new motel on the hill behind Civil Officers' Row overlooking the rear of the Model Prison and the whole site.

After years of delays, the motel finally opened in 1960. Two years later, the Tasman Peninsula Board, a new group within the SPB, assumed responsibility for site conservation after years of ineffective management.

In 1971, the Tasmanian State government dissolved the SPB and replaced it with the National Parks and Wildlife Service (NPWS), which then assumed responsibility for the management of Port Arthur. In 1973, the Tasman Municipal Council vacated the town hall / asylum building and moved to Nubeena. At that time, the NPWS had a policy that excluded residential use within the historic site. The council's relocation and conversion of the town hall to a visitor center was symbolic of the community's displacement from the historic site. As discussed in the following section, the 1970s and succeeding decades saw increased state investment in conservation and creation of more dedicated management regimes for Port Arthur as a heritage site. A regular ferry service began transporting tourists from the site to Dead Island. At the request of the ferry operator, the island's name was officially changed to the Isle of the Dead.[6]

In 1979, the Tasmanian State government announced the first substantial commitment of monies from the Commonwealth and the state (A$9 million over seven years) to conservation at the site in the form of the Port Arthur Conservation and Development Project (PACDP). This project, which continued until 1986, funded the extensive restoration of historic buildings, the stabilization of ruins, and the development of visitor-related facilities and infrastructure, and provided for the conservation and development of historic resources throughout the Tasman Peninsula as well. Based on input from Australia ICOMOS (International Council on Monuments and Sites), the NPWS revised and expanded the recognized significance of Port Arthur as a historic site to include the township period (roughly 1880 to 1930).[7] The PACDP was at the time the largest heritage conservation and development project undertaken in all of Australia. It also served as a significant training ground for Australian heritage professionals. This training component has produced a nationwide interest in the ongoing conservation work and protection of the cultural resources at Port Arthur.

As the seven-year project came to a close, the Tasmanian Minister of Arts, Heritage and Environment refused to provide further funding. The Tasmanian Parliament responded in 1987 by passing the *Port Arthur Historic Site Management Authority Act*. This act created and transferred authority over the site to the Port Arthur Historic

Site Management Authority (PAHSMA), a government business enterprise (GBE).

In late April of 1996, tragedy struck when a gunman killed thirty-five people at Port Arthur, twenty inside the Broad Arrow Café and fifteen in the immediate vicinity. Most of the victims were tourists, but many worked and lived at Port Arthur. The event proved to be traumatic to the site staff and the local community. In December of that year, the Broad Arrow Café was partially demolished.[8] The tragedy forged a new chapter in Port Arthur's, and Australia's, history by almost immediately catalyzing the passage and enactment of national gun control legislation in Australia. The Australian prime minister also tapped funds to build a new Visitor Center to replace the Broad Arrow Café.[9]

Shortly thereafter, the Tasmanian authorities commissioned the Doyle Inquiry into the management of Port Arthur. This investigation looked at the workings of PAHSMA since its establishment, including the PAHSMA Board's handling of the development of the new Visitor Center and parking area, its relations with employees in the aftermath of the tragedy at the café, and the conservation and maintenance of historic resources at the site.[10] The inquiry resulted in amendments to the *PAHSMA Act* as well as the reconstitution of the PAHSMA Board. With the 1998 change in the Tasmanian legislature from the Liberal Party to the Labor Party, the state government adopted policies encouraging tourism to improve the economy. This new stance also led to the appointment of high-profile individuals to the PAHSMA Board, including a former executive director of the Australian Heritage Commission (AHC).

In 2000, the Tasmanian premier announced that PAHSMA would receive A$10 million in funding for conservation over the ensuing five years. A condition of the funding was that PAHSMA would submit a new conservation plan to the AHC. The premier also announced that state and commonwealth funding would be provided for the creation of "The Convict Trail," which would reconnect the historic site at Port Arthur with the convict outstations throughout the rest of the Tasman Peninsula, including those at Eaglehawk Neck, Cascades, Impression Bay, Saltwater River, the Coal Mines, and Norfolk Bay. PAHSMA, the Tasman Municipal Council, and local businesses formed a partnership known as Port Arthur Region Marketing Ltd. (PARM) to market the Port Arthur region as a tourist destination. After much debate, a memorial garden also was created in the spring of 2000 at the site of the former Broad Arrow Café, which is now in ruins.[11]

The Management Context

COMMONWEALTH HERITAGE LEGISLATION, POLICY, AND ADMINISTRATION

Though the Port Arthur Historic Site is owned by the Tasmanian (state-level) government, not the commonwealth (federal- or national-level) government, this discussion of management and policy contexts begins with a look at relevant national-level factors.

Australia has separate commonwealth, state, and territory governments, which together compose a fairly decentralized system. Decisions and actions related to most heritage places and their land use are governed by state and local laws. Correspondingly, sites either are funded by state governments or generate revenue on their own. This important political context is a distinctly different one from sites funded by national governments.

The *Australian Heritage Commission Act* (1975) is the commonwealth's primary legislation dealing with the identification, protection, and presentation of cultural heritage places at the national level. This act established the AHC and the Register of the National Estate. The AHC is an independent authority operating under the jurisdiction of the commonwealth government's Environment and Heritage portfolio, and is responsible to the Minister for Environment and Heritage. The minister is authorized to direct the AHC or its chair to provide advice and to enter places into the Register of the National Estate. The AHC is not directly involved in heritage management as an owner and manager of sites.[12]

The purpose of the act is to place responsibility on commonwealth ministers and authorities to take into consideration National Estate values (as defined by the AHC) and professional recommendations concerning the potential effects of proposed actions.[13] It is generally not intended to give the AHC paramount protective authority over National Estate places.

The act defines the National Estate as follows: "The National Estate consists of those places, being components of the natural environment of Australia or the cultural environment of Australia, that have aesthetic, historic, scientific or social significance or other special value for future generations as well as for the present community."[14]

This register acts as a national list of places that reach a defined threshold of significance at a national, regional, or local level, against which proposed commonwealth actions and decisions can be checked for potentially harmful impacts.

AUSTRALIA ICOMOS

The Australian national committee of the International Council on Monuments and Sites (Australia ICOMOS), organized in 1976, promotes good practice in the conservation of cultural heritage places throughout the nation. It is a nongovernmental organization and is affiliated with the United Nations Educational, Scientific and Cultural Organization (UNESCO). Its members are professionals from a variety of fields involved in the practice of heritage conservation.

In 1979, Australia ICOMOS adopted the *Australia ICOMOS Charter for the Conservation of Places of Cultural Significance* (The Burra Charter). The Burra Charter, which was revised in 1988 and 1999, has provided guiding principles for cultural heritage conservation practice in Australia.[15] The Burra Charter consists of principles and procedures that ensure the conservation of a place's cultural significance. It sets out a logical process for articulating the cultural significance of a place and then deciding on conservation policies and measures to protect that significance. The process emphasizes consultation with a range of stakeholders, as well as transparency and clear documentation with regard to understanding and protecting significance. The charter's principles have been widely and voluntarily accepted and followed by heritage agencies and practitioners throughout the nation, and it has been perhaps the most influential document in moving cultural heritage practice in Australia toward a more explicitly values-based approach. As such, it has become a de facto policy.

TASMANIAN HERITAGE LEGISLATION, POLICY, AND ADMINISTRATION

State-level factors are perhaps the most important policy contexts shaping the management of Port Arthur. The first law in Tasmania to address the protection of heritage was the *Scenery Preservation Act* of 1915. This legislation established the Scenery Preservation Board, the first public authority established in the whole of Australia for the management of parks and reserves. Port Arthur was among the lands the SPB held and managed. In 1970, the *Scenery Preservation Act* was repealed through adoption of the *National Parks and Wildlife Act*. This act provided that land may be declared a conservation area to preserve features of historical, archaeological, or scientific interest, or to preserve or protect any Aboriginal relics on that land. The act also created the National Parks and Wildlife Service (of Tasmania) to manage both cultural and natural heritage within Tasmania, although emphasis was

clearly on the latter. NPWS was the managing agency for Port Arthur Historic Site from 1970 to 1987.[16]

In 1995, the Tasmanian Parliament passed the state's first comprehensive cultural heritage legislation, the *Historic Cultural Heritage Act*.[17] This law contains provisions for identification, assessment, protection, and conservation of places deemed to have "historic cultural heritage" significance. The act also provides for the creation of the Tasmanian Heritage Council (THC), which is responsible for advising the minister on issues concerning Tasmania's historic cultural heritage and on measures to conserve that heritage for present and future generations. The THC also works within the municipal land-use planning system to provide for the proper protection of Tasmania's historic cultural heritage (it has statutory review over projects involving properties on the Tasmanian Heritage Register), assists in "the promotion of tourism in respect of places of historic cultural heritage significance," and maintains proper records—and encourages others to maintain proper records—of places of historic cultural heritage significance.

The 1995 law also provided for the creation of the Tasmanian Heritage Register, kept by the THC. The criteria for being listed on the register are based on those used for the Register of the National Estate. Under the *Historic Cultural Heritage Act*, the minister may declare a site to be a heritage area if it is deemed to contain a place of historic cultural significance. Works impacting a registered place must be approved by the state Heritage Council. The council has the authority to set standards for approved works and to require professional supervision of the work. The act also provides for Heritage Agreements, which include provisions for monetary and technical assistance to the owner of the registered place. The council may approve damaging works only if it is satisfied that there are no prudent or feasible alternatives.[18]

LOCAL COUNCILS

In the state of Tasmania, land use and development are regulated by planning schemes, which are legally binding statutory documents. Local councils are responsible for preparing and administering these planning measures, which include provisions governing land use and development.[19]

The *Municipality of Tasman Planning Scheme* (1979), administered by the Tasman Municipal Council, governs use and development of land on the Tasman Peninsula. All lands within Port Arthur Historic Site are classified as a National Park/State Reserve reservation.

The approach to the site, as well as its viewshed, is also regulated by a complex system of zoning.[20]

When the Tasman Municipal Council receives planning applications regarding historic areas, it refers them to the Development Advisory Committee for Historic Areas. This committee is composed of representatives from the council, from the local community, and from the Tasmanian Department of Tourism, Parks, Heritage and the Arts. For projects and reviews on the Port Arthur reserve, the Tasman Municipal Council focuses on straightforward infrastructural matters, such as sewer and water provision, deferring to PAHSMA (and THC reviews of PAHSMA's activities) on most heritage-specific matters.[21]

PORT ARTHUR HISTORIC SITE
MANAGEMENT AUTHORITY

In 1987, the Tasmanian Parliament passed the *Port Arthur Historic Site Management Authority Act* establishing PAHSMA, which assumed management of the site from the Tasmanian Department of Lands, Parks and Wildlife. Since 1995, PAHSMA has been a GBE operating in part under the provisions of the *Government Business Enterprises Act* (1995). A semi-independent government authority with an annual budget provided by the Tasmanian State government, PAHSMA nevertheless operates under the auspices of an appointed board rather than the state. The Port Arthur site faced perpetual funding shortfalls, and through PAHSMA the Tasmanian government hoped to create an entity capable of independently generating its own revenue. One of the first steps was to start charging admission fees to the site.

The PAHSMA Board reports directly to the Tasmanian premier, and there is state representation on the board as well as state budget oversight and control. The *Port Arthur Historic Site Management Authority Act* defines the functions of PAHSMA as follows:

• Ensuring the preservation and maintenance of the Historic Site as an example of a major convict settlement and penal institution of the nineteenth century;

• Coordinating archaeological activities on the Historic Site;

• Promoting an understanding of the historical and archaeological importance of the Historic Site;

• Consistent with the management plan, promoting the Historic Site as a tourist destination;

• Providing adequate facilities for visitors' use;

• Using its best endeavors to secure financial assistance by way of grants, sponsorship, and other means, for the carrying out of its functions; and

• Conducting its affairs with a view to becoming a viable commercial enterprise. (A further act of parliament in 1989 amended this requirement to read: "Conducting its affairs with a view of becoming commercially viable."[22])

In the wake of the 1996 Port Arthur massacre, the management of PAHSMA came under close scrutiny and was found to be in serious need of reorganization. According to the Tasmanian State government's report of the Doyle Inquiry,[23] PAHSMA's economically self-sufficient mandate was at odds with the conservation values and goals recognized (in the 1985 plan and thereafter) as the foundation of the site's management. PAHSMA is not likely to generate sufficient income to fully fund its conservation activities; however, its tourism operation endeavors to generate a sustainable stream of income within its broader conservation, economic, and community objectives.

In 1997, PAHSMA convened the Port Arthur Heritage Advisory Panel (HAP), consisting of heritage experts. Its chair was a senior Canberra-based heritage consultant. The chair reported directly to the PAHSMA Board. HAP's role was to advise the board on matters regarding heritage at Port Arthur. The panel took a hands-on approach at the outset, initiating and drafting the brief for the site's current conservation plan, which was completed in 2000. As the PAHSMA Board acquired members with greater heritage expertise and hired more professionally trained heritage conservation individuals on its staff, the panel has stepped back and focused primarily on reviewing secondary plans and providing a broader level of advice to the conservation staff.[24]

Port Arthur Historic Site Facilities and Services

One of the most striking aspects of the Port Arthur site is the beauty of the surrounding landscape and its contrast to the horror of the events and penal-industrial system of nineteenth-century convictism. By some accounts, the beautiful landscape works against the conservation and interpretation of the main messages and related historic and social values of the site. However, this quality of the site was noted early on—indeed by the convicts themselves—and thus could be considered one of the important historic elements in the site's past. For some visitors, the serenity of the landscape makes it difficult to imagine the brutality of the convict period. For others, that same serenity actually helps them reflect on the site's past. Buildings such as the penitentiary and the Separate Prison—where the convict experience is immediately felt—have the most potential for conveying the historic experience.

MAJOR BUILDINGS AT PORT ARTHUR[25]

The Asylum

The asylum (1868) housed the mentally ill, older convicts, and ex-convicts—some transported from locations other than Port Arthur. From 1895 to 1973 it was home to the Carnarvon Town Board (later known as the Tasman Municipal Council). Today it houses a small museum and a cafeteria.

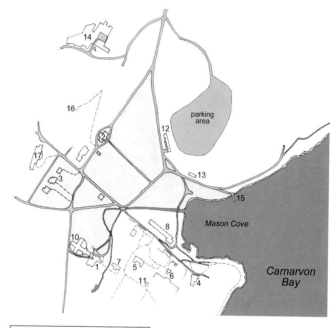

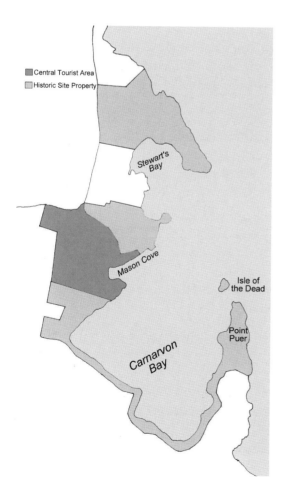

Figure 3.7. Map of the current property boundaries of the Port Arthur Historic Site and the central visitors' area.

Key:
1. Asylum
2. Church
3. Civil Officers' Row
4. Commandant's House
5. Hospital
6. Military Compound
7. Paupers' Mess
8. Penitentiary
9. Point Puer
10. Separate Prison
11. Smith O'Brien's Cottage
12. Visitor Center
13. Broad Arrow Café
14. Administrative Offices
15. Jetty
16. Overlook
17. Motel

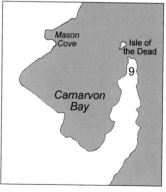

Figure 3.8. Map of the central visitors' area and its major structures and features. It should be noted that the motel (17) sits on a small, privately owned parcel of land adjoining the site.

The Church

The church, constructed in 1836–37, was gutted by a fire in 1884 that left only its walls standing. The ruins of the church are perhaps the most recognizable symbol of Port Arthur today.

Civil Officers' Row

The structures remaining along this row housed civilian officials at Port Arthur. These include the Accountant's House (1842); the Junior Medical Officer's House (1848); the Parsonage (1842–43), which housed the Anglican parson; and the Magistrate's and Surgeon's Houses (1847).

The Commandant's House

The Commandant's House (1833) was home to the highest-ranking official at Port Arthur. It was enlarged several times, extending up the hill. It served as the Carnarvon Hotel from 1885 to around 1904, and then as a guesthouse until the 1930s.

The Hospital

The hospital, which housed up to eighty patients, was opened in 1842. It served convicts and soldiers in separate wards. The structure was severely damaged by bushfires in the 1890s, leaving only the ruined façade and northwest wing standing today.

The Military Compound

Soldiers lived, ate, and engaged in recreation at the military compound. It included a parade ground for military exercises. The compound also housed civilian officers and military families. The soldiers' barracks were demolished after the settlement was closed, and other buildings in the precinct were lost in bushfires in the 1890s. One of the dominant structures today is the guard tower (1835). Other extant structures are Tower Cottage (1854), which housed married officers and their families, as well as some wall sections, two small turrets, and some foundations.

Paupers' Mess

Ex-convicts who were too old or infirm to work gathered at the Paupers' Mess, built in 1864. Only the walls of the building remain today.

The Penitentiary

This substantial four-story structure was built between 1842 and 1844 and originally served as a granary and flour mill for about a decade. In 1857, it was converted to a penitentiary and held prisoners until the closure of the Port Arthur convict settlement. It housed 136 convicts on its first two floors in separate cells and 348 in dormitory-style accommodations on the fourth floor. The third floor housed a library, mess, and Catholic chapel. Sometime

Figure 3.9. The asylum. Photo: Marta de la Torre

Figure 3.10. The ruins of the hospital lie behind those of the Paupers' Mess. Photo: Marta de la Torre

Figure 3.11. The exercise yards of the Separate Prison. The exercise yards lie in ruin today. Conservation and interpretation plans call for partial reconstruction of these yards. Photo: Marta de la Torre

after 1877, the structure was ravaged by fire and looted. Today, several of its main wall sections have been stabilized to prevent collapse, and it is visually the most dominant structure in the Mason Cove area.

Point Puer

Only scattered ruins remain of the former boys' prison at Point Puer (1834), located across the harbor from Mason Cove. Point Puer was created to separate boys ages eighteen and under from older prisoners. The boys' prison ceased operations in 1849.

The Separate Prison

The Separate Prison, originally called the Model Prison, was modeled after London's Pentonville Prison and was typical of a number of other prisons, such as Lincoln Castle, where sensory deprivation was used to break inmates' resistance to reform. The complex comprised two wings of parallel rows of cells, where prisoners were isolated for twenty-three hours per day and performed tasks such as shoemaking. It was first occupied in 1849.

Smith O'Brien's Cottage

This cottage, built to approximately its present configuration in 1846, was named for the Irish political prisoner held there in 1850. It also was once a stable and the military hospital.

Today, most visitors to the site arrive by car or bus via the Arthur Highway and park at the main parking area in front of the Visitor Center, where they may purchase an entry ticket valid for two days. The ticket includes access to the Interpretation Gallery in the Visitor Center; entry to the Port Arthur Museum located in the former asylum building, which has a small collection of convict artifacts; admittance to the site's more than 40 hectares (100 acres) of landscaped grounds and gardens, including more than thirty historic buildings, ruins, and restored period homes; and a guided introductory historical walking tour and harbor cruise. The twenty-minute cruise sails past the dockyards, the site of the Point Puer boys' prison, and the Isle of the Dead. Visitors' options include a thirty-minute tour to the Isle of the Dead and the ninety-minute Historic Ghost Tour. The latter consists of a lantern-lit walk at dusk around the site as tour guides tell of sightings, apparitions, and strange occurrences reported at Port Arthur from the convict period until the present.

Visitor activity is concentrated in the Mason Cove area, which was the center of development of the penal settlement and later the town of Carnarvon. A number of historic buildings, ruins, gardens, and memorials are situated in a verdant landscape occupying the basin surrounding the harbor and defined by small ridges. Visitors navigate through this area on paved roads and surfaced walkways. Use of the roads within Mason Cove is restricted to PAHSMA vehicles. One exception is vehicle access to the public jetty, where locals are permitted to drive through the site to fish. Recently, small electric vehicles have been introduced to enable visitors with mobility difficulties to access most areas of the site.

In the northwest part of the site, secluded from the tourist areas on a forested hilltop, is the administrative complex. It includes management offices, the Radcliffe Collection and Archaeological Store, nursery and forestry facilities, and the works yard. Most of the site's service infrastructure, such as sewers, storm drains, water supply, electricity supply, and telecommunications, is concealed.

Entry fees are listed below. Tours to the Isle of the Dead, as well as the evening ghost tours, are ticketed separately. Tickets may be purchased at the Visitor Center, by phone or fax, or at the Port Arthur Historic Site Web site.[26] Group and school-group bookings are also available. School-group tours last one to two hours. In addition to the standard tour, students get the chance to dress up in nineteenth-century-style clothing, learn how to use a semaphore, observe the site's historic architecture, and learn about early building materials and methods.

Entry ticket fees (valid for 2 days):[27]

A$ 22.00	Adult
17.50	Pensioner, senior, full-time student
10.00	Child (4 to 17 years)
48.00	Family (2 adults and up to 6 children)

Ghost tour fees:

A$ 14.00	Adult
8.60	Child
36.30	Family

Isle of the Dead tour fees:

A$ 6.60	Adult
5.50	Child
19.50	Family

The Port Arthur site is open from 9 A.M. to 5 P.M. The grounds and ruins are open from 8:30 A.M. until dusk. Visitor Center hours are 8:30 A.M. until the last ghost tour at night. Services at the Visitor Center include a desk of the Tasmanian Visitor Information Network, operated by Port Arthur Region Marketing Ltd. Staff at the desk provide information on accommodations, activities, and other services available in the region, including information on other convict-related heritage reserves in the area. They also assist visitors with booking reservations both inside and outside the region. Food, refreshments, and catering facilities at the site include Felons Restaurant and the Port Café in the Visitor Center, and the Museum Café located in the former asylum building. The Visitor Center also houses a gift shop that sells books, videos, souvenirs, and Tasmanian arts and crafts. Some items may be purchased online at Port Arthur's Web site.

In the Visitor Center, a model of the site as it was in the 1870s is used to orient visitors. The placement of the model allows visitors to gaze through a glass wall overlooking Mason Cove and the heart of the site. One of the main activities in the Interpretation Gallery is the "Lottery of Life," a game in which visitors are given a playing card containing the identity of a former prisoner at the penal settlement. As they move through the Interpretation Gallery, they trace the path of that convict from the United Kingdom to Tasmania.

Port Arthur maintains meeting facilities that accommodate groups from six to thirty-five. In addition, the site can host conferences by special arrangement that can include specialized tours, sunset harbor cruises, convict role-plays, and catering. Several structures in Mason Cove are used to house staff.

Facilities at the Mason Cove harbor area include a boat ramp and a public jetty completed in March 2002. The harbor is quite popular for recreational activities, such as scuba diving and boating.[28] A private company, which operates the Isle of the Dead tour, also offers cruises to Port Arthur on a catamaran.[29] One such excursion, the Hobart to Port Arthur Cruise, follows the same route that convicts traveled, and on the way allows passengers to catch glimpses of marine wildlife and observe dramatic coastlines, including those of Storm Bay, Cape Raoul, and Tasman Island. A second excursion is the Tasman Island Wilderness Cruise, which departs from Port Arthur to Tasman Island. Another private operator offers seaplane flights. The Flight to Freedom, offered in three different lengths, gives passengers aerial views of the site and the region's towering cliffs, blowholes, caves, and geologic formations.

Hobart to Port Arthur Cruise, including coach return:[30]

A$ 120.00	Adult
99.00	Pensioner
85.00	Child (ages 4 to 17)
350.00	Family (2 adults and up to 2 children)
68.00	(additional child)

Tasman Island Wilderness Cruise:

A$ 49.00	Adult
43.00	Pensioner
35.00	Child
145.00	Family (2 adults and up to 2 children)
30.00	(additional child)

Seaplane flights:

A$ 80/110/160	Adult
40/66/85	Child
200/280/395	Family (2 adults and up to 2 children)

During the period covered by the 2001 *PAHSMA Annual Report* (1 July 2000–30 June 2001), the number of daytime entries to the Port Arthur site was 203,600, and the Historic Ghost Tour took in more than 46,000 visitors.[31] Visitation is considerably higher in the summer months. Most visitors come from other states in Australia, rather than from within Tasmania.[32]

Understanding and Protecting the Values of the Site

Port Arthur has been recognized, in every way imaginable, as having a great deal of value as a heritage place. This section identifies the various assessments and statements of value[33] made for the Port Arthur site in conservation planning and policy documents. Secondarily, this section identifies values of the site that are implied in policies, but not explicitly assessed and described (for the most part, these implied values are the economic values generally excluded by the Burra Charter values framework).

Values Associated with Port Arthur Historic Site

For forty-seven years Port Arthur was a convict site, but it has been a historic site for more than a hundred years. Thus, some articulation of the site's values is traceable back to the 1870s. Until the contemporary era of heritage professionalization (starting in the 1970s), most articulation of heritage values was implicit and indirect, more discernible in actions and policies taken on the site than in deliberate pronouncements. Some of the major, earlier instances of value identification are outlined in the earlier section on Port Arthur's history as a heritage site. In this section, emphasis is placed on the most recent official statements of the value of Port Arthur.

HISTORICAL ARTICULATION OF VALUES

Immediately following the convict period, the site's values were seen to be both utilitarian (the establishment of a new township and village, a productive rural landscape rising from the remnants of the convict landscape) and social (symbolic). These social values were contradictory: negative, in feelings of shame about the convict period, leading to efforts to tear down, reuse, or otherwise erase traces from the convict era; and positive, in seeing the economic potential of the convict resources, leading to the first efforts to promote tourism on-site.

Aesthetic values, too, were clearly perceived, motivating visits from outsiders even before the penal colony was shut down in 1877. Visitors were drawn to the romantic aspect of the building ruins, the gardened English landscaping, and the remoteness of the Tasman Peninsula. Aesthetic values have remained among the most clearly articulated values throughout the management history of the post-penal colony site. Developing simultaneously was the realization that the Port Arthur story (as told and as symbolized and represented in some of its remaining structures) had value as an economic resource: to draw tourists. From the last third of the nineteenth century to the present, many projects have been undertaken to develop the Tasman Peninsula's tourism economy, often centered on Port Arthur as the main attraction.[34] Attempts to cultivate the site's economic values in effect kept alive the historic, aesthetic, and social values of the site (and also changed them in a way), which in the 1970s became the object of concerted site management and conservation efforts. Only since the 1940s has conservation of the historic, symbolic values of the site—what are these days grouped under the rubric of cultural significance—been the focus of site development.

Historic values relating to convictism were articulated selectively, until more-rigorous, professional efforts were made to document them in the 1979–86 Port Arthur Conservation and Development Project (PACDP). Certain historic values were explicitly recognized in the early twentieth century, in particular those that inspired popular narratives such as the novel and subsequent film *For the Term of His Natural Life*, as well as stories told by local tour guides. However, these values lacked a contextual understanding of the role of convictism in Tasmanian and Australian history and identity, and they did not have the base of scholarly research underlying the historic values recognized today. At the time, historic values were selected on the basis of what resonated with popular culture and consumerism (i.e., fascination with the horror of the penal system and stories of criminals) and what was marketable. Nevertheless, Port Arthur took its place in the popular national memory through the assertion of such consumer-oriented values.

A wide range of values has been associated with Port Arthur, both historically and in contemporary practice. In the hundred-plus years that Port Arthur has been a heritage site, negative values as well as positive values have been very much in evidence and have shaped site management quite clearly. Conflicts between positive and negative values, or among efforts to develop different positive values, have been recognized in the 2000 Conservation Plan and other policy, planning, and legislative documents.

Over time, and especially in the past several decades, the values articulated in Port Arthur's management plans have fluctuated in response to external conditions, particularly the amount of public funding provided by different government sources. When funding has been in abundance (as it was for PACDP from 1979 to 1986), plans and management focused more exclusively on cultural significance values. When public funding has been cut back substantially, emphasis shifted toward economic values, as management necessarily turned its focus on generating revenue from the site through tourism and associated commercial activity. This situation occurred in the early 1990s, when a surplus-generating expectation was imposed on PAHSMA, which responded with greater focus on earning revenue at the expense of conservation.

In the last few decades, the articulation of site values has become an explicit goal of heritage professionals, managers, and policy makers.[35] A number of plans have been formulated (described below), and it is important to realize the external forces shaping these plans. In each case, plans for Port Arthur were formulated not only according to the best practices of the conservation field at the time, but also to secure funding for the site's conservation from a particular government source. The abiding purpose of securing funding through political channels has shaped the goals, methods, and outcomes of the various plans.

The 1975 Draft Port Arthur Site Management Plan, formulated by the Tasmanian NPWS, was the first modern professional plan for the site. It called for fairly aggressive restoration and for the concentration of development (including infrastructure and residences for site staff in historic buildings) on the historic core around Mason Cove. This has been referred to as the Williamsburg approach, focusing on the convict period and removing buildings associated with the post-convict Carnarvon era. Little of this plan was implemented, though it marked one end of the development-conservation spectrum of management planning.

PACDP represented a major shift in attitude toward site values as well as a shift in the conservation philosophy that drove the treatment of values and fabric. Strongly influenced by national heritage organizations, the AHC, and Australia ICOMOS, this concentrated effort of heritage professionals from across Australia resulted in the recognition and management of a broader range of heritage values than solely those of convictism. The considerable on-site presence of PACDP personnel over several years built a strong cadre of professionals who, today, continue to hold a stake in the conservation of Port Arthur from their far-flung positions. The project relied on substantial government funding, which allowed focus on conservation, not development. No sustained emphasis was therefore paid to the future role and cultivation of commercial values.[36] When the temporary infusion of Tasmanian State funds ended, there were few resources, strategies, or expertise available to sustain the site and its conservation.

Through the development of a statement of significance, PACDP focused more explicitly on values. The project also brought about a shift in viewpoint, advocating strongly that both the convict and Carnarvon periods were important aspects of Port Arthur's heritage significance. Informal changes embodied in this new, heritage-professional approach were codified in a 1982 draft management plan, which in turn was the basis for the official 1985 Port Arthur Historic Site Management Plan.

The Burra Charter was the primary guide for the 1985 plan, but there was no explicit articulation of "values" or an explicit process of investigating different values. "The cultural significance of Port Arthur is readily apparent."[37] The planners codified the site values in a four-point statement of cultural significance:

i. The site's value as physical remains—of penal settlement and of Carnarvon

ii. The site's associations with the Australian convict system, and the role of the system in the development of Tasmania and the nation

iii. The townscape/landscape values [referring to aesthetic values]

iv. The "buildings and structures are important and scarce examples of their type."[38]

The "economic importance of tourism" to the state—speaking to the site's economic value—was noted on page 1 of the plan as a context of the study, but not as one of the values or variables per se.

"The principal direction of management for the Port Arthur Historic Site will be towards conservation of the fabric of the settlement to enable the historic realities of the Site to be accurately and continuously understood at many levels, while providing visitor and management requirements with minimal impact."[39] Based on these value priorities, arresting physical decay of the historic fabric was the paramount goal. Reconstruction, advocated strongly in the 1975 scheme, was to be undertaken only when it was the sole means of arresting decay.

The 1985 plan represented an important shift in philosophy to value the post-convict-era historical layers and fabric, capturing, as Brian Egloff puts it, "the transformation of a convict landscape into an Australian township."[40] This avowedly pro-conservation statement of site values (not to mention the clear "value the layers" conservation philosophy) swung the pendulum toward conservation of heritage values and has since been viewed as a benchmark. It proved difficult to execute this level of conservation activity, however, without the extended commitment of Tasmanian State funds on which the plan was premised.

After 1987, state funding for PACDP ceased, and the creation of PAHSMA was naturally accompanied by a swing of the pendulum back toward economic values and generating revenue through tourism. Site management turned its attention once again toward obtaining revenue and away from research and physical conservation of heritage resources. "Given the significant economic, social, and political impacts following the events at Port Arthur in April 1996, the Authority has recognised the need to bring forward plans concerning visitor facilities and services within the Site," including a sound-and-light show, a new Visitor Center, an access road, and parking areas.[41] This change in management strategy and prioritization of values was not accompanied by a new articulation of values. The 1996 amendments to the 1985 management plan (done by PAHSMA) codified these changes (many of which came before the writing of the 1996 amendments) but contained no statement (or restatement) of site values.

The shifts in values resulting from the changes in management between 1970 and 2000 set an important context for understanding the new, explicit articulation of values in the conservation planning process completed in 2000. The 2000 Conservation Plan kept in motion the swinging pendulum of values, bringing site management back from the revenue-centered model toward what the planners view as a clear prioritization of heritage values. In practice, of course, conservation activities must be balanced with the revenue-generating tourism activities on the site, and this important challenge defines many of the site management issues discussed below. In fact, several plans for Port Arthur formally recognized the need to work on both conservation and tourism, but different levels and sources of funding contributed to the swings between management regimes focused on conservation and those focused on tourism. Currently, the management of Port Arthur seems to have achieved a fairly balanced position, one that gives conservation a clear, but not exclusive, priority over commercial activities.

The current regime of value articulation and site management is the subject of the sections that follow, which focus on the 2000 Conservation Plan.

OFFICIAL STATEMENT OF SIGNIFICANCE

At present, the values of the Port Arthur site are referenced in the Tasmanian Heritage Register's statement of significance:

> Port Arthur Historic Site is of great historic cultural heritage value to Tasmania and Australia for its ability to demonstrate the convict period from 1830 to 1877 and its ability to demonstrate the subsequent developments of the site, particularly as a tourist attraction and the attempts to downplay the site's convict history. Port Arthur Historic Site is one of only three convict settlements in Tasmania. It is a rare and endangered place. Port Arthur Historic Site has considerable potential for scientific and social research to contribute to the understanding of Tasmania's history. Port Arthur is a prime example of the British colonial penal system, the evolution of that system during the 19th century, and the effects of that system in shaping Australian society. The site has the ability to demonstrate a high degree of technical and creative achievement for the time, including industrial enterprises such as shipbuilding, saw milling and brick making. Port Arthur Historic Site, as the most famous convict site in Australia, has a strong and special meaning for the Tasmanian as well as the Australian community as a place of secondary punishment in the convict system. The place also has a special meaning to Tasmanians for its association with the 1996 mass killing by Martin Bryant. The site has particular associations with Governor Arthur and political prisoner Smith O'Brien.[42]

As a statement of the site's values, the preceding quote touches on all four Burra Charter categories and speaks strongly to the values attributed to the different historic layers of the post-European-contact Port Arthur landscape: from the founding of the convict period to the 1996 tragedy, including the continual reinterpretation of the site's history in the decades between the end of the convict era and the beginning of the modern conservation era in the 1970s. This statement paves the way for assessing the values of the site by value-type or by historical layer.

THE 2000 CONSERVATION PLAN[43]

The values of the Port Arthur site have been articulated most exhaustively in the 2000 Conservation Plan, one of two main management documents formulated by PAHSMA, the other being the annual Corporate Plan. The Conservation Plan's detailed and rigorous breakdown of the site's values was generated according to research and the multiple significance criteria applicable to the site (from Tasmanian State legislation and from the AHC).[44] Broadly, the values are articulated according to the Burra Charter categories of aesthetic, historic, scientific, and social value, with equivalent categories added for Aboriginal and World Heritage values. The values are summarized below.[45]

Aesthetic Values:
• A beautiful and picturesque landscape, combining buildings and landscape.
• Harbor location and water-boundedness of the landscape is part of the valued aesthetic (also true of other places of secondary punishment), so this aspect of aesthetic value relates closely to historic (convict) values.
• Visual "landmark qualities" as represented by the church ruins, the penitentiary ruins, and the views to Point Puer and Isle of the Dead.
• Individual buildings and elements of the English/bush landscaping each convey particular aesthetic values (for example, Georgian colonial style of the Royal Engineers, use of local materials, or lack of craftsmanship in a building's convict labor).

Historic Values:
• Port Arthur (PA) is a premier convict site relating to the nation's convict history; this takes precedent over other historic values.
• Drawing directly on this, several subvalues are identified, such as the historic value of the Separate Prison

(vis-à-vis penal history and changes in confinement philosophy) and the different parts of the penal system spread across the Tasman Peninsula (the probation stations).
• The combination of the picturesque landscape and the paradoxical representation of convict history in this setting is specifically called out as a value.
• PA is "a complex layered cultural landscape."
• On an international scale, PA is an important part of the British penal/colonization/forced-labor system (this relates to the World Heritage nomination; see below).
• PA is an early and leading example of a heritage-based tourist destination.
• PA illustrates changing approaches to heritage conservation philosophy and practice (both in management and in conservation/restoration work).
• PA's settlement was an important event in the history of Tasmania.
• As part of the penal system, PA was also an industrial complex.
• The April 1996 tragedy added "an additional layer of tragic significance" to the site; it is now associated with national gun laws.
• PA is evidence of the probation system, and later as a welfare institution (lunatics, the poor, etc.).
• After 1877 (especially the post-1894 renaming), Port Arthur/Carnarvon has historic value as a typical Tasmanian local community or small township.

Scientific Values:
• Above- and below-ground historical and maritime resources have "exceptional research potential" to yield insight into the convict experience; this extends to the cultural landscape itself, individual structures, and archival collections.
• Aboriginal sites are separately acknowledged as having research value.
• Natural resources of the site "are also an important scientific research resource."
• These scientific values refer to PA site and the outliers (e.g., Point Puer).
• The combination of "oral tradition [including family links], documentary evidence, collections, structures, engineering relics, archaeological features and landscape at Port Arthur have unparalleled potential for community education."

Social Values:
- PA is a symbol of the convict past of Australia.
- PA is a symbol of Tasmania's role in Australian history.
- PA is a foundation for Tasmanians' self-identity.
- PA is a marker of family history for some (especially those cultivating links to convictism) and of Anglo-Celtic heritage for a larger group.
- "PA is a significant local landmark" and stands as an image of the Tasman Peninsula area as a whole.
- "The Arcadian qualities of the Port Arthur landscape are of significance to generations of Tasmanians and other visitors."
- PA "holds an important place in the history of modern heritage conservation in Australia."
- The 1996 tragedy has made PA a poignant political symbol at a national level [and a poignant marker of grief for those locally and those directly associated with the tragedy].
- PA is of contemporary social significance to Tasmanian Aboriginal people.
- PA represents the identity of the Tasman Peninsula community; this strong association is positive (a reason to recognize and celebrate community life) and negative (signaling the estrangement that has been felt from the site itself).
- The strong community attachment to PA is today "underscored" by the economic importance of the historic site for the peninsula.
- PA is a place of enjoyment, reflection, and catharsis with regard to convictism.

Aboriginal Values:
- Associational values
  - General associational value with Aboriginals due to their occupation of the Tasman Peninsula.
  - The value of some Aboriginal sites on the peninsula, though it is now a highly modified landscape.
  - Negative value, to Aboriginals, owing to their dislocation from this place.
  - Weak associational values in the post-European era.
- Social values (meanings felt by the contemporary Aboriginal community)
  - Existence of traditional Aboriginal resources (though there apparently is little physical evidence of such).
  - The Aboriginality of the area has been crushed by the post-invasion convict era.

- Scientific, educational, and other values (meanings for the non-Aboriginal community)
  - (Potential) scientific value
  - As historic value, Aboriginal values help demonstrate that the significance of PA goes beyond the convict era.

World Heritage Values:[46]
- PA is one of eight sites included in the thematic nomination that has been drafted (but not forwarded) for Australian Convict Sites.[47]
- The values identified to support the World Heritage Convention criteria are in accord with the other values identified above, though they focus mostly on historic values and ignore values and significance for the local communities, a real source of complexity and challenge in managing PA.

The Burra Charter methodology was employed to articulate, research, and assess these values, and they are the result of a deliberate process of investigation, research, consultation, and synthesis. The value categories necessarily overlap (e.g., some historic values also appear under Aboriginal values and World Heritage values), as it is impossible to fully separate one kind of site value from all others. Seeing the Conservation Plan as the product of Burra Charter methodology is important for understanding the particular concept of "social values" used (to encompass all the different senses of place attachment, historical and contemporary) and the absence of "economic values," which are largely excluded from considerations of cultural significance.[48] In keeping with Burra methodology, the articulation of site values is centered on the four primary types: historic, aesthetic, social, and scientific.

Value articulation is also organized according to stakeholder communities: the mainland Australian community, the Tasmanian community, the Tasmanian Aboriginal community, the local Tasman Peninsula community, the tragedy community, and the heritage community. This effort to look at values from multiple perspectives maximizes the articulation of the site's values.

Based on the values articulated in the Conservation Plan, Port Arthur's current statement of significance—PAHSMA's benchmark policy statement on cultural values—reads as follows:[49]

STATEMENT OF SIGNIFICANCE

Port Arthur Historic Site is an outstanding convict place—an important foundation for Australia's sense of identity.

Port Arthur is significant in a World context because it exemplifies a worldwide process of colonial settlement using labour provided by forced migration. The place symbolises an expansionist period of European history and British strategic objectives. It displays key aspects of penal philosophy and the social structure that produced it.
In conjunction with other Australian Convict places, Port Arthur demonstrates aspects of the British penal system, in particular, concepts of religious instruction, secondary punishment and segregation as adopted in Australia. It is a focal point for understanding the convict history and convict-period operation of the Tasman Peninsula. The place also represents changing community attitudes to the notion of convict heritage.

At Port Arthur, a sense of scenic beauty is heightened by the paradox of a grim past. Topography and layers of history reflected in indigenous and introduced plantings and an array of structures combine in an evocative and picturesque cultural landscape. The Arcadian qualities of this landscape contrast with its historical role as an industrial penal site. The form and location of built elements display deliberate design and arrangement, reflecting the initial order and hierarchy of Port Arthur's civil, military and penal settlement and subsequent post-convict history. The place retains a high degree of integrity and authenticity.

Port Arthur is an important element in Australian identity, invoking intense and, at times, conflicting feelings.
The place has traditionally been an important centre of economic activity and work in the Tasman Peninsula and Tasmania—initially as a convict workplace, later a town and premier tourist destination.

For the Tasman Peninsula community, Port Arthur has strong and enduring associations and meanings as a landmark and as the symbolic centre of the community.

Port Arthur's physical evidence, both above and below ground, has exceptional scientific research potential arising from the extensive resource itself, the integrity of archaeological deposits and the ability of material culture to provide valuable insight into the convict experience. In combination, the oral tradition, documentary evidence, collections, structures, archaeological features and landscape at Port Arthur have great potential for research and community education. Port Arthur is a landmark place in the history and

[continued on page 137]

The Broad Arrow Café and the 1996 Tragedy

In April 1996, a gunman entered the Broad Arrow Café in Port Arthur and opened fire, killing twenty people. After firing more shots outdoors in the parking area, he got into his car and continued his killing spree. The tragic event added another layer to the dark history of Port Arthur and presented a number of challenges for site managers.

From the perspective of several distinct stakeholder groups, the heart-wrenching events associated with the Port Arthur massacre have had a marked effect on the values of the site. In the words of one interviewee, the tragedy has "drawn a line" in the history of the site, between what came before and what comes afterward.[1] The incident has made Port Arthur both a poignant contemporary political symbol and a symbol of grief for locals and others directly associated with the tragedy.

The shooting impacted not only the café and its staff (some of whom were among the victims) but also the entire site by recasting the image of Port Arthur in the public mind. Opinions differ as to how the values associated with the 1996 tragedy relate to the core cultural values of Port Arthur (those related to convictism). Although the tragedy is mentioned in the Conservation Plan's statement of significance, the plan's main focus is on convictism. The crime at the Broad Arrow added an ironic note to the cultural values that were already driving the convictism theme. For some visitors, the shooting overshadowed convictism and its industrial, penal, and landscape stories. The 1996 tragedy is thus deliberately not promoted to visitors.

Different groups held different opinions about how the café site should be handled. Some wanted all evidence of the event destroyed. Indeed, the café was partially demolished as an act of mourning. Others sought to mark the site: memorials appeared soon afterward. The different social values of the café, corresponding to different communities / stakeholder groups, were a source of real conflict.

Site managers tried to ensure that the range of values was fully researched and that no group's values were excluded. In deciding what ultimately would happen to the physical remains of the café site, a careful study of the social values associated with the tragedy and the site was undertaken.[2] The study followed a methodology developed specifically for understanding the different social values ascribed to heritage sites, and which depended on identifying and interviewing the broad range of stakeholder groups. The study's findings illuminated what course of action to take. By using a deliberate and detailed process of consultation to deal with an emotionally charged situation, the study was praised as a successful effort to document and address stakeholders' values.

The social-value study discerned national values, some of which, though, were expressed uniquely by local communities (e.g., the mourning of those directly affected by the event). These local and national values, however, were conflicted as much as they were related. The negative site values held by those in mourning sensibly led to the partial destruction of site fabric—an attempt to remove traces of the horrible events. Those focused on a more long-term and more positive view of site values (e.g., that the Port Arthur tragedy represented a turning point in gun control laws, or that the Port Arthur tragedy represented an additional layer of history) wished to preserve the remains as a way of preserving the positive social value.

In the context of this case study, a number of conflicts over values and fabric can be identified:

- Different stakeholders, some representing local constituencies (relatives of victims, local residents, Port Arthur staff) and others representing more national (nonlocal) constituencies, construed the values of the café differently.

- Finding value in a building (or, ascribing values to fabric) does not always lead to a policy of conservation. In some instances, negative values suggest destruction or neglect of the fabric as the preferred course of action.

- Divergent values held by different groups and individuals pointed to different ways to handle the fabric of the café: negative social values led to a desire to destroy the physical remains; positive social values (e.g., the institution of national gun control legislation) suggested conserving the physical remains of the tragedy site.

The resolution of these conflicting values— a painful process that involved a number of stakeholder groups and a site management team in transition—was multifarious. Some parts of the site were conserved in accord with each set of values. A new memorial was installed (a cross made of huon pine, initially intended as a temporary marker); the demolition of the café, begun immediately after the tragedy, was halted; and the remaining shell of

Port Arthur Memorial Garden. Demolition of the café was started shortly after the 1996 tragedy but was halted by court order. The structure remained in ruins until it was reconstructed as a memorial. The memorial, however, is not given prominence in the interpretation schemes of Port Arthur and serves primarily as a quiet testimony to the senseless killing of staff and visitors. Photo: Marta de la Torre

the building was preserved in a state of stripped-down ruins, cleared of any physical evidence of the shooting, yet clearly marking the actual site as a literal memorial.

By putting Port Arthur on the front page nationally and internationally, the tragedy immediately heightened the contemporary social values of Port Arthur, and it likely brought more visitors too. In an economic sense, there is another connection between the tragedy and site values: post-tragedy government funding led to the debate about the siting and form of the Visitor Center, which in turn helped stimulate the design and commissioning of the Conservation Plan and the new articulation of values and values-based planning for the whole site (though a revised conservation plan had already been in the works).

Over time, it is likely—perhaps inevitable— that the values associated with the café, and the strength with which they are felt, will change. In the years since the stabilization of the café ruins and the creation of memorials, site managers have placed an interpretive marker at the site and published a modest brochure in response to visitor inquiries. Such interpretation would have seemed inappropriate in the immediate aftermath of the tragedy, when no one wished to draw attention to the site. As local memory becomes less immediate and locals deal with their grief, the national memory will likely become predominant, and the Port Arthur tragedy will likely take on value

as another layer of national significance—as opposed to the extraordinary, conflicted, and particularly local values of the place that were felt immediately after.

Notes

1. Scott 1997 is a powerful and detailed account of the tragedy and its effects on local citizens and those associated with Port Arthur.

2. Jane Lennon and Associates 1998; Johnston 1992.

development of Australian heritage conservation philosophy and practice.

Port Arthur and the Tasman Peninsula have contemporary significance for Tasmanian Aboriginal people, arising from the perceived intactness of the natural landscape and the presence of pre-contact Aboriginal sites that connects the present-day Aboriginal community to the pre-contact past.

The events of 28 April 1996 make Port Arthur a symbol of continuing tragedy, suffering and gun law reform for all Australians.

Port Arthur is a nationally-significant symbol of Australia's convict past, a highly revered icon that symbolically represents Tasmania's place in Australian history.

The statement of significance touches on all categories of value articulated in the planning process and begins to prioritize them simply by ordering the brief narrative. It also succeeds in interpreting site values in a number of ways: by capturing the different cultural values (aspects of cultural significance) identified in the Burra process and suggesting the character of the Port Arthur landscape as thickly layered with historic values; by introducing economic values into the mix; by referring to various stakeholder communities that hold these values; and by suggesting the regional nature of Port Arthur's significance—it is the peninsular landscape, not just the Mason Cove core, that holds significance.

Along with the Conservation Plan, other documents look at the values of Port Arthur from perspectives other than those involved in the overall, conservation-focused plans.

BROAD ARROW CAFÉ CONSERVATION STUDY

The Broad Arrow Café Conservation Study[50] was commissioned to research, articulate, and assess the heritage values associated with the April 1996 tragedy. This study, which preceded the 2000 Conservation Plan concerning the entire Port Arthur Historic Site, elicited the values of the café site according to established Australian social-value methodology.[51]

The following excerpts from the statement of significance resulting from the Broad Arrow Café study speak to the values identified specifically for this part of the Port Arthur site in the wake of the tragedy. Further detail and discussion can be found in the accompanying sidebar (see p. 134). Most significantly, the study found strong negative and positive social values associated with the café.

The Café has nation-wide social value because of its connection with the tragedy.

• For some communities this value is related to deceased friends and relatives;

• for others it is related to the nature of the tragedy, evoking both negative and positive responses;

• for others such as historians, writers and cultural tourists, it is part of the ongoing history of the site.

The study also found minor or negligible aesthetic and scientific values associated with the Café. The historic values were seen to be significant in two senses. First, the 1996 tragedy added another layer to the history of the site, though the relationship between the 1996 tragedy and the tragic aspects of convictism is the subject of some uncertainty. Second, many observers believe the Broad Arrow Café as tragedy site will acquire greater historic value in subsequent years in association with the shift in national gun laws and attitudes, and may even eclipse the locally held negative social values that were so strong in the tragedy's immediate aftermath.

UNIVERSITY OF TASMANIA
ECONOMIC IMPACT STUDY

The economic impact study commissioned by PAHSMA and completed in 1999 is the most direct and deliberate analysis and statement of the site's economic values.[52] The study included dollar estimates of the contributions of Port Arthur Historic Site operations to the state economy and an exploration of how the heritage values of the site (construed more broadly but still in economists' terms) could be described and estimated. The first aspect of the study showed that Port Arthur clearly has a positive economic impact on the state economy, yielding positive multiplier effects as gauged through job creation, PAHSMA expenditures, and tourism outlays in connection with visits to the site.

As part of the second aspect of the study, a distinction was drawn between direct-use values of the site (the impacts of which are fairly straightforward to measure economically, as was done in the first part of the study) and indirect "preservation values," such as bequest value and existence value, which are more difficult to measure or estimate and are therefore only outlined in the document. These kinds of economic value are briefly described in the report but are not estimated or analyzed in detail.[53]

The report concludes that the "large increases in conservation expenditures on the Port Arthur site can be justified on economic grounds"—that is, on the basis of economic impacts that could be measured within the limits of the study. It also recommended that "a full scale heritage valuation" be completed in which the full range of economic values can be analyzed. Ultimately, the goal of this study was to articulate and analyze the economic values of the heritage site in their own right, employing the various quantitative analytics "native" to the economics field.

SUMMARY OF THE VALUES ASSOCIATED
WITH PORT ARTHUR

Whether one looks at the values that have been articulated for the Port Arthur site, or at recent planning and policy documents, it is clear that both cultural and economic values have been recognized and that both have formed the basis for decision making over time.

In keeping with the Burra Charter model, cultural and economic values are treated differently and separately. Cultural values have been analyzed and articulated most explicitly, and to one extent or another have remained at the center of all discussions of Port Arthur's value as a place. Economic values have been influential in shaping decisions and determining the management for the site, but they have been articulated and analyzed more implicitly, as they are considered to be derived values and not inherent conservation values.

Cultural values center on the remains of the convict period, but over the past several decades conservation philosophy has shifted to emphasize the value of other historic periods of the site—the Carnarvon period, in particular—and set up management schemes in which convict-period values are not permitted to obscure or erase these other cultural values.

Economic values have long been part of Port Arthur's identification and management as a historic site. This is made abundantly clear in David Young's *Making Crime Pay*[54] and in the summary history of Port Arthur in the earlier part of this case study, and remains so today. The tourism development activities initiated over the past hundred-plus years were never based on a deliberate assessment of economic values and potentials. Nevertheless, these activities have been formative factors in the management of the site as well as in subsequent appraisals of the site's values, which now include the history of these tourism activities.[55]

The next section explores how the articulated site values have been incorporated into management policies for Port Arthur. It is followed by a discussion of the implications of management decisions on site values and vice versa.

How Management Policies and Strategies Take Values into Consideration

From the foregoing, it is clear that Port Arthur has a great depth and breadth of values and that the Conservation Plan and other documents articulate values in support of the widely agreed-upon cultural significance of the site. Further, it is evident, implicitly and explicitly, that the economic values of Port Arthur are an important factor in its management. In exploring how these values are reflected in the current management strategies for the site, some patterns emerge:

• First, cultural significance values are clearly articulated and addressed in PAHSMA's Conservation Plan and have become the basis for conservation policy at a general level.

• Second, both cultural and economic values strongly shape the management strategies and decisions regarding the site.

• Third, in accordance with the site's Ministerial Charter and the Conservation Plan, conservation has priority over other activities and issues in the management of the site.

• Fourth, economic values are assessed or analyzed in the course of day-to-day management of the site, whereas cultural values are assessed and analyzed as part of the deliberate forward-planning scheme represented in the Conservation Plan.

• Fifth, the decisions of PAHSMA's executive and board are the vehicle for integrating the various cultural and economic values. The board oversees the preparation of the Corporate Plan each year. It is a formal document endorsed by the government and the vehicle for carrying out on a yearly basis Conservation Plan and board policies and priorities relating to the site as well as various government obligations. However, the board also makes significant conservation and management decisions more informally, based on the need to integrate the various cultural and economic values on a day-to-day basis.[56]

This section describes how site values are reflected in policies by analyzing the main site management documents. Such an analysis seems appropriate given that the overall management of the site has been organized by PAHSMA around the processes that have generated these plans—primarily the Conservation Plan and Corporate Plan. These two instruments, along with

the factors stemming from the institutional and regulatory settings of PAHSMA, overwhelmingly constitute the formal management strategies.[57]

Our interviews revealed the opinion of many on site that these older plans are not relevant to the present management of the site. They were originally required for statutory reasons and crafted to attract funding as well as ensure conservation. Although they do not guide day-to-day, site-by-site decisions today, the 1985 plan in particular has shaped the development of site values and the current management by adjusting the balance between cultivating cultural and economic values. The plan also helped shaped the management of values today by, for instance, valorizing Carnarvon-era resources, ensuring conservation of the remaining heritage resources, and preventing development and overzealous reconstruction at the center of the site.

THE 1985 AND 1996 MANAGEMENT PLANS

Together, the 1985, 1996, and 2000 plans reflect the pendulum swings management has taken in order to balance conservation and the access/tourism activities required to operate the site (in other words, balancing the dual goals of conserving cultural significance and funding operations). The main factor in determining which way the pendulum swings has been the availability of external government funding.

The comprehensive 1985 Management Plan was written near the end of the seven-year PACDP, which used A$9 million of state and national funds to carry out a variety of conservation works. The plan was prepared in accord with the Burra Charter and identified as management objectives conservation of fabric and cultural significance, as well as tourism and ancillary commercial development. Cultural significance centered on the convict system as the basic vector of European settlement in Tasmania. Different layers of history were described and acknowledged—convict, Carnarvon, modern—but as the plan stated, "[T]he potential of Port Arthur as an authentic historic site" lies with convictism.[58]

The cultural significance of Port Arthur was defined in the 1985 plan as "readily apparent":[59]

(i)   because the site is a major physical demonstration of the lives, customs, processes and functions of an early Australian penal settlement, and its transformation into the township of Carnarvon, which is of particular interest and in danger of being lost.

(ii) because of the inherent associations of the site with the Australian convict system, and the role this system played in the economic, social and cultural development of the state of Tasmania in particular, and the nation in general.

(iii) because of the townscape and landscape values of the Site, and in particular the degree of unity of materials, form and scale, and the contribution of the setting in the landscape.

(iv) because many of the buildings and structures within the site are important and scarce examples of their type.

Management policies in the 1985 plan recognize the need to achieve a balance between "the dual requirements of the site with respect to conservation and tourism." Although the national and Tasmanian significance of the convict/penal site "as an historical document" is given priority, "[a]t the same time, the Historic Site is one of the principal tourist destinations in Tasmania, and as such is of vital importance to the State's economy. It is imperative therefore that the enjoyment and interest of visitors to the Site be a principal concern of management to be balanced with the need to curate the Historic site."[60] The policies implementing this strategy, however, continued in the direction of conservation and did not result in strong revenue-generating measures. The eleven policies almost entirely cover guidance of conservation, with little attention paid to tourism development or access. Also included is a statement about the exclusion of community facilities from the site, apparently prioritizing the conservation of the core convict/penal landscape, and tourist access to it, over the social values embodied in community use of the site, which had grown over time.

Safely focused on conservation of cultural significance given the steady stream of government funds, the 1985 plan was essentially a continuance of the PACDP years. As PACDP funds ceased and Port Arthur strived to become more economically self-sufficient, that practice gave way to years of reorientation toward economic values and efforts to generate revenue. This marked a turning point in how management policies took values into consideration.

The 1996 Management Plan reflected this shift in values. Not a full plan, but rather an eighteen-page set of amendments to the 1985 Management Plan, the 1996 plan did not rearticulate values but revised and changed some of the policies set in 1985. "The Authority finance program is reducing its dependence on government and the general limited availability of funds from that source. . . . the overall impact [of this shift] can be mitigated through

[continued on page 144]

The Separate Prison

The Separate Prison is one of the most valued structures at Port Arthur. It is relatively intact, highly imageable, and directly related to some of the most dramatic chapters in the history of Tasmanian convictism. The conservation strategy for the prison is of great interest. As of this writing, the recommendations currently being considered include a combination of preservation, repair, and reconstruction of some elements, as well as correcting some past reconstructions. The plan provides a glimpse into how the general conservation policies of the Conservation Plan are being integrated and applied to the details of a single building—particularly, how significance and values are related to specific fabric interventions.[1]

The 1840s shift in incarceration philosophy represented by the Separate Prison—separation and isolation—is historically significant and resonates today.[2] Through the many decades of Port Arthur's life as a tourist site, the Separate Prison has been the most visited. The building has endured several substantial episodes of construction, conservation, reconstruction, destruction, and reuse. Much of the fabric of the prison is in serious need of repair; overall the building is in poor condition and does not present an authentic or contemplative experience for visitors.

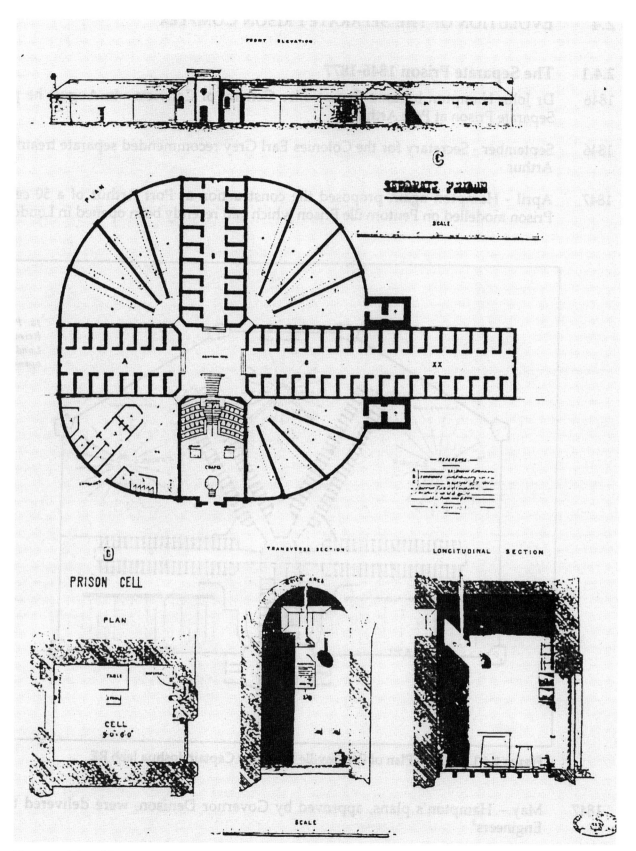

The original plan of the Separate Prison, showing individual cells, exercise yards, and chapel. (Source: 2002 Conservation Plan.) Reproduced with permission of the Archives Office of Tasmania, PWD 266/1822.

The planning process behind the 2000 Conservation Plan provides guidance for the specific treatment of particular areas of conservation activity through secondary plans and specific conservation projects formalized in "individual element plans," master plans, and projects. The Separate Prison Project Report, which is in the draft stage, is a full-scale conservation plan for the building. The plan was undertaken by outside consultants (Design 5 Architects) and has been reviewed by the Heritage Advisory Panel and staff of the Conservation Department. Prior to implementation of the project, the plan and the proposed scope of work must be approved by the Tasmanian Heritage Council.

The Separate Prison Project Report is being developed as a derivative of the Conservation Plan and fleshes out the overall site values and significance statements articulated in the Conservation Plan. The Separate Prison Project Report includes documentation, historical research, and condition assessment of the structure. Issues of interpretation and visitor access are carefully integrated with decisions on the care of fabric; the plan focuses on making an interpretable building, not merely on conserving the fabric.

The planned treatment of some major building elements includes the following:

- Some walls that historically separated exercise yards will be reconstructed.
- The main entrance, where convicts historically entered the building, was incorrectly reconstructed from the 1930s through the 1950s (the opening faced north whereas it originally faced south) and will be reconstructed again.
- Some cell interiors and doors will be reconstructed for the sake of interpretation (no original doors are extant).

The aesthetic impact and historical narratives of the Separate Prison—the power of being in a stark setting, representing a notorious turn in incarceration philosophy—are compelling. Creating an "immersion" experience through which this can be conveyed to visitors is the driving force behind the decisions for selective reconstructions—which, as the Burra Charter and Conservation Plan policies clearly state, is acceptable only under the most stringent conditions. For instance, the principles guiding specific decisions on the prison's fabric state, "It is essential to at least partly reinstate the historical 'opacity' of the building, whereby an outsider could not see in, and an inmate could not see beyond his controlled space." Meanwhile, however, the overall policies of the Conservation Plan set a context for these decisions: "Evidence of later (e.g., post-convict) uses of the building will be conserved and interpreted, but will not be emphasized."[3]

The Separate Prison plan strikes a balance between conservation of cultural values and creating an interesting visitor attraction by reconstructing some lost building elements, removing some layers of previous restoration, and stabilizing other fabric elements. The decisions seem motivated by a clear understanding of the central role this structure should play in the realization and management of the site's cultural significance values (particularly the convictism themes), as well as the financial imperative realized by attracting visitors.

The proposals follow the recommendations for restoration and reconstruction set out in the Conservation Plan. Two types of building elements are slated for reconstruction: some elements of the building made incomplete over time are being restored (the exercise yards and cell interiors); elements incorrectly reconstructed in the past will be demolished and reconstructed. In both cases, this work will enhance the interpretive value of the building through "reinstatement of those functional and spatial relationships which have been missing since closure of the prison."[4] All reconstruction would be based on thorough research and documentation,[5] and all original (pre-1877) material would be kept.

The interiors of the prison's chapel wing are largely a reconstruction. The individual stalls, pulpits, ceiling, and other elements were recon-

structed—too speculatively—in the 1950s. Now known to be inaccurate, removal and reconstruction of these elements has been contemplated but is not currently planned. The benefit of vivid interpretation seems to be the driving force behind these interventions. Decisions for reconstructing elements fall within the boundaries of sound conservation practice (reconstructing only when there is evidence of the original, and/or where the existing reconstruction is inaccurate or misleading) and do not sacrifice any fabric associated with key aspects of cultural significance.

Clearly, the plan's specific decisions about building fabric are intended to directly shape the historic values represented by the building and communicated to visitors. The elements to be reconstructed are judged to be critical in conveying the main interpretive themes of convictism. A secondary concern involves retaining enough fabric to interpret the conservation process itself, though this is secondary to enhancing the core cultural significance values. The plan also pays close attention to visitor access, paving the way for greater and equitable visitation to the building and thus greater realization of its economic value within the framework of conservation.

Notes

1. As of this writing, the plan policies were not complete, though research and documentation phases of the plan are finished.

2. For a detailed description of the philosophy behind the Separate Prison and convict life in this structure, see page 119.

3. Port Arthur Historic Site Management Authority n.d.(c).

4. Design 5—Architects Pty. Ltd. 2001, 116.

5. One of the difficulties encountered was the dearth of documentation available on the major reconstruction and repair projects carried out over the decades.

success in having Port Arthur perceived as the primary desirable destination in the State and as a value-for-money attraction. A higher level of visitor services, enhanced visitor programs, expanded evening programs and a continued commitment towards conservation works will assist the Authority in achieving improved market share."[61] To implement these policies, the 1996 plan amends the 1985 plan to "instigate an immediate capital development program" for improved visitor facilities, including a Visitor Center, vehicle access, and "a new visitor Night Entertainment Experience."[62] Even though it was spurred by the April 1996 tragedy, that event only heightened the need to attract more visitors and thus generate revenue.

THE 2000 CONSERVATION PLAN AND ITS SECONDARY PLANS

The most direct, exhaustive, and deliberate translation of values into policy is found in the 2000 Conservation Plan. These policies follow and build on the articulation of values and statement of significance in the original Conservation Plan.[63] They have been successfully institutionalized as the basis for site management and as the focal point for discussions of all site values, the treatment of all site elements, and decisions regarding programs.

The written policies that form the core of the Conservation Plan—the touchstone document for managing the cultural values of the site—are presented below. As noted many times in print and in interviews, the Conservation Plan has been wholly adopted by PAHSMA's board and executive as the primary policy to guide management decisions. PAHSMA has made a substantial investment in the plan, and it intends to play a large role in management of the site.

Philosophy and Principles

The plan outlines the philosophical approach and principles that underlie policies. In keeping with Burra philosophy, retention and conservation of cultural significance are the overarching goal.

> The outstanding heritage value of the place imposes an overarching obligation for retention of cultural significance of the place.
>
> [T]here is nothing more important or pressing about the management of the Port Arthur Historic Site than the obligation to conserve it. The existing site is the only one that there will ever be. While it is important to recognise that interpretation of the site and communication of information about the place to the wider community is an integral element of conservation, primacy must be given to

caring for the place, rather than to tourism and provision of visitor services.

This is not to say that the importance and legitimacy of visitation and supply of positive visitor experiences is not important—it is. However, as a matter of overwhelming and fundamental importance, the conservation requirements must prevail.

The following principles are identified as the fundamental philosophical basis for the Port Arthur Historic Site Conservation Policy.[64]

• The primacy of conservation over other management objectives must be recognized;

• Port Arthur Historic Site must be a center of excellence in heritage management;

• Essential conservation activities and works should not be accepted as determined by the current limits imposed by funding generated through visitor numbers, or other similar financial constraints. If site-generated resources are inadequate, it is imperative that, once essential actions are known and resource implications quantified, sources of external resources are obtained;

• Conservation must extend to the total resource, tangible and intangible;

• Decision making must be based upon proper understanding of cultural significance;

• A cautious approach is required where actions may have adverse heritage impacts; abide by principles of reversibility and the precautionary principle;

• Conservation should be undertaken in accordance with well-accepted guidelines, such as the Burra Charter and other international declarations;

• The social and environmental condition of Port Arthur Historic Site should be monitored, to measure the effectiveness of conservation actions and provide essential data for future decision making. This relates to the visitor experience and to impacts on the local community;

• Interested persons, organizations, and other stakeholders should be involved in the conservation of PA; wide consultation yields benefits to the management of the site;

• Visitation and interpretation are integral elements of conservation. Provision of a positive, informative and interactive experience for visitors to the historic site, and those who wish to learn about it, remote from the place itself, must continue to be a fundamental aim.

Conservation Policy

Based on the foregoing philosophy and principles, and with guidance from the Burra Charter, the General Conservation Policy for Port Arthur Historic Site is outlined in section 5.1, volume 1, of the Conservation Plan:

Port Arthur Historic Site is a place of outstanding heritage significance, where excellence in heritage management is the primary aim.

The Port Arthur Historic Site Statement of Significance provides the basis for natural and cultural resource management at the site.

Retention of identified significance and conservation of the Port Arthur Historic Site has primacy over all other management objectives.

Port Arthur Historic Site will be managed and conserved in accordance with the following principles and guidelines:

• the Australia ICOMOS Charter for the Conservation of Places of Cultural Significance (the Burra Charter and associated guidelines);

• the ICOMOS–IFLA International Committee for Historic Gardens Charter;

• the ICAHM Charter for the Protection and Management of Archaeological Heritage;

• the Australian Natural Heritage Charter and associated guidelines; and

• the Draft Guidelines for the Protection, Management and Use of Aboriginal and Torres Strait Islander Cultural Heritage Places.

Conservation of the Port Arthur Historic Site will adopt a total resource approach and will extend to all areas and elements such as landscape, built structures, cultural deposits, artefacts, records, memories and associations along with uses and activities. Conservation will be directed at biodiversity as well as social values and cultural heritage, consistent with a commitment to ecological sensitivity.

Conservation of the Port Arthur Historic Site will make use of the full array of available expertise and knowledge and will adopt a scientific approach to materials conservation.

Caution will be applied in making decisions, which may damage the natural or cultural environment over time. The precautionary principle will be adopted, where appropriate, in relation to management actions with potential to result in a loss of significance. If there is any threat of serious or irreversible environmental damage, lack of full scientific certainty will not be used as the reason for postponing measures to prevent environmental degradation.

However, any actions which may result in a loss of cultural significance must be reversible.

The Port Arthur Historic Site will be protected from physical damage by appropriate security and maintenance measures.

The effectiveness of conservation management of the Port Arthur Historic Site will be monitored.

Interpretation of the history and significance of the place is fundamental to its conservation.

Port Arthur Historic Site will set national and international standards in best practice conservation.

Ultimate responsibility for decision making in relation to the Port Arthur Historic Site is vested in the Port Arthur Historic Site Management Authority.

In addition, a separate statement of policy is given for each of the following areas: Landscape; Aboriginal Heritage; Archaeology; Built Elements; Collections (curatorial and archaeological); Records; Research; Financial Resources for Conservation; Human Resources for Conservation; Planning Processes; Use; Visitors; Interpretation; Associated Communities; Other Interested People; The Peninsula; Future Development; Monitoring; and Land Holding.

The Conservation Plan lays out a deliberate and comprehensive approach to translating values and significance into strategies. The policies are inclusive and clear, and comprehensive in regard to cultural values. This is associated with the value types contributing to cultural significance, the functional elements of the site, and the disciplines and professions engaged in its management (landscape, archaeology).

All in all, the plan establishes the primacy of cultural values in managing the site. It is a major achievement that PAHSMA has invested in the entire plan, as has the Tasmanian State government, which has allocated A$10 million over five years for implementation of the plan.

The policies of the Conservation Plan form a strong base for decision making. Its outstanding feature is the strategy of giving seemingly undiluted primacy to conservation (over tourism and economic concerns), especially in light of the institutional arrangement of PAHSMA as a quasipublic corporation and the commercial imperative this requires (even if the imperative is no longer, after 1995, for PAHSMA to be a profitable enterprise; the GBE imperative calls for PAHSMA to lead the region in attracting tourism and setting a high standard for conservation and tourism experience). The policy that articulates this priority—"Retention of identified significance and conservation of the Port Arthur Historic Site has primacy over all other management objectives"— sets a high bar. It decrees that retention of cultural significance always takes precedence over other (i.e., tourism, access, utilitarian) policies and actions. (This high standard was formed in response to the Doyle Inquiry and other reaction against the pre-1996 management goal imposed on PAHSMA to make the site economically self-sustaining. Furthermore, it is in accord with the Burra Charter model.) This expectation would be unrealistic if seen only as a short-term, day-to-day guide to decision making. In reality, some short-term decisions to invest resources in tourism/access infrastructure (and therefore not in direct conservation work) are actually made in conjunction with a long-term decision regarding the site's conservation—keeping in mind that PAHSMA's long-term view and mandate includes ongoing tourist access and commercial activity. The inclusion of both access and conservation as goals is what makes the overall conservation strategy sustainable in the long term.

The policies clearly set the broad strategic course for PAHSMA's conservation work, providing guidance on such issues as consulting with stakeholder communities, relating the Port Arthur site to the whole Tasman Peninsula, preventing the building of new structures in the core areas, and placing a value on monitoring. As policies, they remain quite general and address the direction and management of conservation activities; specific conservation actions on the site and its buildings and other elements are addressed in the secondary and tertiary plans. Creation of secondary plans will take several years to complete. The Conservation Plan is clearly designed to work with the secondary plans and is not intended to stand on its own as a guide to making detailed decisions. The secondary plans complement the Conservation Plan and treat landscape, particular buildings, and archaeological resources in the detail required.

Except in broad terms, the Conservation Plan does not prioritize the identified site values. The full range of values is well articulated, but how and when one takes precedence over another is not addressed. Again, these decisions are left to the secondary plans. Operationally, these problems are resolved by senior management and the board, who assess the priorities set out in each secondary plan and integrate them into a workable yearly program of conservation activities.

Finally, the Conservation Plan does not take economic values into consideration in any detailed way other than stating the policy that economic values take a back seat when choosing between conservation and commerce. Further, the plan policies keep separate concerns such as archaeology, landscape, and built elements. The mechanism for making and policing decisions according to these policies—for managing the site holistically—is the set of relationships forged among the core management team members. These relationships are largely informal and are an intentional result of the conservation planning process. By working with one another, various departments can intelligently resolve complicated management issues using broad parameters to which all staff subscribe. This process was seen as equally important as the production of a written plan, and to date it appears to have largely succeeded.

THE SECONDARY 2001 INTERPRETATION PLAN

This secondary plan, called the Interpretation Plan, revisits the historic values and broad interpretive policies of the Conservation Plan and produces a detailed plan of action that flows out of stated interpretation philosophy and strategies. The Interpretation Plan does not identify new values so much as it revises and renders the historic values (as well as audiences, delivery mechanisms, etc.) to a level of specificity called for in the Conservation Plan. It takes a critical approach to making plans for future interpretation and provides a thorough summary of its theoretical underpinnings.

This plan carries out the general prescriptions in the Conservation Plan. However, it departs from the latter's guidance in one important way. Whereas the Conservation Plan establishes that "the primary message of on-site interpretation will convey the significance of the place and the physical evolution of the site including conservation processes,"[65] the Interpretation Plan provides a variety of options—aimed at different audiences and at different specialty visitor groups—instead of a "primary message." The reasons for this change are justified in the Interpretation Plan's succinct review of theories guiding the design of interpretive programs.

The themes and topics[66] advance the values as literally set out in the statement of significance. They integrate the values for the understanding of visitors (presenting different aspects of the site but also connecting historical insights with contemporary issues) as opposed to using them for purposes of maximizing revenue or harvesting scientific values. For example, the plan calls for

interpretation of the "paradoxes" of the landscape (juxtaposing the ugliness of convictism with the beauty of the landscape) and of the different interpretations of Port Arthur's past over time, as opposed to focusing on the straight chapter-and-verse of convictism history. The plan also specifies interpretation of "crime and punishment" at Port Arthur in terms of how society deals with these issues today.

The amended [interpretation] policy is as follows:[67]

- Interpretation of the Port Arthur Historic Site will be undertaken in accordance with this Plan.
- Interpretation programs and messages will have primary regard to the significance of the site.
- The approach to interpretation will extend beyond the Port Arthur Historic Site itself, providing an understanding of the place in its historical, geographical and social context. [this brings the interpretation in alignment with the Conservation Plan's regional strategy—regionalism is one way that all the policies line up]
- Messages to be conveyed in interpretation will be developed in consultation with all involved in developing, managing and delivering that interpretation.
- Interpretation will be based only on sound, contemporary and scholarly research.
- Interpretation programs and initiatives will be undertaken in a manner that minimises impact on the fabric of significant elements.
- Interpretation will extend to historic activities, structures, places and landscapes and will, where possible, focus on real historic elements. The introduction of new, purpose-built interpretive elements will be minimised.
- Regular evaluation will continue to inform our interpretive activities.

The interpretive policies form a robust strategy that does not suggest prioritizing some heritage values over others. Rather, the policies mandate development of a number of specialized messages, programs, and products based on specific values and oriented to a correspondingly wide range of general and specialist audiences.

THE SECONDARY 2001 LANDSCAPE PLAN

As of this writing, the Landscape Plan is the second of the Conservation Plan's secondary plans.[68] It follows the basic conservation planning methodology (understanding the landscape's natural and cultural features, codifying significance, identifying issues and threats to significance, and formulating policies) in addressing the interaction of landscape and cultural significance at Port Arthur. Broadly, it reinforces the cultural values articulated in the Conservation Plan and asserted in the statement of significance. It adds the notion of natural (environmental-ecological) values to the mix and examines them in detail. Ultimately, the Landscape Plan focuses on the cultural landscape aspects of Port Arthur, with the intention of conserving natural and cultural values and preserving their visual impact on the significance of the site.

One goal of the Landscape Plan is to describe the cultural and natural values of the Port Arthur landscape, and how the landscape (as a whole entity, not only as a collection of elements) contributes particularly to the values articulated in the Conservation Plan. This document gives a more detailed history and background of the cultural features of the landscape. It describes how the values identified in the Conservation Plan are expressed in the various landscape elements (cultural and natural) that have been inventoried. The plan also includes a more detailed analysis of the "paradox" in values of comforting pastoral landscape images juxtaposed with the uncomfortable historic values of convictism. In general, the inventories and significance assessments reinforce the quality of Port Arthur as a site with a deeply layered, eclectic landscape—a place with many values, none of which predominates.

But the Landscape Plan is not merely an analysis of already articulated values. By articulating natural values, the plan in effect adds a set of ecological values to the Conservation Plan. The Landscape Plan encourages the preservation and re-creation of more native plant ecology and identifies landscaping measures to prevent the erosion of the natural environmental qualities. It also asserts the historic and aesthetic values related to (or even stemming from) topography and other aspects of the natural environment.

Another departure from the system of value accounting is reflected in the Landscape Plan's five-page "Statement of significance for the landscape," which articulates site values by describing the values and significance of individual, physical areas (i.e., Mason Cove, Point Puer, Isle of the Dead, Garden Point, and Carnarvon Bay). Specifying values in this manner is one way in which the secondary plans advance the articulation of value. A similar level of specification is evident in the other secondary plans that have been undertaken for the Separate Prison, the asylum/town hall, and the harborside area.

THE 2001/2002 CORPORATE PLAN

PAHSMA's Corporate Plans are the strategic programs for comprehensive site management. Done annually, they set each year's policies and, to a lesser extent, specific project priorities. In devising the Corporate Plan, the board uses the Conservation Plan and its secondary plans as guides. The board also takes into account government requirements and relevant documents such as human resources plans; financial, visitor numbers, and commercial operations targets; and community obligations, as long as these do not conflict with policies in the Conservation Plan. The Corporate Plans imply values without articulating them, and spell out how values are to be realized and cultivated through management decisions and priorities. The plans record the results of PAHSMA decisions but give little insight into the process by which the decisions were made.

For a given year, the Corporate Plan communicates to the Tasmanian Minister of State Development how all the activities of PAHSMA, commercial and conservation, will be carried out. "The Conservation Plan is a broad overriding document of general policy: the Corporate Plan is a yearly statement of what will be achieved. Every year as more secondary plans are completed, the Corporate Plan grows more detailed."[69] In practice, the Conservation and Corporate Plans together define and capture the strategic direction of PAHSMA. They could also be interpreted as addressing two different audiences: the Conservation Plan relating to internally focused decisions about matters inside the site boundaries (conservation and development decisions about site elements); and the Corporate Plan relating to externally focused matters, such as partnerships with government, the local community, and Port Arthur Region Marketing Ltd. (PARM).

Although the Corporate Plan describes the goals and priorities of the same organization as the Conservation Plan does, it takes a different approach, envisioning PAHSMA as an organization to be run as a business, rather than as a set of conservation projects. Nothing is included about specific historic, aesthetic, social, or scientific values other than clarifying that "conserving the cultural value of the site" is the first point in the statement of purpose.[70] (These values are articulated in the Conservation Plan.)

Striking a balance between these two sets of values, these two institutional mandates, these two perspectives, is left to the collaborative work of the management team and the board. The Corporate Plan's strategies and statements are expressions of how different aspects of site management, opportunities, and constraints are integrated. These annual documents report on how the site is managed to ensure that the overriding goal of PAHSMA—conservation—is met, and to ensure that PAHSMA holds itself accountable for the many aspects of its mandate—financial accountability, commercial performance, community engagement, and transparency of decision making, all necessary means to achieving the goal.

In the Conservation Plan and in many other discussions and documents, PAHSMA clearly states that conservation of cultural values is the central goal of its site management. The Corporate Plan does not contradict this, but it views PAHSMA more as a business, creating the possibility that the priority of conservation and the focus on cultural values could be hedged in favor of generating revenue. PAHSMA works actively to prevent this. Whatever disconnects might potentially exist between the Conservation Plan and the Corporate Plan are resolved through managers' deliberations. The means of resolving such hypothetical conflicts are not outlined on paper. The site's leaders and managers have great confidence in the management culture instilled and cultivated in recent years ("the Port Arthur way"[71]), and in managers' commitment to consultation and truly collaborative problem solving.

The 2001/2002 Corporate Plan is organized around six "strategic drivers of [PAHSMA's] business":

STRATEGIC DRIVER	OBJECTIVE
(1) management of heritage values	• conserve cultural and natural fabric and landscape
	• enhance understanding of cultural meaning and value
	• establish PA as a centre for research and expertise in cultural management
(2) increased visitation	• increase visitor numbers to PA by 2%
(3) developing quality visitor experience	• improve visitor experience and increase perception of "value for money" and customer satisfaction
(4) improve organisational capability	• improve financial outcomes of PAHSMA
	• continue to develop human resource function and staff development
	• improve opportunities for education and training on site
	• increase/improve utilisation of IT opportunities on site
	• [improve] corporate governance
(5) maintain government support	• increasing awareness and support for PAHSMA endeavors at Government level
(6) strengthening community interaction	• increasing awareness and support for PAHSMA endeavors in the broader community

As PAHSMA's organizational goals, the strategic drivers are meant to define, connect, orient, and integrate conservation work and the development of tourism. These two spheres are seen by management as interrelated: additional tourism revenue is sought to fund conservation work; conservation work is intended, among other goals, to create a better visitor experience and thereby increase tourism. The extent to which this cycle changes how site values are assessed and acted upon is not addressed in the Corporate Plan and is covered in the last section of this study (see, for instance, the sidebar on the next page, on the Historic Ghost Tours). In some cases, investments are made to improve visitor experience, which could be seen as pre-empting investing in conservation. In a short-term time frame, some might view such decisions as contrary to the Conservation Plan's conservation-first policy. However, PAHSMA clearly sees them as long-term investments to guarantee the conservation of the site (a vision of conservation that integrates tourism and access as one ingredient of successful, sustainable conservation). The Corporate Plan recognizes the need to think carefully about these relationships by pointing out, for instance, the need to "ensure commercial activities on site are consistent with interpretive objectives."[72]

SUMMARY

Based on the foregoing analysis, the findings regarding how different site values are represented in Port Arthur policies are summarized below.

Aboriginal values are acknowledged but not considered a key management issue. This group of stakeholders is absent (attention to these values is legislated), and little material is available to curate. Aboriginal values are not detailed, and their management is not discussed in site documents in deference to the Tasmanian Aboriginal community, which does not wish outside management to be undertaken and prefers to carry out this work itself in the future.

Historic values are well represented and dominated by convictism. There is acknowledgment that layers of meaning are still accumulating, and that post-convict-era layers are significant alongside the values directly related to convictism.

Aesthetic values are considered in policies that call for the perpetuation of the existing aesthetic landscape, and thus the paradox of convictism in an Arcadian landscape.

Social values are described and listed in the Conservation Plan, and a range of policies in the plan relate to their conservation, though they do not seem to attract as much attention as historic values do. Social values emerge as strong factors in specific circumstances, the most striking instance being the Broad Arrow Café tragedy. In the sense that the Conservation Plan defines the economic concerns of the local community and the state as social values, they are omnipresent and enter into many of the decisions about the site. Social values related to specific stakeholder groups also factor into site management of specific site elements, such as the desire of veterans' groups to preserve a World War I memorial avenue of trees.

Scientific values are behind the well-articulated policies dealing with archaeological activities.

Economic values are recognized implicitly in site decisions, policies, and planning documents—through wide recognition of the tension between commercial and conservation uses of the site's values—and explicitly documented in a supporting study (the University of Tasmania's economic impact study). In keeping with the Burra Charter process, however, they remain on a separate plane from the cultural significance values that form the basis of the Conservation Plan's policies.

There is no one document in which all of the site values are articulated. Values tend to be dealt with separately—usually according to the main Burra Charter categories—with little formal analysis of the trade-offs that must occur in practice. Holistic treatment of all site values is addressed in the Conservation Plan only at a general level; the secondary plans (Interpretation, Landscape, Separate Prison, etc.) do achieve a good deal of integration vis-à-vis the specific activities or resources to which they pertain. The integration of values is achieved analytically in work such as the Landscape Plan's statement of significance written for different geographic areas of the site. The

[continued on page 152]

Historic Ghost Tours

Port Arthur's nighttime Historic Ghost Tours are a long-standing part of the site's offerings. As an alternative form of interpretation—distinct from the more scholarly, canonical forms of site interpretation—and a commercial activity, the ghost tours depart from the Conservation Plan and Interpretation Plan. The tours highlight a number of issues related to site interpretation: how commercial and cultural values are balanced, how site values are communicated to visitors, the variety of interpretive forms used to reach diverse audiences, and how the forms of communication shape the perceived values of the site.[1]

On a ghost tour, visitors are led in the dark by flashlight or torch through the site and several of its buildings, entertained with scary stories of "ghosts" who have been spotted at the site. Guides convey some historical information about the place, and the "ghost" characters take their cues from site history, but the content is driven more by entertainment than by Port Arthur's well-researched cultural significance. Ghost tour interpretation is not focused on the significance and values of the site as currently defined in the Conservation Plan, but instead complements the standard daytime offerings of Port Arthur.

Formally organized since 1988, the tours are a popular interpretive program for visitors. They harken back to the immediate post-convict era, when local residents (some of them former inmates) guided visitors around the ruins, regaling them with stories of the convict days.[2] The tours have become central to the commercial strategies of PAHSMA and PARM: because they take place in the evening, they attract and retain overnight visitors, which contributes to the local and state economies. Priced at A$14 per adult, the Historic Ghost Tours attracted 46,000 visitors in 2001, producing nearly A$600,000 in direct revenue.

The ghost tours also advance the cultural values of the site. They represent a different approach to interpretation from that outlined in the Interpretation Plan—less scholarly or informed by theories of education, more entertainment- and commercially driven, cued to the emotional connections that are more accessible in a nighttime visit. PAHSMA's research suggests that the tours are an important means by which visitors learn about the site and its significance. One-third of the evening visitors overlap with the 200,000 annual visitors to the site and thus have additional exposure. For more than 30,500 evening visitors, the ghost tour is their only contact with the site. Even though they are a de facto form of interpretation, the tours are managed not as part of the interpretive offerings of PAHSMA but by

Visitor Services, a separate unit in the Conservation Department. In effect, the tours are a separate, independent interpretative operation. The board has begun reviewing the Historic Ghost Tours program, consulting with the various stakeholders (including the guides who created and continue to deliver the tours) and incorporating their feedback into the site's other interpretation policies and activities. The tours also represent social values. Some PAHSMA staff (particularly those who created the tours and have managed them over the years) identify with the tours as a tradition and feel strongly about allowing them to continue. Indeed, the tours represent the contributions of staff who have worked on the site for years, well before the 1996 tragedy and the changes that followed, and whose interpretations of Port Arthur's history are a de facto part of the site's significance.

Despite the tours' popularity and financial success, some heritage professionals criticize their lack of interpretive rigor and question their relation to the cultural significance and values of the site as identified in the Conservation Plan. While the tours deliver some information about the site itself, conforming to the main interpretive themes, the tours seem tooled to elicit emotional reactions to the place. Some see the ghost tours as potentially undermining the cultural values of the site by representing them to the public as entertainment rather than as complex historical issues. Such a critique undervalues the real benefits of the tours. PAHSMA's board and staff express strong support for the tours as an alternative means for engaging visitors with the site's cultural significance as well as for their economic contributions. They believe that the Historic Ghost Tours fill a valuable and idiosyncratic niche in the management of Port Arthur's many values.

Notes

1. This assessment is admittedly anecdotal and based on limited exposure to the ghost tours.
2. Young 1996.

board's decisions rely on secondary plans to a large extent. Regarding areas or issues for which no secondary plan is yet completed, informal means of integrating site values are more important and flow from the input and expertise of site managers, a topic discussed further in the last section of the study.

Impact of Management Policies and Decisions on the Site's Values and Their Preservation

This section addresses the following questions: How are values considered in decision making? What have been the implications of decisions and policies on the values of the site? Are there discrepancies between what is stated in the documents and what actions are actually taken? What effects do institutional arrangements have on the management of site values?

GENERAL POLICIES AND DECISION MAKING
The management of Port Arthur, in general and in its details, is carried out according to PAHSMA's plans and policies. It seems well served by the plans themselves, and more so by the planning processes (collaborative, inclusive, and exhaustive).

One of the overriding themes in this section is PAHSMA's focus on formulating general policies that set strategic direction, while carrying out (over time) a series of more detailed secondary plans and leaving specific decisions about fabric to informal processes managed on an ad hoc basis by the executive team. This approach is in keeping with the nature of management plans as guidance documents rather than as specific work plans.

Port Arthur's Conservation Plan, for instance, establishes the range of values of the site and states clearly that conservation is more important than attracting and serving visitors. But it does not specify, for example, how the fabric of the Separate Prison should be handled; this is the subject of its own secondary plan. Nor does the Conservation Plan specify exactly what conservation projects should be undertaken and in what order. Such specifics are left (1) to the actions called for in the secondary and tertiary plans, and (2) to the day-to-day, year-to-year judgment of the managers themselves—abiding by the overall policy of conserving the site's cultural significance value first—as to which actions to take and in what order.[73]

These arrangements, within the limits agreed to as overall policies, allow the managers to react according to circumstances and seize opportunities as they present themselves. The decentralized, somewhat privatized institutional setup of PAHSMA, and its Conservation Plan scheme, embodies this approach. Constant consideration is given to what actions are most urgent, most relevant, and most suitable for implementation, given the ever-shifting availability of funding and partners.

THE EFFECTS OF GOVERNMENT POLICY

PAHSMA's fairly independent status has a significant effect on how site values are managed. In general, state and commonwealth bodies have become less influential as PAHSMA has become more independent, well funded, and professionally staffed. PAHSMA has clearly won the confidence and support of the THC and the AHC for its policies and programs, and hence is seen not to warrant the detailed scrutiny previously necessary. The exception is the enormously influential role of PAHSMA's home ministry, which is providing the A$10 million of funding (over five years) for the site's conservation program. This and other Tasmanian State policies—such as investing in the new Bass Strait ferry service between Tasmania and mainland Australia—continue to be important influences on the management of site values.

Policy changes at the state and commonwealth government levels can have a great effect on site values and their management. In the case of Port Arthur, these effects can be summarized as (1) shaping the institutional setup of the managing entity (PAHSMA's status as a GBE, a quasigovernmental corporation);[74] (2) providing/controlling access to financial resources (direct state funding, subsidiary funding of tourism development as one of the preferred means of postindustrial public investment in economic development); and (3) creating expectations and performance targets for the benefits created by these public investments.

The institutional setup directly affects values by setting the general goals of the organization and enabling it to undertake certain activities. Quasipublic corporations enjoy latitude in specifying how institutional goals are to be pursued, and PAHSMA's, for example, are quite broad and diverse. By design, it operates as a business and as a government stewardship agency to pursue both economic and conservation goals in managing the site, in contrast to the institutional setup of a straightforward government agency, which is often constrained by bureaucratic structures and interagency relationships. Traditional government agencies have fairly narrow (if extensive) mandates (e.g., conservation of cultural heritage) and often rely on other government entities and rules in order to perform functions outside that mandate

(procurement, personnel, tourism promotion, forming partnerships with the private sector; in other words, the separation of sectoral responsibilities in different agencies works against holistic management). Quasigovernment corporations are more flexible and can be opportunistic and responsive to external conditions.

Changes in membership of the governing body and external conditions can also have a strong impact on such relatively small, relatively independent organizations. The management troubles at Port Arthur by the time of the 1997 Doyle Inquiry were brought on in part by attempts to respond to external factors. They were also symptomatic, however, of what can happen in a small, freestanding management group in which the impact of individuals is strong and susceptibility to external funding and other factors is high.

Another major effect on Port Arthur's values in the recent past has been the state government's shift in thinking about the resources it provides to Port Arthur and the benefits it expects from the site. Continuing the pendulum swings between conservation and commercial orientations at the site from the 1970s through the 1990s, government policies have led the most recent shift, which started in 1998. The chief executive of the Department of State Development stated that the government's expectations of getting returns on their investment were "not simply economic."[75] The state government and the PAHSMA Board work on the assumption that the site has a variety of economic and cultural values—or, aspects of significance—and that investment in these different values yields different kinds of returns. In other words, the government supports the emphasis on conservation as long as the "returns" continue to be both cultural (good conservation work, excellence of visitor experience, plenty of visitors, maintenance of Australian and Tasmanian identity) and economic (reasonable economic performance of PAHSMA, and economic benefits of Port Arthur activities to the peninsula and the state).

The investment of Tasmanian authorities in Port Arthur is part of the state's decision to eliminate reliance on extractive and agricultural industry (the export of timber and apples) and become more of a green, tourist-oriented state. Port Arthur's management, a linchpin of this strategy, is key to the broader marketing of Tasmania for tourism. This change in government policy—raising the profile of Port Arthur as an economic development resource—shapes the de facto prioritization of site values. The economic values realized on-site through commercial activities, as well as the positive economic externalities to the region, are more explicitly recognized. Government policy is further reflected in the handling of values through site management: the economic values are dependent on the conservation, protection, and presentation of the site's cultural significance values, which puts everything in alignment for the managers. Conserving cultural values enables the realization of economic values.

The Corporate Plans and Conservation Plan provide a clear mandate: Do not sacrifice conservation to commerce. Nevertheless, the board has shown that it is also willing to respond to opportunities and carry out such initiatives within the guidelines of the Conservation Plan. Measures are in place to gauge the impact of individual projects such as the new ferry service and harborside plan. However, there are no established processes to monitor the cumulative impact of all projects, nor have limits of acceptable change been articulated. Either one would allow the board and management to assess impact on the whole site over time.

PAHSMA must continue to prove that state funds are needed and well spent, and that this government investment yields benefits beyond the site itself. PAHSMA has demonstrated the social and economic benefits of a well-conserved and -interpreted heritage site to the local and wider community.

DEALING WITH CONFLICTING VALUES

Dealing with conflicting values is a major issue in values-based management and of major interest to the didactic purposes of this case study. The potential for economic values to trump or undermine cultural values, and the potential for different cultural values to compete, is an issue faced at many sites.

As is made clear in the Conservation Plan, the Corporate Plans, and in conversations with PAHSMA Board and staff, the primary goals and values for Port Arthur's site management are conservation and cultural significance. Yet the financial requirements for managing the site require a fairly aggressive courting of economic values through commercial and tourism activities and courting political-governmental sources of funding. The policy documents for Port Arthur do not detail specifically how to achieve a balance when the realization of economic and cultural values seems to conflict. Because these documents address different sets of site values, gaps may appear when they are put together. To the extent that such gaps raise uncertainty about value priorities, conflict and competition can crop up.

Staff and board appear to share a clear working understanding about how PAHSMA is supposed to perform as a commercial operation and government economic-development investment, and also as a paragon of conservation work—standards set out in the Corporate and Conservation Plans. The only specified decision regarding the relation of these two sectors and site values is the Conservation Plan's philosophy/policy that conservation takes priority when commercial activities are in conflict.

A case in point was the decision not to privatize and outsource commercial operations on the site (e.g., restaurants, gift shop). This decision stemmed in part from the state government's commitment (related to its political position not to privatize the Tasmanian State hydro company) and has been part of the CEO's mandate from the board. Privatization might have been more lucrative, but it would have taken quality control out of PAHSMA's hands and would not have been in accord with the Conservation Plan's values and policies, which put conservation first. "We often make decisions a private business would not," one executive said, citing examples such as not putting a McDonald's restaurant in the Separate Prison, or not stocking certain products in the gift shop that the conservation staff would consider inappropriate. Conflicts arise between commercial and conservation mandates from time to time—such as those regarding special events and the ghost tours—but the conflicts were worse when private operators and contractors were on-site. Fewer conflicts crop up now that PAHSMA controls all decision making and implements these decisions through its management team—a "whole-of-site" approach.

In interviews, board members and staff communicated clearly that conservation is the fundamental goal of management, and that achieving this goal requires integrating management of tourism with other economic aspects and commercial activities of the site. This integration, or trading-off, happens not through structured planning or according to routinized decision making but "around the table" in board and executive deliberations. Integration of economic and cultural values is handled informally and guided by general policies—it is left not to chance but to the managers. For instance, the staff heading different departments (commercial as well as conservation operations) work well together as a team. This executive group, representing all management areas and different values, meets weekly and ensures that there is collaboration between conservation and commercial entities. The importance of this integration process was acknowledged and addressed more formally through the workshops presented to the staff, and specifically the scenarios used to train staff. Staff were asked to consider, for example, what would happen if someone proposed staging a rock concert on the site, or if someone donated funds for reroofing the church. These exercises were in effect management "practice" for the process-based solutions (as opposed to prescribed plan-based solutions) on which PAHSMA relies to resolve conflicts and set priorities vis-à-vis site values.

The executive staff are quite clear about their duty of confronting and heading off potential conflicts between conservation and commerce, dealing with them "around the table" guided by the "general conservation policy." This model of decision making depends a great deal on the personalities sitting at the table. As the people change, the "Port Arthur way" is intended to be the system for educating and integrating newcomers and sustaining the management practices set in place by the Conservation Plan and the board. The Port Arthur way is described by board vice chairperson Sharon Sullivan: "The Port Arthur way is the way in which the Conservation Plan was developed with full staff input, including the workshops which continually reinforce the conservation planning process and in which conservation plan policies are worked through as they apply to particular issues. It is not an accident that the Port Arthur staff act the way they do. It is an intended outcome of the conservation planning process and it is intended to ensure that priority is given to long-term site conservation in every issue which is considered by the Executive and the staff."[76]

In setting PAHSMA's course, the Corporate Plan leaves room for political maneuvering and opportunistic development decisions on the part of the board. Any gaps perceived between the strategic Corporate Plan and the more-specific Conservation Plan (including the secondary plans) appear to be by design. This gives the board and executive flexibility in setting priorities, allocating resources, and so forth, and enables them to respond more effectively to opportunities, disasters or other unexpected events, changing macroeconomic conditions, and changing political fortunes.

The leadership of the board continues to recognize the importance not only of integrating the management of different values but also of continually revising Port Arthur's statement of significance and reexamining the relation between commercial and conservation strategies. One board member stated, "If we were doing the Conservation Plan starting now, we would integrate commercial and conservation activities/policies in the same plan." Other members explained that the Burra Charter methodology and the dominance of economic values during the previous administrations are reasons why economic values are not a more-explicit part of the Conservation Plan.

THE CONSERVATION PLAN'S EFFECT ON SITE VALUES

"The Conservation Plan is the basis for all our decision making."[77]

The philosophy behind the Conservation Plan, mirrored in PAHSMA policies overall, is the primacy of conservation and, by extension, the cultural values comprising the site's cultural significance. As reported by several interviewees, the single most important moment in the Conservation Plan process was the approval of this philosophy by the PAHSMA Board and Tasmanian State government.

Economically, the plan helped secure the A$10 million in state funding for Port Arthur (along with the Tasmanian State government's confidence in PAHSMA's board and management). The political objectives of the process were successfully addressed: a targeted effort was made to shape state policy and gain financial and political support. In this material sense, the Conservation Plan obviously advances all the values of the site.

The balance of this section explores issues related specifically to management of cultural values.

Articulating Values According to Type
By employing the heritage value typology of the Burra Charter process, the Conservation Plan privileges those value types. This approach yields benefits in exhaustively dealing with the four canonical types of cultural significance value—historic, social, scientific, and aesthetic—backed by an established process of research, consultation, and synthesis into an overall statement of significance. At the same time, the process raises some potential difficulties by, for instance, excluding economic values, and handles Aboriginal values awkwardly by segregating them.

The Conservation Plan's method of examining values by type and not by chronology may work against the understanding of Port Arthur as a deeply layered site. Contrast this with a way of assessing values (historic or "conservation" values at least) according to the periods or layers of the site (Aboriginal, convict-era, Carnarvon, SPB, Parks/PACDP, PAHSMA, post-1996). A value elicitation framework based on historic periods can lead to a different management strategy, privileging the values related to a particular era, which may have a beneficial effect on the scientific value related to it.

The idea of chronological layers is central to visitors' understanding of the site and has been the traditional way of looking at the site's significance and conservation.[78] How are values of different periods prioritized when they coexist in a particular building? In the penitentiary, for instance, future conservation to allow reading of the 1840s fabric and create performance space may sacrifice the integrity of the 1970s conservation work. Ideally, values would be organized both by type and by historical layer, so that one way of valorization does not dominate.

Port Arthur conservation planning efforts respond to this issue by trying to mitigate this kind of unavoidable, chronological valorization of value types. Different value schemes are used in secondary plans—organized, for instance, around geographic areas, as in the Landscape Plan; around interpretive themes, as in the Interpretation Plan; or around eras in built-element plans. These "alternative" value schemes cut across the main typology and enrich the articulation of values without undermining the values-based rigor of the Burra Charter framework.

Assigning Priorities among Cultural Values

The Conservation Plan articulates the wide range of cultural values, yet assigns no priority or hierarchy to them. When decisions must be made between, hypothetically, a project centered on conserving research values (documenting archaeological resources) and a project to stabilize reconstructed built fabric, the value articulation and significance statements provide little guidance. The Separate Prison (see sidebar on page 140) presents the option of removing earlier conservation work (from the twentieth century) to restore the nineteenth-century convict experience.

Section 6.3.10 of the Conservation Plan offers general guidance (first, work on things that are dangerous or that threaten operations, then prioritize according to the significance of the specific elements in question), and individual site elements are rated in broad categories for their significance.[79] The decisions are left in the hands of PAHSMA managers and their annual works budget. Yet PAHSMA policy for spending A$10 million in government funds on conservation works has not been codified; it is decided on a rolling, year-to-year basis. A scheme for phasing of conservation and development projects has been drafted as an internal planning tool, identifying planning projects and major and minor works, and scheduling these projects over a five-year period. This document provides a guideline for decisions and is continually rethought and refined.

Tying Values to Fabric

Values articulated in the Conservation Plan are not tied to specific elements of fabric. It is left to the secondary plans to establish the more-detailed policies about conservation and operational priorities and treatment of fabric, and to set out steps for implementation. The tertiary plans spell out actual works procedures. The secondary and tertiary plans are not actually hierarchical, even though their names suggest they are. They are intended to cut across one another, enabling project planning to focus either on subject areas (e.g., archaeology) or on specific site elements (e.g., the Separate Prison).

Instances arise, however, when the general policies—in concert with the specific value assessments—seem to prefigure a decision regarding the conservation of a site resource. For example, the church, like many site elements, has several kinds of value. Given the overall value assessments and conservation policies, the scenic (aesthetic) qualities of the church as a roofless ruin seem to take precedent over the historic values that would be realized by roofing and reconstructing it. (Such reconstruction would also raise the issue of adversely affecting the authenticity of the structure.)

The Conservation Plan's Effect on the Process

The process of formulating and approving the Conservation Plan has had a very strong and salutary effect on management within PAHSMA. The process helped manage the huge post-1996 transition of staff; it helped manage and guide the recomposition of the board; and it helped reduce tension by improving communication among different stakeholders and within the PAHSMA organization.

In another sense, the Conservation Plan raises questions about the role of outside agencies vis-à-vis PAHSMA in managing the site, and what kinds of oversight are enabled. The flexibility of the decision-making process gives PAHSMA a significant amount of autonomy and oversight. The Conservation Plan has helped secure confidence and a priori buy-in by staff, local leaders, and state officials on PAHSMA site development and conservation decisions. Local council approval is still needed to approve physical projects, but this concerns mainly infrastructural issues (not heritage issues—on this the local

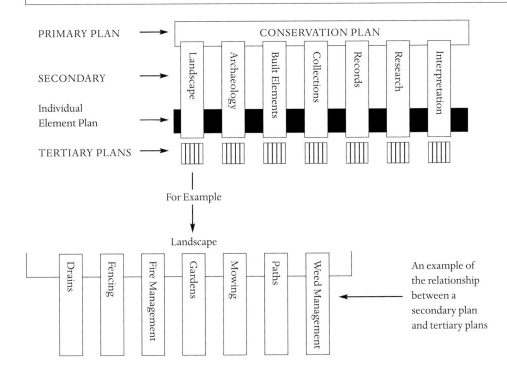

PORT ARTHUR HISTORIC SITE
Conservation Plan and derived plans

PRIMARY PLAN →

SECONDARY →

Individual
Element Plan →

TERTIARY PLANS →

CONSERVATION PLAN

Landscape · Archaeology · Built Elements · Collections · Records · Research · Interpretation

For Example

Landscape

Drains · Fencing · Fire Management · Gardens · Mowing · Paths · Weed Management

An example of
the relationship
between a
secondary plan
and tertiary plans

Figure 3.12. Port Arthur Historic Site Conservation Plan and derived plans. (Source: Adapted from Richard Mackay, "Conservation Planning Presentation," January 2001)

council defers to the THC). The THC has statutory review responsibilities and sometimes attaches conditions to projects. But PAHSMA and the THC have a close working relationship,[80] and there has been discussion over granting PAHSMA blanket exemption from THC review on the basis that self-review would be sufficient to ensure the quality of conservation work.

THE INTERPRETATION PLAN
AND ITS EFFECTS ON VALUES

The Interpretation Plan will shape cultural values directly as it packages them for public understanding.[81] For the most part, the measures called for in the plan will build on the values and significance outlined in the Conservation Plan. There are some departures, though. Instead of seeing the values according to the categories used in the Conservation Plan, the Interpretation Plan views the site first as "a complex layered cultural landscape." In this sense, it presents a different, more holistic way of looking at cultural values.[82]

The main interpretation strategies remain those identified in the Conservation Plan, although their content has been significantly revised. The guided tour remains the most important interpretive activity, but the number and variety of offerings is to be increased to address niche audiences.

The Interpretation Plan dispenses with the idea of one "primary message" and in particular with a primary message "too fabric-focused" and centering on the physical evolution of the site. "[R]ather, Interpretation will aim to offer a range of presentations that will cater to audience types and interests," and the interpretation policies and activities will be more "visitor-focused." This significant departure of interpretation strategy will likely affect how the values are managed. By catering to the interests of visitors, the interpretation policies are turning away from a consensus view of historic values (centered on convictism and national character) and toward the recognition that all visitors see the values of the site differently and should not be expected to accept a singular message. Such a strategy raises the potential for conflict with the notion of a single statement of significance for the site—and indeed, the Port Arthur Statement of Significance (see p. 134) is lengthy and incorporates, in effect, a number of different "significances."

The Interpretation Plan also builds in mechanisms of feedback and responsiveness to visitor experiences that, in time, may shift the kinds of values being presented. Hence there is an intentional reshaping of values—or at least an opening to different views—built in to the management strategy. Presumably, as visitors' perceptions of value shift, interpretation policies would shift to address them, perhaps changing the priorities of the values being transmitted. Visitor feedback is a potential factor of change in which values are interpreted; another is research, which is intended to continually improve and update the specific values and messages available to visitors and the public.

In more specific terms of handling fabric, values, and interpretation strategy, one of the plan's most interesting points is the notion that the stark contrast between two of the main cultural values of the site—the aesthetic values of the landscape juxtaposed with the historic and social values of convictism and its dreadful narratives—is singled out for interpretation. Also, reconstruction and reinstatement of missing but historic features is encouraged, as allowed within the boundaries of Conservation Plan policy. Such interpretation improvements have potential effects on the aesthetic values if yards, fences, fieldlines, pathways, and footprints are reinstated, for instance. This is a clear example of a secondary plan giving one type of cultural value priority over another in order to achieve the overall goals for the site.

THE TASMAN PENINSULA REGION AS RESOURCE AND AS STAKEHOLDER

The articulation of values and statement of significance in the Conservation Plan pave the way for this multifaceted approach to seeing the cultural significance of Port Arthur on a regional scale (including the peninsula, the island, and the waters). This rightly encompasses the peninsula-wide system of convict stations, probation stations, penal sites, and other sites of production to support the main convictism values. Like many others, the "regional" issue stems from the cultural significance of the site as well as from its economic values.

The significant cultural landscape being conserved and interpreted at Port Arthur is the Tasman Peninsula, not just the Port Arthur site itself. Plans and scholars going back at least to the PACDP years (1979–86)

agree that the peninsula, stretching to places like Saltwater River and the Coal Mines, is the true resource and is not confined to the boundaries of Port Arthur. The value of the historical probation relics has been recognized on the peninsula—the buildings and routes are protected under the Tasman Municipal Council planning scheme. Commercial activities and economic benefits being managed by PAHSMA are intended to encompass and spill over to the whole peninsula. To advance the commercial and conservation goals of PAHSMA, management has already begun adopting regional strategies and actions, including Port Arthur Region Marketing Ltd. (PARM) and the Convict Trail interpretive scheme. The site's regional significance is being addressed proactively and successfully, largely through activities and organizations outside the Conservation Plan, and by strengthening informal relationships with the community and with owners of the other peninsular sites.

PARM was formed in 2000 to coordinate and advance efforts to market Port Arthur along with other tourism activities in the Tasman Peninsula region. It has forty-three members. PAHSMA is PARM's primary benefactor and holds two of the group's six seats on the board. The organization builds on the widely held notion that the Port Arthur site is the competitive advantage of the region in tourism marketing and should be marketed to benefit the entire region. Tourists experience the region as a whole; their satisfaction does not begin or end with the site experience. If the tourist experience in Port Arthur can be linked to other resources beyond the site, overnight visits to the region can be increased—a primary means of increasing economic benefits.

The character of the whole peninsula—its marketing, services, ownership, and land-use control—is out of PAHSMA's control, yet the overall success of promoting Port Arthur depends on these regional/peninsular connections. Initiating and supporting PARM is a step toward managing these relationships/partnerships. Even the direct stewardship responsibilities of PAHSMA may soon extend to the secondary punishment station at Coal Mines.[83] What are the implications for values and their management of this multifaceted effort to treat Port Arthur as a regional entity as opposed to a strictly bounded site?

Apart from PARM, there are currently no formal relationships between PAHSMA and other owners and partners. Any strong assertion of PAHSMA control over the greater peninsula would be resented by locals, though they seem to enjoy a productive relationship at present.

Broader control would have to be achieved carefully, in a partnership framework and through a deliberate collaborative process. PAHSMA seems to be paving the way toward this—the Conservation Plan and PARM are two examples of effective collaborative processes.[84]

Conclusions

The management of Port Arthur brings to light a number of important lessons and principles. A summary is offered here as didactic points and themes relevant to heritage site management in general.

Port Arthur provides an opportunity to observe a deliberate and thoughtful conservation planning framework—the pioneering Burra Charter process—applied to a site with varied cultural heritage significance, an extensive and complex set of physical resources, and a progressive set of institutional arrangements made for the site's management. Port Arthur is of particular interest because it has been managed as a heritage site for more than one hundred years, much longer than the forty-seven years it was operated as a prison.

The ownership, control, and funding sources for Port Arthur have changed a great deal over its history, resulting in a variety and number of plans—each one completed not only to outline conservation strategies but to satisfy the goal of securing resources either from the governmental agency in control at the time or from the tourism market. The imperative to secure funding, in ever-changing political and administrative climates, explains in large part the shifts in valuing strategies over time—from the conservation-centered, government-funded priorities at one end of the spectrum to the commercial-centered, market-oriented strategies at the other. At present, PAHSMA has stopped the pendulum somewhere in the middle of the spectrum, balancing physical conservation and interpretive needs with tourism access and other revenue-generating activities that also contribute to the long-term conservation of the site.

The 1996 tragedy at the Broad Arrow Café added another significant layer of values to the site without obscuring the core cultural values related to convictism and its aftermath. Dealing with the impact of the tragedy was a major challenge for site management. It helped pave the way for the 2000 Conservation Plan and planning process, which turned the site around. The management philosophy changed to include true collaboration across management areas, incorporate lateral management, and focus on external partnerships, while simultaneously emphasizing the conservation and presentation of core cultural significance values.

The recent history of Port Arthur disproves the idea that commerce is the bane of conservation, and that the separation of economic and cultural values is legitimate in dealing holistically with site management. The model of sustainable conservation practiced by PAHSMA advances both sets of the site's values.

POLICY AND VALUES FRAMEWORK

Port Arthur has a well-developed policy framework. The overarching frameworks of the Conservation and Corporate Plans, plus the more detailed decisions worked out and recorded in the secondary and individual elements plans, give managers a good deal of latitude as well as sufficient levels of policy guidance and empirical information to make sound decisions.

Values are articulated completely and explicitly. Economic and cultural values are assessed differently and at different levels of detail. More important is how these values are integrated, and the management regime at Port Arthur—the "Port Arthur way"—has done this quite well. The current management clearly understands the primacy of conservation of cultural significance values, while fully recognizing the essential role of economic values and efforts to realize them (through direct tourism, business development related to tourism and site operations, and the positive economic externalities generated for the Tasmanian economy by visitation to Port Arthur).

MANAGEMENT ARRANGEMENTS AND INSTITUTIONAL ARCHITECTURE

The institutional arrangements of the site represent an important, emerging model in heritage management— a quasipublic corporate model.[85] The salient feature of this institutional arrangement is that the primary management entity—PAHSMA, in the case of Port Arthur— enjoys the benefits of some government funding without the strictures (oversight, for instance) of operating as a governmental department nested within a large hierarchical bureaucracy. In a small, independent entity, decisions can be made more quickly and with more flexibility, and with a larger range of public, private, or nongovernmental organization (NGO) partners. These entities also bear responsibility for generating some of their revenue.

However, this independence is a double-edged sword. In its initial form, when annual profit was required, the GBE institutional format was found to be deeply flawed. It has been used to excellent effect in recent years, when, in response to post-1996 challenges and opportunities, PAHSMA's mandate was modified to replace profit making with the more reasonable goal of ensuring the conservation and presentation of the site while pursuing a policy of commercial viability.

By relying on a mix of dedicated government funding and self-generated revenue, this kind of institutional setup exposes the site and its values to a level of risk. If visitation drops off, and/or if government support is threatened, the site would become vulnerable. There would likely be pressure to become more commercial at the expense of conservation values. The PAHSMA institutional framework enables the pendulum to swing either way in favor of commercial or cultural values. Port Arthur has less of a safety net to guard against overdevelopment, though it has the same exposure to public-sector disinvestment in conservation. Moreover, in its commitment to the 2000 Conservation Plan, PAHSMA has accepted the primacy of its obligation to protect the cultural significance of Port Arthur over all other considerations. The key, of course, is balancing certainty and risk taking to act entrepreneurially within the bounds of retaining cultural significance, a course PAHSMA has charted well.

THE PORT ARTHUR WAY, MANAGEMENT STYLE, AND PLANNING PROCESS

Port Arthur is a good example of the salutary effect of thoughtful, deliberate planning processes. The Conservation Plan process enabled and stoked collaboration among PAHSMA's departments and has positively shaped the ongoing, everyday management of the site. Establishment of the Port Arthur way is counted among the major accomplishments of the past few years. The collaboration of business and conservation staff at Port Arthur is remarkable. Developed as part of the Conservation Plan process, the Port Arthur way relies on flexible policies to guide day-to-day management, and on avid consultation and staff involvement.

The managers of PAHSMA have succeeded in collaborating with external partners as well. They have been opportunistic, attracting the new ferry service from Hobart and carrying out the successful Islands of Vanishment conference, and also have been avid partnership builders, forging relationships with the Tasmanian State government, the heritage community, and PARM. This collaborative approach is applied more generally throughout the site, and it is one of the primary ways in which decisions about economic and cultural values are integrated. The management style of the CEO has set an important tone: reaching consensus, building a management team, building ties to government, and breaking down barriers among the different levels of staff. All of these tools and habits create a management strategy that is not easily recorded or captured in documents, making them hard to study outside of case studies. Nevertheless, they are important to the effective, sustainable management of the site.

It is difficult to get a well-rounded view of the effect of this management and planning regime on site values. This is particularly so with Port Arthur, given the relatively short time the current management team has been in place. In recent years, however, PAHSMA has largely succeeded in creating a values-centered management regime in the sense that it has deliberately identified a range of site values, placed them at the center of policy, and managed flexibly and creatively to achieve overall goals within policy frameworks.

Ultimately, the question is, What benefits have stemmed from the use of values-based planning and management for Port Arthur? On the basis of this case study, one can conclude that the values orientation of Port Arthur's management has created a clear mandate of protection of a widely understood set of cultural values centered on convictism; flexible internal management habits and principles, allowing creativity and opportunism within the overall conservation-focused management policy; and good partnership building, leading to strong relations in the region and the creation of solid resources at the state government level.

Notes

1. Further details about the site's geography and features are available in the 2000 Conservation Plan, particularly Godden Mackay 2000b.

2. See appendix A for a time line of Port Arthur from 1877 to 2001.

3. Simpson and Miller 1997, 15.

4. Brand 1998; Godden Mackay 2000b; Design 5 Architects Pty. Ltd. 2001; and Young 1996 were used as sources of information for this section.

5. Much of the information in this and the following sections was taken from Young 1996.

6. Egloff 1986, 4.

7. Ibid., 19.

8. Jane Lennon and Associates 1998.

9. Briggs 1996.

10. Michael 1997.

11. AAP Information Services Pty. Ltd. 2000.

12. For a full description of the role and responsibilities of the Australian Heritage Commission, please log on to http://ahc.gov.au/ (8 May 2003).

13. Marshall and Pearson 1997, 46.

14. Government of Australia 1975, section 4(1).

15. Australia ICOMOS 1999.

16. In 1987 (the year PAHSMA was created), the NPWS (of Tasmania) merged with the Department of Lands to become the Department of Lands, Parks and Wildlife. Five years later, this department was subsumed within the Department of Environment and Land Management (DELM). After the Labor government was re-elected in August 2002, the Tasmanian premier created a new Department of Tourism, Parks, Heritage and the Arts, which reported to him. Source: Tasmania National Parks and Wildlife Service 2000.

17. The act became effective in early 1997. Tasmania was the last state in Australia to adopt such legislation.

18. Government of Tasmania 1995a.

19. Tasmanian Premier's Local Government Council 2001, 5.

20. Context 2001, 85–86.

21. Ibid., 87.

22. Government of Tasmania 1987, 1995.

23. Tasmanian Audit Office 1997.

24. D. Young, "Re: Port Arthur," e-mail correspondence, 26 February 2002.

25. Information for figure 3.8 was gathered from the Site Tour section of the Port Arthur Historic Site Web site, http://www.portarthur.org.au/site-tour.htm (8 May 2003) and from Temple 2000.

26. The Bookings section of the Port Arthur Web site is found at http://www.portarthur.org.au/bookings.htm (8 May 2003).

27. All prices are given in Australian dollars; current as of January 2002.

28. Context 2001, 105.

29. Information regarding transportation to Port Arthur and other areas in the vicinity can be found at http://www.portarthurcruises.com.au/ (8 May 2003).

30. All prices are given in Australian dollars; current as of January 2002.

31. PAHSMA 2001a.

32. Context 2001, 100.

33. Use of the term *values* herein follows the precedents set by the Burra Charter unless otherwise noted.

34. The ebb and flow of these many decades are carefully documented in Young 1996.

35. Brian Egloff's work was a valuable source for this summary.

36. In the context of this study, *commercial values* refers to a particular type of economic value, specifically the kind of economic use value realized by the commercial activities directly related to the site—user fees, food and other products purchased on site, and so on. Secondarily, it also refers to the economic values generated as positive externalities to site activities, and again are realized through specific commercial operations—for instance, nearby restaurants and lodging.

37. Tasmania National Parks and Wildlife Service 1985, 22.

38. Ibid.

39. Ibid., 1.

40. Egloff 2002, 15.

41. Port Arthur Historic Site Management Authority 1996, 1–2.

42. Quoted from the Australian Heritage Places Inventory entry found at www.heritage.gov.au/cgi-bin/ahpi/record.pl?TASR1 (no date given). The statement of significance at the commonwealth-level Register of the National Estate is not considered current. It identifies, indirectly, the 1830s to the 1870s as the primary period of significance. It refers mainly to buildings of the main site, with only a passing reference to open spaces. The register's Web site notes that pre-1991 listings such as this are in need of updating.

43. The Conservation Plan was developed by Godden Mackay for the Port Arthur Historic Site Management Authority.

44. Godden Mackay 2000a, section 3.2.

45. The summaries are derived from Godden Mackay 2000b, section 3.0.

46. "World Heritage" values cannot be articulated for Port Arthur because it has not been designated a UNESCO World Heritage Site. They are listed in the Conservation Plan because of an ongoing effort to nominate Port Arthur and other convict-related Australian sites for World Heritage status. Nevertheless, these values are shaped by the nomination criteria set out in the *World Heritage Convention and Operational Guidelines*.

47. Government of Australia 1999.

48. Economic values are, however, mentioned in passing in other parts of the Conservation Plan: for example, in section 5.9, volume 1, on policies for financing of conservation: "Recognising the economic value of the PAHS to the economies of Tasmania and Australia, State and Common-

wealth Governments will be asked to commit to ongoing recurrent financial contributions." As noted elsewhere in this case, the site's economic values are recognized—often implicitly—in documents other than the Conservation Plan.

49. Godden Mackay 2000a, Section 3.3.

50. Jane Lennon and Associates 1998.

51. This social-value methodology is an outgrowth of the Burra Charter methodology. See Johnston 1992. The use of this methodology for the BAC study was advocated by the HAP.

52. Unitas Consulting Ltd. 1999. This work is an economic impact study based on input-output modeling.

53. For a full description of economists' frameworks for understanding and measuring the value of cultural heritage, see Frey 1997; Mason 1999; Throsby 2001.

54. Young 1996.

55. These tourism activities are classic examples of "valorization" of a heritage site, even in the absence of deliberate articulation and valuation of economic values.

56. The suggestion here is not that decisions or policies reached "informally" lack the qualities of formal decision-making processes. It would be useless to judge whether formal or informal processes are a priori "better." The point we wish to make here is that informal decision-making processes are important in the management of the values of any site and should not escape our attention or emphasis just because they are not formally specified or documented. As noted in the final section of this report, the informal aspects of PAHSMA's management are critical to its success.

57. The operations of the site, by contrast, are organized more by value-type. If this section were analyzing operations, not strategies, value-type would be a more sensible way to organize the discussion.

58. Tasmania National Parks and Wildlife Service 1985, 9–10.

59. Ibid., 22.

60. Ibid., 43.

61. Port Arthur Historic Site Management Authority 1996, 6.

62. Ibid., 8.

63. This sequence of progressively more detailed policies—contained in the 2000 Conservation Plan and following into the secondary plans—is summarized in the diagram in figure 3.12 (see p. 157).

64. These are excerpted and/or paraphrased; for full text, see Godden Mackay 2000a, section 4.8.

65. Ibid., section 5.14.

66. Port Arthur Historic Site Management Authority 2001b, 4–5.

67. Ibid.

68. The latest draft does not include recommendations, and the policies have not yet been finalized. The Draft Landscape Plan was prepared by Context Pty., part of the team that created the Conservation Plan.

69. Sharon Sullivan, personal communication, February 2003.

70. Port Arthur Historic Site Management Authority n.d.(b), 24.

71. The collaborative process instilled during the management planning process, and cultivated assiduously by the board and executive since then.

72. Port Arthur Historic Site Management Authority n.d.(b), 24.

73. The Conservation Plan, for instance, does not contain a list of conservation projects to be undertaken over the life of the plan. Instead, the conservation manager keeps a list of projects phased over a five-year span but not ranked in order of priority. This list is revisited annually as the year's work program is devised—but not followed strictly—in deciding how to spend each year's A$2 million of funding from the state.

74. The Conservation Plan calls for exempting PAHSMA from the GBE Act, leaving it an independent, quasigovernmental agency but giving it a statutory focus on conservation. PAHSMA was exempted in 1997 from providing a financial return to the government, although it remains a GBE. It was also recommended that PAHSMA be given delegation under the *Tasmanian Heritage Act* so that referral of conservation decisions to the THC is not necessary.

75. Personal communication, January 2002.

76. Sharon Sullivan to Marta de la Torre, e-mail correspondence, 13 January 2003.

77. Peter Romey, personal communication, January 2002.

78. Consider, for instance, the difference between the 1972 plan to conserve the convict era versus the PACDP philosophy to assess the Carnarvon-period values and site elements.

79. Godden MacKay 2000a, section 6.3.10.

80. Being that the Tasmanian heritage community is small, there is a membership overlap between the THC and PAHSMA.

81. The future tense is used in this section because few parts of the Interpretation Plan have been implemented to date. Any effects are projected, not actual.

82. The benefit of having different perspectives on cultural values is discussed in the section "How Management Policies and Strategies Take Values into Consideration," noting reasons to have alternatives to the type-driven articulation of values in the Conservation Plan.

83. This transfer of stewardship to PAHSMA from the state parks and wildlife agency was under discussion at the time of the Getty team's visit; it has since been agreed to.

84. It should be noted that the research team did not talk extensively with people in the community, related and/or unrelated to the site, who could give a different perspective.

85. Technically a government business enterprise in the case of Australia. Elsewhere they are known by such titles as public-benefit corporations and community development corporations.

Appendix A: Time Line after the Closing of the Penal Colony[1]

1877   Port Arthur penal settlement closed. The site almost immediately became a destination for interested tourists.

1881   The Whitehouse brothers began a biweekly steamer service between Hobart and Norfolk Bay to transport tourists to Carnarvon.

1883   The Whitehouse brothers opened the first hotel at the site in the former Commissariat Store to cater to visitors.

1884   A bushfire sets ablaze the church, leaving little save for its walls. The ruined remains, which became overgrown with ivy, added to the site's picturesque appearance.

1889   The Tasmanian government made plans to auction for demolition and salvage all Port Arthur buildings previously reserved from sale. Opposition from residents of Carnarvon and Hobart provided that the buildings could remain if converted into factories or showplaces. The Carnarvon town board was formed.

1890s   The Port Arthur Museum, which included many photographs of the site, opened in Hobart at the photography studio of J. W. Beattie.

1890   Four-horse carriage service between Taranna and Carnarvon was initiated. Roads throughout the peninsula were generally upgraded, and work began on a new road between Carnarvon and Wedge Bay.

1891   The Union Steamship line launched Easter tours of Port Arthur and other Tasmanian penal settlements.

1892   Beattie published the first edition of *Port Arthur, Van Diemen's Land,* a collection of photographs.

1893   The volunteer Tasmanian Tourist Association was formed to promote and develop Tasmania as a destination of tourism. Its work was instrumental in promoting tourism in Tasmania, and included the preparation and distribution of leaflets about Port Arthur.

1895   A bushfire spread into Carnarvon and burned the old asylum, then the town hall; the Model Prison; the hospital; the Government Cottage; and several houses. The hospital and town hall were rebuilt.

1898   Another bushfire blew into the settlement, destroying the roof and floor of the penitentiary and burning the rebuilt hospital, leaving only its stone walls.

1905   In response to increased demand for tourist visits to Port Arthur, the Whitehouse brothers increased the frequency of their steamer service between Hobart and Norfolk Bay, and later to Taranna, from two to three trips per week.

1907   The Tasmanian Tourist Association began to organize overland and steamer trips to Port Arthur.

1908   The first film version of *For the Term of His Natural Life,* based on the Marcus Clarke convict tragedy novel of the same name, was filmed at the site. The overland route to the site was improved to make it accessible to motor vehicles.

1912   Motor bus service to Port Arthur began.

1913   The Tasmanian Tourist Association put forth the first proposal to the Tasmanian government for management of the ruins at the site.

1914   After an inquiry concerning financial deficiencies, the Tasmanian Tourist Association was replaced by the state Department of Tourism.

1915   The Scenery Preservation Board (SPB) was created through passage of the *Scenery Preservation Act* by the Tasmanian Parliament. This body represented the first Australian authority created for the management of parks and reserves, although its primary focus was protection of the natural environment.

1916   The SPB provided for the first formal protection of the ruins at Port Arthur through the creation of five reserves there—the sites of the church, the penitentiary, the Model Prison, Point Puer, and Dead Island. These reserves were Australia's first gazetted historic sites. The SPB gradually began to acquire land at the site.

1925   As the SPB's financial resources became scarce, it responded by accepting the Tasman Municipal Council's offer to take over management of the reserves at the site, subject to certain conditions set by the board. The council managed the site until 1937.

1926   The second version of *For the Term of His Natural Life* was filmed at the site. This film, which was a box-office success, had a significant impact in attracting tourism to the site.

1927   The community at the site changed its name from Carnarvon to Port Arthur, in large part due to the growing tourist industry there. The Port Arthur Tourist and Progress Association also was formed with the purpose of developing the site as a tourist center.

1930   Tasmanian novelist Roy Bridges published in the Melbourne *Argus* a short essay arguing that the Port Arthur ruins were significant mainly for the convict suffering that had occurred there, rather than for aesthetic qualities.

1935   The Port Arthur Room was created at the Tasmanian Museum in Hobart to house relics as well as documents, photos, and other items related to the site from a second collection amassed by J. W. Beattie, who had died in 1930. The collection was purchased primarily for its economic value in terms of attracting tourists.

1938   Control over the site was taken away from the local Tasman Municipal Council and turned over to the Port Arthur and Eaglehawk Neck Board, a new sub-board of the SPB.

1939–40   The government acquired the Powder Magazine, the Government Cottage, the Commandant's House, and the cottage in which Irish political prisoner William Smith O'Brien was held in 1850.

1946   Following the recommendations of a document known as the McGowan Plan, the Tasmanian government purchased the town of Port Arthur to better preserve the site and to have control over its future development. In a stark change from the past, the McGowan Plan called for valuing the history and architecture of the site rather than focusing solely on its economic value.

1959   The first car ferry service from mainland Australia to Tasmania began, providing a significant boost to the number of tourists visiting the state.

1960   After years of construction delays, a motel was opened overlooking the site to the rear of the Model Prison and within the viewshed of the site.

1962   A new sub-board of the SPB, the Tasman Peninsula Board, assumed responsibility for site conservation.

1971   The SPB was dissolved and replaced by the newly created National Parks and Wildlife Service (NPWS), which assumed responsibility for management of Port Arthur.

1973   The Tasman Municipal Council offices moved from the town hall / asylum building to Nubeena, marking the permanent removal of the local community from the site.

1979–86   Extensive conservation work was conducted through the Port Arthur Conservation and Development Project (PACDP) and was carried out with commonwealth and state funding. PACDP was a regional development project that provided for the conservation and development of historic resources throughout the Tasman Peninsula. PACDP also served as a significant training ground for Australian heritage professionals. In addition, it was involved in the relocation of the Port Arthur township and the construction of roads bypassing the site.

1983   Based on comments from Australia ICOMOS, the NPWS revised and expanded the official significance of Port Arthur as a historic site to include the township period (roughly 1880 to 1930).

1986   In response to uncertainty concerning the future of Port Arthur as PACDP came to a close, members of the local community founded Friends of Port Arthur Historic Site. The organization was formed to promote the site and lobby the state and commonwealth governments with the objective of ensuring sound management practices at Port Arthur.

1987   The Tasmanian Parliament passed the *Port Arthur Historic Site Management Authority Act*, which created and transferred authority over the site to the Port Arthur Historic Site Management Authority (PAHSMA). The act also erected a toll booth at the site to collect visitor entrance fees for the first time.

1996   In April, a lone gunman killed twenty people inside the Broad Arrow Café (and fifteen more in the vicinity). Most of the victims were tourists, although a number of the remaining victims both worked and lived at Port Arthur.

In June, the Australian prime minister announced the provision of A$2.5 million for the construction of a new Visitor Center to replace the Broad Arrow Café.

In December, the Broad Arrow Café was partially demolished as a reaction to the tragedy.

1997   The Doyle Inquiry, a state audit, investigated the management of Port Arthur since the establishment of PAHSMA and examined issues including the board's handling of the development of plans for the new Visitor Center and parking area, its relations with PAHSMA employees in the aftermath of the 1996 tragedy, and the general handling of conservation and maintenance of historic resources at the site. The inquiry led to the reconstitution of the PAHSMA Board as well as amendments to the *PAHSMA Act*.

1998   The site's new Visitor Center opens after much controversy.

2000   The Tasmanian premier opened the Convict Trail, which connects the historic site at Port Arthur with the convict outstations at Eaglehawk Neck, Cascades, Impression Bay, Saltwater River, the Coal Mines, and Norfolk Bay. The premier simultaneously announced that PAHSMA would receive A$10 million in funding for conservation over a five-year period.

Conservation Plan completed and adopted by PAHSMA.

A memorial garden was created at the site of the former Broad Arrow Café.

Port Arthur Region Marketing Ltd. (PARM) began operations with the "overall objective to increase the economic input of tourism to the Port Arthur Region through an effective market-

ing and sales program." PAHSMA and the Tasman Municipal Council are the main financial contributors to PARM.

2001   Work was completed on the reconstruction of the Government Cottage gardens.

Notes

1. This time line was derived from the following sources: Young 1996; Egloff 1986; Briggs 1996; Jane Lennon and Associates 1998; Michael 1997; as well as other PAHSMA documents and personal communication with PAHSMA staff.

References

AAP Information Services Pty. Ltd. 2000. "Tasman Peninsula Receives Double Boost," 25 May.

Armstrong, H. 1997. "Recognition of Landscape Values Workshop: A Summary." *Historic Environment* 13(3–4): 63–64.

Australia ICOMOS. 1999. *The Burra Charter: The Australia ICOMOS Charter for the Conservation of Places of Cultural Significance*. Australia ICOMOS. The full text of the charter is found at www.icomos.org/australia/burra.html (8 May 2003).

Australian Heritage Commission. 1981. *The Heritage of Australia: The Illustrated Register of the National Estate*. Melbourne: Macmillan Company of Australia.

———. 1994a. *More Than Meets the Eye: Identifying and Assessing Aesthetic Value*. Barton, ACT: Australian Heritage Commission.

———. 1994b. *People's Places: Identifying and Assessing Social Value for Communities*. Barton, ACT: Australian Heritage Commission.

———. 2000. *Australian Heritage Commission Annual Report 1999–2000*. Canberra: Australian Heritage Commission.

———. 2001. *Australian Historic Themes: A Framework for Use in Heritage Assessment and Management*. Canberra: Australian Heritage Commission.

Australian Heritage Projects and K. Winkworth. 1998. *Review of Existing Criteria for Assessing Significance Relevant to Movable Heritage Collections and Objects*.

Beck, H. 1995. "Social and Aesthetic Values: New Assessment Methodologies for Involving the Community." *In Place: A Cultural Heritage Bulletin* (Bulletin of the Australian Heritage Commission) 1: 15–18.

Boyer, P. 1995. "An Interpretation of Port Arthur." In *Cultural Conservation: Towards a National Approach*. Canberra: Australian Heritage Commission, Australian Government Publishing Service.

Brand, I. 1998. *Penal Peninsula: Tasmania's Port Arthur and Its Outstations, 1827–1898*. Launceston, Tasmania: Regal Publications.

Briggs, J. 1996. "$2.5m Welcomed for Port Arthur Reconstruction." *Hobart Mercury*, 14 June.

Casella, E. C. 1997. "To Enshrine Their Spirits in the World: Heritage and Grief at Port Arthur, Tasmania." *Conservation and Management of Archaeological Sites* 2: 65–80.

Context. 2001. Port Arthur Historic Site Landscape Plan (Draft 2).

Coombs, C. 1998. "Port Arthur Historic Site Management Authority Response." *Australian Journal of Emergency Management* 13(1): 16–19.

Design 5 Architects Pty. Ltd. 2001. *The Separate (Model) Prison Port Arthur Conservation Project Report (Conservation Analysis—Final Draft)*.

Egloff, B. 1986. *The Port Arthur Story: 1979 to 1986 (Being a True and Accurate Account in Brief of the Port Arthur Conservation and Development Project)*. Hobart: National Parks and Wildlife Service.

———. 1995. "Conservation Project Units at Home and Abroad." In *Cultural Conservation: Towards a National Approach*. Canberra: Australian Heritage Commission, Australian Government Publishing Service.

———. 2002. "Port Arthur Historic Site and Australia ICOMOS: The Formative Years." Paper presented at Islands of Vanishment conference, Port Arthur, June.

Egloff, B., and R. Morrison. 2001. "'Here Ends, I Trust Forever, My Acquaintance with Port Arthur': The Archaeology of William Smith O'Brien's Cottage." *Australian Historical Archaeology* 19: 1–11.

Frey, B. S. 1997. "The Evaluation of Cultural Heritage: Some Critical Issues." In *Economic Perspectives on Cultural Heritage*, ed. M. Hutter and I. E. Rizzo, 31–49. London: Mac Millan.

Gardiner, J., and S. Knox. 1997. "Identifying, Assessing, Conserving and Managing Elements of a Cultural Landscape: A Case Study of the Alstonville Plateau, North-Eastern New South Wales." *Historic Environment* 13(3–4): 45–53.

Godden Mackay. 2000a. *Port Arthur Historic Site Conservation Plan, Volume 1: Overview Report*. Prepared for the Port Arthur Historic Site Management Authority.

———. 2000b. *Port Arthur Historic Site Conservation Plan, Volume 2: Supporting Information*. Prepared for the Port Arthur Historic Site Management Authority.

Government of Australia. 1975. *Australian Heritage Commission Act of 1975 as Amended*. The text of this legislation can be found at http://scaletext.law.gov.au/html/pasteact/0/227/top.htm.

———. 1999. *Australian Convict Sites: Nomination by the Government of Australia for Inscription on the World Heritage List (draft)*.

Government of Tasmania. 1987. *Port Arthur Historic Site Management Authority Act*. The full text of this legislation can be obtained through www.thelaw.tas.gov.au/scanact/acttitle/F/A (3 June 2003).

———. 1995a. *Historic Cultural Heritage Act*. The full text of this legislation can be obtained through www.thelaw.tas.gov.au/scanact/acttitle/F/A (3 June 2003).

———. 1995b. *Government Business Enterprises Act*. The full text of this legislation can be obtained through www.thelaw.tas.gov.au/scanact/acttitle/F/A (3 June 2003).

Jane Lennon and Associates. 1998. *Broad Arrow Café Conservation Study*.

Johnston, C. 1992. *What Is Social Value? A Discussion Paper*. Canberra: Australian Government Publishing Service.

Kaufman, P. 1997. "Community Values in Cultural Landscape Decision Making: Developing Recommendations for Ensuring Planning Processes Include Differing Expectations of Communities of Interest." *Historic Environment* 13(3–4): 57–62.

Marquis-Kyle, P., and M. Walker. 1994. *The Illustrated Burra Charter: Making Good Decisions about the Care of Important Places.* Sydney: Australian Heritage Commission.

Marshall, D., and M. Pearson. 1997. *Culture and Heritage: Historic Environment.* Canberra: Department of the Environment [Australia: State of the Environment Technical Paper Series (Natural and Cultural Heritage)], 46.

Mason, R., ed. 1999. *Economics and Heritage Conservation.* Los Angeles: The Getty Conservation Institute. Available at www.getty.edu/conservation/resources/econrpt.pdf (8 May 2003).

Michael, L. 1997. "No Board Could Have Anticipated the Impact of April 28/ Doyle Opens Can of Worms." *Hobart Mercury,* 28 June.

Pearson, M., et al. 1998. *Environmental Indicators for National State of the Environment Reporting—Natural and Cultural Heritage.* Canberra: Department of the Environment.

Pearson, M., and D. Marshall. 1995. *Study of World Heritage Values: Convict Places.* Canberra: Department of the Environment, Sport and Territories.

Pearson, M., D. Marshall, and S. Sullivan. 1995. *Looking After Heritage Places.* Carlton, Victoria: Melbourne University Press.

Port Arthur Historic Site Management Authority. N.d.(a). *Briefing Note: Government Gardens Reconstruction.*

———. N.d.(b). *Port Arthur Historic Site Management Authority Corporate Plan 2001/2002.* Port Arthur Historic Site Management Authority.

———. N.d.(c). *Separate Prison Conservation Project Principles.*

———. 1996. *Port Arthur Historic Site Management Plan 1996 (Amending the Port Arthur Historic Site Management Plan 1985).*

———. 1998a. *Port Arthur Historic Site Management Authority Corporate Plan 1998/99 to 2000/2001.*

———. 1998b. *Port Arthur Historic Site Management Authority Draft Business Plan.*

———. 2000a. *Port Arthur Historic Site Management Authority Annual Report 2000.* May be found at www.portarthur.org.au/paannrep-2000.pdf (8 May 2003).

———. 2000b. *Port Arthur Historic Site Management Authority Corporate Plan 2000/2001.*

———. 2000c. *Port Arthur Historic Site Management Authority Government Cottage Gardens Landscape Masterplan Rationale.*

———. 2000d. *Port Arthur Historic Site Management Authority Government Cottage Gardens Masterplan: Accompanying Notes.*

———. 2000e. *Port Arthur Historic Site Management Authority Museum Conservation Stage II: Proposal for the Reinstatement of the Entrance Portico (For Consideration by the Tasmanian Heritage Council).*

———. 2001a. *Port Arthur Historic Site Management Authority Annual Report 2001.* May be found at www.portarthur.org.au/paannrep.pdf (8 May 2003).

———. 2001b. *Port Arthur Historic Site Management Authority Interpretation Plan 2001.*

Purdie, R. W. 1997. *The Register of the National Estate: Who, What, Where?* Canberra: Department of the Environment.

Russell, J. 1997. "The Upper Mersey River Valley, Tasmania: Assessing Cultural Values in a Natural Area." *Historic Environment* 13(3–4): 42–44.

Scott, M. 1997. *Port Arthur: A Story of Strength and Courage.* Sydney: Random House.

Simpson, L., and B. Miller. 1997. *The Australian Geographic Book of Tasmania.* Terrey Hills, New South Wales: Australian Geographic Pty. Ltd.

Strange, C. 2002. "From 'Place of Misery' to 'Lottery of Life': Interpreting Port Arthur's Past." *Open Museum Journal* 1 (August). Available at http://amol.org.au/omj/volume2/strange.pdf (8 May 2003).

Tasmania National Parks and Wildlife Service. 1975. *Port Arthur Historic Site Management Plan.*

———. 1985. *Port Arthur Historic Site Management Plan.* Sandy Bay, Tasmania.

———. 2000. "A Brief History of the Parks and Wildlife Service," 25 January. Available at www.dpiwe.tas.gov.au/inter.nsf/WebPages/SJON-57K8UB?open (8 May 2003).

Tasmanian Audit Office. 1997. *Special Investigation into Administrative Processes Associated with Preservation and Maintenance of Port Arthur Historic Site.* Auditor-General Special Report No. 21. Hobart, August.

Tasmanian Premier's Local Government Council. 2001. *Simplifying Planning Schemes: A Discussion Paper about Common Key Elements for Planning Schemes.* Available at www.dpiwe.tas.gov.au/inter.nsf/Attachments/JCOK-5E58TU?open (8 May 2003).

Taylor, K. 1997. "Is Aesthetic Value Part of Social Value?" In *Place: A Cultural Heritage Bulletin* (Bulletin of the Australian Heritage Commission) 3: 15.

———. 1999. "Reconciling Aesthetic Value and Social Value: Dilemmas of Interpretation and Application." *Association for Preservation Technology (APT) Bulletin* 30(1): 51–55.

Temple, J. 2000. *Port Arthur: Tasmania, Australia.* Launceston, Tasmania: Archer Temple Pty. Ltd.

Throsby, D. 2001. *Economics and Culture.* Cambridge: Cambridge University Press.

Unitas Consulting Ltd. 1999. *The Economic Contribution of the Port Arthur Site to the Tasmanian Economy.*

Young, D. 1996. *Making Crime Pay: The Evolution of Convict Tourism in Tasmania.* Hobart: Tasmanian Historical Research Association.

Persons Contacted during the Development of the Case

Ian Boersma
Conservation Project Manager
Port Arthur Historic Site Management Authority

Julia Clark
Interpretation Manager
Port Arthur Historic Site Management Authority

Brian Egloff
Associate Professor
School of Resource, Environmental
and Heritage Sciences
University of Canberra

Greg Jackman
Archaeology Manager
Port Arthur Historic Site Management Authority

Barry Jones
Chairman
Board of the Port Arthur Historic Site
Management Authority

Jeff Kelly
Director
Board of the Port Arthur Historic Site
Management Authority, and
Chief Executive
Tasmanian Department of State Development

Wendy Kennedy
Director
Board of the Port Arthur Historic Site
Management Authority

Stephen Large
Chief Executive
Port Arthur Historic Site Management Authority

Richard Mackay
Principal
Godden Mackay Pty.

Peter Romey
Conservation Manager
Port Arthur Historic Site Management Authority

Margaret Scott
Director
Board of the Port Arthur Historic Site
Management Authority

Maria Stacey
Visitor Services Manager
Port Arthur Historic Site Management Authority

Sharon Sullivan
Director
Board of the Port Arthur Historic Site
Management Authority

David Young
Chair
Port Arthur Historic Site Advisory Committee

Hadrian's Wall World Heritage Site

Randall Mason, Margaret G. H. MacLean,

and Marta de la Torre

About This Case Study

This case study looks at the management of Hadrian's Wall World Heritage Site. Hadrian's Wall is a remarkable, extensive Roman ruin that has been valued as an archaeological remain for more than two centuries. Today the designated World Heritage Site includes the Wall; its associated archaeological features, such as forts, milecastles, and vallum ditches; and the "setting," a "visual envelope" and buffer zone extending from 1 to 6 kilometers (.6 to 3.7 miles) from the Wall itself. A number of agencies, government bodies, and private landowners are involved in the management of the site under the coordination of English Heritage. This study focuses on the values-based management of these resources since the site's World Heritage listing in 1987.

Throughout this case study, references to "the site" indicate the entire World Heritage Site—the Wall, its associated remains, and its immediate surroundings. According to planning documents, the site and the setting are understood as distinct geographic entities in this report.[1]

However, most of the general references to the site refer also to the setting. If some uncertainty remains in these definitions, their use in this case study closely mirrors that in the 2002 Hadrian's World Heritage Site Management Plan. In the plan, the setting is considered part of the site and is described as distinct from it. When referring to some overarching aspect of the site—for example, "visitors to . . . ," "perception of . . . ," or "government policies toward . . . "—the setting is implicitly included. In other instances, the setting is referred to specifically as a terrain separate from and enveloping the Wall. The lack of a rigorous and clear distinction in the plan seems intentional in that it conveys the loose, flexible nature of the partnership-driven management structure of the site. In the end, the values according to which the Hadrian's Wall landscape is managed are understood as pertaining to the whole entity, site and setting. It is possible that if the plan defined the setting as part of the core managed territory of the site—instead of defining it as a "visual envelope"— it would engender political opposition. Such was one of the lessons learned during the boundary-setting debate raised by the 1996 plan.

The long history of Hadrian's Wall as a heritage site provides an excellent illustration of how values emerge and evolve with changing use and new knowledge as well as how they are influenced by changing values in society. More specifically, this case explores how the values of an extensive site, with a complex set of landowners and stakeholders (and where there is no unified ownership of the land or historical features of the World Heritage Site), are conserved and managed in collaborative arrangements. Of interest are issues arising from the large-scale partnership model of management as well as issues related to the conservation and development of specific sites within the regional management framework.

An analysis is presented in the next two sections. The first of these, "Management Context and History of Hadrian's Wall World Heritage Site," provides general background information on the site and its management, gives a geographic description of the site, and summarizes the history of Hadrian's Wall. Also discussed is the management environment of the site, including the numerous partners involved at national and local levels as well as relevant legislation and policy.

The last section, "Understanding and Protecting the Values of the Site," looks at the connections between values and management in three ways. First, the values ascribed to the site are summarized, as they have been reflected in successive planning and management documents. Second, the role of values in determining the management policy of the current World Heritage Site regime is examined. Finally, management policies and decisions are analyzed as to their impact on the site's values.

This case study of Hadrian's Wall World Heritage Site is the result of research, interviews, site visits, extensive consultation, and frank discussion. Colleagues at English Heritage and the Hadrian's Wall Tourism Partnership have been particularly helpful in the research, production, and refinement of this study. They have been forthcoming and generous, and have participated energetically in the extensive tours and discussions that took place during the Steering Committee's visit to the Hadrian's Wall region in April 2002.

In preparing this case study, the authors consulted the extensive documentation produced by English Heritage, the Hadrian's Wall Tourism Partnership, and various local governments and regional organizations with stewardship responsibilities for some aspect of the World Heritage Site. Site visits and tours of the region were indispensable in understanding the scope of effort and depth of understanding that go into managing the Hadrian's Wall landscape.

Digital reproductions of the following supplementary documents are contained within the accompanying CD-ROM: Planning Policy Guidance 16: Archaeology and Planning (1990); Planning Policy Guidance 15: Planning and the Historic Environment (1994); Hadrian's Wall World Heritage Site Management Plan 1996; and Hadrian's Wall World Heritage Site Management Plan 2002–2007.

Management Context and History of Hadrian's Wall World Heritage Site

Physical and Geographic Description

Hadrian's Wall World Heritage Site is located in northern England. The site extends approximately 118 kilometers (73 miles) east to west, following the line of Hadrian's Wall across the Tyne-Solway isthmus and spreading down the Cumbrian coast to include Roman coastal defenses. The specific geographic boundaries of the site[2] are based on the extent of the Wall and associated sites and ruins that are protected as scheduled monuments under the *Ancient Monuments and Archaeological Areas Act* of 1979.[3] The setting consists of the viewshed around the site itself.

The Romans, in search of a location on which to build a defensive military network against hostile inhabitants to the north, chose the narrowest east-west path in this region of Britain and used many of the area's topographic features to their advantage. Today, the archaeological remains of the Wall and its associated structures take many forms, and a great deal of archaeological research has been conducted on them. Features of the Wall have been adapted, altered, reused, dismantled, and conserved on an ongoing basis since its construction began in 122 C.E.

In many places, the Wall stands aboveground in its original position, though not in its original dimensions (nowhere does the Wall survive at its full height). On the western and eastern ends there are few aboveground remains. Wall features are best preserved and most readable in the central section of the site, where a significant portion, called the Clayton Wall, has been conserved and

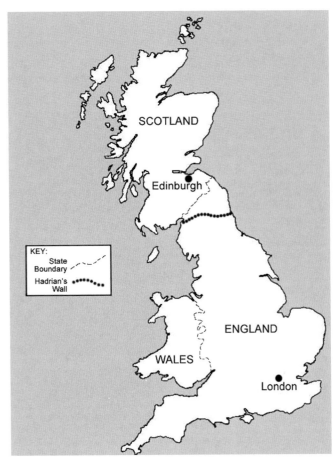

Figure 4.1. Map of the United Kingdom, indicating the location of Hadrian's Wall. The Wall was built by the Roman army in 122 C.E. across the narrowest part of its island territory.

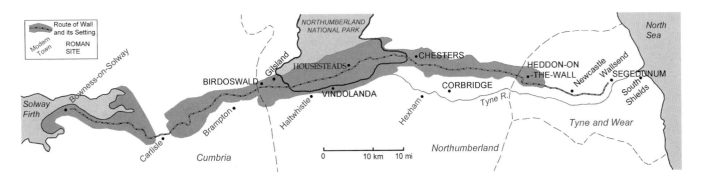

Figure 4.2. Map of the Wall and its setting.

Figure 4.3. A long view of the Wall. This portion of the Wall is typical of the central section of the World Heritage Site. Photo: Margaret G. H. MacLean

Figure 4.5. The exposed foundations of a fort at South Shields. Photo: Margaret G. H. MacLean

rebuilt.[4] Many landscape features—vallum ditches and other earthworks—survive. Dozens of milecastles, forts, and fortlets are still evident in excavated and conserved remains, and many of these are interpreted for the public. Since the 1880s most of the Wall's visible remains have been conserved and consolidated in some measure. The Wall has been totally destroyed in only a few places, where highways, pipelines, or quarries cross or cover its line.[5]

Topographically, the site can be divided roughly into three regions. The first is the eastern lowland region known as the Tyne and Wear Lowlands, which lie between South Shields and Chollerford. From Wallsend, the Wall runs westward from the North Sea coast across low-profile terrain and through the lower Tyne River valley. After the industrial revolution, the urban center of Newcastle upon Tyne emerged as the commercial capital of England's northeast, a position the city still maintains.

This sprawling urban area (now called Tyneside) dominates the eastern region of the site. Within Tyneside, the Wall exists mostly as belowground or excavated/conserved ruin.

The continuous course of aboveground Wall runs westward, beginning at Heddon and extending toward Birdoswald, and forms the second, central region of the site.

The third region lies to the west and consists of lowlands between Brampton and the Solway Firth, a tidal estuary characterized by marshes and mudflats. Today, this area is dominated by livestock pastures and agricultural cultivation. Farther inland is the Carlisle Basin, a broad valley drained by the rivers Irthing, Eden, Esk, and

Figure 4.4. One of numerous sections of the Wall that cuts through working farms. Photo: David Myers

Figure 4.6. The remains of a well-preserved regimental bathhouse associated with the Roman fort at Chesters, situated astride the Wall on the North Tyne River. Photo: Margaret G. H. MacLean

Figure 4.7. Detail of a conserved section of the Wall near Birdoswald. The stone contains an original Roman inscription. Photo: David Myers

Caldew, all of which flow into the Solway Firth. Rural land in the basin is used mainly for livestock grazing. Situated at the head of the Solway Firth is the historic city of Carlisle, the region's urban hub. Between the basin and the central region of exposed uplands is a transitional zone of rolling hills divided by valleys.

Although the Wall ends at Bowness-on-Solway along the Solway Firth, remnants of the Romans' defensive network, in the form of freestanding fortlets and towers, are found to the southwest along the Cumbrian coast as far as Maryport at the periphery of the Lake District. Here the landscape becomes more rolling, with the coast marked by sea cliffs. Occasional fort sites continue as far south as Ravenglass, the southernmost point of the World Heritage Site.

Figure 4.8. The Romans took advantage of the landscape's natural barriers, situating the Wall atop the high ridges of Whin Sill, east of Housesteads. Photo: Marta de la Torre.

A maritime influence creates a temperate climate year-round in Great Britain, in spite of its relatively high latitude.[6] The region of the site is characterized by regular high humidity, cloudiness, and a high percentage of days with precipitation.[7]

History of Hadrian's Wall[8]

The history of the Wall's creation by Roman legions, and of the Roman period of British history, has been extensively documented.[9] This section focuses on the post-Roman period and emphasizes the history of the Wall as a heritage site and the gradual acknowledgment of the landscape in which the Wall is situated as part of the site.

In the centuries following the Romans' abandonment of the Military Zone, the stones of the masonry structures of the Wall and its associated fortifications were removed and reused in the construction of castles, churches, dwellings, field walls, and other structures. Thus the Wall provided great utilitarian value as a source of building material. Land records dating back to the Norman period also show that the Wall was an important boundary between property holdings, agricultural fields, and parishes. In addition, it inspired place-names throughout the region, giving rise to Walton, Walwick, Thirlwall, and Walby.

Although the Wall has been described in written and cartographic works dating back to the eighth century, the first relatively large-scale account appeared in 1599, when the antiquarian William Camden published a survey and explanation of the Wall and its structures in the fifth edition of his *Britannia*.

Throughout the eighteenth and nineteenth centuries, the Wall continued to be used as a source of building material. The 1750s saw the construction of the Military Road, which is approximately 48 kilometers (30 miles) long, between Newcastle and Carlisle.[10] The road was built on the top of the Wall to minimize damage to the fields of local landowners and to save costs by using the Wall's remnants as a road foundation and as a source for stone.[11]

The steady erosion of the Wall led to concerted efforts to study it as well as a growing interest in conserving it. In the eighteenth century, several antiquarian studies were made, including William Hutton's *The First Man to Walk Hadrian's Wall* in 1801. Ten years later, Hutton saved a section of the Wall at Planetrees from being pillaged to make field walls, an event considered the first successful effort of conservation.[12]

John Clayton was an important figure in the understanding and conservation of the Wall. In 1832, he inherited land containing Chesters Roman Fort. The nineteenth century was a period "when [Wall] sites were owned by privileged individuals…who could use them for their own research—and the pleasure of themselves and of their friends."[13] For nearly six decades, Clayton funded the excavation, protection, and reconstruction of remains of the Wall. In the process, he amassed a collection of Roman objects from various locations along the Wall. Clayton acquired and worked on five Roman sites in the area of Chesters and led excavations at the fort sites of Housesteads (1849–present), Carrawburgh (1873–76), and Carvoran (1886).

The nineteenth century was also marked by the establishment of "learned societies" for the study of antiquities. This development came at a time when there was a strong interest in all things Roman and the view that the Roman Empire was a model for England's own vast imperial holdings. These societies increased interest in, and access to, the Wall, introducing it to broader audiences, although membership was limited to the social and economic elite. The proliferation of these groups coincided with the emergence of the Romantic movement, which fostered an appreciation for the aesthetic qualities of the ruins and the natural or naturalistic landscapes in which they were situated.[14] In 1849, the first pilgrimage traveling the full length of Hadrian's Wall was led by John Collingwood Bruce. Two years later, Bruce published the first edition of *The Roman Wall*, which summarized the results of Clayton's excavations at Chesters Roman Fort and publicized John Hodgson's theory of the Wall's construction under the emperor Hadrian.[15] In 1863, Bruce also published his *Handbook of the Roman Wall*, an important historical guide to this day.[16]

The latter part of the century saw the first public acquisition of part of the Wall and the creation of the first museum to display its Roman relics. In 1875, the South Shields Urban District Council established the Roman Remains Park at South Shields, marking the first public acquisition and display of part of the Wall by a public authority.[17] Later, in 1896, the museum at Chesters Roman Fort was constructed to house John Clayton's collection of Roman objects.

Government efforts to protect the Wall increased through further public and trust ownership in the twentieth century. These decades also witnessed an extraordinary growth of tourist visitation. A new generation of academically trained, professional archaeologists rose to prominence in Wall studies and replaced the amateur antiquarians. With the passage of national legislation providing for the protection of archaeology, a first portion of the Wall was scheduled as an ancient monument in 1927.

In 1932, continued quarrying threatened the archaeological fabric of the Wall, motivating the national government to introduce new, more powerful national ancient monuments legislation. This led to the adoption of the Hadrian's Wall and Vallum Preservation Scheme, a first step toward comprehensive public protection of the central part of the Wall and some buffer areas surrounding it.[18] The National Trust also received as a donation the core of its Hadrian's Wall holdings at Housesteads in the central region, a Wall site that has proven to be the most popular among tourists. In 1935, the National Trust opened the Housesteads Museum to the public.[19]

Mass tourism began in the years following World War II, when the growth in automobile ownership and increases in leisure time brought more and more visitors to the Wall. Visitation peaked in 1973, then quickly dropped as a result of a spike in fuel prices (see fig. 4.9). From the start, the experiences available to tourists have been quite varied and remain so today, ranging from well-staffed and thoroughly managed sites with interpretive schemes, gift shops, and amenities, to large stretches accessible informally by simply walking through the countryside.

In 1970, the Vindolanda Trust, an independent archaeological charitable organization, was founded at the fort site of Vindolanda (formerly Chesterholm). Its mission was the excavation, preservation, and presentation of the Roman remains. Later, in the mid-1980s, another fort site went into public ownership when the Cumbria County Council acquired the Birdoswald estate. Likewise, Rudchester was acquired by Northumberland County, North Tyneside acquired Wallsend, and South Tyneside expanded its holdings at South Shields. English Heritage (EH), created by Parliament in 1984, has served as an active force in the conservation, management, and presentation of the Wall. The agency opened the Corbridge Museum in 1984 and launched its Wall Recording Project the following year. The project provides detailed documentation of the visible remains of the Wall and its associated features.[20] EH continues to care for many parts of the Wall.

As a culmination of its long history of heritage and stewardship, Hadrian's Wall was inscribed by the United Nations Educational, Scientific and Cultural Organization (UNESCO) as a World Heritage Site in 1987.

The inscription cites criteria C (ii), (iii), and (iv) (see box at right). Since this designation, a number of measures have been implemented to coordinate management of the site. The Hadrian's Wall Tourism Partnership (HWTP) was created in 1993 to coordinate the development of sustainable tourism for the Hadrian's Wall World Heritage Site area. Early work focused on coordinating marketing and visitor information. Shortly thereafter, the secretary of state approved a proposal for the Hadrian's Wall Path, a new National Trail enabling visitors to walk the length of the Wall. The path opened in 2003. In 1996, a Hadrian's Wall World Heritage Site management plan for the period 1996–2001 was published after extensive consultation. The first plan to coordinate management of the entire site, it established the World Heritage Site Management Plan Committee (WHSMPC, or MPC) "to act as the primary forum for issues concerning the management of the World Heritage Site."[21] EH established the Hadrian's Wall Co-ordination Unit, based in Hexham, to oversee implementation of the plan. The plan was updated in 2002.

In recent decades, local entities have implemented a variety of strategies to attract more visitors to the site. These efforts have been motivated in part by the weakening of other industries in the region, such as shipbuilding, coal mining, iron making, and steelmaking. In 1986, the Tyne and Wear Museums completed reconstruction of the West Gate at Arbeia Roman Fort at South Shields, which Ewin notes was "the first reconstruction of a standing remain associated with Hadrian's Wall and was consequently controversial."[22] Work is now under way to reconstruct the Commanding Officer's quarters and a soldiers' barracks block. At the eastern end of the Wall in Maryport, the Senhouse Museum Trust opened the Senhouse Roman Museum in 1990, which houses the Netherhall collection of Roman artifacts. In 2000, the Segedunum Roman Fort, Bath House and Museum in Wallsend opened to the public. The development, which reuses part of a shipyard on the Tyne River, is operated by the Tyne and Wear Museums and includes a working reconstruction of a Roman bathhouse as well as a viewing tower approximately 34 meters (112 feet) in height.

Faced with rising numbers of visitors to the Wall, the 1996 Management Plan expressed concerns about the negative impact on historic resources by increased tourism (especially by walkers and other informal visitors[23]). That upward trend was reversed, however, in 2001 with the outbreak of foot and mouth disease (FMD). The epidemic caused the closure of the countryside in many rural areas of the region to avoid the spread of the

World Heritage List Criteria for Cultural Properties[24]

A monument, group of buildings or site—as defined above—which is nominated for inclusion in the World Heritage List, will be considered to be of outstanding universal value for the purpose of the Convention when the Committee finds that it meets one or more of the following criteria and the test of authenticity. These criteria are defined by the Committee in its Operational Guidelines. Each property nominated should:

i. represent a masterpiece of human creative genius; or

ii. exhibit an important interchange of human values, over a span of time or within a cultural area of the world, on developments in architecture or technology, monumental arts, town-planning or landscape design; or

iii. bear a unique or at least exceptional testimony to a cultural tradition or to a civilization which is living or which has disappeared; or

iv. be an outstanding example of a type of building or architectural or technological ensemble or landscape which illustrates (a) significant stage(s) in human history; or

v. be an outstanding example of a traditional human settlement or land-use which is representative of a culture (or cultures), especially when it has become vulnerable under the impact of irreversible change; or

vi. be directly or tangibly associated with events or living traditions, with ideas, or with beliefs, with artistic and literary works of outstanding universal significance (the Committee considers that this criterion should justify inclusion in the List only in exceptional circumstances and in conjunction with other criteria cultural or natural).

disease. Access to sections of the Wall on farmland was impeded, and the most popular managed site—Housesteads—was closed to the public all but ten days during that year. Urban sites suffered indirectly via general downturns in the numbers of overseas and education/group visits to the region.

FMD severely damaged the region's agricultural economy, necessitating the slaughter of all infected or potentially infected livestock, and had a secondary negative impact by reducing tourism to the site to a fraction of its pre-existing levels. Latest figures indicate that tourism promotion and other efforts to recover from FMD have been effective vis-à-vis tourism traffic. Total visitation to

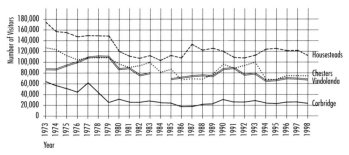

Figure 4.9. "The graph shows some longer term trends. Whilst the numbers of visitors to the forts and museums shown have declined since the 1970s, the numbers of people out walking around the Wall area, particularly in the central sector have increased. ... Approximately 23% of visitors in the central sector of Hadrian's Wall are from overseas. Approximately 69% of visitors in this area are on holiday." Source: "Tourism Facts & Figures," http://www.hadrians-wall.org/

staffed sites in the region reached 562,571 in 2002—a 23.7 percent increase on 2001 figures and a 5.1 percent increase on 2000 figures.[25]

The Management Context

Heritage preservation in the United Kingdom began with modest efforts to protect individual archaeological sites of interest. The preservation movement became more formalized in 1882 with the passage of the *Ancient Monuments Protection Act*. Over time, historic buildings, landscapes, parks, battlefields, and other places attracted the interest and concern of preservationists and government, and efforts proliferated to record, restore, and preserve such places for posterity. The main legislation concerning archaeological resources at this time is the *Ancient Monuments and Archaeological Areas Act* of 1979. Other protections now in place are numerous, flexible, and almost entirely integrated into the planning processes from the national level down to the county council level, and are supported by the various governmental and nongovernmental organizations that administer heritage places.

Hadrian's Wall is a constellation of scheduled monuments and listed buildings with unique status at the national level; it is also inscribed as a World Heritage Site, more as a conceptual entity than as a particular place. It is subject to a broad range of protections afforded by government authorities through statutes, regulations, and policy directives, and by the international community through the World Heritage Convention and its operational guidelines. Below is a brief description of the heritage classifications, agencies, and statutory authorities, which inform the management discussions that follow.

A primary means of heritage protection in England is statutory designation. The categories of heritage places covered by separate legislation are: scheduled ancient monuments, listed buildings, and conservation areas. World Heritage Sites, registered parks and gardens, and battlefields are protected through the integrated planning processes administered at the local to district levels.[26]

Scheduled Ancient Monuments

As prescribed by the *Ancient Monuments and Archaeological Areas Act*, a scheduled ancient monument is one that meets specific criteria of age, rarity, documentation, group value, survival, fragility or vulnerability, diversity, and potential. The secretary of state approves those monuments meeting these criteria as well as the criterion of national importance, in consultation with EH.

Of the three types of designated heritage, scheduled ancient monuments are the most rigorously protected by legislation. By law, the treatment of scheduled ancient monuments is handled at the national level and is not integrated into town and country planning policies. Scheduled monument consent must be obtained from the secretary of state for all works to scheduled monuments, including maintenance.[27] Planning guidance for work on such monuments—including that proposed in these management agreements—is provided in *Planning Policy Guidance 16: Archaeology and Planning (PPG 16)*.[28]

Today, there are more than 13,000 such monuments under protection around the world. After being scheduled as an ancient monument, Hadrian's Wall later acquired status as a listed building and as a World Heritage Site.

Listed buildings

The primary means of acquiring national protection of buildings is through listing. The secretary of state, again relying on the counsel of EH, is responsible for maintaining a statutory list of buildings determined to have special architectural interest, historic interest, close historical association, and group value. *Planning Policy Guidance 15: Planning and the Historic Environment (PPG 15)* contains the definitions, selection criteria, procedures, and considerations relevant to this designation, and provides guidance concerning the treatment of listed buildings.[29]

Listed buildings are ranked according to grades I, II* ("two starred"), and II. Any works (repairs, upgrades, restorations, etc.) being considered for listed buildings must obtain consent. The secretary of state has delegated to local authorities most decisions concerning these consent applications. Applications for works to grade I, grade II*, and demolitions of grade II buildings must be reviewed by EH or other relevant national bodies.

Conservation areas

A conservation area is a territory that has been determined to have special architectural or historic interest. Conservation areas may be designated by local planning authorities, and local development plans contain descriptions of them and policies for their protection. Local authorities determine whether proposed new development will negatively impact a conservation area's character and appearance. No conservation areas have been created to protect any part of the Hadrian's Wall World Heritage Site or its setting.

World Heritage listing

Since becoming a signatory to the World Heritage Convention in 1984, the United Kingdom has added twenty-four World Heritage Sites to the list in the natural and/or cultural categories. The operational guidelines of the World Heritage Convention include a recommendation to develop site management plans for each site being nominated to the list: "States Parties are encouraged to prepare plans for the management of each natural site nominated and for the safeguarding of each cultural property nominated. All information concerning these plans should be made available when technical co-operation is requested."[30]

While there is no British legislation or regulation pertaining solely to World Heritage Sites or nominations, some official guidance makes specific reference to the operational guidelines that implement the Convention. For example, *PPG 15*, issued by the Office of the Deputy Prime Minister, requires local authorities to devise policies to provide for the long-term protection of these sites, and that any development proposals be evaluated with regard to their potential impact on the prospective site and its setting, from an aesthetic as well as an environmental perspective.

Thus, national policy works with the guidelines so that World Heritage designation serves to stimulate the development of integrated conservation planning across the United Kingdom. Hadrian's Wall has the distinction of having the first World Heritage Site management plan to be completed in the country (1996) and the first to be updated (2002).

NATIONAL HERITAGE–RELATED AGENCIES

At the national level, heritage is managed by several departments and agencies. The Department for Culture, Media and Sport (DCMS) holds primary responsibility for the built heritage through its Architecture and Historic Environment Division.[31] Advised by EH, the secretary of state for culture, media and sport is responsible for the scheduling of ancient monuments, ruling on applications for scheduled monument consent and listing buildings of special architectural or historic interest. The secretary also works specifically with UNESCO on issues related to World Heritage Sites in the United Kingdom.

Land-use planning falls under the aegis of the Office of the Deputy Prime Minister, including national legislation and guidance documents, such as the PPGs, (see statutes, regulations, policy directives, and guidelines below). The Department of Environment, Food, and Rural Affairs (DEFRA), which handles countryside issues, also plays a significant role in the management and conservation of heritage. The Countryside Agency, which operates under DEFRA, is the national agency responsible for rural matters. It plays a less direct but noteworthy role in heritage affairs.

English Heritage serves as the government's statutory adviser concerning all issues related to the conservation of England's historic built environment. EH is classified as "an Executive Non-Departmental Public Body sponsored by the DCMS."[32] It is responsible for the management (i.e., repair, maintenance, and presentation) of more than four hundred properties in public ownership and, more commonly, guardianship. EH interfaces with many aspects of the planning and consent system, as discussed further below. Funded in part by the government and in part by self-generated revenues, it also re-grants funding for the conservation of the built heritage. (Other key nongovernmental financial supporters of heritage in the United Kingdom include the Heritage Lottery Fund and the European Union.)

The National Trust was established as a private charity in 1895 to safeguard threatened natural and cultural heritage sites.[33] Today, it holds in perpetuity more than 248,000 hectares (613,000 acres) of countryside in England, Wales, and Northern Ireland, almost six hundred miles of coastline, and more than two hundred buildings and gardens. It is a particularly important force in the region of Hadrian's Wall.

LOCAL HERITAGE AUTHORITIES

At the local level, responsibility for conservation of the historic built environment resides with 34 county councils, 238 district councils, and 46 unitary councils. These authorities handle most decisions regarding buildings and conservation areas, including consideration of applications for listed building consent and conservation area consent. Local authorities also issue monetary grants to outside groups and vendors for the repair and improvement of both designated and nondesignated elements of the historic built environment. In some cases, the local authorities own and manage their own heritage sites. Ten national parks in England and Wales also are independent local authorities with statutory responsibility for heritage. These include Northumberland National Park, a large portion of which coincides with the Hadrian's Wall World Heritage Site.

In addition to their role in determining the outcome of consent applications, the councils provide active protection of the historic built environment by placing specific policies into local town and country plans. A number of local authorities have incorporated specific provisions into these policies as a way of implementing the otherwise advisory and partnership-based Management Plan. As of summer 2002, thirteen local authorities at various levels had incorporated measures specific to Hadrian's Wall, based on the Management Plan, into local policies.[34]

NATIONAL HERITAGE STATUTES AND POLICIES

Provisions for the national government's conservation of heritage are found in acts of Parliament, regulations, and policy documents. Statutory protection of heritage in Great Britain began with the enactment of the *Ancient Monuments Protection Act* of 1882. Since that time, the adoption of new national statutes and policies has greatly expanded the extent of government control over cultural heritage, including towns and landscapes. Starting in the late 1960s, national conservation activities have been folded into the planning process. Rather than enforcing fixed rules, this discretionary planning system allows for flexible and responsive decision making. A listing of the principal statutes follows; those with annotations bear a specific relation to designation, enhancements of protection, and new approaches to planning and management.

Historic Buildings and Monuments Act (1953)

Civic Amenities Act (1967). This act launched the trend of embedding heritage preservation in the planning processes at the county and district levels. It also legalized the group value of buildings and acknowledged the importance of conserving areas as opposed to individual buildings. Local planning authorities were given the responsibility of designating as conservation areas those places within their jurisdiction that were of special archi-

tectural or historic interest, the character or appearance of which it was desirable to preserve or enhance.

Town and Country Amenities Act (1974). This act makes it the responsibility of local planning authorities to review designated conservation areas and determine if other elements should be designated.

Ancient Monuments and Archaeological Areas Act (1979). This act refined the definition of protected status designations—adding the category of archaeological area—which could be made either by the secretary of state or by local planning authorities, subject to confirmation by the secretary. The criterion of national-level significance remained in force. The act also strengthened protections by making certain offenses against scheduled monuments subject to criminal prosecution.

National Heritage Act (1983). This act established English Heritage as a public body with responsibility for all aspects of protecting and promoting the historic environment.

Town and Country Planning Act (1990). The latest in a series that began in 1947 with the establishment of the English planning system, this act recognizes and assigns planning jurisdiction in various contexts. Any development of land or change in land use warrants an application for permission from the planning authority in force, thus reducing the individual landowner's ability to change the character of a townscape or countryside in unacceptable ways.

Planning (Listed Buildings and Conservation Areas) Act (1990).[35] This act recognizes that the primary responsibility to list significant buildings lies with the secretary of state and his or her advisers. However, it emphasizes the roles and responsibilities of local planning councils to monitor the historic fabric in their jurisdictions, recommend buildings for listing, and limit changes that can be made to listed buildings.

Heritage Lottery Fund (HLF) (1993). The *National Lottery Act* of 1993 allowed for the creation of a revenue stream to support conservation projects for the physical upkeep of buildings and sites of national importance. While the legislation relating to the *National Lottery Act* is not prescriptive in regard to the heritage itself, 1998 saw the introduction of the requirement for a conservation plan for a site requesting HLF funds for works on historic sites.

Planning Policy Guidance (PPG). "Planning policy guidance notes set out Government policy on planning issues and provide guidance to local authorities and others on the operation of the planning system. They also explain the relationship between planning policies and other policies which have an important bearing on issues of development and land use. Local planning authorities must take their content into account in preparing their development plans."[36]

PPG 15: Planning and the Historic Environment (September 1994; updated frequently) focuses on the planning processes involving listed buildings and other aspects of the historic environment, including World Heritage Sites, parks and gardens, battlefields, conservation areas, associated roadways and traffic, and the broader historic landscape. No special statutes pertain specifically to World Heritage Sites. Rather, this PPG (section 2.22) articulates that local authorities must devise management plans that include policies to provide for the long-term protection of sites. Development proposals must be assessed with regard to their potential impact on a site and its setting, including the assessment of environmental impacts for development of significant magnitude.

PPG 16: Archaeology and Planning (1990) is a parallel manual for planning processes involving archaeology. It is directed at planning authorities, property owners, developers, archaeologists, amenity societies,[37] and the general public. "It sets out the Secretary of State's policy on archaeological remains on land, and how they should be preserved or recorded both in an urban setting and in the countryside. It gives advice on the handling of archaeological remains and discoveries under the development plan and control systems, including the weight to be given to them in planning decisions and the use of planning conditions."[38]

OWNERSHIP AND MANAGEMENT DISTRIBUTION

Ownership and management within the site is varied and complex. There are approximately seven hundred private owners, accounting for 90 percent of the site. Land use is similarly diverse and includes urban neighborhoods, farms and pasturage, towns and villages. Many of the prime archaeological sites, however, are publicly owned or otherwise managed for conservation and public access.

Approximately 10 percent of the site is managed specifically for heritage conservation, access, presentation, research, and recreation. These owners and managers include seven local authorities, English Heritage, the National Trust, and the Vindolanda Trust. The local authorities with the most substantial holdings and management roles for particular Roman heritage sites are the Cumbria County Council (owns and manages Birdoswald), Northumberland County Council (owns and manages Rudchester), North Tyneside Council (owns Wallsend), and South Tyneside Metropolitan Borough Council (owns South Shields). Both Wallsend and South Shields are managed for their owners by the Tyne and Wear Museums. Northumberland National Park Authority also leases Thirwall Castle and manages a visitor center and car parks. The Allerdale District Council and Carlisle and Newcastle City Councils also own areas of Roman ruins related to Hadrian's Wall.

English Heritage manages approximately 8 kilometers (5 miles) of the Wall, three forts and parts of their civil settlements (including Roman Corbridge), two bridges, and most of the visible milecastles and turrets. It should be noted that many EH guardianship properties are owned by the Cumbria County Council, the National Trust, and the Vindolanda Trust, resulting in considerable overlap in management activities.

The estate of the National Trust in the site's central sector covers approximately 1,100 hectares (2,718 acres). Its main holdings include the fort at Housesteads, approximately 8 kilometers (5 miles) of the Wall, lengths of the vallum, two visible milecastles, and the fortlet and marching camps at Haltwhistle Common.

The Vindolanda Trust owns the forts and civil settlements at Vindolanda and Carvoran, and operates museums at both sites. The Senhouse Trust also operates a museum of Roman relics located next to the Roman fort at Maryport. Both the Newcastle Museum of Antiquities and Tullie House hold major collections related to Hadrian's Wall. A number of related Roman sites lie within the World Heritage Site but are under varied ownership.

MANAGEMENT COORDINATION

Coordination among the many owners, managers, stewards, and users of Hadrian's Wall and its setting is one of the leading challenges in conserving and managing the site. The 1987 designation of the Wall as a World Heritage Site clearly recognized the value of the Wall and its setting as a whole, not simply as a collection of individual sites and features. In addition, it highlighted the importance of coordinated management to preserve the Wall's values. Groundwork was laid for the present efforts of the Hadrian's Wall World Heritage Site Management Plan

Committee (MPC) as far back as the 1976 Darlington Amenity Research Trust (DART) report and the 1984 Hadrian's Wall Consultative Committee document *Strategy for Hadrian's Wall*. Both documents were based on the intellectual-historical tradition of understanding the Wall and its associated features holistically and asserted that the Wall should be managed as a whole.

The notion of Wall-wide management gained further momentum in 1990–91 as a result of major development proposals for open-cast coal mining and oil drilling in what would later be designated as the setting. Opponents of the development (including English Heritage and the Council for British Archaeology) prevailed, and the experience provided an important validation of the Wall's acknowledged values as well as the values of its landscape/setting. Furthermore, it emerged that *management* of the Wall and its surroundings—not just its designation and protection—would be key to its survival and development.

Prior to these pro-conservation outcomes, World Heritage designation had not been explicitly addressed in the legislation regarding the management of the historic built environment. These public controversies occurred before *PPG 15* was published in 1994; indeed, the inquiries that were held helped lead to the inclusion of specific World Heritage sections in *PPG 15*.

Around 1993, three distinct but related initiatives were developed, each bringing together a variety of partners and focusing efforts on the Wall and setting as an integrated whole. These three initiatives were the Hadrian's Wall Tourism Partnership (HWTP); the Hadrian's Wall Path National Trail, led by the Country-

Figure 4.11. View of a structural wall of Housesteads Fort in the foreground with Hadrian's Wall extending eastward into the distance. Photo: David Myers

side Agency; and the start of the Management Plan process, led by English Heritage. Historically, ownership and control of the territory making up the site and setting had been fragmented. In response, these initiatives created institutions and partnerships to manage Wall and setting resources in ways that were coherent geographically and

Figure 4.12. View of the excavated area at Housesteads Roman Fort looking south into the valley. Visitors cross this area as they walk from the car park up to the fort. Photo: Randall Mason

Figure 4.10. The English Heritage museum building just below the fort at Housesteads. Photo: Margaret G. H. MacLean

across sectors. They have led quite directly to the current management and planning regime. Behind the initiatives is a core set of individuals, connected informally and formally, who remain involved in the management of the site to this day.

In 1996, the first comprehensive management plan was adopted to provide a framework reconciling and balancing the variety of interests in the site, to articulate agreed-upon objectives, and to generate programs of work. Among the central provisions of this plan was the creation of the Management Plan Committee, which represents the stakeholders in the site and its setting. The 1996 plan spells out the MPC's responsibilities:

1. to oversee the implementation of general and specific recommendations made within the Management Plan, and to monitor the success in meeting the targets it sets;

2. to establish a forum for management issues, and to continue to co-ordinate efforts towards concerted management within the Hadrian's Wall World Heritage Site;

3. to receive reports from responsible bodies and agencies on projects which affect the Hadrian's Wall area;

4. to agree action programmes and priorities for developing specific aspects of the management plan;

5. to monitor the condition of the World Heritage Site, and develop and agree on appropriate action to deal with threats to its well-being;

6. to develop and agree further policies and codes of practice for protection, recording and research, access, interpretation, and preservation of the World Heritage Site, as well as safeguarding the livelihoods and interests of those living and working within the zone, and to encourage the adoption of such policies by responsible bodies and agencies;

7. within the overriding need to conserve the World Heritage Site, to promote the economy of the region;

8. to agree the work programme of, and provide general direction for the proposed Hadrian's Wall Co-ordination Unit;

9. to review the conclusions and recommendations within the management plan, to determine the frequency of the necessary updating of the plan, and to oversee this process when it occurs.[39]

The members of the MPC are:

Allerdale Borough Council

Association of Northeast Councils

Carlisle City Council

Carlisle County Council

Castle Morpeth Borough Council

Community Council of Northumberland

Copeland Borough Council

Council for British Archaeology

Country Land & Business Association

Countryside Agency

Cumbria County Council

Cumbria Tourist Board

Department of Culture, Media and Sport

Department of Environment, Food, and Rural Affairs

Durham University

English Heritage, Hadrian's Wall Co-ordination Unit

English Heritage, London

English Nature

European Liaison Unit

Forest Enterprise

Government Office North East

Hadrian's Wall Tourism Partnership

ICOMOS UK

Lake District National Park

National Farmers Union

The National Trust

Newcastle City Council

North Tyneside Metropolitan Borough Council

Northeast Museums, Libraries and Archives Council

Northumberland County Council

Northumberland National Park

Northumbria Tourist Board

Tyne & Wear Museums

Tynedale District Council

University of Newcastle

The Vindolanda Trust

Voluntary Action Cumbria

The MPC convenes biannually to review progress on the plan. The 1996 plan also created the Hadrian's Wall Co-ordination Unit (HWCU), which oversees implementation of the management plan on a day-to-day basis. Another important entity is the HWTP, which, like the HWCU, handles day-to-day responsibilities for managing activities at the site. The HWTP works to coordinate sustainable tourism marketing and development; it is discussed in more detail below.

THE ROLE OF ENGLISH HERITAGE

English Heritage is a key organization in this management scheme. It plays several roles simultaneously. At one level, it serves as partner and coordinator; at another level, it is the national authority that advises and approves or prevents certain interventions or activities of other partners. EH's core mandate—and its historical mission and raison d'être—as well as its statutory responsibilities identify it closely with the historic, archaeological, and research values of the Wall. The management functions it has taken on for the Hadrian's Wall World Heritage Site (and others in England) have, however, more fully clarified its role in contemporary values. Congruent with this broadening of mandate and of the types of values it recognizes in its site-specific work, EH sees itself as steward, advocate, and protector of historic landscapes and environments, rather than of sites and monuments.[40]

Of central importance to the success of management is the HWCU, set up in 1996 by EH to lead the implementation of the first Management Plan.[41] Currently, the HWCU consists of two staff members on loan from EH who, in collaboration with other individuals from other institutions, lead the implementation of this scheme across the totality of the site, aided by dozens of partner organizations and more than seven hundred landowners.

EH is the government's "lead body for the historic environment" and is the only national body with the remit to protect and conserve the World Heritage Site. Based on the 1979 *Ancient Monuments and Archaeological Areas Act* and the 1983 *National Heritage Act*, EH has statutory review authority for planning consent regarding scheduled monuments. EH also offers advice to owners of scheduled monuments and listed buildings and is the manager of several museums/historic sites and museums at the site (Corbridge, Housesteads, and Chesters).

Because of its key role in the HWCU and its legal mandate at a national level, EH is somewhat more than an equal partner in the scheme, and this creates an imbalance of power among the partners. EH holds a trump card in the form of its statutory review authority. If in certain situations the negotiation, consultation, and collaboration of the partnership fails to bring a result acceptable to EH, the organization has the authority to change the outcome. Evidently, this action is avoided to the largest extent possible. EH fills the complicated roles of manager, regulator, archaeologist, business partner, and referee. Furthermore, as an operator of historic sites, the organization needs to cultivate the site's economic and use values, and it is sometimes seen to be in competition with other sites. This puts EH in the position of advocating—and needing to balance—different kinds of values. Recognizing the complexity, EH and its partners have established other organizations, such as the HWTP and the National Trail, to bolster the sitewide presence and perspective and hedge reliance on one sole, coordinating entity.

Reconstruction at Archaeological Sites: A Lens on Cultural Resource Policy

Reconstruction of aboveground features at archaeological sites is a source of great controversy in professional circles, and yet it is a fairly common practice. In situ reconstruction proposals often highlight conflicts of value: while reconstruction usually destroys archaeological and research value to some extent and may damage perceptions of a site's "authenticity," the "realism" suggested by the new structure can increase the number of visitors and therefore the economic and social value of the site. Ex situ reconstructions are less controversial because, in principle, they are not placed over archaeological deposits. The strategies and intentions behind reconstruction vary consid-

The bathhouse of Segedunum at Wallsend. In addition to a broad, excavated area and a new, award-winning museum, the site includes a Roman bathhouse reconstructed ex situ. The project has captured considerable interpretive and research values through the process of researching, constructing, and presenting the working Roman-style bathhouse. Since it was not built above archaeological resources and is presented as a modern structure, it does not undermine the research value of the site. Photo: Marta de la Torre

erably from site to site along Hadrian's Wall, making reconstruction an excellent lens through which to view the varying, sometimes opposing, approaches to cultural resource policy that exist within the Management Plan framework.

Several examples of reconstructed buildings and features are present at individual sites across the World Heritage Site, and more are planned for the future. Even the Wall itself is an in situ reconstruction in some places. Partners have different standards for reconstruction, ranging from a strict avoidance of reconstruction as a conservation strategy, to its free use to generate interpretation and visitor attraction.

Reconstruction has been justified either as research in the use of construction materials and techniques or as a means of helping the visitor imagine the original appearance of a site. The reconstructions illustrated here were conceived and executed to create stronger images and interpretive tools for conveying the central historic values of the Wall and its features as representing the Roman military frontier that so strongly shaped this part of the United Kingdom.

In general, the conservation field does not embrace reconstruction. The Venice Charter[1] states, "All reconstruction work should ... be

Panoramic view of the actual remains of the fort at Sege-dunum, as seen from an observation tower, showing the reconstructed bathhouse at the far left. Photo: Margaret G. H. MacLean

ruled out 'a priori.'" *PPG 15* terms reconstruction "not appropriate." The 1998 British Standard on the Principles of the Conservation of Historic Buildings[2] instructs, "A presumption against restoration is a hallmark of the British approach to building conservation." However, some experts believe reconstructions increase

The West Gate at Arbeia at South Shields. Located near Newcastle, the site of Arbeia has several reconstructions. The West Gate, reconstructed in 1988, was initially challenged by English Heritage and resulted in a public inquiry. Reconstruction was eventually approved, along with tacit approval of the idea of using reconstructions as a bold visitor attraction strategy. It is interesting to note that the same individual developed the plans for South Shields and Sege-dunum using reconstruction, excavation, and museum display methods but different overall approaches to each. Photo: Margaret G. H. MacLean

public understanding, bolstering the marketability of sites, creating jobs, and boosting tourism expenditures and associated economic externalities.

Recently revised EH policy on reconstruction maintains basic conservation principles while carefully circumscribing certain conditions under which it can be accepted as conservation policy, and therefore in the interest of sustaining heritage values. Emphasis, however, remains on discouraging speculative reconstruction and precluding in situ reconstructions that damage original fabric.

The 2002 Management Plan adopts a policy generally supportive of reconstruction, citing several successful examples at the site and listing several advantages of selective reconstructions (in situ and otherwise). This marks a change from the traditional approach to archaeological values.

All in all, a lack of consensus still remains on reconstruction among the Hadrian's Wall partners. The issue has been divisive. Already in

The reconstructed barracks at Arbeia at South Shields. At present, additional in situ reconstructions of barracks and houses are being undertaken within the excavated fort walls at Arbeia. Photo: Marta de la Torre

The private Vindolanda Trust pursues an active program of excavation, research, conservation, and reconstruction with a strong entrepreneurial visitor orientation. Some of the Trust's initiatives have proven controversial. These include a number of ex situ reconstructions, for example this temple and segments of stone-and-turf wall. The Trust plans to reconstruct a large Roman fort on its properties, in a location that would have a strong visual impact on the setting. Photo: Marta de la Torre

Clayton's Wall, near Steel Rigg. Many segments of Hadrian's Wall could be considered reconstructions. For example, in some places much of the wall was mined for building stone in the post-Roman era. The extensive sections of Clayton's Wall reconstructed in the nineteenth century (followed by similar conservation in the twentieth century) consist of a core of excavated and reassembled Roman-era dry-laid wall with nineteenth-century course layered on the top. Few, if any, truly authentic segments of exposed wall survive. Photo: Marta de la Torre

1984, prior to World Heritage designation, approval of the proposal for the reconstruction of the West Gate at South Shields did not come until after a public inquiry, the last step in resolving a reconstruction disagreement. The interests in favor of reconstruction and its economic-development benefits won out over heritage conservation interests, led at that time by EH. Proposals for reconstruction are expected to continue as conservation and development activities proceed in the World Heritage Site. The absence of consensus is seen as an indicator of the health of the overall partnership: partners can disagree on specific approaches even though they agree on the general framework of values and their protection. "Generally, there can be no objections to reconstruction which is not in situ provided the setting of the World Heritage Site is protected," and, further, that principles of historical accuracy and reversibility are respected.[3] Hadrian's Wall policy therefore reflects a branching away from rigid ideological pronouncements against reconstruction toward a more situational decision making based on recognition of the multiplicity of values involved. Future proposals for reconstruction present potentially divisive decisions for the partnership.

In the end, the key question about reconstruction is whether it threatens the overall integrity and authenticity of the Wall and setting, and therefore the heritage values of the entire site. Decisions ultimately will be made within the planning controls system—the scheduled monuments review conducted by EH to advise the consent decisions of the DCMS.

Notes

1. ICOMOS, The Venice Charter, 1967.

2. British Standard on the Principles of the Conservation of Historic Buildings (BS7913, 1998), cited in *English Heritage Policy Statement on Restoration, Reconstruction, and Speculative Recreation of Archaeological Sites Including Ruins*, February 2001.

3. English Heritage 2002, 65–66.

Understanding and Protecting the Values of the Site

Values Associated with Hadrian's Wall

HOW VALUING OF THE WALL HAS EVOLVED

Since the departure of the Roman legions centuries ago, local people and communities have valued and made use of the Wall in a variety of utilitarian ways: as a source of quarried stone, as field boundaries, and so on. Antiquarian interest in Hadrian's Wall, and the conscious understanding of archaeological and historic value, began around 1600 and increased throughout the nineteenth century. Thus, use values *and* heritage values of the Wall stretch back over centuries.

Legislation protecting the Wall has been enacted over time, reflecting the changing values attributed to the site. The original legislation scheduling most of the Wall as a national monument dates from 1927 and focused exclusively on the Wall's Roman archaeological and historic values. This scheduling was updated by the 1932 Hadrian's Wall and Vallum Preservation Scheme, which extended the protected area.

The 1976 Darlington Amenity Research Trust report on conservation and visitors services, organized by the Countryside Commission, formulated a strategy to deal with the Wall in a geographically comprehensive way. It also addressed both the threats and opportunities presented by tourists drawn to the Wall, and recognized real and potential constraints presented by reconciling agricultural, tourist, and conservation uses of the Wall and its landscape. The DART report was the basis for the 1984 document *Strategy for Hadrian's Wall*, produced by the Hadrian's Wall Consultative Committee, which consisted of a few dozen national, regional, and local government agencies, as well as nonprofit groups representing a wide variety of stakeholders.[42] The balanced view of resources and / or conservation and development opportunities presented in the DART report were extended by the *Strategy*. The latter focused on sites directly on, or related to, the Wall itself, and proposed a strategy of strengthening tourism use of larger, central sites along the Wall (Carvoran, Birdoswald, Chesters, and Corbridge). While concentrating on safeguarding the Wall, the document suggested efforts to protect and enhance its landscape setting. The four points of the strategy are:

a. to safeguard the splendid heritage of Roman monuments and all associated remains so that they are not lost or spoilt for future generations;

b. to protect, and where possible enhance, the quality of landscape setting of the Wall sites;

c. to encourage appropriate public visiting of the Wall area, with convenient access and high-quality experience and (for those who seek it) understanding of the Roman monument and way of life;

d. to ensure that local people derive the best possible benefits from tourism by way of income and employment, whilst ensuring that all appropriate steps are taken to minimise the adverse effects of tourism, particularly on agriculture.[43]

Though both the DART report and the *Strategy* had little immediate, practical effect, they did set a precedent for partnership building and a broadened view of the Wall's values. Both acknowledged contemporary and heritage values, and valued the Wall itself as well as the surrounding landscape. Equally important, these early initiatives launched an evolutionary process of conceiving the Wall and its values as *a whole entity* comprising the core archaeological resources as well as the landscape setting. Monument scheduling under the 1979 *Ancient Monuments and Archaeological Areas Act* revised the original designations. The Wall is now almost entirely scheduled.

UNESCO World Heritage inscription of Hadrian's Wall Military Zone in 1987 was based on Roman-era heritage values. "Built under the orders of Emperor Hadrian in about 122 A.D. on the border between England and Scotland, the 118-kilometer long wall is a striking example of the organisation of a military zone, which illustrates the techniques and strategic and geopolitical views of the Romans."[44] The inscription was a catalyst for understanding *and managing* the Wall as a zone, not simply an archaeological resource.

Managing the site in a comprehensive and holistic way became the major challenge. The primary vehicle has been the Management Plans of 1996 and 2002. The plans dealt with contemporary-use values and the long-recognized, iconic archaeological and historic values of the Wall. They have stimulated the development of the partnership-based management model employed today, and in their formulation even embodied such an approach.

CURRENT UNDERSTANDING OF VALUES

The current understanding of the site's values is explicitly represented in the two Management Plans. The values are not listed per se in the 1996 plan, but the site's historical and contemporary significance is well summarized as follows: "The Hadrian's Wall corridor is important … both for the concentration of Roman sites and for their survival and effect on today's landscape."[45] An articulation of values is presented in the significance of the Hadrian's Wall Military Zone:

- archaeological values of the Roman Wall remains, as well as its associated features (vallum, etc.), and outlier sites (e.g., fortlets and Stanegate features);
- the historical values associated with the Roman northern frontier and its subsequent influence;
- the varied surrounding landscape along the 80-mile length of the Wall;
- aesthetic and natural values of the surrounding landscape are also noted briefly; and
- the additional layer of World Heritage value is described.

Economic and other contemporary values were not explicitly articulated as a contributor to the site's significance in 1996, though they are tacitly addressed in plan policies and through the partnerships formed. In section 3.1, "Need for a Management Plan," the central management challenge is clearly defined as involving "four major factors which need to be balanced": (1) conserving archaeological resources (and associated landscape); (2) protecting the working agricultural landscape surrounding the Wall; (3) ensuring public access for visitors and local users, and making this access sustainable; and (4) recognizing the important contributions of the Wall to the local and regional economies.

A first-draft plan was issued in July 1995 and generated strong reactions during the public consultation period, resulting in revisions and a plan more responsive to the concerns of a wider range of stakeholders.[46] Hundreds of copies of the draft and 35,000 summary leaflets were distributed to a wide range of partners and individuals. The three-month consultation period was extended, and eventually more than two hundred responses were received. Most of the concerns were expressed by the archaeological community and by landowners and farmers, often channeled through local authorities. The overall number of responses was not large, and few were hostile, but specific concerns were strongly articulated:

- Fear of additional controls on farming throughout a wide zone
- Fear of widespread enforced change to farming practices
- Fear of increased bureaucracy and additional English Heritage controls
- Concerns over traffic management on road B6318 (the Military Road)
- Fear of impact of tourism and of the National Trail on farming activities and archaeological remains.

English Heritage's response, as captured in the revised plan, was described by lead planner Christopher Young: "We rewrote the plan [after the public comment cycle] and made it more accessible. We also spent a lot of time talking to people and groups with concerns. In the end, apart from the boundaries, there was comparatively little difference in substance between the policies set out in 1995 and 1996, but we had achieved better understanding of what was intended as a result of the consultation process."[47]

The final 1996 plan addressed the primary concerns as follows:

- It adopted a tiered approach to land-use and monument controls, using normal ancient monument powers for archaeological cores and appropriate planning policies to protect the setting.
- It recognized the need for change in the agricultural landscape (not the fossilization of particular farming methods), and the development of positive landscape management on a voluntary basis with appropriate grant support.
- It clarified that EH sought no additional powers in establishing the Co-ordination Unit; the role of the unit was to provide a focus on the Wall as a whole, as well as coordination of efforts and carrying out of tasks that did not fall to other agencies.
- It formalized the boundaries of the World Heritage Site and defined its setting.
- It pursued "sustainability" of tourism through working with the HWTP and through maintenance and management of traffic throughout the region.

The revised 2002 Management Plan is not a significant departure from the 1996 plan; rather, it is a refinement and continuation of it. The 2002 plan includes a point-by-point analysis of the progress accomplished on the nineteen objectives of the 1996 plan. Adjustments to "regulatory and administrative measures" for putting the plan into effect were considered to have been largely achieved. For the most part, objectives in the area of conservation and research were estimated not to have been achieved. Finally, in the areas of sustainable tourism and visitor access, it was determined that significant progress had been made both at specific sites and at the Wall-wide scale.[48] In the 2002 plan, the approach to value articulation was revised to suggest a new balance between heritage values (the basis of conservation policies) and contemporary-use values (the basis for access and development policies).

The core statement of significance makes the connection between archaeological values and their uses, both cultural and economic: "[Hadrian's Wall Military Zone] is of significant value in terms of its scale and identity, the technical expertise of its builders and planners, its documentation, survival and rarity, and also in terms of *its economic, educational and cultural contribution to today's world*."[49]

Following are elements of the 2002 Statement of Significance:[50]

- Archaeological and historical values: tightly tied to Roman period, with some acknowledgment of the nineteenth- and twentieth-century values created by conservation . . . although the values are clearly centered on the Roman, the aboveground remains have (almost exclusively) been conserved, consolidated, and restored in situ over the last 150 years.

- Natural values: seven key types of habitat are represented in the World Heritage Site, many of them recognized as significant ecological resources at the national and international levels.

- Contemporary values: economic, recreational and educational, social and political.

- World Heritage values. The rationales for meeting WHC criteria (ii), (iii), and (iv) stem exclusively from Roman fabric and associations. [Though stated last, these in fact are at the center of articulated values for the Wall and its setting.]

Current management and policy are clearly focused on the archaeological values and associated historic values of the Wall. Secondary to this, but integrated as bases for policy, are the aesthetic values of the setting and the economic values. The latter is perhaps the most important contemporary value of Hadrian's Wall and represents a departure from the 1996 plan.

The latest Management Plan does not reflect *all* the values held by *all* the partners. What are represented are the values and policies on which there is consensus, and which have emerged from the process of consultation and negotiation that created the multipartner plan. Each of the partner organizations and / or landowners is likely to have projects and hold values that are not accounted for in the plan.

Each partner sees management of the site from the perspective of its particular stake in the Wall and its value priorities. The core significance, range of values, and general policies for the World Heritage Site are shared by all. As expected, the values are arranged and prioritized differently by different partners as each pursues its goals within the Management Plan framework. For example, the 2002 bid for Single Regeneration Budget (SRB) regional economic development funding highlights economic values. These documents were submitted by the HWTP and reflect a collective decision by the members of HWTP (which include EH).[51]

How Management Policies and Strategies Take Values into Consideration

This section describes how the evolving values of the Wall have been reflected and taken into consideration in the policies and strategies of the World Heritage Site Management Plans. The discussion is organized around several types of policies or management issues that provide a perspective on the particular challenges faced by management. These challenges include the setting of boundaries; the value shifts between the 1996 plan and the 2002 plan; tourism strategies and the creation of the HWTP; agricultural policy; and the central role of partnerships in management of the site.

SETTING BOUNDARIES

Boundaries for the site were not included in the original nomination of Hadrian's Wall to the World Heritage List in the mid-1980s. The boundaries were set later, during formulation of the 1996 Management Plan. This lag gave the multipartner collaboration the opportunity to grow and develop before the contentious subject of boundary setting was addressed.

Primarily, boundaries were determined in accord with the parts of the Wall that had been scheduled as ancient monuments. Secondarily, the setting was established as a viewshed of the Wall resources (from 1 to 6 kilometers distant) and as the areas that potentially contained significant archaeological resources. The resulting discussions and negotiations revealed the different values held by various groups and stakeholders. Disagreements arose with local authorities or landowners about specific properties to be included in the setting, and strategic decisions had to be made to exclude particular agricultural, town, or other lands lest landowners perceive even more regulatory controls and reviews were being imposed.

The 1995 draft plan proposed boundaries that approximated roughly the area now defined as the Setting of the World Heritage Site. Also proposed, more tentatively, was the inclusion of a wide zone down the Cumbrian coast, down the north coast of the Solway estuary, and through a large area of the Tyne River valley around Corbridge and north of Hexham. This reflected an approach that viewed the World Heritage Site very much as a cultural landscape.

In practical terms, the 1995 draft plan presented a tiered approach to the management of this broadly defined site. The innermost tier, the archaeological core, would be protected by powers under ancient monuments legislation since it consisted of scheduled sites only, while developments in the outer part of the site would be controlled through planning policies in local authority plans. This was effectively the position reached, after exhaustive public consultation, in the 1996 plan—a tightly defined Site composed of the archaeological core and a Setting under local control. The end result was virtually the same.

Some argued in the 1995–96 public discussions that the World Heritage Site should not be concerned with the landscape as a whole since that landscape is not Roman and therefore not of outstanding universal value. This argument did not win out, owing to the logic that the Wall is where it is because of the landscape and has greatly influenced the development of the landscape since its construction.

The most powerful arguments offered regarding boundaries were not about the cultural value of the landscape, but rather about the potential impact on modern land management and the interests and freedoms of current landowners. There was widespread concern that formally designating such a large area as a World Heritage

Site would lead to further controls. This issue was taken up at senior levels of government, and the eventual decision on boundaries was made at the ministerial level.

In the end, the practical management effect of setting the boundaries was very small—the planners' original conception and the eventual result are quite similar. Psychologically, though, many people felt more comfortable with a closely defined Site along with a broad Setting, which might be easier to alter in the future.[52]

FROM THE 1996 PLAN TO THE 2002 PLAN

There are some subtle but significant differences between the 1996 and 2002 Management Plans, which reflect on the continuing evolution of site values.

Conceptually, over the course of this period, focus shifted from the Military Zone to "the Wall and its Setting." Although the notion of Hadrian's Wall as a landscape and not simply as an archaeological resource was indicated in the 1995 draft and the 1996 plan, this central idea is much more evident in the 2002 plan. This shift reflects a broadening of the types of values toward a greater inclusion of aesthetic and contemporary values of the wider setting landscape. It also was a response to the FMD disaster and its impact on the values of the World Heritage Site. In addition, it symbolized a move toward a broader-scale and more holistic approach to planning. One could say that the older model of planning for an archaeological resource had been replaced by a model of planning for a living landscape that counts the 118-kilometer (73-mile) archaeological resource among its dearest elements.

Access, tourism revenue, tourism impact, agricultural viability, and economic development—issues that form the social context of conserving the Wall—have been discussed and debated since the 1970s. The Management Plans have grown progressively more detailed and proactive in dealing with these diverse issues that constitute the social context of the Wall's conservation, and integrating them with the more heritage-centered values and issues. The values articulated in the 2002 plan more explicitly recognize the importance of contemporary-use values. Correspondingly, the policies are more strongly shaped by contemporary values in the 2002 plan, though not at the sacrifice of heritage values (which already were well articulated in the 1996 plan).

THE CENTRAL ROLE OF PARTNERSHIPS

Recognition and engagement of many diverse stakeholders are key to values-based management. The Hadrian's Wall plans are inclusive in this regard, taking into consideration the interests of future generations, of the world at large (universal value), of archaeologists and researchers, of tourists and visitors, and of government, landowners, farmers, and local communities. Development and implementation of management policies have relied strongly on the formation of institutional partnerships, with the HWCU, HWTP, or the Countryside Agency playing the coordinating roles. At one level, this regime of partnerships is a straightforward response to the decentralized patterns of ownership and stewardship in the territory of the Site and Setting—namely the seven hundred or so owners and dozens of government and nonprofit agencies with a stake in the site.

Fragmented landownership remains a prevalent pattern. Under the current partnership regime, there is no single manager for the whole site, but rather a fluid but fairly stable group of organizations led by a small core of coordinating partners.[53] This has been called a *partnership park* management model, in contrast to the traditional model of unified site ownership.[54] The core group of partners per force spends a great deal of energy managing the partnerships. These partnerships provide benefits beyond those that would accrue from individual partners acting alone and without coordination. That these benefits are seen as outweighing the costs holds true even for some individual partners—foremost, the Vindolanda Trust—who disagree with some of the main policies guiding the Management Plan.

By making it a priority to coordinate and integrate the actions of partners at all geographic levels, the Management Plan serves the *range* of the landscape's values well. One risk of such a large partnership park is that of uncoordinated action, which not only can damage resources and threaten values directly but also can send a message that the entire partnership is not fully supported by all partners. Maintaining a spirit of cooperation and partners' ultimate deference to the values of the whole site, as discussed and recorded in the Management Plan, is central to the success of the partnership.

The overriding goal of the Hadrian's Wall partnerships has been to create a balanced program of conservation and development, as evidenced in the collaboration of three different organizations leading the effort: EH, a conservation-driven agency; the HWTP, primarily an economic development agency; and the Countryside Agency, a statutory agency involved in many countryside issues and in developing the Hadrian's Wall Path National Trail. This is a departure from traditional conservation practice—which generally resisted or ignored develop-

ment and its benefits, and too often focused on monuments rather than whole landscapes—and is aligned with similar efforts in other countries seeking to manage large heritage resources, complexes, or landscapes (for example, French regional parks and American heritage areas).

Through partnering and overlapping of responsibilities, the site's values have been well acknowledged in both depth and breadth. This acknowledgment probably comes more easily when the partners have diverse interests and values than in a case of centralized ownership and management. For instance, some partnerships focus on archaeological values, others on natural values or recreational use. With these collaborations spread out across the region, a critical task for management is one of coordination. The Wall's status as a World Heritage Site plays an anchoring role, keeping archaeological values, and historic value related to the Roman archaeology, as the focus of all efforts. Such buy-in on "Roman" values brings together all the stakeholders—not just the partners for which Wall-wide value understanding and management is the primary goal, but also local authorities, individual heritage sites, government agencies with divergent mandates, national government, and World Heritage stakeholders.

TOURISM STRATEGY

Tourism development activities and the economic values realized by tourism play a strong but not primary role in site management. The leading tourism strategy pursued has been spearheaded by the tourism development agency HWTP. The HWTP is itself a partnership, with an executive and more than a dozen funders and partners (government agencies, local councils, and others). The agency seeks to increase the economic benefits and sustainable uses of the heritage resources and other amenities available to visitors.

Since its formation in 1993, the HWTP's efforts have been closely coordinated with those of the HWCU and other Wall-related entities, as reflected in the Management Plan.[55] This integration of tourism and management activities is evident in the list of HWTP objectives:

• To develop a high quality tourism product which meets the needs of identified target markets, within the overall objectives of the World Heritage Management Plan;

• To generate and spread benefits for businesses in the area, by improving communication and access to markets, attracting more high spending domestic and overseas visitors, and developing the 'shoulder' seasons;

• To encourage more people to leave their cars at home and to travel into and around the area by public transport and other means such as cycling and walking;

• To stimulate visitor interest in, and support for, the management and conservation of the World Heritage Site;

• To influence visitor behaviour, to spread the load in support of agreed site management objectives, to maximise benefits and minimise any adverse impacts on the host community.[56]

The agency engages in traditional marketing activities and plays an important part in regional branding and identity for both the Northeast and the Northwest (two governmental regions across which HWTP's work spans). It works with local businesses to improve their understanding and connections with the site and also organizes the Wall-wide bus service.[57]

The HWTP's involvement reflects the attitude that tourism values must be integrated with heritage values. The agency takes the lead in tourism promotion and Wall-based economic regeneration—within the framework of the Site's conservation mandate. It has launched a wide variety of successful services and initiatives (from the aforementioned bus service to a Web site to winning and administering a large government grant for tourism-led regional economic regeneration) to work toward these goals, operating on the idea that "heritage is a driver of economic regeneration." What sets the HWTP apart from other tourism agencies is its close partnership with EH and its full buy-in to the Management Plan, including the primacy of heritage conservation.

Through its objectives and activities, the HWTP defines and pursues what the Management Plan calls sustainability. *Sustainable*, as defined by the HWTP and its World Heritage Site partners, means (1) staying within the overall (conservation) objectives of the World Heritage Site and (2) balancing the pursuit of the various values recognized in the plan, both contemporary and historic. As the Management Plan states on its very first page, it is "to provide a means for establishing an appropriate balance between the needs of conservation, access, sustainable economic development, and the interests of the local community."[58] Indeed, sustainability is anchored in values: "An underlying principle [of the plan] is that of 'sustainability' which strikes a balance between maximising enjoyment and use of the WHS while still preserving the values and fabric of the Site and its Setting and ensuring that their universal significance is not impaired for future generations."[59]

AGRICULTURAL POLICY, VALUES, AND USES

The practice of agriculture and agricultural policy has a significant effect on the Hadrian's Wall landscape and its management, especially in the central sections of the site. Agriculture has shaped the landscape for centuries and plays an exceedingly important role in the regional economy, rivaling tourism and tourism-related development as the most important contemporary-use values in the Setting.

The 2002 plan recognizes the interdependency between agriculture and heritage conservation. As part of the articulation of contemporary values, the plan's statement of significance notes the contribution of agriculture to the World Heritage Site's economic values.[60]

Sustaining agriculture, difficult in itself given economic pressures and globalization, is yet more complex in the context of the World Heritage Site. The maintenance of traditional agriculture (especially pasturage) is a powerful lever for managing the landscape, which has become an increasingly valued part of the site, as well as for conserving the archaeological resources of the Wall itself. Great aesthetic and historic value lies in the landscape of pasturage, stone walls, and sheep. Likewise, agriculture is essentially an economic activity, and economic pressures on agriculture are addressed by a number of government programs, such as the Countryside Stewardship Scheme, which provides grants and advice on diversification.

Farmers tend to see conservation and tourism as costs to bear, and even as a threat to economic sustainability. Nevertheless, they are partners in managing the site as a heritage place. DEFRA's Countryside Stewardship Scheme is one program used to manage the threats and opportunities of changing agricultural practices and their effect on heritage places. The scheme gives grants to farmers to encourage the conservation of landscape and ecological values. For example, by helping start farm-stays instead of converting pasturage to tilled land or forestry, stewardship grants help farmers manage their land to conserve valued environments and cultural features while diversifying operations to achieve greater financial stability. The site is a target area for this national program, and applicants from within the area receive preferential treatment. Another benefit is the barn scheme, through which farmers secure grants to construct barns that are appropriate to the aesthetic values of the landscape and that allow them to shelter stock during winter and therefore manage a more lucrative operation. This program was strongly promoted by Northumberland National Park and is a good example of what can be achieved through partnership; indeed, such a program would not have been created by any one organization working independently.

Heritage protection is an important public good, and restricting some of the rights of private property holders is a reasonable trade-off for guaranteeing public access to heritage. Heritage conservation of any kind thus has some perceived disadvantages, for instance, the constraints that monument scheduling might impose on free use of one's land. Although World Heritage designation brings advantages to some farmers, others see it as further constraint.

The FMD crisis of 2001 reduced farming incomes some 60 percent in the region and pushed agricultural values to the forefront.[61] The impact on tourism, access, and the regional economy—along with the direct threat to agriculture—shaped the creation of the 2002 plan. The 2002 plan takes agricultural values into consideration more seriously, given that it was written when this region was recovering and responding to the FMD disaster. Even though the decimation of animal stocks threatened the very practice of pasturage in these places, the crisis is thought to have accelerated the pressures on agriculture but not to have changed them fundamentally. Economic pressures on farming will continue to spur diversification, changes in ownership (both fragmentation and amalgamation of farms), and conversion of farmland to other uses altogether.

At the regional scale and in the long-view time frame, the interrelationship between agricultural policy and management of the World Heritage Site is evident in several ways. Consider a scenario in which agriculture ceased to be viable in its traditional modes: open land would likely revert to scrub or forest, vastly changing the aesthetic of the landscape and the perception of its values. Or, consider the wholesale transfer of pasture land to cultivation (although it is unlikely for reasons of climate and soil). This would result in potentially damaging effects of plowing on several kinds of site values, physically disturbing archaeological remains, accelerating erosion, and, again, changing the look of the landscape.

In the end, economic decisions of individual farmers must be reconciled with local effects as well as regional effects, not only on the Wall and Setting but also on environmental/ecological values. At the local level, coordinated conservation of archaeological resources, ecological resources, and economically robust agricultural practices is difficult for so few staff to manage.

[continued on page 199]

Foot and Mouth Disease: The Effects of External Forces

The agricultural economy and pastoral landscape that predominate much of the central section of the Wall are important contributors to contemporary values of the World Heritage Site and its setting. These came under direct threat in 2001 with the outbreak of foot and mouth disease (FMD) among livestock populations in the United Kingdom. FMD is a viral disease that is deadly to some livestock and other mammals, including cattle, sheep, pigs, goats, and deer.[1] The outbreak had disastrous economic effects in the area of Hadrian's Wall, along with a number of secondary effects on the values and management of other aspects of the site.

The FMD crisis effectively closed large areas around the Wall for months. It dealt a major blow to the agricultural and tourism economies of the region and has had lasting effects on the surrounding communities and landscape. Cumbria was the county hardest hit: "Approximately 80% of farms within the World Heritage Site and its setting had their stock destroyed."[2] Visitor traffic to much of the site came to a virtual halt as parts of the country were quarantined, although some sites along the Wall remained open. Fear and negative perception kept people away perhaps as much as the actual closures did.

Assisting farmers and rescuing the agricultural economy and landscape—a fundamental part of the World Heritage Setting and perhaps the key contributor to its widely perceived aesthetic value—were the necessary, immediate responses to the crisis. In the longer term, FMD heightened partners' perceptions of the importance of agriculture in managing the landscape. Farmers, who are important stewards of historic and aesthetic values, are economic operators and key participants in the production and enjoyment of the site's contemporary values. Thus, threats to their livelihood translated into threats to their stewardship roles: if they could no longer farm, how would that impact the management of the site? A new agricultural farming economy based on tillage or forestry instead of pasturage, or new kinds of commercial or industrial development seen as alternatives to pasturage, could drastically affect the character of the setting. The Countryside Stewardship Scheme, developed by the Department of Environment, Food, and Rural Affairs (DEFRA), has been addressing these types of transitions for a decade, but FMD dramatically emphasized how serious the effects could be.

The FMD crisis also highlighted the importance of tourism to the regional economy—particularly in rural areas along the Wall—and the relationship between agricultural practices and management of the site. For decades the Wall had provided economic value as a tourist attraction; balancing this with conservation of heritage values was the central challenge for planning and management. The external force of FMD threatened this balance by focusing attention on economic values. Tourism (which suffered its own 40 percent drop in activity in the aftermath of the outbreak) became identified more fully as the "replacement" economic development strategy for agriculture, much as it had been for industry a generation earlier. Conservation of cultural values was not directly undermined by the FMD crisis, though damages to the tourism economy highlighted the vulnerability of the cultural sector to fluctuations in tourism-market revenue.

The most relevant lesson was learned through the difficulty encountered in responding to this kind of "slow-burn" disaster, given the much decentralized power structure of the partnership. A quick and sure response was hindered

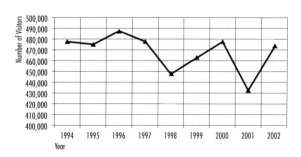

Visitation to major sites near Hadrian's Wall. There was a significant decrease in the number of visitors as a result of foot and mouth disease affecting the area during 2000–2001. However, the number of visitors increased quickly once the crisis had passed.

by the need for consultation and coordination among the partners. This factor would also come into play in the wake of similar natural disasters, environmental accidents, or economic dislocations. Though the FMD disaster is still quite recent and adjustments are still being made by landowners, organizations, communities, and other groups, a few insights can be drawn from the experience.

The 2002 Management Plan was greatly influenced by the fact that it was written during the FMD recovery period—illustrating that the conditions under which a plan is formulated have a strong impact on it. The emphasis on economic recovery and, consequently, on contemporary-use values has been the most obvious impact of the FMD crisis. Planners and partners have participated and continue to participate in determining the adjustments needed to find a new balance of diversified, sustainable agriculture that does not have adverse effects on the heritage resources of the site.

This balance of values has changed in response to the FMD tragedy and the resulting stresses on the Hadrian's Wall landscape and stakeholders. The Management Plan goals remain focused on sustainable management— which is to say, development within a conservation framework—but this sustainability has been redefined by FMD. By bolstering the economic use of the landscape for diversified

agriculture as well as for heritage tourism, the heritage values of the site and setting were protected. The basic structure of the site's management regime—flexible policies and a wide latitude for the actions of individual partners, held together by a mutual commitment to a common core of values—allowed participants to respond the way they did. At the same time, the decentralized partnership structure prevented a swifter response. The need for partners to act in concert and inform one another takes time and resources. Coming to an agreement on novel, contentious, unexpected issues also causes delays. There was much debate, for instance, on the pros and cons of which Wall venues would stay open during the crisis. And a great deal of effort was put into informational campaigns and discussions among agencies and institutions, which helped foster a mutual understanding between institutions with very different mandates and missions (e.g., DEFRA, HWTP, individual farmers, and heritage site operators).

Brought on by FMD, the heightened awareness of the connection between agricultural use/policy and management of the Wall and setting has been a learning experience for the management group of the Hadrian's Wall World Heritage Site. Management has accommodated a shift toward emphasizing the economic values of the Wall in the context of conserving the core heritage values. In the new climate, the focus is now on tourism rather than on the crippled agricultural sector.

Notes

1. Accessed at http://www.defra.gov.uk/footandmouth/about/index.htm (5 April 2003).

2. Accessed at http://www.24hourmuseum.org.uk/nwh/ART13762.html (10 July 2003).

Impact of Management Policies and Decisions on the Site's Values and Their Preservation

This section outlines some of the impacts that the Management Plans, policies, and decisions have had on the site's values. The discussion highlights major innovations of, and lessons learned from, the Hadrian's Wall experience and identifies issues relevant to managers of similar sites and projects. In reality, of course, the effects of the site's management extend beyond what is covered here. The topics selected for discussion in this section are the impact of World Heritage designation on values; the balance between the values of the Wall and the values of the wider landscape; the effects of the partnership-driven model of management; and the nature of Management Plan policies.

IMPACT OF WORLD HERITAGE DESIGNATION ON VALUES

World Heritage designation has reinforced, and even helped expand, the values of Hadrian's Wall. It has generated planning processes that have engaged a full range of values and integrated these into the management of the surrounding landscape. As a policy decision taken by the government, the World Heritage nomination has directly affected the perception and assessment of the values of this landscape and its resources. In primary ways, it has clearly articulated the site's "universal value," and in myriad secondary ways it has prompted value assessment, planning, and management action.

World Heritage status functions as both a conservation strategy and a marketing strategy and furthers the efforts of existing local, regional, and national bodies. It does so by creating the mechanisms for Wall-wide management through partnerships, which have resulted in a series of affirmative relationships and development opportunities, while reinforcing existing statutory controls and refraining from imposing additional ones.

By adding an explicit layer of universal value, World Heritage status continues the decades-long evolution of the understanding and management of the Wall and its landscape. It facilitates moving from a narrow focus on the Roman archaeological remains to a more holistic, encompassing view of the heritage values. Because it has enabled and fostered regional cooperation, World Heritage designation has indeed added value in each of the categories articulated in the Management Plan.

The management planning activities have resulted in a broad articulation of the values of Site and Setting (i.e., including natural, contemporary, and non-Roman cultural values along with the core Roman/universal values). By institutionalizing the connection between the management of the site *and* the setting, World Heritage status has reinforced the values of the living landscape, such as ecology and nature, visual qualities, and contemporary use.

The designation has also brought prestige to the Wall and probably helped attract the substantial amounts of government funding devoted to projects at the site (£10 million to £12 million from the Heritage Lottery Fund, for instance; more recently, £3.6 million in regional SRB grants). The result has been a more proactive, incentive-based attitude toward site development, as opposed to the traditional regulatory, restrictive approach.

World Heritage designation has been a unifying force, creating incentives (and in some ways requirements) for collaboration. Projects such as the HWTP programs or the National Trail benefit all and provide additional opportunities to enjoy, use, and understand the site. Inscription of the site is seen as the force behind the continuing exchange between different stakeholders—from different parts of the Wall, and from different perspectives on the value of the Wall. Given the fragmented ownership pattern, the number of government and other agencies involved with land management, and the competition for tourism and grant revenue in times of economic stress, it is reasonable to think that there would not have been a Wall-wide plan or management scheme without the designation. Opinions on this interpretation differ, however. Some of those involved feel that some regional scheme would still have emerged without the designation's catalyzing effect.

All these benefits should not lead one to think that World Heritage status has been a panacea. The designation has not eliminated divisiveness and competition among stakeholders in the Site and Setting. Conflicts between owners and regulatory agencies remain, as do conflicts between conservation-driven interests and development-driven interests. The essential nature of this place's heritage and contemporary values—extraordinarily rich and very diverse—makes such disagreements inevitable, and a planning system in which this is recognized and dealt with collectively is a productive arrangement. Various agencies will continue to compete for resources. Indeed, various groups—the Roman archaeology community, or the

[continued on page 202]

Limits of Acceptable Change Conference

A number of resource-, project-, and place-specific plans have been initiated under the rubric of the Management Plan, including a local interpretive plan at Gilsland and conservation plans for the Roman fort sites of Chesters and Housesteads. The plans have been spearheaded by the particular partners involved, but, dictated by the Management Plan, efforts have been made to incorporate them into the larger regional framework of significance, values, and general policies.

Two overarching implementation issues must be addressed. The first is how to specify and implement the broad insights and decisions of the regional planning and management scheme at a local level, or for specific resources. The second is how to monitor values at such local, empirical scales that their improvement (or erosion) "on the ground" can be gauged and management can respond.

To address both these challenges, the Countryside Agency and English Heritage are leading an effort to complete a limits of acceptable change (LAC) study for the most highly visited and traveled stretch of the Wall—Housesteads to Steel Rigg.[1] This area is under the most intense use and pressure, and it also has a complicated, overlapping stewardship and ownership pattern involving a number of institutions, including EH, the National Trust, and Northumberland National Park. An adaptation of carrying-capacity planning and impact assessment, LAC methods acknowledge the reality of landscape change and focus on identifying acceptable ranges of change. They are based on managing outcomes so that the different values and functions of a landscape remain balanced, as opposed to setting particular values as a priori targets for protection. These tolerances are not based on scientific studies, but rather are established through extensive consultation among the stakeholders.

The Housesteads LAC conference looked at five factors, each relating loosely to the heritage and contemporary values articulated for the World Heritage Site: archaeological resource quality; natural resource quality; disturbance to farming; recreational path quality; and quality of visitor experience. For each factor, clear benchmarks are outlined as limits— for example, "no deterioration in the archaeological resource" or "a maximum of 40 complaints from farmers per annum." Monitoring is built in: "The LAC process relies upon a system of continual environmental monitoring that demonstrates when a quality threshold has been breached or is about to be breached."[2] The five elements chosen for monitoring correlate well with World Heritage Site values and goals. With the points for unacceptable change having been defined, a series of "management prescriptions" is drawn up to guide responses to specific changes (e.g., whom to consult before constructing a fence around a scheduled monument, or when it is acceptable to close certain parts of the walking path).

As with other plans in the World Heritage Site, the linchpin of the LAC approach to microlevel heritage landscape management is not the specific limits or actions described in the plan but the system of collaboration. The Housesteads LAC "brings together organisations and individuals with diverse interests (subsequently referred to as the Conference) to agree on limits of acceptable change for specific parameters, how they should be monitored and the measures to be taken to prevent them being reached or if they are reached." With the conference done and the plan in place, the actual work of monitoring and reporting is shared by the main stakeholder agencies.

The LAC stresses collaboration among partners as the key to balancing the values of the landscape, while also demonstrating detailed understanding of the resources and their use. This effort has nonetheless engendered criticism for being too exhaustive, intensive, and expensive to be pragmatic and useful as a widely adopted management method.

Notes

1. The source for much of the information on the LAC efforts is Rimmington and McGlade 2001.

2. Ibid., 4.

owners of one or another site / attraction, for example—have selectively used the statement of significance to advance their own interests. This study, however, suggests that World Heritage designation and the management efforts that have resulted substantially outweigh these real and potential conflicts. The World Heritage efforts have led to effective management of the full range of the Wall's values.

BALANCING WALL VALUES AND LANDSCAPE VALUES

The Wall and its landscape are closely related but also distinct. The Wall is primarily an archaeological resource,[62] whereas the Setting is a working landscape defined by economic production, ecological values, aesthetic judgments, and so on. Site and Setting are valued differently yet managed in concert.

From the onset of modern historical interest in the eighteenth and nineteenth centuries, the values of the Wall were overwhelmingly construed in terms of Roman-era archaeological and historic remains. More recently, the perceived values have evolved and broadened quite dramatically to encompass a richly layered historic landscape representing many periods and narratives and carrying important contemporary values. Without diminishing the value of the Wall, the clear trend over the past thirty years or so has been to value the Wall *and* its surrounding landscape for both their heritage values and their contemporary-use values. This broader conception represents the consensus today—that the Roman Wall is the core but not the totality of what is significant about this place—and the diversity of values presents a challenge for management.

A two-tiered geographic scheme was devised from the beginning of World Heritage inscription, identifying the core archaeological resources (including some associated resources not on the line of the Wall itself) as well as a substantial buffer zone (the Setting). Such a territorially broad conception necessitates a broad consideration of values, given that much of the land is in active, nonconservation use and under the control of many separate owners. Today, the site is understood and described primarily as a landscape, though it is clear that the roots of the site's value lie in the archaeology and over time have evolved to include the landscape.

The key element of Hadrian's Wall—and the set of values leading to the various legal protections and official recognition—is clearly the history of the Wall and its associated features as a Roman imperial frontier. In the years following the 1987 inscription and the new management structures and initiatives formed in the 1990s, the strict focus on Roman archaeological and historic values has evolved to incorporate a broader range of values. This expanded range includes other heritage values (post-Roman uses of the Wall, or the nineteenth-century agricultural landscape) as well as contemporary-use values (associated with the practice of agriculture or tourism development). Today's management scheme endeavors to maintain a balance among the different kinds of values.

For instance, historic values related to the agricultural landscape created in the nineteenth century seem to be of little consequence in the planning and management of the landscape, though these values are reflected in much of the territory. Features related to these values form a large portion of the landscape—pasturage, stone field walls, farmhouses, and barns—and there is ample evidence of ongoing medieval habitation along and on the Wall.[63] The Roman focus on conservation and management can work against understanding and managing these post-Roman values. Defining the landscape as a "setting" for the Roman/Wall resources puts it in a secondary position. While this is rightly seen as necessary in terms of prioritizing values (identifying the ones of universal value and putting them at the center of management), the implications as to how the other, non-Roman historic values are recognized are not clear.

Contrary examples are evident in the several layers of post-Roman historic values that are well preserved and represented. The Birdoswald site has maintained buildings dating from the sixteenth to nineteenth centuries, carrying out conservation and interpretation within this context. The efforts to develop access and interpretation at this site are held up as a model in the framework of the Management Plan. The need for sensitivity and subtlety in balancing values is well-recognized, and wrestled with, across the site.

These values coexist almost everywhere in the landscape. For example, the Roman historic values relate directly to contemporary values through tourism: the Wall is the source of many kinds of value and is perhaps the most important resource for regional economic development and regeneration. The values are protected explicitly as a matter of policy, and many of the current and planned efforts to improve management are focused on the visual and other experiential qualities of the Wall setting. These have been the subject of the "limits of acceptable change" analyses done by the National Trail, the National Trust, and Northumberland National Park to manage the Housesteads area at a more local scale. Using

the conserved archaeological and historic values of the Wall as a visitor attraction has been a driving force not only in the Wall-wide management scheme committed to paper but also in the creation of partnerships (especially with the HWTP and with national and local governments) and the attraction of funding to sustain all activities associated with the Wall (from strict conservation to more development-oriented schemes).

What has been the impact of the shift toward valuing the setting as well as the site? Highlighting World Heritage values—explicitly "universal"—seems largely to have bolstered the advancement of local and regional values associated with the landscape. The current management regime acknowledges that the Wall has shaped this landscape for the last nineteen hundred years, and that a broader story of landscape evolution and a broader range of values are the basis for its current value to society. While the expansion of geographic scope and universal significance of the values to be conserved may have introduced more complexity and conflict, the more important result is positive: a greater range of values is assessed and conserved, and a more holistic framework for recognizing the significance of different kinds of values has become broadly accepted. The Management Plans reflect a balanced approach to managing the core heritage values (those associated with the Wall) and the other, often equally important, values of the context (i.e., the Setting).

THE EFFECTS OF A PARTNERSHIP MODEL ON VALUES

The partnership management structure used for Hadrian's Wall has an important impact on values.[64] In a general sense, involving more partners of varied kinds broadens the values that are being championed. For instance, including private landowners along with conservation groups and archaeologists places economic and other contemporary-use values on par with historic and research values. Some particular examples arise in the following discussion.

The MPC emerged in the 1996 plan, but such cooperation and collaboration can be traced back to reports and plans formulated in the 1970s and 1980s. Similar arrangements have been employed elsewhere in the world over the past twenty years, but they reach a high level of articulation and refinement in the management of Hadrian's Wall.[65]

The institutionalized partnership of these agencies constitutes a comprehensive effort to manage a range of values larger than that held by any one partner. This range is clearly reflected in the Management Plans as well: archaeological, historic, aesthetic, economic, and other contemporary-use values are all accounted for at the regional scale. Such a thoroughly horizontal process of management, it could be said, leads to a continuous rebalancing of values and thus to plans well adjusted to achieving longer-term stewardship goals as well as shorter-term development goals. At one level, this approach is a response to the mosaic of complicated ownership and stewardship responsibilities. A generation ago, the list of potential partners was smaller (EH and landowners), but under the current regime the number has increased dramatically. The territory is controlled by more than six hundred owners and dozens of different organizations and agencies. The only sensible management model depends on partnership among the existing owners and stakeholders.

How does the partnership-dependent management structure affect values? Regional coordination works in at least two ways. First, raising awareness of the integrity of the whole Wall as a Roman archaeological resource—not the individual, excavated sites—abets the conservation of this overarching, regional-scale cultural value, which otherwise would be difficult to achieve under a piecemeal arrangement of disparate sites. Second, marketing the Wall as a whole to visitors increases economic values. A collaborative marketing effort can create an image for the region as a whole, rendering it more distinctive to visitors in distant markets. Regional coordination also is spreading visitors elsewhere along the Wall, guiding them to lesser-known places. In some sites this is perceived as "reducing tourism pressure" and in others as "siphoning off visitors."

Underlying the plans is an ethic of cooperation, and there is much evidence of cooperative work on the ground as well. Nearly every organization and site contacted for this study reported some kind of partnership as essential to its current activities and goals. The partnership model has also been successful in securing funds for new initiatives and cooperative projects. But the partnership structure also leaves room for competition among partners for funding, visitors, credit and visibility, control over land use, and other issues. A cooperative ticketing scheme with several participating sites was introduced but failed, as some operators felt the cross-promotion was not working and opted out. There are indications that the older, prevailing attitude of competition among sites has not faded, although new managers tend to fall in line with the cooperative philosophy of the Management Plan.

Partnership models in general, and the Hadrian's Wall efforts in particular, are not without their inherent difficulties. There is no single accountability for the site's overall well-being. The organizations with sitewide mandate are coordinating or development entities, not management units. Some partners are involved in several different aspects at once—as owner, regulatory agency, financially interested party, neighbor—leaving ample room for conflicts of interest to develop, or the perception of them. One organization, or core of partners, has to take the lead yet must never appear too far out in front of the consensus on various issues. Recognizing individual partners who are taking uncoordinated actions or following divergent policies requires constant vigilance. Such difficulties and complications are best resolved not by exercises of raw power—though sometimes the need arises—but rather by a continuing series of discussions, exchanges, negotiations, compromises, and dispute resolution, all of which demand a great deal of resources (staff time, energy, material costs, etc.). Indeed, only landowners and EH have and exercise raw power. The partnership model operates under the hypothesis that the time and effort needed to manage complex partnerships are worthwhile.

The benefits of the partnership model speak directly to other issues that have arisen vis-à-vis values and management of the site—for instance, striking a balance between Wall values and setting values. DEFRA and the Countryside Agency wield the influence and have the incentive to manage the broader landscape, whereas the power of EH is fairly well focused on the Wall and its immediate surroundings. To manage the site and setting together requires a collaborative partnership.

MANAGEMENT PLANS AND THEIR POLICIES

It has already been pointed out which values are articulated in the Management Plans for Hadrian's Wall. The intent here is to describe how the approach to management and planning (1) is reflective of the broader, more inclusive attitude toward values that has evolved, and (2) is a response to the large scale of the resources and the need to foster local and resource-specific control over resources and their values.

Management Plan policies set the vision and provide direction, but they do not prescribe or proscribe actions. The plan differs from what is traditionally seen as a master plan in that it establishes principles of operation and general guidelines but does not chart out the specific work to be done. Instead, the plan creates a framework for and anticipates the creation of the regional- and local-level plans and contributions to determining local land-use policy. Specific regulatory controls remain in the hands of local authorities and, for national scheduled monuments themselves, with EH. For instance, the plan is designed to be implemented through adoption in existing local plans and regulations—and to a large extent, local and regional authorities have endorsed the Management Plan and incorporated its provisions into their own planning policies and schemes.[66]

The Management Plans for the site carry no statutory authority and are not tabled in Parliament (i.e., passed or endorsed officially by the government). The 2002 plan is "endorsed" by the MPC and "adopted" by the individual partners. In other words, the plan gains authority only to the extent to which it is adopted or implemented by local authorities. These local controls, the adoption of which is negotiated and not required, are complemented by existing national statutory controls (cf. *PPG 15* and *16*; scheduled monuments reviews) and are seen as sufficient legal protection. By endorsing the World Heritage listing of the site, however, the national government tacitly endorses the provisions of the plan. As a result, the intentions of the plan are backed by various statutory authorities, but these are neither centralized in any particular institution or agency nor tied directly to the MPC.

The primary focus is on the means (the process) of continuing to work together, pursue common goals, and/or pursue individual goals within the bounds of the agreed-upon framework. Some typical results of this flexible policy approach include the use of LAC methods to manage access to the Housesteads-Steel Rigg segment of the Wall, and the different approaches taken to creating local/small-area interpretive plans, carried out under the rubric of the regional scheme but performed by the local partners themselves. In all these types of local planning, the key value added by the MPC is the coordination of actions so that consistency and cooperation lead directly to leveraging all investments for positive, Wall-wide impact.

Conclusions

The Hadrian's Wall management and planning scheme represents a highly developed, thoroughly consultative, and thoughtful system of values-based conservation. It has two hallmarks of sustainability: it encompasses the many types of values associated with the core resources and their contexts, and its implementation is based on partnerships. The scheme is explicitly driven by the identification of heritage and other values, and by actions undertaken to ensure their existence and sustained use. The current scheme has evolved over the past thirty years through the efforts of many organizations and has been strengthened by World Heritage designation and the United Kingdom's efforts to generate a thorough management response to this recognition of universal value.

Over the generation or so of planning and management examined in this case study, there has been a clear and progressive recognition of the breadth of values to be managed for this heritage place. What was once considered an archaeological resource tracing a line across the country has been transformed in a few decades into a complex, layered cultural landscape rich in both heritage and contemporary values. Management practices and plans have evolved as well and have helped shift attitudes toward values at every step. Overall, the recognition of partners' collective interests outweighs the importance of individual goals. The partnership has come to an agreement that Hadrian's Wall is a landscape and not a discrete monument. The two-tiered structure of boundaries follows the partnership model for managing the landscape: the core is agreed upon and protected tightly and uniformly, and the setting is managed according to the wishes of the local jurisdictions or owners, who have differing views of what should be protected and how. In seeking inclusion and recognition of the site's policies in local land-use policies and plans, the whole scheme recognizes the limits of a partnership model. Ultimately, control over the resources resides with the individual partners.

The collaborative, "horizontal" management scheme seems well suited to the resources and the patterns of landownership and control, and has resulted in benefits equal to (if not exceeding) its costs (real and metaphoric). Its significant achievements have included the founding of the HWTP and its Wall-wide programs of marketing, transportation, and education; the establishment of the National Trail; the attraction of substantial grant funds; and the successful conservation and interpretation of a large and complex set of cultural resources. The Management Plan provides a framework and guidance for all partners and actors to carry out their work.

The partnership model has several features abundantly in evidence for Hadrian's Wall and contributing to its success:

- The positive results of the partnership since the mid-1990s are clear. With the partners working in concert, a number of objectives have been achieved which, in the opinion of those on the ground, would not have been reached by organizations working independently.

- Managing by consensus is an exceedingly important principle and a major learning point. It is a replacement, one can say, for management by regulation and direct statutory control. There is a remarkably wide buy-in among partners on the protection of the setting as well as the Wall.

- There are a lot of "calculated ambiguities" in planning and management. The planning has remained at a strategic level, avoiding the prescription of particular actions for particular sites. This is appropriate given the extensive scale of the whole venture and the need to recognize (and perhaps decentralize) the distribution of power among the various partners and individuals who wield ultimate control over land and resources. It is also flexible and allows the partnership to respond to changing external forces, whether those forces are welcome opportunities (regional regeneration funds) or unwelcome threats (the ravages of FMD).

An integrated planning and management regime has been implemented at Hadrian's Wall that addresses a variety of situations and sets a framework for integrating policies and actions at different geographic scales. The approach used is also a "learning" system, as seen in the evolution from the 1996 plan to the 2002 plan. The latter is by no means a finished plan; it explicitly calls for the implementation of policies (which necessarily relate to the region and the whole resource) at a local, actionable scale. Further, the partnership recognizes that one goal over the next several years should be the creation of monitoring mechanisms—ways to understand and track how values are being shaped, and to use this information in the management of the Wall and Setting.

The institutional arrangements seem well suited to managing values as well as conservation and development activities. The Hadrian's Wall scheme seems neither centralized nor decentralized. An effective center exists in the combination of the HWCU and the HWTP. This combination also includes partners from the private sector but is not so privatized as to be overly susceptible to market fluctuations. EH has a unique and complicated set of roles: for the region, it is a coordinator, convener, and consultant; for the Wall as an archaeological resource, it is a regulatory agency; for certain sites, it is a day-to-day manager; and for other sites, it is also the owner. As such, EH is potentially at odds with some of its own partners, but this has not proven to be a liability. It is not clear, however, whether this makes EH more or less effective in playing the lead coordinating role.

The partnership model is not without its downside. Competition among partners remains. There is little centralized or statutory authority to force resolution of issues when necessary. The partnership's successes have relied on large infusions of funds; if the incentives for funding and marketing dry up, there would be little more than the power of good ideas to hold together the whole partnership. Persuasion and perseverance are among the most important managers' tools in such a scheme, and these require enormous investments of time and human capital.

Notes

1. English Heritage 2002, 2 and part 5, "Maps."

2. Reiterating what is noted in the introduction, *site* refers throughout to the World Heritage Site in totality—the Wall, associated remains, and the setting.

3. These include forts, fortlets, and other monuments to the south of Bowness (the western end of the Wall) along the Cumbrian coast, and other Roman sites near, but not adjacent to, the line of the Wall.

4. The Clayton Wall was rebuilt not to its original height but to that sufficient to serve as a barrier to keep out livestock and create a property boundary.

5. Details on the archaeological remains and extant remains in the site can be found in the Management Plans, in particular section 1.2.6 of the 2002 plan [and guidebooks].

6. Hadrian's Wall World Heritage Site is situated at a latitude of 54°N.

7. McKnight 2001, 224–26.

8. A detailed time line appears in the appendix.

9. For a detailed history and description of the Wall, see Birley 1961; de la Bedoyere 1999; Breeze and Dobson 2000; and Ewin 2000.

10. Watson 1997, 23. Today, the Military Road is known as B6318.

11. Ewin 2000, 41.

12. English Heritage 2002, 13.

13. Ewin 2000, vii.

14. Ibid., 2.

15. Hadrian's Wall Tourism Partnership, "Hadrian's Wall World Heritage Site: Research and Archaeology: Rev. Dr. John Collingwood Bruce, 1998–99." http://www.hadrians-wall.org/randa/jcb.htm (16 May 2002).

16. Ibid.

17. English Heritage 2002, 13.

18. Ewin 2000, 44. The archaeological protection acts passed during this period were the *Ancient Monuments Protection Act* of 1882, the *Ancient Monuments Act* of 1910, the *Ancient Monuments Consolidation and Amendment Act* of 1913, and the *Ancient Monuments Act* of 1932.

19. English Heritage, "Hadrian's Wall Museums." http://www.eng.-h.gov.uk/ArchRev/rev95_6/hwmuseum.htm (23 May 2002).

20. Hadrian's Wall Tourism Partnership, "Research and Archaeology: Wall Recording Project." http://www.hadrians-wall.org/ (23 May 2002).

21. English Heritage 1996, paragraph 9.4.2.

22. Ewin 2000, 31.

23. This concern was based on the perception that more walkers would come and have a negative impact. Once formal counts of footpath traffic were conducted, fears of overuse by walkers proved unfounded, illustrating the notion that accurate information and monitoring are essential for site management. Christopher Young, English Heritage, e-mail correspondence, 19 June 2003.

24. Quoted from http://whc.unesco.org/nwhc/pages/doc/mainf3.htm. World Heritage List criteria for natural heritage properties are also available at this URL.

25. Jane Brantom, Hadrian's Wall Tourism Partnership, e-mail correspondence, 19 June 2003.

26. Kate Clark, personal communication, 2001, citing Mynors 1999.

27. If such consent is denied, the applicant has the right to public inquiry or informal hearing prior to a final ruling concerning the application.

28. *PPG 16: Archaeology and Planning*, Department of the Environment, 1990. Her Majesty's Stationery Office, London. May be found at http://www.planning.odpm.gov.uk/ppg/ppg16/index.htm (May 2003).

29. *PPG 15: Planning and the Historic Environment*, section 6.10. Department of the Environment and Department of National Heritage, 1994. Her Majesty's Stationery Office, London. Found at http://www.planning.odpm.gov.uk/ppg/ppg15/pdf/ppg15.pdf. Recent amendment may be found at http://www.planning.odpm.gov.uk/circulars/0101/09.htm (May 2003).

30. *UNESCO Convention Concerning the Protection of the World Cultural and Natural Heritage: Operational Guidelines*, part I.21.B.

31. This department is also responsible for matters related to the arts, sport, and recreation; the National Lottery; libraries, museums, and galleries; licensing for the export of cultural goods, film, broadcasting, and the royal estate; and regulation of the press.

32. Accessed at www.english-heritage.org.uk.

33. See http://www.nationaltrust.org.uk/main/.

34. These measures are summarized in appendix 4 of the 2002 Management Plan.

35. This document is found at http://www.hmso.gov.uk/acts/acts1990/Ukpga_19900009_en_2.htm#mdiv1.

36. *PPG 15*, explanatory note. http://www.planning.odpm.gov.uk/ppg/ppg15/pdf/ppg15.pdf.

37. Amenity societies in the United Kingdom include the Ancient Monuments Society, the Council for British Archaeology, the Georgian Group, the Society for the Protection of Ancient Buildings, the Victorian Society, and the Twentieth Century Society.

38. *PPG 16*, introduction.

39. English Heritage 1996, section 9.4.2.

40. It should also be noted that this change is congruent with philosophical shifts in the heritage field and related disciplines that more seriously recognize the geographic and value contexts of what are traditionally seen as historic resources.

41. English Heritage 2002, 20–21.

42. *Strategy* 1984.

43. Ibid., 9.

44. Accessed at http://whc.unesco.org/sites/430.htm (5 April 2003).

45. English Heritage 1996, paragraph 1.1.9.

46. Accessed at http://www.eng-h.gov.uk/ArchRev/rev95_6/hadrian.htm.

47. Christopher Young, English Heritage, e-mail correspondence, 11 April 2003.

48. English Heritage 2002, section 2.1.1, 33–42.

49. Ibid., 28, emphasis added.

50. See English Heritage 2002, 28–32, for the full text of the statement of significance.

51. This document is available at http://www.hadrians-wall.org/. Click on Hadrian's Wall Tourism Partnership.

52. The source for much of the information in this section is drawn from correspondence with Christopher Young, English Heritage.

53. The core of the partners group is represented by the MPC.

54. This term is used increasingly, for instance, in the U.S. National Park Service to refer to the increasing decentralization of authority and funding through the inclusion of private, public, and nonprofit partners in the management of parks and historic sites. As an example, see the press release at http://data2.itc.nps.gov/release/Detail.cfm?ID=355.

55. Available at http://www.hadrians-wall.org/.

56. Available at http://www.hadrians-wall.org/. Click on Hadrian's Wall Tourism Partnership.

57. The operation of the bus is funded by a number of bodies—not solely HWTP—including Northumberland National Park, which underwrites any losses.

58. English Heritage 2002, 1.

59. Ibid.

60. Ibid., 57.

61. Ibid., 26.

62. It should be noted that "the Wall," as used here and throughout, also encompasses related archaeological resources and sites not technically part of the Wall itself.

63. English Heritage 2002, section 1.2.4.

64. Similar kinds of partnership-driven models have been used in other countries, and the increasing reliance on partnerships in all types of planning has been an area of innovation for at least the last thirty years.

65. In the United Kingdom, such partnership arrangements involving different national agencies as well as local and regional partners are quite common now, but those involving Hadrian's Wall have been a trendsetter.

66. Appendix 4 of the 2002 Management Plan lists the specific local plans and policies through which the plan is already being implemented.

Appendix A: Time Line for Hadrian's Wall during Heritage Status

1599   Antiquarian William Camden visited the length of Hadrian's Wall except the central sector due to its dangerous condition. The following year he published his survey and explanation of the Wall and its structures in the fifth edition of his *Britannia*.[1]

1732   The Rev. John Horsley's work *Britannia Romana*, the first systematic study of Hadrian's Wall, was published.

ca. 1750   The Military Road was constructed between Newcastle and Carlisle. Approximately 48 kilometers (30 miles) of the road was built on top of Hadrian's Wall between Newcastle and Sewingshields.[2]

1801   William Hutton walked the length of the Wall and wrote an account, now published under the title *The First Man to Walk Hadrian's Wall*.

1811   William Hutton saved a section of the Wall at Planetrees from being pillaged to make field walls.[3]

1832–90   In 1832, John Clayton inherited ownership of Chesters Roman Fort. From that time until his death in 1890, Clayton excavated and protected remains of the Wall and amassed a collection of Roman objects from various locations along the Wall. One conservation technique Clayton developed was encasing the surviving Wall remains in drystone facework topped with turf. Sections of the Wall built over in this fashion are today known as the Clayton Wall.[4]

1840   John Hodgson published his *History of Northumberland*, the first work to argue convincingly that the Wall had been constructed under the Roman emperor Hadrian. Hodgson also was the first to record thoroughly and in detail the structure of the Wall and its associated forts in the central sector.[5]

1849   The Newcastle Society of Antiquaries and the Cumberland and Westmoreland Antiquarian and Archaeological Society, led by John Collingwood Bruce, held their first pilgrimage along the length of the Wall. A second pilgrimage took place in 1886, and since that time the groups have led such pilgrimages every ten years.[6]

1851   John Collingwood Bruce published the first edition of *The Roman Wall*, which summarized the results of John Clayton's excavations at Chesters Roman Fort and publicized John Hodgson's theory of the Wall's construction under the emperor Hadrian.[7]

1863   John Collingwood Bruce published his *Handbook of the Roman Wall*, which has since served as an important guide to the Wall. Its thirteenth edition was published in 1978.[8]

1875   The South Shields Urban District Council established the Roman Remains Park at South Shields, marking the first public acquisition and display of a part of the Wall.[9]

1896   The museum at Chesters Roman Fort, which housed John Clayton's collection of objects, was opened to the public.

1927   A first section of the Wall was scheduled as a monument.

1932   The *Ancient Monuments Act* was enacted in part as a result of threats to the Wall.[10] The Hadrian's Wall and Vallum Preservation Scheme was adopted. The British government acquired its first parts of the Wall.[11]

1935   The Housesteads Museum was opened to the public.[12]

1970   The Vindolanda Trust, an independent archaeological charitable trust, was founded to excavate, preserve, and present the Roman remnants associated with land owned by the trust at Vindolanda.

1972   The Vindolanda Trust acquired the Roman site known as Carvoran, located 8 miles to the west of Vindolanda.

1973   Tourist visitation to the Wall peaked.

1976   Darlington Amenity Research Trust report was published, articulating the need for a Wall-wide conservation strategy, tourism scheme, and management attention.

1984   The document *Strategy for Hadrian's Wall* was published, proposing a regionwide framework for conservation and tourism.

English Heritage opened the Corbridge Museum at Corbridge Roman site.

The Cumbria County Council acquired the Birdoswald estate for the purpose of developing the remains of the Roman fort and other archaeological features there as a heritage site that would be open to the public.

1985   English Heritage began its Wall Recording Project, which provided the first detailed record of the visible remains of the Wall and its associated features. The finished drawings are used in the management and conservation of the Wall.[13]

1986   The Tyne and Wear Museums completed reconstruction of the West Gate at Arbeia Roman Fort at South Shields.

1987   Hadrian's Wall Military Zone inscribed by UNESCO as a World Heritage Site under criteria C (ii), (iii), and (iv).

The first visitor center opened at Birdoswald Roman Fort.

1990   The Senhouse Museum Trust opened the Senhouse Roman Museum, which houses the Netherhall collection of Roman artifacts, in Maryport.

1993   The Hadrian's Wall Tourism Partnership was created.

1994   The secretary of state approved proposals for the Hadrian's Wall Path, a new National Trail.

1996   The Hadrian's Wall World Heritage Site Management Plan for the period 1996–2001 was published after extensive consultation. The plan established the World Heritage Site Management Plan Committee "to act as the primary forum for issues concerning the management of the World Heritage Site."[14] English Heritage established the Hadrian's Wall Co-ordination Unit, based in Hexham, to oversee implementation of the plan.

2000   The Segedunum Roman Fort, Bath House and Museum in Wallsend opened to the public. The development, operated by the Tyne and Wear

Museums, included a working reconstruction of a Roman bathhouse and a viewing tower approximately 34 meters (112 feet) in height.

2001   The Hadrian's Wall region was severely damaged by the foot and mouth disease epidemic.

2002   Management Plan 2002–2007 was released.

Notes

1.   English Heritage 2002, 23.

2.   Watson 1997, 23.

3.   English Heritage 2002, 13.

4.   English Heritage 1999, 42–43.

5.   Hadrian's Wall Tourism Partnership, "Hadrian's Wall World Heritage Site: Research and Archaeology: Rev. John Hodgson." http://www.hadrians-wall.org/ (23 May 2002).

6.   English Heritage 2002, 24.

7.   Hadrian's Wall Tourism Partnership, "Hadrian's Wall World Heritage Site: Research and Archaeology: Rev. Dr. John Collingwood Bruce, 1998–99." http://www.hadrians-wall.org/randa/jcb.htm (16 May 2002).

8.   Ibid.

9.   English Heritage 2002, 13.

10.   English Heritage 1996, 13.

11.   English Heritage 2002, 13.

12.   English Heritage, "Hadrian's Wall Museums." http://www.eng-h.gov.uk/ArchRev/rev95_6/hwmuseum.htm (23 May 2002).

13.   Hadrian's Wall Tourism Partnership, "Research and Archaeology: Wall Recording Project." http://www.hadrians-wall.org/ (23 May 2002).

14.   English Heritage 1996, paragraph 9.4.2.

References

Bidwell, P., ed. 1999. *Hadrian's Wall 1989–1999: A Summary of Recent Excavations and Research Prepared for The Twelfth Pilgrimage of Hadrian's Wall, 14–21 August 1999*. Carlisle: The Cumberland and Westmoreland Antiquarian and Archaeological Society and the Society of Antiquaries of Newcastle upon Tyne.

Birley, E. 1961. *Research on Hadrian's Wall*. Kendal, England: T. Wilson.

Breeze, D. J., and B. Dobson. 2000. *Hadrian's Wall*. 4th ed. New York: Penguin.

British Standard on the Principles of the Conservation of Historic Buildings (BS7913, 1998). In *English Heritage Policy Statement on Restoration, Reconstruction, and Speculative Recreation of Archaeological Sites Including Ruins*, February 2001.

Darlington Amenity Research Trust. 1976. *Hadrian's Wall: A Strategy for Conservation and Visitor Services*. DART Publication no. 25, August.

de la Bedoyere, G. 1999. *Hadrian's Wall: History and Guide*. London: Tempus Publishing Ltd.

Dore, J. N. 2001. *Corbridge Roman Site*. 1989. Reprint. London: English Heritage.

English Heritage. "Hadrian's Wall Museums." http://www.eng-h.gov.uk/ArchRev/rev95_6/hwmuseum.htm (23 May 2002).

English Heritage. 1996. *Hadrian's Wall World Heritage Site Management Plan*. London: English Heritage.

———. 1999. *Chesters Roman Fort*. London: English Heritage.

———. 2002. *Hadrian's Wall World Heritage Site Management Plan, 2002–2007*. Available as a pdf file at http://www.hadrians-wall.org/HWTPMgmtPlan2002.pdf.

Ewin, A. 2000. *Hadrian's Wall: A Social and Cultural History*. Lancaster: Centre for North-West Regional Studies/University of Lancaster.

Fairclough, G., G. Lambrick, and A. McNab. 1995. *Yesterday's World, Tomorrow's Landscape: The English Heritage Historic Landscape Project, 1992–94*. London: English Heritage.

Hadrian's Wall Tourism Partnership. 2002. *Beyond the Final Frontier: Projects in Progress and Proposed, Hadrian's Wall World Heritage Site*. January.

———. "Hadrian's Wall World Heritage Site: Research and Archaeology: Rev. Dr. John Collingwood Bruce, 1998–99." http://www.hadrians-wall.org/randa/jcb.htm (16 May 2002).

———. "Research and Archaeology: Wall Recording Project." http://www.hadrians-wall.org/ (23 May 2002).

———. "Research and Archaeology: Rev. John Hodgson." http://www.hadrians-wall.org/ (23 May 2002).

Hadrian's Wall Tourism Partnership/SRB Steering Group. 2000. *Enrichment and Enterprise. Round 6: Single Regeneration Budget Bid*. 23 May.

Historic Buildings and Monuments Commission for England. N.d. *World Heritage Convention, Cultural Properties: UK Nomination Hadrian's Wall Military Zone*.

Johnson, J. S. 1999. *Chesters Roman Fort*. 1990. Reprint. London: English Heritage.

Land Use Consultants (in association with Heritage Site and Landscape Surveys Ltd). 1995. *Hadrian's Wall Landscape and Planning Study: Final Report*. June.

Mason, R., ed. 1999. *Economics and Heritage Conservation*. Los Angeles: The Getty Conservation Institute. http://www.getty.edu/conservation/publications/pdf_publications/econrpt.pdf.

McKnight, T. 2001. *Physical Geography: A Landscape Appreciation*. 4th ed. Englewood Cliffs, N.J.: Prentice Hall.

Mynors, C. 1999. *Listed Buildings, Conservation Areas and Monuments*. 3rd ed. London: Sweet and Maxwell.

Ordnance Survey. 1975. *Map of Hadrian's Wall*. 2d ed. Southampton: Ordnance Survey Publication.

Pearson, M., and S. Sullivan. 1995. *Looking After Heritage Places: The Basics of Heritage Planning for Managers, Landowners*. Melbourne: Melbourne University Press.

Rimmington, N., and D. McGlade. 2001. "Limits of Acceptable Change Conference: Defining and Managing Quality—Housesteads Roman Fort to Steel Rigg Section of Hadrian's Wall." Consultation draft, 5 November.

The Strategy for Hadrian's Wall. 1984. Hadrian's Wall Consultative Committee.

U.K. Department of the Environment. 1990. *Planning Policy Guidance 16: Archaeology and Planning*. Her Majesty's Stationery Office, London. Found at http://www.planning.odpm.gov.uk/ppg/ppg16/index.htm (May 2003).

U.K. Department of the Environment and Department of National Heritage. 1994. *Planning Policy Guidance 15: Planning and the Historic Environment*. Her Majesty's Stationery Office, London. Found at http://www.planning.odpm.gov.uk/ppg/ppg15/pdf/ppg15.pdf. Recent amendment may be found at http://www.planning.odpm.gov.uk/circulars/0101/09.htm (May 2003).

UNESCO Convention Concerning the Protection of the World Cultural and Natural Heritage. Accessed at http://whc.unesco.org/nwhc/pages/doc/mainf3.htm.

UNESCO Convention Concerning the Protection of the World Cultural and Natural Heritage: Operational Guidelines for the Implementation of the World Heritage Convention. Accessed at http://whc.unesco.org/opgulist.htm.

Watson, I. 1997. *Hadrian's Wall: A Teacher's Handbook.* London: English Heritage.

Persons Contacted during the Development of the Case

Julian Acton
National Farmers Union
Northumberland

Lindsay Allason-Jones
Director of Archaeological Museums
Museum of Antiquities
University of Newcastle

Paul Austen
Hadrian's Wall World Heritage Site Co-ordinator
English Heritage Co-ordination Unit

Patricia and Robin Birley
Directors
The Vindolanda Trust

Jane Brantom
Manager
Hadrian's Wall Tourism Partnership

Bill Griffiths
Curator
Tyne and Wear Museums / Segedunum

Nick Hodgson
Principal Keeper of Archaeology
Tyne and Wear Museums / South Shields

Paget Lazari
Project Manager
Northumberland National Park

David McGlade
Hadrian's Wall Path National Trail Officer
Countryside Agency

Emma Moody
Sustainable Transport Officer
Hadrian's Wall Tourism Partnership

David Murray
National Farmers Union
Cumbria

Karen Parker
Administration and Newsletter Editor
English Heritage Co-ordination Unit

Georgina Plowright
Curator
English Heritage
Corbridge Roman Site

Andy Poad
Property Manager
The National Trust

Neil Rimmington
Earthworks Officer
English Heritage

Brian Selman
Parish Council
Heddon-on-the-Wall

Peter Stone
Senior Lecturer
Newcastle University

Lynn Turner
Chief Leisure and Tourism Officer
Tynedale Council

Elaine Watson
General Manager
Birdoswald

PART THREE Issues Raised by the Case Studies

Marta de la Torre

The four case studies included in this publication illustrate how different organizations have dealt with the challenges of managing sites with multiple values. The cases shed light on the approaches dictated by the administrative and political environments of each organization, and the solutions they found to accommodate the specific resources and circumstances of the sites.

This section compares how some of the issues and challenges were handled at the different sites. Every aspect of management illustrated in the cases could be the subject of these comparisons. However, this section focuses on those issues that seem to illustrate the challenges of management particularly well. Those selected for consideration are: the management planning requirements and the guidance available for it and for its implementation; the application of these guiding principles to individual sites; the treatment of values, including how they are recognized and the role played by stakeholders; the handling of the often difficult subject of economic value; the resolution of conflicting values and the tensions between local, national, and international values; the recognition of the landscape as a cultural value; the importance of the fabric; the concept of "quality of the visitors' experience"; and the monitoring of values.

Management Planning

The organizations involved in this study operate in complex environments and engage in elaborate planning processes to assure that they move ahead in a concerted manner to fulfill their mandates. In all systems the planning processes are intended to result in written documents used to guide and explain decisions and actions. The number of documents available and their currency varied among the sites, but in all instances the management guidelines called for primary and secondary plans, as well as implementation and reporting documents.

PLANNING GUIDELINES

The Canadian and U.S. sites are part of national systems of parks and historic places. Their governing agencies have developed policies and guidelines to be applied in the man-

agement of all the units in the systems to assure consistent practices of conservation and management.[1]

Justification and rationale for planning are clearly explained in the two North American systems. The U.S. National Park Service (NPS) documents state that the agency "plans for one purpose—to ensure that the decisions it makes are as effective and efficient as possible in carrying out the NPS mission. That mission is to preserve unimpaired the natural and cultural resources and values of the national park system for the enjoyment, education, and inspiration of this and future generations and to cooperate with partners to extend the benefits of resource conservation and outdoor recreation throughout this country and the world."[2] Current NPS guidelines specify the development of a series of sequential plans, starting with a General Management Plan that will "ensure that the park has a clearly defined direction for resources preservation and visitor use." Guidelines indicate that "general management planning will constitute the first phase of tiered planning and decision-making. It will focus on why the park was established, and what management prescription (i.e., resource conditions, visitor experiences, and appropriate types of management actions) should be achieved and maintained over time."[3]

In the Canadian system the preparation of management plans is mandated by the act that established Parks Canada.[4] This obligation is reflected in the agency's Guiding Principles and Operational Policies, which states that "[E]ffective planning sets out the ways and means by which cultural resources will be cared for and presented. Planning activities flow from policy objectives and adhere to policy principles. Through these activities Parks Canada ensures that the elements of good cultural resource management practice are in place in all systems and processes."[5] It further specifies that "the goal of management planning for national historic sites is to ensure the commemorative integrity of national historic sites and the application of cultural resource management principles and practice."[6]

Port Arthur Historic Site Management Authority (PAHSMA) is a government business enterprise (GBE) established by a ministerial charter of the State of Tasmania.[7] As such, it is able to set its management policies within the parameters specified in the charter but without the guidance of a higher authority. PAHSMA adheres to the *Australia ICOMOS Charter for the Conservation of Places of Cultural Significance* (the Burra Charter), which endorses very specific planning processes.[8]

In England, responsibility for the protection of recognized heritage sites is assigned to various levels of government, to both public and private agencies, and to private citizens. World Heritage Sites, registered parks and gardens, and battlefields are protected through integrated planning processes administered at the local to district levels by national legislation to protect designated sites and by policies in land-use development plans. The Office of the Deputy Prime Minister issues Planning Policy Guidance notes (or PPGs, currently being replaced by Planning Policy Statements—PPSs), which set out government policy on the relevant legislation and give detailed guidance for decision makers. These planning guidelines define terms and direct all planning activities and are meant to consider a scope of concerns much broader than the values and circumstances of a specific cultural site. *PPG 1: General Policy and Principles*[9] clarifies that "the planning system regulates the development and use of land in the public interest. The system as a whole and the preparation of development plans in particular, is the most effective way of reconciling the demand for development and the protection of the environment. Thus it has a key role to play in contributing to the Government's strategy for sustainable development by helping to provide for necessary development in locations which do not compromise the ability of future generations to meet their needs."[10] There are currently twenty-five PPGs,[11] all of which must be taken into consideration when planning in historic sites; however, only two relate specifically to heritage sites: *PPG 15: Planning and the Historic Environment* and *PPG 16: Archaeology and Planning.*[12]

SPECIFIC PLANS

In the sites studied, the main management documents are called management plans, general management plans, or conservation plans. While their content and organization vary from site to site, these documents usually include statements about the legal status of the site, its significance, and main management objectives. Today, these primary plans are strategic documents, and site authorities see them as a tool for change containing a vision of the future and outlining the rules and principles that will be followed to achieve it. In this they differ from the master plans popular a few decades ago, with their long lists of specific actions and activities.

Chaco Culture National Historical Park (CCNHP) has the management plan of longest standing among all the sites studied. Its 1985 General Management Plan is not considered by site staff to reflect current policies of the NPS even though the plan proposed "a course of action for management and use of CCNHP for the next 10–15 years." Since the plan was constructed around very specific issues considered critical in 1985, such as mining and development of surrounding lands, it became obsolete soon after when the anticipated threats did not materialize. The usefulness of the plan has been limited since then. Currently the plan is used mainly as a checklist of "action items" from which the authorities select for implementation those that are considered relevant and ignore those that are not, awaiting the development of a new General Management Plan in accordance with current NPS policies. Currently, the directives and regulations established for the NPS system as a whole seem to be more important for the management of CCNHP, and Park management spends considerable resources on "compliance" activities.

The first management plan for the National Historic Site of Grosse Île was started shortly after its designation as a national historic site. The presentation of a development concept to the public in 1992 launched an important phase of public consultation detailed in the case study.[13] In accordance with Parks Canada policy, when the plan was published in 2001, it focused on ensuring the commemorative integrity of the site. From the management plan flow a series of documents, which study the values and the resources in detail and formulate specific strategies and identify actions to preserve them.[14]

The 2000 Conservation Plan is the latest in a series of management documents that have been prepared over the years for Port Arthur Historic Site. The preparation of the latest plan was led by external consultants and followed closely the guidelines provided in the Burra Charter. The staff was very involved with the development of the plan, since the process is seen as the means of transmitting and institutionalizing the policies set out in the plan. More so than at any of the other sites, PAHSMA staff constantly referred to the Conservation Plan as justification for management decisions.

The 2001 Management Plan of Hadrian's Wall is the second one prepared for this World Heritage Site. It reflects the broad social considerations mandated by the United Kingdom's planning guidelines, and considers the protection of heritage resources in the context of societal needs. This is different from the three other sites, where the purpose of planning was the protection of the sites themselves and their values. A greater purpose is recognized in the plan for Hadrian's Wall, where it is stated that "[M]anagement Plans provide the means for establishing an appropriate balance between the needs of conservation, access, sustainable economic development and the interests of the local community."[15]

In contrast to the other three sites, this management plan does not have "statutory status," since Hadrian's Wall and its Setting exist as a unit only in the context of the World Heritage Convention. Nevertheless, in spite of, or perhaps because of, its exclusive strategic nature, the plan has enormous importance for the development of activities in the area of the World Heritage Site, although not legally binding. "Its purpose is to draw together into one document the description and significance of the Site, to identify the organisations and individuals with an interest in the Site, including the existing relevant frameworks that can be used to protect it, to identify the pressures on the values of the Site and to set out an agreed overall guiding strategy for the partner organisations, to address the issues which are of concern through their individual remits and by working cohesively together."[16]

The management systems used in all four sites rely on a primary planning document that records the mission of the place and the mandate of the governing authority and establishes general principles of operation. These conservation plans or management plans are supported by secondary or tertiary plans that focus on implementation methods and work plans. In the NPS system, strategic, implementation, and annual performance plans constitute the next tiers of documents. Parks Canada staff has prepared plans dealing with visitor experience and care of the resources; business plans; and periodic reports for Grosse Île and the Irish Memorial National Historic Site. The 2000 Conservation Plan for Port Arthur Historic Site specifies a complex set of secondary and tertiary plans that deal with specific buildings as well as areas of operations. Finally, the Management Plan for Hadrian's Wall World Heritage Site acts as an umbrella for more specialized management plans for the various places that exist within the site as well as business and tourism plans for the region.

One of the questions raised in the study was how much latitude did system-wide directives allow local authorities to tailor decisions to their own circumstances. The answer seems to be that the Canadian and the U.S. national parks systems give sufficient discretion to local

managers to address the needs of their sites. Most interventions on archaeological remains within Hadrian's Wall World Heritage Site are governed by principles established for English Heritage, including reconstructions. Nevertheless, as indicated in the case study, there is a great variety in the approach to reconstruction and the extent to which it is used by different owners. In short, the study found instances when the guidelines, policies, and directives appeared to have left so much leeway to local authorities that some of their decisions seemed to be outside the parameters set by the prescribing documents.

In a couple of instances, policies and regulations were seen to be a source of conflict. Some of the directives of the NPS—having been formulated independently to deal with specific issues—provided contradictory guidance. For example, the directives guaranteeing respect of traditional uses of the parks by Native Americans, particularly in relation to religious ceremonies, and the system-wide prohibition to remove any materials from the national parks created a dilemma for authorities. The NPS's recently updated management policy documents attempt to address these inconsistencies through more comprehensive approaches and considerations of management issues.

Values

The case studies show that the management approaches used in all four sites are based on the conservation of values and the significance of the places, and demonstrate that values-based management can take different forms. The main differences lie in the ways in which values are prioritized, how values are considered during the planning and management processes, and the means to resolve conflicts between them.

SIGNIFICANCE

The official significance of the sites included in this study stems from the values of their archaeological or historic resources. Until recent times, few documents elaborated on the values of a site, since it was assumed that their antiquity or history, their beauty, their scientific potential, and in many instances, their uniqueness were self-evident. However, the arrival of new stakeholders with demands that other values also be recognized brought with it the realization that values can be in conflict and that, at times, protecting all of them simultaneously can be impossible.

All four cases illustrate how the values of the sites have evolved over time and how new values have emerged. The significance of what is today Chaco Culture National Historical Park was recognized in a presidential proclama-

tion in 1907 that mentioned the importance of the archaeological remains due, seemingly, to their scientific, aesthetic,
and age values. At that time, the site already had value for
other groups, but these values were not recognized as
being sufficiently important to make the place significant
for the emerging nation. To this day, the official "purpose of
the park" remains anchored to its archaeological and aesthetic significance. However, in managing the site, the
National Park Service must take into consideration also the
ecological value and the spiritual and cultural values to
Native American and other groups. Within the NPS, new
values are recognized mainly through legislation that often
is not directly related to the site or even to the national
parks. For instance, the natural value of Chaco became
more prominent as the regulations established by the *Environmental Protection Act* were enforced, and Native American values (and the involvement of these groups with the
site) were strengthened by the passage of the *Native American Graves Protection and Repatriation Act (NAGPRA)* in 1990.

The values of Grosse Île and the Irish Memorial—
with a shorter history as a heritage place—have yet to fully
evolve. Its significance is based on the island's importance
to the history of immigration to Canada; as a site of the
great tragedies of Irish immigrants, especially due to the
1847 typhus epidemic; and finally as a quarantine station
for the port of Quebec. The statement of commemorative
intent of the site mentions these three aspects of its history. However, even in its short history as a national historic site, the island's association with Dr. Frederick Monti-
zambert—who ran the quarantine station and did important work in the field of preventative medicine and public
health in Canada—has been recognized as an additional
element of significance. Furthermore, Parks Canada's concept of commemorative integrity requires that all heritage
values of a place be identified so that they can be protected. Thus, Grosse Île is recognized as having other historic values and natural values as a special habitat.

Port Arthur has had a history as a heritage site
that spans more than a century, and its significance has
fluctuated during that time in accordance with the
value—positive or negative—attributed by Australians to
their convict past. Similar changes can be seen in the
attention paid to the economic value of the site, determined in this instance by the availability of external support or the need to rely on earned income. Today, as a government business enterprise that is not dependent on a
government agency, Port Arthur Historic Site Management Authority seems to have the most flexibility to recognize and take into consideration the largest number of val-

ues. The process of creating the 2000 Conservation Plan
started with a series of values identified in the Burra Charter and established their existence in Port Arthur, resulting
in the longest list of values of any of the sites studied.

The nomination of Hadrian's Wall for World
Heritage listing focused on the universal value of the
Roman remains as testimony of the technical and architectural accomplishments of an ancient civilization. The
site's most recent management plan specifically mentions
the archaeological and historical values of the Wall and
associated features, and the importance of the landscape
and setting in which they exist. This strict definition of the
values is dictated by its World Heritage status and is probably salutary, since the other, nonheritage values of the
place—such as its economic value through tourism—are
significant, and attempts could be made to give them priority when making certain decisions. However, as a place
composed of many individual sites and encompassing
large urban and rural areas, it has a complex set of values.
As the case study of the English site explains, the tension
between the values and interests of many varied stakeholders is one of the challenges of management.

STAKEHOLDERS

It is evident that the broad involvement of public groups
provides legitimacy to the results of the planning process
and can assist authorities in the implementation of the
plans. However, the involvement of new groups is not
always an easy process. In the sites studied, as authorities
sought to identify the values of a site, the identification of
stakeholders presented a number of challenges, including
determining the legitimate spokesperson for a group and
maintaining a balance among stakeholders.

The case of Grosse Île and the Irish Memorial
National Historic Site illustrates the difficulties of the
former. Early in the planning process, Parks Canada recognized that Irish Canadians have a special affinity to the
island through which many of their ancestors entered
the country. In determining the views of the place during the initial planning phases, the authorities consulted
individuals who had a long-term involvement with the
place and whom they thought could speak to the values
of this group. Nevertheless, when the plans were set out
to the public for consultation, other Irish groups across
Canada felt that the proposed interpretation did not
reflect their values. The strong reaction that ensued
caught Parks Canada by surprise and threatened to derail
the consultation process by turning it into a confronta-
tion. The position taken by some Irish Canadians—and it

is not clear even today whether it was a group representative of the whole community or only a faction—resulted in a name change for the historic site and a delay in the planning process. This episode illustrates how important it is to identify the spokesperson for a stakeholder group. However, unless a group is structured formally and can designate a spokesperson (as could be the case of a tribe or a religious group), it will continue to be difficult to identify a legitimate representative who is capable of speaking on behalf of the whole group.

EVOLUTION OF VALUES

There are heritage places whose values appear to remain unchanged. However, the evolution of values over time is an important characteristic of sites studied. The cases of Port Arthur, Chaco, and Hadrian's Wall illustrate this well.

When Hadrian's Wall lost its utilitarian value as a military defense in Roman times, it retained utility as its material components were reused in other constructions. Starting in the eighteenth century, antiquarians and historians brought forth a different set of values, and today, the economic (and thus utilitarian) value of the Wall is again recognized by all stakeholders. Port Arthur's significance shifted from a key element in the Tasmanian economy to an important cultural site for all Australians over a period of a century.

Sometimes, a particular value of a site comes to be appreciated by new groups. In the mid-twentieth century, New Agers started to find spiritual value in Chaco Culture National Historical Park, a place that had been spiritually significant to Native American groups for centuries. Today, the aesthetic and scientific values coexist with spiritual values for Native American and New Age groups, and with expanding ecological values.

Important events or situations can also modify the values attributed to a place. This was the case for Port Arthur, where a gunman randomly killed thirty-five people at and around the site in 1996, creating a new significance for Port Arthur as a place of mourning. Immediately after the tragic killings, many questions were asked about the future of the site, from possible closure to how to interpret the tragedy, if at all. The individuals who were most touched by the tragedy in many cases lived nearby or worked at the site, and had great influence over the reevaluation process that followed the tragedy. The initial reaction of wanting to obliterate evidence of the event, by tearing down the Broad Arrow Café where most of the killings took place, later evolved into a desire to remember the lost lives. Today, the massacre is memorialized in

an abstract garden surrounding the ruins of the Café, and interpretation to the visitor is low-key. In addition, Port Arthur is now closely associated at the national level with strict gun control laws that were passed after the massacre. These values are very recent, and it can be anticipated that they will evolve as time goes by. This newer tragic value of Port Arthur and the national significance of the gun control legislation are likely to be interpreted differently by generations to come.

The foot and mouth disease (FMD) that infected herds in the United Kingdom in 2001 originated in farms around Hadrian's Wall. The measures taken by government and farmers to avoid the spread of the infection included the destruction of many herds and the closure of the region to visitors. These measures had a terrible impact on the economy of the area. These events, which coincided with the development of the second Management Plan for the World Heritage Site, resulted in an altered perception of the values of the site. For one, the risks inherent in herding led the farmers to discuss alternative uses for the lands around the archaeological resources. Those discussions made evident the important contribution and value of the landscape—in its present condition—to the integrity of the World Heritage Site. Second, the importance of Hadrian's Wall to the economy and welfare of the region had been recognized in the past, but in the crisis created by FMD it was cruelly highlighted. (It is conceivable that the role that Grosse Île played after World War II as a research center for bacteriological warfare, and later as a quarantine station, might acquire special significance through societal changes or special circumstances.)

ECONOMIC VALUE

There is great concern in the cultural world that consideration of the economic value of heritage sites could lead to overemphasizing this aspect of the place at the expense of the cultural values. However, although none of the planning processes carried out at the sites in this project considers economic values on par with cultural ones, most planning and management documents contain some form of acknowledgment of the economic value of the site to stakeholders. It would be impossible not to do so in a world where cultural and natural sites, like many other public goods, are increasingly being asked to cover their own costs.

Tourism and visitor-generated income are generally behind the economic value of most cultural sites. The economic contribution of the site of Port Arthur to the local economy was quickly recognized when shortly after the closure of the penal colony people started to visit the place. The Tasmanian Tourist Association was the first group to express interest in protecting the ruins in 1913. The 2000 Conservation Plan for the site does not consider economic value when establishing the significance of the place. Nevertheless, the current statement of significance acknowledges that the site "has traditionally been an important centre of economic activity and work in the Tasman Peninsula and Tasmania—initially as a convict workplace, later a town and premier tourist destination."[17] Economic considerations are important in Port Arthur, not only because of its contribution to the region but also because the act that created the PAHSMA specifically mentions that it should operate "with a view of becoming commercially viable."[18] Similarly, the Management Plan of Grosse Île and the Irish Memorial National Historic Site acknowledges the economic value of the site to the region, particularly as a result of increased tourism. Hadrian's Wall partners, as has been mentioned before, consider the economic dimension of the site to be of great importance.

In the management of all the sites included in this study, the economic and cultural values are kept separate conceptually and to a large extent also in planning and management. The result of this separation in the case of Port Arthur is that in a management setting where the Conservation Plan provides detailed guidelines for the "cultural" decisions on the site, it does not address the "economic" activities of the place, apart from the overriding policy that commercial decisions must not impact adversely the conservation of the site.

The economic value of CCNHP is completely different. It is not based on tourism or on economic activity generated by the site, but rather on alternative uses of the land. The case study discusses in detail the economic potential of the energy resources that lie under the park and surrounding lands. In contrast with the other sites, where the stakeholders can realize the benefits of the cultural and economic values simultaneously, in Chaco, the exploitation of energy resources would certainly have a very negative impact on the cultural values of the site.

In Port Arthur and Hadrian's Wall, where the importance of the economic value for the region and its inhabitants has been explicitly recognized, stakeholders and site authorities have created separate entities to pursue the benefits of tourism. Port Arthur Regional Marketing Ltd. and Hadrian's Wall Tourism Partnership are independent from the sites. However, their objectives and actions are carefully monitored and coordinated so as not to damage the cultural significance of the sites, and the site authorities are intimately involved with their operations. The roles of these agencies are discussed in the case studies.

CONFLICT RESOLUTION

The purpose of values-based management is to respect the many values attributed to any given cultural site. As the case studies demonstrate, there are instances when values held by different stakeholder groups come into conflict. Sometimes, these conflicts can find resolution through compromises and adaptations. Other times, however, the conflicts are irreconcilable, and one or another of the values has to be given priority. These are some of the most difficult decisions that cultural managers must make, and for this reason the governing agencies often provide guidance.

CCNHP documents state that "while both cultural and natural preservation efforts are generally compatible, they may be in conflict in some situations. In these instances, given the legislated purpose of the park, management of cultural resources will be favored over management of natural resources."[19] In Parks Canada, maintaining the integrity of the commemorative intent of a site (i.e., the values that make the place significant in Canadian history) is the primary management objective. Commemorative integrity means healthy resources supporting national significance and effective communication of the commemorative intent, and it also requires that "the site's heritage values (including those not related to the reasons for designation as a national historic site) are respected in all decisions and actions affecting the site."[20] (It should be noted that among the sites studied, only Parks Canada considers communication of significance an integral part of the protection of the values of a site.)

In CCNHP some of the practices introduced by the New Age stakeholders were seen by some Native American groups to violate their religious beliefs. Faced with this conflict among stakeholders' values, the NPS prohibited all religious ceremonies in places considered sacred. This decision eliminated the conflict from park grounds but affected the spiritual value the place had for both groups. It can be argued that NPS had only two alternatives: to allow every group to carry on their practices and rituals or to ban the acts completely. According to the Constitution of the United States, favoring one group over another would have constituted discrimination on the basis of religion.

Some conflicts have simpler solutions. At Grosse Île, the protection of the very important Lazaretto required eliminating bat colonies in the eaves. Bats, however, are a protected species in Canada, and closing access to their habitat would have inflicted damage. The solution found by the authorities was to close the eaves but to construct small structures nearby to which the colonies could migrate. These structures are moved further from the Lazaretto each year, leading the bats away from the historic building.

Sometimes a particular value can be given more or less importance in different decisions. The ruins of the church of Port Arthur have acquired iconic meaning for the site, and the church has remained unroofed for decades. Meanwhile, plans are proceeding to reconstruct parts of the Model Prison to make it more easily comprehensible to the visitors. Clearly, the aesthetic and historic values are considered very important in relation to the church, while at the Model Prison, the educational value and probably the architectural forms seem to be given priority over the others.

LOCAL VERSUS NATIONAL AND INTERNATIONAL VALUES

Two of the sites studied in this project—Chaco Culture National Historical Park and Hadrian's Wall—were inscribed in the World Heritage List in 1987, and the nomination of a third—Port Arthur—is in preparation. The choice of justification for the listing is left to the country nominating the site, but the site must meet the criterion or criteria selected at a universal level. This restriction, by definition, will not allow all values of a site to be part of the World Heritage Nomination, as mentioned earlier, and could be seen as giving less importance to some of the values that do not have "universal importance."

Chaco was listed as a place that "bear[s] a unique or at least exceptional testimony to a cultural tradition or to a civilization which is living or which has disappeared."[21] Hadrian's Wall was inscribed under broader criteria, which, in addition to the criterion used for Chaco, included "exhibit(ing) an important interchange of human values, over a span of time or within a cultural area of the world, on developments in architecture or technology, monumental arts, town-planning or landscape design" and "be(ing) an outstanding example of a type of building or architectural or technological ensemble or landscape which illustrates (a) significant stage(s) in human history."[22] Evidently, these criteria leave out important values of the sites.

There have been attempts to enlarge the World Heritage guidelines to include all the values of a nominated site, not only those that are considered of international significance. If this were to happen, all of the site's values would be protected by the World Heritage listing. However, this change has been opposed by some state parties who do not want to be subject to international oversight with respect to local or national issues and values.

Although the designation as World Heritage is considered important by U.S. and English authorities, it has been used very differently in each case. Park staff at CCNHP indicated that the site's World Heritage status is invoked usually to obtain resources or special consideration.[23] In Hadrian's Wall, on the other hand, the UNESCO listing is the force behind, and often the justification for, planning and coordination.

The Value of the Landscape

The values recognized by the criteria of the World Heritage Convention and national heritage schemes are traditional ones, generally historic, archaeological or scientific, artistic and aesthetic. Social values have started to be recognized in the heritage field only lately and have been the subject of important recent research.[24]

The expansion of the concept of what can constitute "heritage" has led to the recognition of the significance of landscapes. The natural values of the environment have been part of the natural conservation field since its inception. However, the concept that landscapes are also cultural heritage emerged in recent decades. Starting from an increased awareness of the need to protect the setting of the traditional "monuments," it has expanded to include vast areas that encompass both natural resources and human creations. This extension of the scope of heritage is leading to recognition of social and economic values as "nonmonumental," and utilitarian areas are included in heritage resources. This was the case in Port Arthur Historic Site and Hadrian's Wall World Heritage Site, where, once the "site" was recognized as reaching beyond the strict confines of the monuments to include land, villages, and cities, new social and economic considerations came into play.

At the same time, landscapes are acquiring importance in and of themselves, and different strategies for their protection can be seen in the cases of this study. As this has happened, the "setting" of the cultural resources often extends beyond the official boundaries of the site, and changes in the use of those lands could affect the other values of the heritage site. In CCNHP, the significance of the setting and the need to protect it crystallized in the 1970s as a result of anticipated expansion of mining activities around the park. It was feared that coal and uranium mining and the exploitation of natural gas would create atmospheric pollution that would obscure the views from the site, and at the same time bring an increase in the population and development around the site. In many places of Hadrian's Wall World Heritage Site, the horizon is visible for many kilometers beyond the protected areas. The importance of these landscapes and views had been recognized well before the FMD crisis focused national attention on it.

In both places it is acknowledged that legal protection of such vast extents of land would be unreasonable and impossible. English Heritage, as the national agency mandated to protect the heritage of Hadrian's Wall, has reserved the right to comment on development in places with a high impact on the setting. In recent years, for example, it opposed a proposal to establish wind farms in the hills visible from parts of the site and found an unexpected ally: military authorities in a nearby airbase who saw the windmills as a hazard to military flights.

Chaco authorities have adopted a more passive approach to the protection of the views from the site. Once the energy crisis of the 1970s passed and with it the threat of mining, NPS has carefully avoided raising questions about the use of lands around the site. The rationale, as explained by the former superintendent, is that restrictions on land use in that region of the U.S. are a very sensitive issue, and even discussing it would polarize factions. As long as the potential threats do not become real, the NPS is following a policy of "letting sleeping dogs lie."

The Importance of Fabric

Another big challenge presented by values-based management has been establishing the connection between the values identified and their protection in the operations of the site. The four cases illustrate different means of integrating values into practice, and various degrees of success. The old conundrum of access versus conservation emerged as perhaps the most common conflict of values, leading several of the site authorities to use a concept of "quality of the visit" as an arena for tradeoffs.

The tangible/intangible duality of the concept of significance is recognized in guidance documents. The NPS states that "to be significant, a cultural resource must have important historical, cultural, scientific, or technological associations and it must manifest those associations in its physical substances. Put another way, the significance of cultural resources is based on two interrelated qualities. A cultural resource consists of a number of physical, chemical, or biological features; at the same time, it consists of ideas, events, and relationships. The physical and social dimensions of a cultural resource are inseparably interwoven. For a resource to be significant, its meaning must be indelibly fixed in form and fabric."[25]

The Burra Charter also clearly states that "[C]ultural significance is embodied in the place itself, its fabric, setting, use, associations, meanings, records, related places and related objects." It makes a distinction between "conservation," defined as "all the processes of looking after a place so as to retain its *cultural significance*" and "preservation," said to mean "maintaining the fabric of a place in its existing state and retarding deterioration."[26] Volume 2 of the 2000 Conservation Plan of Port Arthur Historic Site looks at the resources of the site in relation to the values identified and the significance established for the place.

The Canadian system highlights the importance of making the connection between fabric and values by specifying that "[I]n order to guide design decision-making in practical fashion, heritage character must be clearly defined by linking the primary areas of heritage value to related character-defining elements, patterns and relationships."[27]

In accepting the intangible dimension of significance, some organizations have developed new methods to establish the connections between values and the site itself and are making these connections between values and fabric very explicit. An excellent example of this is the analysis carried out for the resources of Grosse Île, which examined the various aspects of the commemorative intent (significance) in relation to what was on-site and what the visitor would see.[28]

At CCNHP the protection of the values and significance of the site has been equated for almost a century with the physical protection of the resources. According to NPS mission, the resources should be maintained unimpaired. In fact, since becoming a national monument and later a park, the resources have been changed by excavations and enhancements for interpretation and the enjoyment of visitors. Some values, such as those attributed to the ruins by Native Americans, can be denied or receive less recognition if they are seen to have an impact on the physical materials of the ruins.

Heritage agencies use different means to determine where "values" reside. Traditionally, work was conducted as if values resided in any material that was "authentic" and any structure that had "integrity." The values-based planning process calls for two steps that focus on the physical aspects of the site.[29] These two steps—documentation of the site and assessment of the conditions of the resources—provide a clear understanding of the place, which is fundamental to the connection between "values" and fabric.

Quality of the Visitors' Experience

The management documents in all four sites address the imperative of providing a high-quality experience to visitors. Some of the factors seen to influence that quality are common to all four sites, such as interpretation of the significance of the place. Nevertheless, there are differences in emphasis, which reflect the management philosophies of the individual sites.

The Conservation Plan of Port Arthur Historic Site determines that management will "endeavor to provide high quality visitor experience, consistent with the conservation requirements and enabling visitors an understanding of the meanings and significance of PA."[30] It then goes on to mention that nonessential facilities that could have adverse effect on cultural significance will be avoided, but that those that are provided will be "consistent with industry best practice." These directives clearly echo the priority of protection and conservation. At the same time, "industry best practice" seems to refer to its mandate to "conduct its affairs with a view of becoming commercially viable."[31]

Hadrian's Wall's plan calls for "providing visitors with an overall experience of the WHS worthy of its special values and significance."[32] The plan, however, never fully defines what a quality experience would be, although it mentions excavations and display of archaeological remains; good interpretation, both in sites and in museums; access, such as that provided by the new National Trail; conservation of the archaeological resources; and better facilities. Among the facilities mentioned are wet-weather facilities, shops, visitor centers, refreshments, and toilets sited adjacent to car parks. There is special importance attached to the quality of these facilities, expressed in the plan as: "It is important that visitors to the WHS are welcomed by facilities that immediately communicate to them the significance of the Site through their quality."[33]

In Grosse Île, a balanced emphasis on various factors such as access, facilities on-site, interpretation, and conservation is the hallmark of the definition of a quality visitor experience. As dictated by the elements of commemorative integrity, successful communication of the significance of the site is given a lot of importance. Of all the sites studied, Grosse Île had the most complete analysis of the visitors' experience, which considered issues such as transportation, time needed on-site, and optimal itinerary.

On the other hand, CCNHP is the site that seems to most frequently use the "quality of the visitors' experience" as a management and monitoring tool. The authorities at Chaco have identified the visitors' ability to be in direct contact with the resources, a reflective atmosphere, and a pristine environment as the elements that provide quality to the visitors.[34] In this instance, good facilities on-site are not a factor contributing quality. As a matter of fact, development of facilities is seen as potentially having a negative impact on the environment and the atmosphere.

Monitoring Values

The effort to identify and protect values would be incomplete if the condition of these values could not be monitored. Monitoring, the final stage in many management planning processes, seems always to be left last when it comes to devoting time and resources to management. Many managers admit the need to put more thought and resources into monitoring values. At the end of the day, good management is evident in healthy and sustainable values. Monitoring the physical resources is the most common method of monitoring sites, but this is useful only if the relation between values and fabric is established and well understood. Although there are today very sophisticated tools that can detect minute changes in the material, this does not guarantee that the underlying values of the place are not being eroded. For example, while a site might retain total integrity of its fabric, it might lose some values through intense (but well-managed) visitation, noise pollution, or improper use of the place. Monitoring intangible values is difficult and can only be done indirectly. The organizations involved in this study are employing methods that hold promise.

Parks Canada's concept of commemorative integrity was developed in the 1990 State of the Parks Report "as a framework to evaluate and report on the health and wholeness of national historic sites."[35] Part of the process of preparing the commemorative integrity statement includes an in-depth analysis of the relationship of the commemorative intent (i.e., the values and significance of the site) and the physical place. In addition, the process includes the preparation of objectives related to each of the three elements of the statement. These objectives should uphold "the desired state of the site, its resources and their historic values," "describe the ideal field conditions sought through management," and "provide a framework for management activities and performance indicators for measuring the state of a site's commemorative integrity."[36] Periodically, the agency issues a report on the conditions of the heritage areas, where various indicators associated with the objectives of the statement are examined and evaluated.[37]

The NPS regularly monitors and carries out periodic reviews of its units but has not done a comprehensive, system-wide evaluation of them. In 1999, the National Parks Conservation Association launched a four-year program that "assesses the health of our national parks by objectively examining the resource conditions and threats in selected park units."[38] As part of the work, it has developed methodologies to assess the natural and cultural resources, as well as the stewardship capacity of its sites.[39] This work is of recent date and had not been applied to CCNHP at the time of the study.

The role of monitoring at Port Arthur takes at least two forms. One of them is the typical monitoring of site-wide physical conditions, which proceeds on a regular annual schedule and is carried out by conservation staff. Monitoring of intangible values—as noted above, a far trickier task—is addressed by some of the habits inculcated as part of what one could call the "management culture" of PAHSMA: the staff are in constant, open communication about the state of the site and threats to values; additionally, constant surveying of visitors and other stakeholders offers an indirect, though meaningful, stream of information on how the values of the site are being transmitted (and by extension, how they are being conserved).

In England, the Countryside Agency and English Heritage are leading a conference to establish the limits of acceptable change (LAC) for the Housesteads area of Hadrian's Wall World Heritage Site—the most intensely visited part of the Wall's archaeological remains. Monitoring change is critical in this vast site with a large number of owners, managers, and environments. The method employed, explained in detail in the case study, works through detailed discussions among a wide range of stakeholder groups to establish minimum conditions of quality necessary to sustain the values of the site and the quality of visitor experiences. As for the question of moni-

toring for the entire World Heritage Site, those involved in planning and managing the overall site maintain that monitoring is one of their foremost priorities in developing the management scheme after recently revising the Management Plan.

Other systems are based on the use of indicators, which provide quantitative data. All these approaches attempt to measure change or success. Often, however, the baselines against which measures are taken are fragmented—they deal only with one aspect of the site, or have no correlation to the values of the place. There is considerable interest in identifying indicators of sustainability. This study suggests that the significance of the site and the protection of its values could be the baseline that could start the process.

Notes

1. U.S. National Park Service, *Management Policies 2001*, Washington, D.C.: National Park Service Policy; Parks Canada, *Parks Canada Guiding Principles and Operational Policies*, Ottawa: Parks Canada, 1994.

2. In http://planning.nps.gov/ (10 Feb. 2004).

3. NPS, *Management Policies 2001*, Section 2.3.1.

4. Statutes of Canada 1998, Chapter 31, "Parks Canada Agency Act," Article 32. Text available at http://laws.justice.gc.ca/en/P-0.4/89014.html (10 Feb. 2004).

5. Parks Canada Agency, "3.2. Planning," in *Parks Canada Guiding Principles and Operational Policies*, 1994. http://www.pc.gc.ca/docs/pc/poli/princip/index_E.asp (10 Feb. 2004).

6. See the case study of Grosse Île and the Irish Memorial National Historic Site in this publication for a detailed discussion of the concept of commemorative integrity.

7. *Government Business Enterprises Act* 1995, Ministerial Charter Enterprise: Port Arthur Historic Site.

8. In the context of a relatively decentralized government, the Burra Charter, although not a legal document, is by consensus the central guidance used by heritage professionals throughout Australia.

9. *PPG 1*, as well as a number of the other PPGs, will be superceded by corresponding Planning Policy Statements in the course of 2004.

10. Office of the Deputy Prime Minister, *Planning Policy Guidance 1: General Policy and Principles*: Part 39. Found at http://www.odpm.gov.uk/stellent/groups/odpm_planning/documents/page/odpm_plan_606895.hcsp (August 2003).

11. For a complete list of PPGs, see http://www.odpm.gov.uk/stellent/groups/odpm_control/documents/

contentservertemplate/odpm_index.hcst?n=2263&l=2 (10 Feb. 2004).

12. *PPG 15* and *PPG 16* are due to be replaced by a single PPS.

13. The Act of Parliament creating Parks Canada Agency in 1998 stipulates that management plans must be revised every five years.

14. This holds true for all the sites studied in this project. Each case explains the network of planning and guidance documents used in the site.

15. English Heritage, *Hadrian's Wall World Heritage Site Management Plan 2002–2007*, 2002, Section 1.1.

16. Ibid.

17. Godden Mackay, *Port Arthur Historic Site Conservation Plan, Volume 1: Overview Report,* prepared for the Port Arthur Historic Site Management Authority, 2000, Section 3.3.

18. The *Port Arthur Historic Site Management Authority Act* of 1987, as amended in 1989.

19. National Park Service, Chaco Culture National Historical Park Resource Management Plan, 10 January 2002 (Draft), 4.

20. Parks Canada, *Guide to the Preparation of Commemorative Integrity Statements,* 2002, Section 1.1.2. http://www.pc.gc.ca/docs/pc/guide/guide/index_e.asp.

21. World Heritage Committee, *World Heritage Convention Operational Guidelines,* Part C, Paragraph 24, a, ii (commonly called Criterion C [iii]). http://whc.unesco.org/nwhc/pages/doc/main.htm.

22. Ibid, C (ii) and C (iv).

23. This can be interpreted as the reflection of the distrust in certain quarters in the U.S. of all United Nations activities, even if filtered through UNESCO. Those who opposed the UN have raised the specter of loss of sovereignty over the land encompassed in World Heritage sites. For whatever reason, the number of WHSs in the U.S. is low compared to other countries. (Of 730 sites in the World Heritage List, only 20 are in the United States. In comparison, Italy has 36 sites, Spain 35, France 28, India 23, and Mexico 22). Even those U.S. places that have been listed do not use their World Heritage status very publicly.

24. See, for example, D. Byrne et al., *Social Significance: A Discussion Paper*, Hurtsville, Australia: NSW National Parks & Wildlife Service, 2001.

25. NPS, *Cultural Resources Management Guidelines,* 1997, 9.

26. Australia ICOMOS, *The Burra Charter,* 1999, Article 1.

27. Federal Heritage Buildings Review Office, *Federal Heritage Buildings Review Office (FHBRO) Code of Practice.* Ottawa: Federal Heritage Buildings Review Office, 1996, 13.

28. Parks Canada, "Lieu Historique National de la Grosse-Ile-et-le-Memorial-des-Irlandais Plan d'Expérience de Visite," December 1998 (unpublished document).

29. For a step-by-step explanation of this process, see M. Demas' "Planning for Conservation and Management of Archaeo-

logical Sites: A Values-Based Approach," in J. M. Teutonico and G. Palumbo, *Management Planning for Archaeological Sites,* Los Angeles: The Getty Conservation Institute, 2000, 27–54.

30. Godden Mackay, *Port Arthur Historic Site Conservation Plan, Volume 1: Overview Report,* prepared for the Port Arthur Historic Site Management Authority, 2000, Section 5.13.

31. The *Port Arthur Historic Site Management Authority Act* of 1987, as amended in 1989.

32. *Hadrian's Wall World Heritage Site Management Plan 2001–2007,* 2000, 76.

33. Ibid., 62.

34. The CCNHP case study contains a discussion of the quality of the visit.

35. Parks Canada, *Guide to the Preparation of Commemorative Integrity Statements,* 2002, Section 1.1.1.

36. Ibid., Section 2.3.3.

37. See Parks Canada Agency, State of Protected Heritage Areas 1999 Report at http://www.pc.gc.ca/docs/pc/rpts/heritage/sphareport_e.pdf (10 Feb. 2004).

38. In http://www.npca.org/across_the_nation/park_pulse/default.asp (10 Feb. 2004).

39. Ibid.

Index

Note: Page numbers in *italic* type refer to illustrations and captions; page numbers followed by an "n" refer to endnotes.

D

E

F

G

About the Authors

Marta de la Torre is the director of the Museum Studies Graduate Certificate Program at Florida International University in Miami. From 1985 to 2002 she worked at the Getty Conservation Institute (GCI), where she was director of training and, later, head of information and communications. While at the GCI, she led a six-year research project on the values of heritage, which produced several research reports and the four case studies presented in this publication. Prior to joining the GCI, she was director of special projects and administration at the International Council of Museums in Paris, France. She holds an M.A. in arts management from American University, a B.A. in art history and design from George Washington University, and a Certificate of Museum Studies from the Ecole du Louvre in Paris.

Margaret G. H. MacLean is a cultural heritage analyst with the United States Department of State, where she is engaged in heritage conservation and management policy, and in the protection of movable heritage from international theft and illegal trafficking. As senior training program coordinator at the Getty Conservation Institute (GCI) from 1989 to 1993, she developed and implemented training programs relating to conservation and management of archaeological heritage materials and sites. From 1993 to 1999, as documentation program director at the GCI, she established a field recording and information management section in support of the GCI's conservation projects. She studied art history, cultural geography, and anthropology and holds a doctorate in anthropology, with a specialization in archaeology, from the University of California at Berkeley.

Randall Mason is associate professor of architecture, Graduate Program in Historic Preservation, at the University of Pennsylvania. Trained in geography, history, and urban planning, he worked previously at the Getty Conservation Institute and was director of the Historic Preservation Program at the University of Maryland. In addition, he is a partner in the nonprofit research group Minerva Partners, which develops projects to strengthen the connections between heritage conservation and social development. His recently published work includes *Giving Preservation a History: Histories of Historic Preservation in the United States* (edited with Max Page; Routledge, 2003).

David Myers is research associate at the Getty Conservation Institute in Los Angeles. He was a Kress Research Fellow at the University of Pennsylvania's Architectural Conservation Research Center from 2000 to 2001. From 1991 to 1995 he served as a legislative assistant to a U.S. representative. He studied historic preservation, geography, and political science and holds a master's degree and an advanced certificate in architectural conservation and site management from the University of Pennsylvania as well as a master's degree from the University of Kansas.

The following supporting documents on the enclosed CD-ROM are gratefully used by permission of the organizations listed below:

Grosse Île and the Irish Memorial National Historic Site

Grosse Île National Historic Site—Development Concept; Grosse Île National Historic Site—Report on the Public Consultation Program; Commemorative Integrity Statement for Grosse Île and the Irish Memorial National Historic Site; Grosse Île and the Irish Memorial National Historic Site Management Plan; Part III (Cultural Resource Management Policy) of Parks Canada Guiding Principles and Operational Policies; and Guide to the Preparation of Commemorative Integrity Statements have all been generously provided by the Parks Canada Agency.

Chaco Culture National Historical Park

The Chaco Culture General Management Plan/Development Concept Plan; Chaco Culture Statement for Interpretation and Interim Interpretive Prospectus; and National Park Service Management Policies 2001 were kindly provided by the U.S. National Park Service.

Port Arthur Historic Site

The Port Arthur Historic Site Conservation Plan, volumes 1 and 2; Broad Arrow Café Conservation Study; and the PAHSMA Annual Report 2001 were reproduced with the permission of the Port Arthur Historic Site Management Authority.

Hadrian's Wall World Heritage Site

Hadrian's Wall World Heritage Site Management Plan 1996 and Hadrian's Wall World Heritage Site Management Plan 2002–2007 were reproduced with the kind permission of English Heritage. Planning Policy Guidance 15: Planning and the Historic Environment and Planning Policy Guidance 16: Archaeology and Planning are Crown copyright materials reproduced with the permission of the Controller of HMSO and the Queen's Printer for Scotland.